The Mughal empire was on[illegible]
pre-modern world history. It [illegible]
the following century the Mughal emperor ruled almost the entire Indian subcontinent with a population of between 100 and 150 millions. As well as military success, the Mughal emperors displayed immense wealth and the ceremonies, etiquette, music, poetry, and exquisitely executed paintings and objects of the imperial court fused together to create a distinctive aristocratic high culture.

In this volume, Professor John Richards traces the history of this magnificent empire from its creation in 1526 to its breakup in 1720. He stresses the dynamic quality of Mughal territorial expansion, their institutional innovation in land revenue, coinage and military organization, ideological change, and the relationship between the emperors and Islam. Professor Richards also analyzes institutions particular to the Mughal empire, such as the *jagir* system, and explores Mughal India's links with the early modern world.

The Mughal Empire offers a concise and up-to-date synthesis of this spectacular period in the history of India, Pakistan and Bangladesh. It will be widely read by students and specialists of South Asian history and civilization and will be of interest to travellers wishing to know more about the background to the great Mughal monuments.

The Mughal empire was one of the largest centralized states known in pre-modern world history. It was founded in the early 1500s and by the end of the following century the Mughal emperor ruled almost the entire Indian subcontinent, with a population of between 100 and 150 million. As well as military success the Mughal emperors displayed enormous wealth and the architecture, poetry, and exquisitely executed paintings and objects of the imperial court fused together to create a distinctive Indo-Persian high culture.

In this volume, Professor John Richards traces the history of the Mughal empire from its creation in 1526 to its breakdown in 1720. He stresses the dynamic quality of Mughal territorial expansion, the imperial centralized system in land revenue, the centralized military organization, ideology of kingship and the relationship between the emperors and Islam. Professor Richards also analyzes institutions particular to the Mughal empire, such as the jagir system, and explores Mughal India's links with the early modern world.

The Mughal Empire offers a concise and up-to-date synthesis of this spectacular period in the history of India, Pakistan and Bangladesh. It will be widely read by students and specialists of South Asian history and civilization and will be of interest to travellers wishing to know more about the background to the great Mughal monuments.

THE NEW CAMBRIDGE HISTORY
OF INDIA

The Mughal Empire

THE NEW CAMBRIDGE HISTORY OF INDIA

Although the original *Cambridge History of India*, published between 1922 and 1937, did much to formulate a chronology for Indian history and describe the administrative structures of government in India, it has inevitably been overtaken by the mass of new research published over the last fifty years.

Designed to take full account of recent scholarship and changing conceptions of South Asia's historical development, *The New Cambridge History of India* will be published as a series of short, self-contained volumes, each dealing with a separate theme and written by a single person, within an overall four-part structure. As before, each will conclude with a substantial bibliographical essay designed to lead non-specialists further into the literature.

The four parts are as follows:

I The Mughals and their Contemporaries.

II Indian States and the Transition to Colonialism.

III The Indian Empire and the Beginnings of Modern Society.

IV The Evolution of Contemporary South Asia.

A list of individual titles already published and in preparation will be found at the end of the volume.

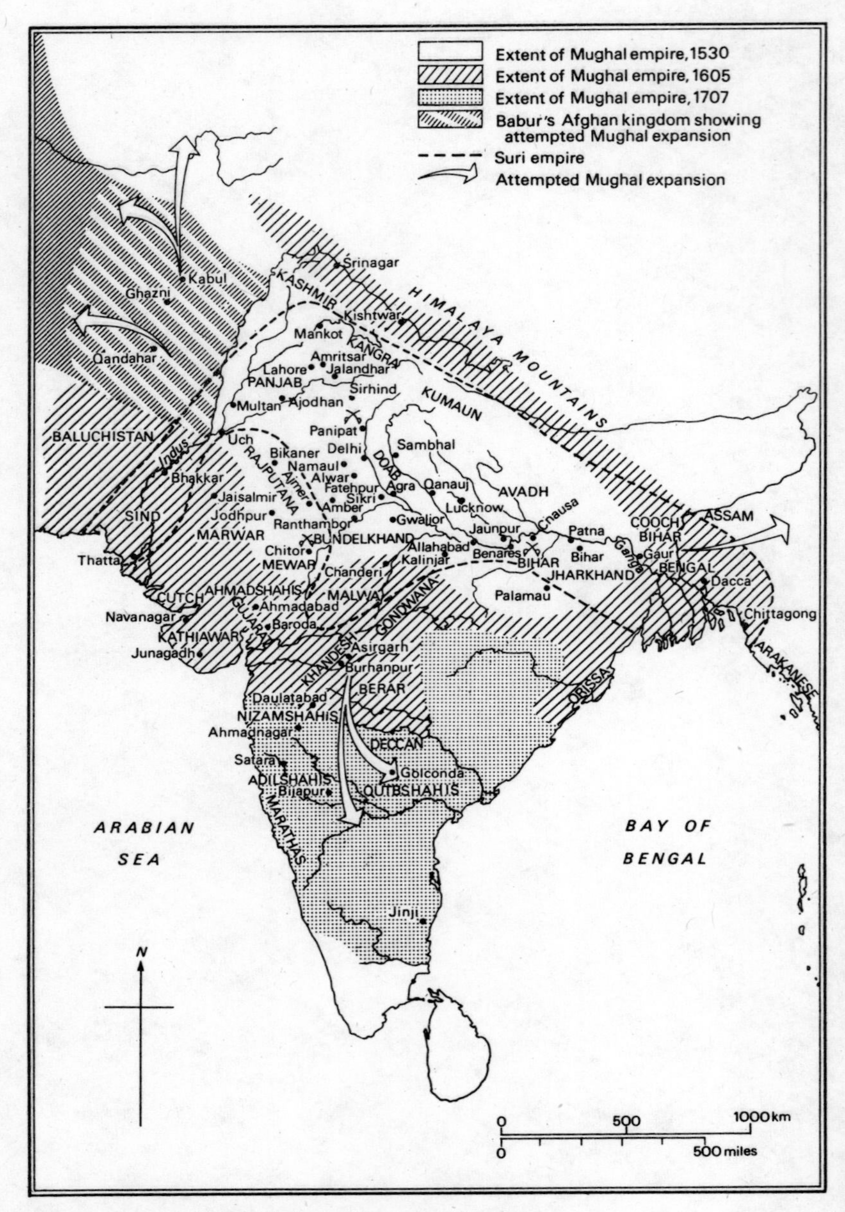

Frontispiece The Mughal empire, 1526 to 1707
Source: F. Robinson, *Atlas of the Islamic World since 1500* (Oxford, 1982), p. 59.

THE NEW CAMBRIDGE HISTORY OF INDIA

I · 5

The Mughal Empire

JOHN F. RICHARDS

PROFESSOR OF HISTORY, DUKE UNIVERSITY

Published in South Asia by

Foundation Books
4764/2A, 23 Ansari Road
New Delhi-110 002

First South Asian Edition 1993
Second reprint 1995
Third reprint 1997
Fourth reprint 1998
Fifth reprint 2000

A catalogue record for this book is available from the British Library
Library of Congress Cataloguing in Publication data

ISBN 81-85618-49-6 Paperback

This edition of "The Mughal Empire by John F. Richards" is published by arrangement with Cambridge University Press, The Edinburgh Building, Shaftesbury Road, Cambridge CB2 2RU, UK.

Published by Manas Saikia for Foundation Books and printed at Rekha Printers Pvt. Ltd., A-102/1, Okhla Industrial Area, Phase-II, New Delhi-110 020.

Dedicated to the memory of my mother

ELLA HIGGINS RICHARDS

1908–1990

CONTENTS

MAPS AND TABLES

MAPS

TABLES

GENERAL EDITOR'S PREFACE

The New Cambridge History of India covers the period from the beginning of the sixteenth century. In some respects it marks a radical change in the style of Cambridge Histories, but in others the editors feel that they are working firmly within an established academic tradition.

During the summer of 1896, F. W. Maitland and Lord Acton between them evolved the idea for a comprehensive modern history. By the end of the year the Syndics of the University Press had committed themselves to the *Cambridge Modern History*, and Lord Acton had been put in charge of it. It was hoped that publication would begin in 1899 and be completed by 1904, but the first volume in fact came out in 1902 and the last in 1910, with additional volumes of tables and maps in 1911 and 1912.

The *History* was a great success, and it was followed by a whole series of distinctive Cambridge Histories covering English Literature, the Ancient World, India, British Foreign Policy, Economic History, Medieval History, the British Empire, Africa, China and Latin America; and even now other new series are being prepared. Indeed, the various Histories have given the Press notable strength in the publication of general reference books in the arts and social sciences.

What has made the Cambridge Histories so distinctive is that they have never been simply dictionaries or encyclopedias. The Histories have, in H. A. L. Fisher's words, always been "written by an army of specialists concentrating the latest results of special study". Yet as Acton agreed with the Syndics in 1896, they have not been mere compilations of existing material but original works. Undoubtedly many of the Histories are uneven in quality, some have become out of date very rapidly, but their virtue has been that they have consistently done more than simply record an existing state of knowledge: they have tended to focus interest on research and they have provided a massive stimulus to further work. This has made their publication doubly worthwhile and has distinguished them intellectually from other sorts of reference book. The editors of the *New Cambridge History of India* have acknowledged this in their work.

The original *Cambridge History of India* was published between 1922 and 1937. It was planned in six volumes, but of these, volume 2 dealing with the period between the first century A.D. and the Muslim invasion of India never appeared. Some of the material is still of value, but in many respects it is now out of date. The last fifty years have seen a great deal of new research on India, and a striking feature of recent work has been to cast doubt on the validity of the quite arbitrary chronological and categorical way in which Indian history has been conventionally divided.

The editors decided that it would not be academically desirable to prepare a new *History of India* using the traditional format. The selective nature of research on Indian history over the past half-century would doom such a project from the start and the whole of Indian history could not be covered in an even or comprehensive manner. They concluded that the best scheme would be to have a *History* divided into four overlapping chronological volumes, each containing about eight short books on individual themes or subjects. Although in extent the work will therefore be equivalent to a dozen massive tomes of the traditional sort, in form the *New Cambridge History of India* will appear as a shelf full of separate but complementary parts. Accordingly, the main divisions are between I. *The Mughals and their Contemporaries*, II. *Indian States and the Transition to Colonialism*, III. *The Indian Empire and the Beginnings of Modern Society*, and IV. *The Evolution of Contemporary South Asia*.

Just as the books within these volumes are complementary so too do they intersect with each other, both thematically and chronologically. As the books appear they are intended to give a view of the subject as it now stands and to act as a stimulus to further research. We do not expect the *New Cambridge History of India* to be the last word on the subject but an essential voice in the continuing discussion about it.

PREFACE

The starting point for this volume is 1526, the date of Babur's victory at Panipat. The ending point is 1720, the date of Muhammad Shah's accession in Delhi. By the latter date the essential structure of centralized empire was disintegrated beyond repair. Behind my choice of 1720, rather than 1739, or 1761, or even 1803, is the belief that the collapse of the centralized formal apparatus of the Mughal empire was an important turning point in Indian history. Three decades of study have convinced me that Mughal centralized power was a reality and that its effect on Indian society was considerable. Whether this was good or bad is a different question. After 1720 the Mughal empire became a substantially different entity.

Within these dates I have tried to describe the construction of the Mughal empire, its operation, and its destruction. One of my aims has been to explain as clearly as possible the design and operation of the imperial system. This is no small matter, for generations of scholars have worked hard to try and decipher the intricacies of this enterprise.

Another goal has been to write a concise, coherent narrative history from 1526 to 1720. The narrative is conventional in that I trace the large public events, primarily political and military, that shaped imperial history. Partly this is because I believe that we ought to take the military history of the Mughal empire more seriously than is our current custom. After all, war was the principal business of the Mughal emperors, who committed by far the bulk of their resources to the military. It is also difficult to understand the nature of the empire without some knowledge of its dynamic growth in territory and resources.

A third aim is to encourage further scholarly work on the Mughal period. We simply do not know enough. The secondary literature on the Mughals is thin despite its great importance in South Asian and world history. Many more detailed local histories need doing. A host of scholarly monographs and lengthy articles on various castes and ethnic groups are waiting for their historian. New sources in different genres and languages need to be identified, authenticated, collated, and published in the original text and in translation. We need better integration of the Indian and European sources by someone who reads Rajasthani, Persian, French, and Dutch, for example. For such new work our best hope lies in the originality of young historians from India, Pakistan, and Bangladesh.

Finally, my most important goal is to offer a one-volume synthesis that will be comprehensible to the non-specialist. I hope that this book can be read with profit by anyone interested in this most fascinating of historical periods. If successful, the volume should create a context for further reading and study.

In writing this volume I have become deeply conscious of my debt to colleagues in this field. I am especially grateful to Irfan Habib, Ashin Das Gupta, Satish Chandra, Tapan Raychaudhuri, and M. Athar Ali for their inspired scholarship and leadership in Mughal history over the past decades. Peter Hardy and Simon Digby have provided warm support and encouragement for my work over the years. A more immediate debt is to my two fellow editors, Gordon Johnson and Christopher Bayly, for their patience and their criticism. I especially wish to thank Muzaffar Alam for his incisive comments on an earlier draft. I have also benefited from discussions with Catherine Asher, Stewart Gordon, Bruce Lawrence, Om Prakash, Sanjay Subrahmanyam, and Ellen Smart. And, as always, I must thank my wife and children for their continuing love and understanding.

INTRODUCTION

The Mughal empire was one of the largest centralized states known in pre-modern world history. By the late 1600s the Mughal emperor held supreme political authority over a population numbering between 100 and 150 millions and lands covering most of the Indian subcontinent (3.2 million square kilometers). Timurid India far outstripped in sheer size and resources its two rival early modern Islamic empires – Safavid Persia and Ottoman Turkey. The Mughal emperor's lands and subjects were comparable only to those ruled by his contemporary, the Ming emperor in early modern China.

The "Great Mughal's" wealth and grandeur was proverbial. His coffers housed the plundered treasure of dozens of conquered dynasties; his regalia and throne displayed some of the most spectacular precious stones ever mounted. Nearly all observers were impressed by the opulence and sophistication of the Mughal empire. The ceremonies, etiquette, music, poetry, and exquisitely executed paintings and objects of the imperial court fused together to create a distinctive aristocratic high culture. Mughal courtly culture retained its appeal and power long after the empire itself had declined to a shell. Today the Mughal style as represented in miniature paintings, or much-admired buildings like the Taj Mahal, has an immediate and powerful attraction.

For nearly one hundred and seventy years (1556–1719) the Mughal empire remained a dynamic, centralized, complex organization. The emperor commanded cadres of officials and soldiers of proven loyalty who carried out his orders in every province. Men, money, information, and resources moved regularly and routinely throughout the empire as official needs dictated. Mughal success was the product of hard-driving, active rulership exercised by extremely capable rulers who acted as their own chief executives. Military victory, territorial expansion, and centralized control rested upon the management skills and strategic vision of the emperors and their advisers.

The empire was more than a superficial canopy stretched over the substantial social life lived in each region. It was an intrusive, centralizing system which unified the subcontinent. Imperial military power imposed an unprecedented level of public order. The scale and level of organized violence diminished perceptibly in the lands within its borders. Imperial demands for revenue and tribute stimulated production and encouraged market growth. The uniform practices and ubiquitous presence of the Mughals left an imprint upon society in every locality and region of the subcontinent. Few persons and communities, if any, were left untouched by this massive edifice.

Although the first two Timurid emperors and many of their noblemen were recent migrants to the subcontinent, the dynasty and the empire itself became indisputably Indian. The interests and futures of all concerned were in India, not in ancestral homelands in the Middle East or Central Asia. Furthermore, the Mughal empire emerged from the Indian historical experience. It was the end product of a millennium of Muslim conquest, colonization, and state-building in the Indian subcontinent.

Muslim and Hindu-Buddhist warriors first clashed in the early seventh century in Seistan on the border between Iran and Afghanistan. Century after century their descendants skirmished, raided, and fought bloody battles along a slowly eastward-moving military frontier. From the western edge of Afghanistan and the shores of Makran and Sind, the area of Muslim political conquest reached Kabul in the ninth century, Delhi in the early thirteenth century, and the cities of the Deccan and South India in the fourteenth century. Behind this frontier line Muslim generals built new states commanded by Turkish, Persian, Afghan, and other foreign Muslim elites. For a few decades in the mid-fourteenth century, the Sultans of Delhi ruled over an empire extending over most of the subcontinent before it broke apart. Thereafter, the locus of Indian Muslim political power reverted to regional kingdoms.

Indo-Muslim rulers appealed regularly to Muslim militancy in the *jihad* or holy war against the idolatrous Hindus of the subcontinent. Indo-Muslim rulers relied heavily upon the support of the Islamic religious establishment for legitimacy and political backing. In return the state supplied money and administrative support for the essential institutions of organized Islam. Theologians, preachers, and judges, often employed by the state, actively sought to retain the orthodox purity of the community in India against the absorptive power of Hindu Brahminical religion. Sufi *shaikhs*, who were influential leaders of the Muslim community and who also received royal largess, met a wide range of religious and social needs among lay adherents. The implicit contract between ruler and religious leaders was an important aspect of Islamic conquest and expansion.

By 1500 Hindu society in nearly every region of the subcontinent save the extreme south was conditioned to accept the authority of an Indo-Muslim ruler – whether of foreign or Indian origin. Generations of Hindu kings, warriors, and priests, fought and lost, rebelled and lost, and finally accepted service within the Muslim political order. Rajput, Maratha, and Telugu and other warrior castes recognized the legitimacy of Islamic political power in return for assurances of continued dominance in the countryside. Men from various secretarial castes, such as the Kayasths or the Khatris, adapted to the new order by learning Persian and becoming experts in the administrative procedures required by Indo-Muslim states. Generation after generation the process of political socialization continued. The Mughals were the beneficiaries of that process when they began to construct their overarching imperial system.

As heirs to the Indo-Muslim political tradition, the Mughals found conditions favorable for political centralization. They could turn to numerous precedents in their efforts to build a reliable yet flexible political and administrative system. All earlier sultans had recruited and maintained a nobility firmly bound to themselves and relatively free of constraining local ties. If continually reinforced, bonds of fealty and personal loyalty imposed open-ended obligations of service for each grandee. Earlier regimes had induced local Hindu warrior-aristocracies to maintain order and help levy taxes in the countryside. Royal officials could obtain cooperation to the limits spelled out in contractual arrangements. These were the two essential joints in the articulated structure of the Indo-Muslim state. Without a reliable imperial elite, no ruler could function. Without cooperating local aristocracies the countryside was lost. An unresolved question was the extent to which powerful armed nobles could be transformed into royal officials at the center and armed lords of the land be transformed into royal officials in the countryside.

Another, often-ignored technological advance aided Indo-Muslim rulers. The introduction and wide use of paper in the eleventh century made the centralized administration of large, complex organizations much easier. Rulers could exercise tighter control over people, land, resources, and money by using paper documents and records.

Information flows became more copious and reliable. Enforcement of standardized rules and regulations became more feasible.

The economy of the subcontinent responded buoyantly to new markets and new demands under the Indo-Muslim states. By the sixteenth century regional economies were linked together in a dense overland and coastal trading network. Agriculture, industry and trade could readily support the economic needs of a rising empire. The wealth of Hind was proverbial in the relatively less fertile and sparsely settled lands of the medieval Islamic world to the west.

In each region on the subcontinent, peasant cultivators living in peasant villages grew dozens of varieties of foodgrains and specialized crops for subsistence and for sale in a hierarchy of cash markets. Wells and riverine irrigation helped to improve production and partially offset years when the annual monsoon rains failed. Industrial production was impressive – especially from the intricately organized textile industry. Weavers, dyers, bleachers, and painters produced an enormous range of cotton and silk cloth for sale in local, regional, and international markets. Markets for commodities and labor were extensive and efficient. Overland, coastal, and deep-water trade routes linked local economies with the wider world. Indian trading communities in Gujarat, North India, and the south could scarcely be equalled for the sophistication of their skills and resources. The Indian population was long-accustomed to a money economy using gold, silver, copper, and mixed silver and copper coinage. Meager domestic production of gold and silver was augmented by large imports paid for by India's trade surplus.[1]

The subcontinent's productivity ensured that it enjoyed a continuing favorable balance of trade. Apart from precious metals, India's only other unmet needs included large numbers of horses (primarily for military use), black slaves and ivory from Africa, and other exotic consumption goods. Exports included much sought-after Indian cotton cloth bound for Southeast Asia, East Africa and the Middle East as well as spices, narcotics, and other agricultural commodities.[2]

In the early decades of the sixteenth century, the compressed social energy of western Europe began to have an impact upon the Indian subcontinent. New ideologies, technologies, products, and markets

[1] See Tapan Raychaudhuri and Irfan Habib, eds., *The Cambridge Economic History of India* (Cambridge: Cambridge University Press, 1982), I, Part I, *c.* 1200–1500, pp. 45–162 for a full description.

[2] Simon Digby, "The Maritime Trade of India," in Raychaudhuri and Habib, pp. 125–162.

pressed upon the subcontinent. These forces traversed long-established overland and sea routes through the Middle East and the Mediterranean to reach northern and western India. In addition, under the impetus of Iberian expansion, new maritime connections with western Europe became the conduit for direct, unmediated transfers to India. Many diffusions originated in Europe's discoveries in the New World. This new conjuncture stimulated growth in the economy of the subcontinent and, indirectly, the growth and expansion of the Mughal empire.

The direct maritime connection was established by the Portuguese, who, sailing around the coast of Africa, entered the Indian Ocean trading world for the first time in 1498. Portuguese round ships equipped with numerous light cannon were far superior to indigenous vessels.[3] In 1509 the first viceroy, de Almeida, destroyed an allied war fleet sent by the Mamluk ruler of Egypt and the Sultan of Gujarat. For the next century or more the Portuguese were the dominant naval power in the Indian Ocean. From a command post on the western coast of India, they administered a new, unprecedented political entity: a maritime empire.

In 1510 Albuquerque occupied the estuarine island of Goa on the Mandovi river and held it against a besieging army commanded by the Sultan of Bijapur whose principal port Goa had been. Goa became the seat of the viceroy and a council appointed by the Portuguese king in Lisbon. Between Goa and Lisbon a new, formal, sea borne linkage was established by which a European state exercised direct control over its subsidiary realm in the east. Each year a flotilla of vessels armed and equipped by the king sailed from Lisbon to Goa; each year a flotilla returned from the Indies. Portuguese and their slaves, precious metals, orders and correspondence, officials, supplies including firearms and other commodities travelled out to India. Returning Portuguese, spices, official dispatches and correspondence, and other commodities made the return voyage. An aggressive early modern state in Europe administered a direct political and economic connection between India and Europe.

[3] Bailey W. Diffie and George D. Winius, *Foundations of the Portuguese Empire, 1415–1580* (Minneapolis: University of Minnesota Press, 1977), pp. 214–219.

CHAPTER 1

CONQUEST AND STABILITY

The legacy of the Indo-Muslim frontier, the medieval Indian economy, and new connections with Europe helped to create conditions favorable to the rise of an imperial state in North India. These conditions by no means assured that such a state would arise, or that it would be ruled by the Timurids. The Mughal empire was the product of a prolonged political struggle whose outcome was in large measure due to the abilities and good fortune of its founders and builders. The two founders of the Mughal empire, Babur and his son and successor, Humayun, eventually won a bitter struggle with the Afghans for supremacy in northern India. In this conflict the Mughals, although kings, were scarcely to be viewed as emperors. They fought, sometimes against overwhelming odds, to create a Mughal domain in the rich Indo-Gangetic plain of north India.

Their principal adversaries were Afghans who had supplanted Turks and Persians to become the most powerful and widely dispersed foreign Muslim group in northern India. Under the Lodi dynasty thousands of Afghan soldiers and traders had migrated from the mountain valleys of Afghanistan to the plains of north India. Many, like the founder of the Lodi dynasty, Buhlul Lodi, could trace their origins to the overland horse trade. North Indian demands for riding and battle horses created a ready market for the hardy horses of the Central Asian steppe. By this point in time many of these Afghan adventurers had settled on the land as local lords who controlled a Hindu peasantry.

BABUR 1526–1530

The Mughal empire was founded by Zahir-ud-din Muhammad Babur, a Chaghatai Turkish ruler, who invaded the Lodi-governed Punjab several times from his capital at Kabul before winning a decisive victory. The unexpected entry of Babur into the Indian scene added a third party to the Afghan–Rajput struggle that had just begun. The Mughal intrusion displaced the indigenous Hindu Rajputs and the

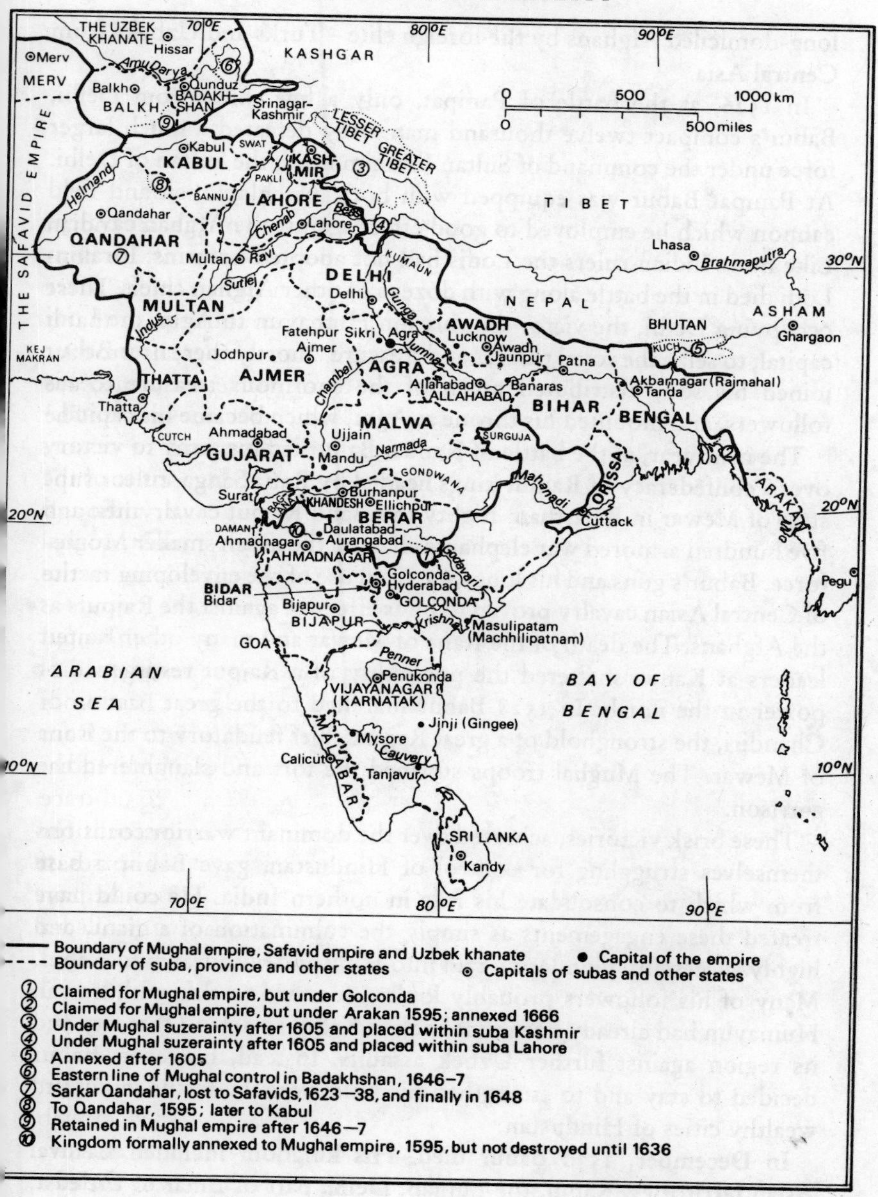

1 The Mughal empire, 1601
Source: I. Habib, *An atlas of the Mughal Empire* (Delhi, 1982), OA

long-domiciled Afghans by the foreign elite – Turks and Uzbeks from Central Asia.

In 1526, at the battle of Panipat, only a few miles from Delhi, Babur's compact twelve thousand man army defeated a much larger force under the command of Sultan Ibrahim Lodi, the Sultan of Delhi. At Panipat Babur was equipped with both matchlockmen and field cannon which he employed to good effect against the Afghan cavalry. Like most Indian rulers the Lodis had not adopted firearms. Ibrahim Lodi died in the battle along with dozens of other Afghan chiefs. After occupying Delhi, the victor sent his son Humayun to Agra, the Lodi capital, to seize the royal palaces and treasure. Shortly thereafter Babur joined his son, distributed much of the enormous treasure to his followers, and mounted his throne at Agra, which became his capital.[1]

The next year, at the battle of Kanua, Babur led his army to victory over a confederacy of Rajput kings headed by Rana Sanga, ruler of the state of Mewar in Rajasthan. Eighty thousand Rajput cavalrymen and five hundred armored war elephants charged the much smaller Mughal force. Babur's guns and his long-practiced use of the enveloping tactics of Central Asian cavalry proved to be as effective against the Rajputs as the Afghans. The death of the Rana of Mewar and many other Rajput leaders at Kanua shattered the possibility of a Rajput resurgence of power in the north. In 1528 Babur marched to the great bastion of Chandiri, the stronghold of a great Rajput chief feudatory to the Rana of Mewar. The Mughal troops stormed the fort and slaughtered the garrison.

These brisk victories, achieved over the dominant warrior coalitions themselves struggling for control of Hindustan, gave Babur a base from which to consolidate his rule in nothern India. He could have treated these engagements as simply the culmination of a giant, and highly successful, plundering raid into Hind and withdrawn to Kabul. Many of his followers probably looked forward to this withdrawal. Humayun had already been sent back to Kabul to defend that city and its region against further Uzbek assaults. Instead, however, Babur decided to stay and to strengthen his hold over the fertile lands and wealthy cities of Hindustan.

In December, 1530 Babur died. His kingdom included Central Asian territories, Kabul, the Punjab, Delhi, part of Bihar to the east,

[1] For further details see Rushbrook Williams, *An Empire Builder of the Sixteenth Century* (Delhi: S. Chand, 1922).

and south to Gwalior. As yet it was a new conquest state with little done to consolidate Mughal rule in the new Indian territories.

Babur bequeathed to his successors a distinguished lineage stretching back to the great Central Asian conqueror Timur, and also through the Chaghatai Turks back to Chingiz Khan. Through Timur, the Mughal dynasty claimed impeccable credentials as rulers and conquerors of extraordinary luster. (Hence the term Timurid used synonymously for Mughal in this volume.) In addition Babur's legacy included Central Asian horsemanship and battle tactics, life lived comfortably under canvas in tents, and the Turki language. He left a persistent and abiding Sunni Islamic faith and a familial connection with the orthodox Naqshbandi Sufi order which had originated in Central Asia. His legacy included a sophisticated cultural style derived from Timur's patronage at Samarkhand and refined at the courts of his successors in Central Asia. Finally, not least of Babur's heritage were his memoirs, written in Turki, which recounted his life adventures from his early youth in the valley of Ferghana to his conquest of India. Copied by distinguished calligraphers and illustrated by the finest painters, manuscript copies of Babur's remarkable journal became a primary source for the familial pride of the Mughal or Timurid dynasty.

HUMAYUN 1530–1556

The emperor Humayun (1530–1556) encountered massive difficulties in his efforts to retain and expand Babur's conquests in India. The source of one of his major problems was another of Babur's legacies. In keeping with the appanage system of the Timurids, Humayun distributed provinces to administer to each of his four brothers. In the northwest Mirza Sulaiman obtained Badakhshan, and Kamran governed Kabul and Qandahar. In India Askari and Hindal each were given large districts to administer. Within a year, Kamran, with the support of his brother Askari, occupied the Punjab and forcibly removed Humayun's governor. He then forced Humayun to agree to his possession of the province.[2] Humayun was thereby denied access to the resources of both the Punjab and the Central Asian bases of the Mughals.

[2] Ishwari Prasad, *The Life and Times of Humayun* (Bombay: Orient Longmans, 1956) pp. 44–45.

Humayun's immediate concerns lay with the Afghans to the east who looked to restore an heir to the Lodi throne. After an initial victory over the Afghan forces in the east, Humayun retreated into nearly a year of profound inactivity at Agra induced, it seems, by a growing addiction to opium taken with wine. During this period two powerful enemies consolidated their positions.

In the south Bahadur Shah, ruler of the prosperous maritime state of Gujarat, challenged Humayun by seizing control of the Sultanate of Malwa. Bahadur Shah was busily negotiating Afghan support in the northeast to try to eject the Mughals from North India. The Gujarat court was the refuge of many Lodi exiles who urged Bahadur Shah to action. Bahadur Shah had built up an extremely large army equipped with the latest cannon. He employed an Ottoman Turkish engineer and Portuguese gunners.[3]

In 1535 Humayun launched a campaign against the Gujarat ruler who was then engaged in his own invasion of Rajasthan. The Mughals defeated and drove back the Gujarat armies and captured the fortress of Champanir in Gujarat in a very short time. But delay and indecision on Humayun's part, largely brought on by opium use, forced him to withdraw from Gujarat without deposing Bahadur Shah or formally annexing the kingdom. Further danger from Gujarat ended with the untimely death of Bahadur Shah at the hands of the Portuguese.

While the Mughals were engaged on the seacoast, an extremely able Afghan nobleman, Sher Khan Sur, had quietly gained control of the military fief of his father in southern Bihar. During the five years consumed by Humayun's campaigns in the south, Sher Khan became the acknowledged leader of the Afghan resistance against the Mughals and a king in all but name. In 1537 Sher Khan invaded Bengal, defeated Mahmud Shah, the ruler of Bengal, and besieged him at Gaur, his capital. Fearing Sher Khan's growing power, Humayun marched to the east to relieve the Bengal Sultan. Unfortunately, Humayun's ill-advised attempt to take Chunar fort rather than pressing on to Gaur permitted Sher Khan to capture Gaur and take control of Bengal. Mahmud Sultan fled his lost kingdom to seek an insecure refuge with Humayun at Chunar.

The fall of Chunar was followed by months of maneuvering which left Sher Khan with strong Afghan support and Humayun in a precarious position in the east. The Mughals and the Afghans met once

[3] Prasad, *Humayun*, p. 71.

again at Chausa, a river town on the Ganges. Three months of inconclusive negotiations between Humayun and Sher Khan were ended by an Afghan surprise attack in June, 1539. The battle became a complete rout in which Humayun himself barely escaped alive. Sher Khan, who had defeated the acknowledged ruler of Hindustan, assumed the title of Sher Shah in a coronation ceremony after the battle.

In May, 1540, the Mughal and Afghan armies met once again near Kanauj. The demoralized Mughal army panicked, ran, and was butchered. Humayun fled to Agra and then on to Lahore with a few followers. At Lahore a confused meeting with Kamran and his other brothers produced no plan of action. Kamran refused to allow his brother to take refuge in Kabul. The Timurids decamped from Lahore just ahead of Sher Shah and left the Afghan leader unchallenged ruler of northern India in 1540.

During the next fifteen years, Humayun remained a royal exile, a refugee seeking a means to recover his throne in India. From Lahore he and his much-depleted army rode to Sind, then back to Rajasthan and to Sind again with varying responses from local chiefs and rulers. In 1544 he crossed the border to Herat and sought refuge with Shah Tahmasp, the Safavid ruler in Iran. At the Safavid court, Humayun, under extreme duress, accepted the Shia faith in order to keep himself and several hundred followers alive. After this initial test, Shah Tahmasp grew more friendly and eventually agreed to underwrite Humayun's attempt to regain power. With fresh troops and funds Humayun led a combined Mughal–Persian force which seized Qandahar and then occupied Kabul. There followed an eight-year war between Humayun and Kamran for dominance in Afghanistan. Finally, in 1553, the royal exile reoccupied Kabul as its unchallenged ruler. Kamran became his brother's captive and was blinded to render him incapable of rule.

From Kabul Humayun turned to duplicate his father's conquest of northern India. Sher Shar had only ruled at Agra for five years before his death in 1545. During that brief period his energetic administration forecast many of the centralizing measures in revenue assessment and military organization that would be carried to completion by the Mughals. The throne at Delhi passed to his son Islam Shah Sur, who in the course of an eight-year reign was not able consolidate his father's administrative reforms or his own centralized rule. At Islam Shah's death in 1553 the Sur domains were divided by treaty into the Punjab; Agra and Delhi; Bihar and the eastern region; and Bengal. Each was ruled by a son or relative of Sher Shah Sur. Everywhere the Sur administrative system was breaking up. Drought in preceding years brought famine conditions by early 1555. Popular distress contributed to Afghan demoralization as mortality from starvation and disease shot up.

Humayun, now fully energized, led his army from Kabul back to the northern Indian plain in late 1554. The Mughals met little resistance until Sikandar Shah Sur, the ruler of the Punjab, assembled a large Afghan army at the town of Sirhind. A hard-fought battle ended with Mughal victory. Sikandar Shah Sur fled the battlefield and with him went any hope of further Afghan resistance. Humayun entered Delhi and restored Babur's monarchy by mid-1555.

The Mughal restoration was complete. But Humayun had little time left. Within seven months, in January, 1556, he met a fatal accident on the steps of his library in the fortress at Delhi. Humayun's nobles concealed the fact of his death for seventeen days until they could secure a stable arrangement for the succession. The agreement arrived at permitted Humayun's young son Akbar, then twelve years of age, to be crowned under the title Jalal-ud-din Muhammad Akbar.

AKBAR 1556–1605

During his long reign Akbar made no emotional or political commitment to a permanent capital. His court, household, chancery, treasury, stables, and armories moved from one urban setting to another to suit changing circumstances. When desired, the Timurid ruler became readily mobile. The massive tents of the imperial encampment, emplaced after the day's march, retained the grandeur and fixed spatial arrangements of a permanent city built of stone. The emperor himself, rather than a physical site, was the capital of the empire.

Akbar's changing strategic foci are reflected in the four successive sites – Agra, Fatehpur Sikri, Lahore, and Agra – adopted as royal capitals. Each phase in his grand strategy is defined by increased Mughal power, resources and territory as the precarious regime inherited by the young Timurid prince grew into a multi-regional empire.

BAIRAM KHAN AS REGENT

Bairam Khan, a dominant member of Humayun's nobility, assumed the role of protector or regent for the young Akbar. Several months after Akbar's enthronement, Hemu, a minister and general of one of the presumptive heirs of Islam Shah Sur, marched with a huge army to attack Delhi. Hemu, a Hindu Vaisya or member of a literate, mercantile caste, who had risen from humble circumstances to be a general for the Sur regime, claimed royal status by employing the ancient Sanskrit title of Raja Vikramaditya. Had he succeeded this would have been a remarkable reassertion of the Sanskritic/Brahminical monarchical tradition in North India – long subservient to Muslim rulers. A much smaller Mughal army assembled by Bairam Khan with Akbar at his side met Hemu's forces at Panipat, the site of the climactic Lodi–Timurid battle three decades earlier. The Sur forces nearly overwhelmed the Mughals but for a stray arrow that wounded Hemu and brought him as a prisoner to the Mughal commanders. Together Bairam Khan and his young protégé slew the helpless Sur general. The dead commander's troops, thoroughly demoralized, rapidly deserted the battlefield to give the victory to the Mughals.

In the next six months the Mughals won another major battle against Sikandar, one of the Sur princes, who then fled east to Bengal. Under Bairam Khan's direction Mughal armies occupied Lahore and seized Multan in the Punjab. In 1558 they took possession of Ajmer, the aperture to Rajasthan, after the flight of its Muslim ruler. Late in the same year a Timurid commander defeated Ibrahim, the remaining Sur prince, and annexed Jaunpur, capital of the former Sultanate of Jaunpur in the eastern Gangetic valley. By early 1557 a Mughal force besieged a Sur commander in control of Gwalior fort, the greatest stronghold north of the Narmada river. After nearly two years the beleaguered Afghan garrison surrendered in January, 1558.

This aggressive flurry of activity put the vital cities and strongholds of a compact region between Lahore, Delhi, Agra, and Jaunpur under Mughal control. This was Hindustan, the old heartland of Muslim political and military power in North India. The Mughals, like their predecessors, now tapped the immense agricultural productivity and busy trade of the epicenter of the Indo-Gangetic plain. Lahore and Delhi stood together as western and eastern redoubts – symbols of Muslim victory and domination in Hindu north India.

By the fourth regnal year Bairam Khan had launched a drive to the south into Rajasthan and Malwa. At this juncture a new political struggle put a temporary halt to expansion. Akbar, then turned seventeen, chafed in adolescent rebellion against Bairam Khan's stern authority. Several clashes with the regent brought the young king to an alliance with a dissident faction of the nobility. This clique consisted of Adham Khan, Akbar's Turani foster brother, the son of his wet-nurse, and a group of his relatives. Hamida Begam, Akbar's mother, actively encouraged the planned coup. Ethnic and religious friction underlay dissatisfaction with the all-powerful minister. The orthodox Sunni Muslim Central Asian (Turani) nobles disliked deferring to a Persian Shia like Bairam Khan. Their dislike intensified when Bairam Khan appointed a fellow Shia theologian as religious minister (*sadr*) who controlled state patronage in the form of gifts, grants and jobs.

In March, 1560, Akbar, who was at Delhi, demanded Bairam Khan's resignation as chief minister. Feeling the erosion of his position, Bairam Khan complied. The disgraced minister could choose between continued personal service at court (but not as regent), or temporary exile in a pilgrimage to Mecca. Choosing the pilgrimage, the unfortunate minister was assassinated on his journey by an Afghan with a long-standing personal grievance, before he embarked for the sea passage.

TOWARD AUTONOMOUS RULE

Between 1560 and 1571, the first period of his mature rule, Akbar remained at Agra. For two years Maham Anaga, Akbar's foster mother, Adham Khan, and Shihab-ud-din, a cousin who served as governor of Delhi, exercised nearly complete political and fiscal powers.

The troika wasted little time in resuming military activity. A Mughal field army under the command of Adham Khan and Pir Muhammad Khan invaded the kingdom of Malwa. The Mughal army defeated Baz Bahadur, the Sultan of Malwa, at the town of Sarangpur. The defeated ruler fled to the Sultanate of Khandesh for refuge leaving his harem, treasure, and war elephants. His principal queen, Rupamati, famed for her beauty, took poison rather than lose her honor in captivity. This tragic theme has inspired many poetic compositions since that date.

Despite its initial success the campaign proved a disaster from

Akbar's point of view. Adham Khan retained virtually all the spoils. The victorious commander then followed Central Asian practice by wholesale slaughter of the surrendered garrison, their wives and children, and many Muslim theologians and Sayyids (descendants of the Prophet). The opprobrium this generated greatly upset Akbar. The emperor rode in person to the army's headquarters to confront Adham Khan and relieve him of command. Akbar sent his other leading general, Pir Muhammad Khan, in pursuit of Baz Bahadur deep into the territory of the Deccan Muslim Sultanate of Khandesh. But the rulers of Khandesh and Berar and the royal fugitive Baz Bahadur allied to beat back the Mughal army.

Baz Bahadur temporarily regained control of Malwa until, in the next year, another Mughal army invaded and firmly annexed the kingdom. Malwa became a province embedded within the nascent imperial administration of the Timurid regime. Baz Bahadur survived as a refugee at various courts until, eight years later, in 1570, he took service with his conqueror as a Mughal noble (*amir*).

Shortly after the return of the Mughal armies, in late 1561, Akbar's conflict with Adham Khan flared up again. Feeling slighted by the appointment of another noble as chief minister (*vakil*), Adham Khan attacked and killed the new minister in his own audience hall in the palace. When the still armed Adham Khan confronted Akbar in the harem, he was struck down by the outraged young emperor and thrown from a terrace into the palace courtyard. Still alive, Adham Khan was dragged up and thrown to the courtyard once again by Akbar to ensure his death. This dramatic event is described in full detail in the histories of the reign and graphically portrayed in miniature paintings. The fate of Adham Khan became part of a growing corpus of stories that together formed the legendary Akbar.

Akbar immediately assumed full executive powers as ruler. In place of the office of chief minister he created four specialized ministerial posts for financial, military, household, and religious affairs. In so doing, he removed one focal point for noble rebellion and discontent. No single member of the Mughal nobility would have unquestioned preeminence and thereby attract dissident adherents. The threat of an over-mighty chief minister had been diverted – at least until the waning days of the dynasty.

Beyond these measures the young ruler faced the problem of political organization. Military victories were not enough; the new regime required a coherent political statement. Somehow Akbar had to interweave the strands of his inherited Timurid charisma and authority, of centralized authority inherited from the Surs and the Sultans of Delhi, and the notion of Islamic legitimacy. If he failed to do so, North India would undergo once again war between Mughals, Afghans, Rajputs, and regional Muslim rulers which had disfigured the previous three decades. Merely to survive as a ruler, he must win over or break the power of two groups: the Muslim nobility with its armed power and wealth, and the religious elites of Islam, the *ulema* and Sufi shaikhs, with their influence over the Muslim community in India.

NEW CONQUESTS

In 1561 Sher Khan Sur, son of Adil Shah Sur, still unsubdued, marched from the great Afghan bastion at Chunar toward Jaunpur with a large army. Two Mughal commanders, Zaman Khan and Bahadur Khan, Central Asian Uzbek nobles, dealt a sharp defeat to the Afghans and seized arms, treasure and war elephants. Zaman Khan duly reported the victory to the emperor, but retained the battle plunder without permission. Akbar was incensed at the violation of royal prerogatives – especially in the case of the war elephants whose use was a royal symbol in India. He marched in person to Kara and confronted the two generals in person. They paid formal homage to him and dutifully handed over the spoils of battle. The seizure of Chunar rounded out the first phase of Mughal expansion in the east.

In the two years after the departure of Bairam Khan, the Mughal ruler, still not past his twentieth birthday, displayed his true political and organizational capabilities. He asserted his position as an absolutist ruler demanding deference from all. Even victorious generals could be brought to submission if prompt vigorous action were taken by the emperor. Akbar became his own comander-in-chief and most capable strategist and field commander.

As a symbol of his new-found autonomy and military prowess, Akbar sent a mission to the Baghela Rajput ruler Ram Chand at Kalinjar, his capital, to induce the famed singer–musician Tansen to come to the Mughal court at Agra. Ram Chand, who had rejected earlier overtures from the Surs, dared not refuse and sent Tansen with his instruments and lavish presents to Akbar's court. Akbar is said to have given Tansen two hundred thousand rupees as a gift on the occasion of his first performance at court. Acquisition of Tansen's services stimulated Akbar's active patronage of music. Tansen, and after him, his sons and other pupils actively cultivated what was to become known as North Indian or Hindustani music.

After Malwa the first major target was the hilly, thinly populated kingdom of Garha-Katanga, or Gondwana, famed for its herds of wild elephants. A Mughal army under Asaf Khan, an Uzbek noble, invaded the kingdom in 1564. The Rajput queen, Rani Durgavati of the Candela lineage, died commanding her armies in a futile defense. The Mughals swept aside the remaining Rajput defenders and marched on the capital at Chauragarh. The young Candela prince Bir Narayan died in battle. Most of his female relatives perished in the bloody rite of suicide and immolation in flames reserved for noble Rajput women and their attendants (*jauhar*). Garha-Katanga became a huge district (*sarkar*) incorporated within the just acquired province of Malwa. As was the case with all such imperial annexations the boundaries and internal divisions of the kingdom remained unaltered.

THE UZBEK REVOLT

In 1564, trouble flared up with the Uzbek nobles, Khan Zaman and his brother Bahadur Khan, who had defeated the Afghans at Chunar. Although most of these nobles had returned with Humayun to India, Uzbek allegiance to the Timurids was not as firm as it might have been. The Uzbek nobles traced their lineage back to Shaiban, the Uzbek ruler, who had been Babur's nemesis a half century earlier and whose descendants continued to rule in Central Asia. Accustomed to a more egalitarian political tradition, these grandees resented Akbar's imperious ruling style. Considerable friction existed also between the staunch Sunni Muslim Uzbeks and the Shia Persian nobles employed in Mughal service. Not surprisingly, the Uzbek dissidents determined to test Akbar early while the young ruler was still solidifying his position.

In 1564 Abdullah Khan, governor of Malwa, went into open revolt. Akbar marched with an army to Mandu and drove the rebel with his followers to seek refuge in the still-independent Sultanate of Gujarat. Early in 1565 Akbar's attempt to recall the senior Uzbek officer in Awadh, touched off a unified Uzbek rebellion. A confused series of battles and negotiations ended in early 1566 with Akbar's withdrawal to Agra and the rebels still holding the eastern provinces.

Akbar also faced a potential challenge from his half-brother, Mirza Muhammad Hakim, who governed Kabul and its surrounding districts. Mirza Muhammad Hakim's hold on Kabul was threatened by the Timurid ruler of Badakhshan (whose kingdom had been restored to him in 1530 by Babur). Despite Akbar's assistance, the Badakhshani armies were besieging Kabul in 1566. Muhammad Hakim left a garrison in place and retreated with his army towards the Indus river in the Punjab plain.

The still unreconciled Uzbek nobles, learning of these events, invited Muhammad Hakim to invade India. They, in turn, proclaimed him the legitimate Mughal ruler by having Muhammad Hakim's name read in the Friday prayers (the *khutba*) in the great mosque at Jaunpur. Encouraged by this, Muhammad Hakim marched through the Punjab and besieged Lahore. At this critical point, a group of Timurid nobles bearing the title Mirza or prince also rebelled and tried to seize Delhi. The elderly leader, Muhammad Sultan Mirza, was descended from Timur's second son (instead of Akbar's descent from the third son). In theory, at least, Muhammad Sultan, or his numerous sons and grandsons, could claim Akbar's throne. This claim was strengthened by intermarriage with Timurid princesses from Akbar's line. Loyalist commanders drove off the rebels and captured Muhammad Sultan Mirza. The remaining Mirzas sought refuge and support from the Rana of Mewar and other Rajput rulers in Rajasthan.

Akbar responded to this crisis by ignoring the Mirzas and marching to confront his half-brother at Lahore. Mirza Muhammad Hakim retreated to Kabul, now cleared of the Badakhshan army. Akbar chose not to pursue him. For the next decade, Mirza Muhammad Hakim acted as a sovereign ruler at Kabul and posed a continuing danger to Akbar's regime in India.

The emperor wheeled his army round and marched east to dislodge the Uzbeks from the cities and fortresses they had seized. In June, in the midst of the monsoon, the emperor reached Manikpur on the bank of the rain-swollen Ganges. The Uzbeks were encamped across the river and unaware that the royal army had arrived so quickly. Akbar led a surprise night river crossing and attacked the rebels at dawn. In the ensuing fracas Akbar's troops killed or captured for execution the Uzbek nobles who had opposed him. In the closing phase of the revolt, the emperor drove the dispirited Mirzas and their followers south to take refuge with the Sultan of Gujarat.

Somehow the young emperor survived one of the most dangerous episodes in his career. Throughout this three-year period he relied as much on negotiation and diplomacy as on force to deter the rebels. His Timurid ancestry was an asset, but it alone could not ensure fidelity from all his nobles. In the end, battle decided the issue.

THE NEW NOBILITY

The Uzbek revolt underscored Akbar's vulnerability vis-a-vis his nobles. These warrior-grandees drew upon inherited positions of power, authority, and influence with their kinsmen. The amirs were heirs to bellicose martial traditions that emphasized personal honor, dignity, and bravery on the field of battle. Always armed themselves, they commanded varying numbers of personal slaves, dependent kinsmen, and paid retainers.

The small cadre of fifty-one nobles who returned to India with Humayun in 1555 were nearly all foreign-born Muslims.[4] Twenty-seven, or over half, were from Central Asia. These were high-status chiefs from Chaghatai Turkish or Uzbek Central Asian lineages. By this time members of both lineages could claim varying degrees of blood relationship with Humayun. All were imbued with the egalitarian and divisive attitudes of the Central Asian Turkish tribes. And they were well aware that Mirza Muhammad Hakim offered a legitimate alternative to Akbar's rule. A second group consisted of sixteen Persian Shi`ite nobles, including Bairam Khan, who formed the primary counterweight to the Turanis or Central Asian *beks*. The Iranis were more willing to accede to the notion of an unchallenged *pad shah* or emperor in the Persian imperial tradition.

Akbar recruited new nobles to serve the needs of his enlarging empire. In the course of twenty-five years the imperial elite had grown six-fold to 222 amirs. The emperor's fixed goal was to reduce the relative numbers and influence of his Central Asian nobles. To do so, he vigorously recruited Persian entrants into the service. By 1580 Persians numbered forty-seven; Chaghatai and Uzbek Turanis forty-eight.

Beyond this, however, the young leader recruited new men from

[4] Iqtidar Alam Khan, "The Nobility Under Akbar and the Development of His Religious Policy, 1560–1580," *Journal of the Royal Asiatic Society* (1968), pp. 29–36. Data on the composition and numbers of nobles are taken from this source.

Indian, rather than foreign, racial, and religious backgrounds. Many Indian Muslim warriors had become landed aristocrats as they put down local roots and seized lands from Rajputs and other Hindu groups in North India. Afghans, probably the most numerous body of Indian Muslims, were necessarily excluded. Continuing bitterness and resistance among Afghan grandees in the east meant that Afghan recruitment was not a feasible option for the Timurids.

Other Muslims long resident in North India, but rarely favored with access to political power at the court of the Delhi Sultans, were more pliable. Such, for example, were the Sayyids of Baraha, invariably referred to as brave warriors, whose names begin to appear in imperial annals in the early 1560s. Their ancestor, claiming descent from the Prophet Muhammad, had migrated from Iraq during the thirteenth century and settled in Sirhind near Delhi. From this original settlement numerous descendants proliferated and peopled other villages and lands in the region. Proverbially loyal, the Sayyid leaders could muster several thousand of their bellicose kinsmen for service under Akbar. Other Indian Muslim nobles enlisted to the point that, by 1580, forty-four men (16 percent) of the enlarged nobility were indigenous Muslims.

More significant was Akbar's recruitment of Hindu Rajput leaders into the Mughal nobility. During the fifteenth century Indo-Muslim rulers of regional kingdoms (but not the Sultans of Delhi) had accepted unconverted Hindu warriors into their elite cadres. Even the Surs had benefited from the services of Hemu, a Vaisya administrator and general. Nevertheless, although scarcely unprecedented, this was a major step for the Timurids. In 1561, a minor Rajput chief, head of the Kachhwaha clan of Amber, sought the emperor's intervention in a bid to keep his power against an unfriendly Mughal governor. Bharamall, the Kachhwaha raja, had actively supported Humayun in the conflict with the Surs. When Akbar was marching near Jaipur, the Rajput suppliant offered one of his daughters in marriage to the young monarch. Akbar agreed, the marriage was performed, and the emperor accepted Bharamall, his son, and grandson as amirs in imperial service. The Kachhwaha raja retained his seat at Amber.[5]

Over the next two decades, Akbar demonstrated the reality of Mughal power by repeated campaigns in Rajasthan. Other Rajput

[5] Kunwar Refaqat Ali Khan, *The Kachhwahas Under Akbar and Jahangir* (New Delhi: Kitab Publishing House, 1976).

chiefs negotiated entry into the imperial elite and offered their daughters as marriage partners for the Mughal emperor. By the sixteenth century a diffuse political system based on the obligations of patrilineal kinship and marriage alliances was ripe for political centralization. Several generations of settlement and frontier expansion, driven in large measure by Islamic conquest in the Gangetic valley, resulted in increased productivity and population densities in Rajasthan. Akbar generally recruited Rajput clan heads who either claimed royal blood, or who were the scions of great noble houses. These *thakurs* or masters were the aristocrats of Rajput society in contrast to the more obscure *bhumiya* warriors who possessed only modest power, land and status.

By 1580, Rajputs (and a few other non-Rajput Hindus) numbered forty-three members of the nobility. Each raja was awarded high rank, pay and perquisities. His adult sons, and other close male relatives and kinsmen, obtained lesser *mansabdari* rank as well. In conformity with imperial regulations, Rajput noblemen organized their kinsmen and non-kin retainers into cavalry contingents armed and equipped for active military service. Rajputs were required to serve the emperor personally wherever he might be sent. At court, Rajputs publicly acknowledged the authority and supremacy of the emperor and became conversant with Persian and imperial manners and etiquette. In so doing they were assured that they could retain their beliefs, customs, and honor as Hindu warriors.

In return for imperial rank and privileges the rajas conceded tight Mughal domination over Rajasthan. By placing a *tika* or vermillion mark on the new raja's forehead in court, the emperor legitimized his position. Simultaneously Akbar stipulated rank and precedence and gave the new nobleman valuable ceremonial gifts. The new raja was expected to offer a substantial tribute or *pishkash* as his part of this gift exchange. The emperor conferred the ancestral lands (*watan*) of the raja as his non-transferable holding. These lands were not subject to tribute but their estimated revenues were applied to the pay expected for imperial service. When Bharamall, the Kachhwaha raja, submitted to Akbar, his domain lands consisted of the villages and towns of Amber *pargana* in eastern Rajasthan.[6] The administration estimated Amber's annual revenues and applied them to the pay and perquisites of the raja according to his rank as a Mughal nobleman. Revenues from

[6] Satya Prakash Gupta, *The Agrarian System of Eastern Rajasthan (c.1650–c.1750)* (Delhi: Manohar, 1986), p. 5.

several additional parganas within and, in some cases, outside Rajasthan, were assigned to Bharamall as a transferable salary assignment. The number and location of these additional lands fluctuated as the rank and pay of Bharamall and his successors varied. The net effect was to secure the Kachhwaha ancestral lands in Amber from external or internal threats and to make available revenues from other lands to the raja. The intent was to thwart any attempt to enlarge the Amber domains and create a larger state. The emperor made similar arrangements with other Rajputs as they submitted to him.

Akbar clamped tight imperial control over the Rajputs and the new province of Rajasthan. The Rajput lands did not become a set of autonomously ruled tributary kingdoms. Instead, Mughal governance of the province was very similar to other directly administered provinces in the Gangetic plain. A Mughal governor with substantial numbers of troops occupied a newly built imperial fortress at Ajmer, which became the provincial capital. Only imperial currency could circulate; only imperial tolls could be levied on the overland caravan traffic to the Gujarat ports. The standard Mughal revenue system, complete with detailed assessments, land survey and registration, and cash payments for each village became the standard. Those areas not held by Rajput amirs were routinely assigned as transferable revenue producing areas to non-Rajput *mansabdars*. A mixed stratum composed of Rajput bhumiyas, Jat and other dominant castes continued to act as intermediaries between the imperial claimants and the producing peasantry.

Submission to the Timurid dynasty did not violate the Rajput *dharma* or inherited code for moral conduct as set out in the bardic literature of the period. The Mughal tie initially encouraged, rather than disrupted, kinship solidarity. Each Rajput nobleman relied heavily upon his kinsmen for military service and advice and counsel. His immediate coterie was formed from his "brotherhood" (*bhaibamdh*) consisting of all males tracing shared patrilineal descent up to six generations.[7] Each brotherhood formed a kinship unit holding intrinsic power to rule its homelands won by colonization, conquest, and settlement. The larger sphere for recruiting lay in the patrilineal clan, composed of several brotherhoods of varying status and power

[7] Norman P. Ziegler, "Some Notes on Rajput Loyalties During the Mughal Period" in J. F. Richards, ed., *Kingship and Authority in South Asia*, (Madison Wisconsin, South Asian Studies No. 3, 1978), pp. 231–232.

who together claimed descent from a common male eponymous ancestor. The brotherhood and the clan rose in prestige and power as warriors in Mughal service.

Rajput thakurs who offered their daughters for marriage created a powerful bond between themselves and the Timurid house. The second primary unit of recognition for each Rajput was the brotherhood to which he gave daughters and from which he received wives. Marriage created an alliance with his wife's male relatives that could be called upon at any time for support and assistance.[8] Although not reciprocal, since no women came from the Mughal side, marriage became an important strand in the ties that bound the Rajputs to the empire. For many thakurs, notably the Rana of Mewar, supplying Rajput noblewomen for the emperor or princes was seen as a disgraceful submission. Those houses who offered brides had made the critical gesture of subordination.

Mughal service was compatible with the ethos of the warrior in service to a great master. Rajputs were enjoined to fight and die in battle in the service of a master. A warrior's service was expressed in acts of complete self-sacrifice and devotion for the earthly master and for god. Salvation for the warrior was the result of such devotion. The Rajput master or thakur acquired his power to conquer and rule by devotion to his god or goddess. The thakur then transmitted the essence of his power and authority to lesser men, also thakurs, who could rule smaller domains within his own. In accepting Akbar's service Rajput thakurs thereby accepted him as a Muslim Rajput who possessed far greater power and sovereignty than even the greatest of Rajput masters. The bardic traditions from this period often "equate [Akbar] with Ram, the pre-eminent Ksatriya cultural hero of the Hindu Rajput."[9]

Both sides benefited by this arrangement. The Timurids won the loyalty of thousands of Rajput warriors, generation after generation. The publicly proclaimed devotion of these prestigious chiefs had its impact on hundreds of lesser Rajput lineages who controlled localities across northern and central India. Akbar preempted the possibility of the rise of another Rajput coalition similar to that which his grandfather had faced at Kanua in 1527. The Rajputs in turn placed themselves within a much wider political arena. Instead of being caught up in local internecine conflicts, they became imperial generals,

[8] Ibid., p. 224. [9] Ibid., p. 235.

statesmen, and high administrators. Instead of being content with the produce of the semi-arid lands of Rajasthan, they diverted streams of wealth from the largess of the empire toward their homelands. Further reinforced by a powerful dynastic appeal, Akbar forged a political bond that would endure for nearly two centuries between Rajput and Mughal.

RANKING

Akbar had created a complex, heterogeneous nobility with divergent experience and cultural expectations. But how could he cope with this diversity? The young emperor resorted to a system of honorific ranks or *mansabs* derived from his Mongol background. These assigned a numerical rank to each officer in imperial service. Each mansabdar or "rank-holder's" status, pay, range of official assignments, and titles were defined by his personal (*zat*) rank. The emperor was the source of all rankings and changes in rankings. As the ranking system evolved, the graded ranks became a supple, powerful instrument to reward or to punish military and civil officers in imperial service.

The decimal ranking order had its origins in the system employed by the Mongols for military commanders. The latter were graded from commanders of ten to those of a hundred, a thousand, and ten thousand troops. The later Timurids continued to employ the terminology although the actual number of troops was often less than the nominal figure in the title. Even the Sur dynasty had employed a similar rank order for its military commanders. From these precedents Akbar created a comprehensive system in which every officer or official was ranked.

In theory, personal rank could be any one of sixty-six even numbered ranks from twenty to five thousand zat (or even ten thousand for princes of the blood). In practice only thirty-three ranks were actually in use. Soldiers and bureaucrats alike were mansabdars although higher ranks tended to fall to military commanders rather than financial or judicial specialists. Increases or decreases in rank followed no set rules but were dependent upon royal favor. Especially meritorious service – such as great courage and devotion in battle – resulted often in large increases in rank. Emigré aristocrats from Persia, Turan or elsewhere were given higher ranks as were Rajput chiefs and other powerful local lords who enlisted with Akbar. But these ranks did not transfer directly to sons and heirs. A mansabdar could see that his son was enrolled in Mughal service, frequently as a member of his own contingent, but the young aspirant obtained a modest rank in relation to that of his father.

Later in the reign, by the 1590s a second decimal ranking came into use. The *suwar* or "trooper" ranking denoted the number of armed heavy cavalrymen each mansabdar was required to recruit, train, command, and pay. In succeeding reigns virtually all mansabdars held suwar ranks expressed in even numbers from as little as ten to as high as five thousand. Numerical trooper rank determined the additional funds paid the mansabdar to permit him to maintain his military contingent. In Akbar's time the trooper rank matched the number of cavalry mustered. The latter varied from a small band of ten retainers led by a petty officer to a field army of five thousand horsemen organized by an amir or noble. All cavalry commanded by mansabdars were at the disposal of the emperor. All had to meet strict imperial standards.

This approach fell short of a centrally recruited and paid, bureaucratic, standing army. Instead, organization by military captains and their followers shifted the burden of recruitment, pay, and command to individual mansabdars. By imposing uniform royal standards, Akbar secured the benefits of a large central army without the crushing financial and administrative burden such an entity usually carried with it.

CHITOR AND RANTHAMBOR

Rajput willingness to accept Mughal hegemony was not won without force. In the early 1560s the most prestigious Rajput ruler, the Rana of Mewar, remained defiant. Udai Singh (1540–1572) was descended from the Sisodia ruler Rana Sanga who had died fighting Babur at the battle of Kanua in 1527. As head of the Sisodia clan he possessed the highest ritual status of all the Rajput rajas and chiefs scattered across the landscape of North and Central India. Unless Udai Singh were reduced to submission, the imperial authority of the Timurids would be lessened in Rajput eyes. Akbar, at this early period, was still enthusiastically devoted to the cause of Islam and sought to impress the superiority of his faith over the most prestigious warriors in Brahminical Hinduism.

Udai Singh's son was in uneasy residence in Akbar's court. When asked by Akbar (in jest as Abul Fazl claims) as to whether he would support his father or the emperor in a confrontation, the young Rajput prince fled back to Mewar. Akbar was enraged and determined on war. In September, 1567, the emperor led his armies in a holy war or jihad toward Chitor, the capital of Mewar, a fortified city rising 200 meters above the Rajasthan plain.[10] As the imperial armies approached, Udai Singh's advisers in council concluded that the Sisodia army could not face the Mughals in open battle. Instead, Udai Singh left a 5,000 man garrison in Chitor with supplies to withstand a protracted siege and retreated to a subordinate fortress in the hills. Within a month Akbar laid his siege lines completely around Chitor. His raiding parties devastated the countryside and captured Udaipur, the other leading city.

After initial assaults on the walls failed, taking heavy casualties, the besieging army set up three large batteries to bombard the fort. Simultaneously, imperial sappers commenced digging tunnels for two mines and an approach trench (*sabat*). The artillerymen cast a large siege cannon on site to be used for breaching the walls when the sabat reached its objective. At this point the garrison tried to negotiate a surrender on terms; Akbar rejected this overture.

Fifty-eight days into the siege, the sappers had reached the walls and exploded the first of the mines. When the second mine went off it killed about 200 of the assault force caught in the breach. The defenders sealed up the walls. Akbar then pushed ahead with his covered trench to bring his siege cannon within range of the walls. On the night of 22 February, the Mughals made several breaches in the wall and began a general assault. During the melee, Akbar killed Jaimal, the Rajput commander of Chitor, with a well-aimed musket shot, whose death broke the morale of the defenders. Rising pillars of smoke soon signalled the rite of jauhar as the Rajputs killed their families and prepared to die in a supreme sacrifice. In a day filled with hand-to-hand struggles virtually all the defenders died. The Mughal troops slaughtered another 20–25,000 ordinary persons, inhabitants of the town and peasants from the surrounding area on the grounds that they had actively helped in the resistance. Only an audacious body of one thousand musketeers, men of Kalpi who had done much damage to the

[10] Abul Fazl, *The Akbar-Nama* (Calcutta: Asiatic Society of Bengal, 3 vols., 1907, 1912, 1939), translated by H. Beveridge II, 464–477.

Mughals in the siege, managed to escape Akbar's wrath. They bound their wives and children and marched them right through the imperial lines as if they were Mughal troops carrying off prisoners.

Although the imperial armies found little treasure to seize, the fortress was destroyed to the point that it remained deserted thereafter. A victory proclamation (*fath nama*) issued in early March celebrates the successful prosecution of the holy war against the polytheists by the Timurid ruler.[11] Udai Singh, however, remained at large, uncaptured by the Mughals until his death four years later. Akbar, for his part, fulfilled an earlier vow by marching on foot to Ajmer in pilgrimage to the shrine of Khwaja Muin-ud-din Chishti. There, during the month of Ramazan, Akbar circumambulated the shrine, gave gifts to the poor and pious, and after ten days returned to Agra.

The next year, in February, 1569, Akbar led his army to an assault on the massive fortress at Ranthambor which, together with Chitor, controlled the major trade corridor to the sea. Rai Surjan, of the Hada lineage, held the fort and its territory as a vassal of Udai Singh. At Ranthambor, the Mughals employed hundreds of bullocks and dozens of elephants to drag fifteen massive siege guns to a hill overlooking the fortress. When, after only a month, these guns started bombarding the fortress and the covered way had reached the walls, the garrison surrendered on terms. Rai Surjan accepted imperial service in return for retention of his ancestral holdings.

The sieges of Chitor and Ranthambor were spectacular public events. The fall of these great forts demonstrated the reality of Mughal power for every warrior in North India. Outright defiance to the Mughal emperor was not possible; submission or death was the only choice.

IMPERIAL STRONGHOLDS

At the same time that he was demonstrating the inability of any fortress, however strong, to defy his assaults, Akbar was busily engaged in constructing his own strategic network of strongholds. His first concern was to fortify his capital at Agra, "which by position is the centre of Hindustan." In 1565 after "lofty minded mathematicians and able architects laid the foundations" the massive walls and four gates of the fort began to rise on the banks of the Yamuna river:[12]

[11] K. A. Nizami, *Akbar and Religion* (Delhi, 1989), pp. 383–399.
[12] Ibid., p. 372.

Every day 3 to 4,000 active builders and strong-armed labourers carried on the work. From the foundations to the battlements, the fortress was composed of hewn stones, each of which was polished like a world-revealing mirror, and was ruddy as the cheek of fortune. And they were so joined together that the end of a hair could not find a place between them. This sublime fortress ... was completed with its battlements, breastwork, and its loop-holes ... in the space of eight years under the faithful superintendence of Musim Khan Mir Barr u Bahr.

The massive red fortress contained over five hundred buildings when completed. Still standing today it "was to be stable like the foundation of the domination of the sublime family and permanent like the pillars of its fortunes."[13]

Over the next two decades, Akbar, as part of his grand strategy, erected two other huge palace fortresses. Allahabad (formerly the Hindu city of Prayag), guarded the conjunction of the Ganges and Yamuna rivers in the eastern Gangetic plain. Lahore, the capital of the Punjab, was the first line of defense against an assault over the northwest passes from Afghanistan or Central Asia – the classic invasion route. These three large fortress and palace complexes, defended by heavy cannon, were virtually impregnable to direct assault. The emperor further anchored this defensive line by building a strongly defended castle (begun 1570) at Ajmer, the gateway to the Rajasthan corridor. He strengthened the strategically placed frontier strongholds in the northwest at Attock and Rohtas on the Indus. In the east the bastion of Rohtas in Bihar stood guard.

The Lahore, Agra, Allahabad, Ajmer quadrilateral formed a protective framework for Mughal imperial power. The great walls of these bastions secured growing hoards of imperial treasure and massive arsenals, and provided ultimate safety for the person of the emperor and his court and household. Fortress commanders, who received their appointments directly from the emperor, were responsible directly to the imperial court. To ensure their autonomy the custom grew up of assigning revenues from those villages and lands surrounding each fortress to meet the needs of the garrison. The Mughals occupied and garrisoned many other famous strongholds as they expanded, including Gwalior, and the great forts of Rajasthan – Chitor, Ranthambor and Mirtha – as well as Asirgarh (near Burhanpur) and the massive hill forts of the Deccan provinces. Nevertheless, imperial security rested on the great strongholds in Hindustan – the very center of the empire.

[13] Ibid., p. 372.

CHAPTER 2

THE NEW EMPIRE

In 1571 Akbar moved twenty-six miles from Agra to Fatehpur Sikri, a newly built city that would be his capital until 1585. During his fifteen year residence at Fatehpur Sikri Akbar directed major conquests and surmounted his most dangerous political crisis. The new city was also the site of significant organizational and administrative initiatives – measures that put an indelible stamp upon the Mughal imperial system. Brilliant innovations in land revenue, coinage, military organization, and provincial administration emerged from the Fatehpur Sikri years.

Why Fatehpur Sikri in preference to the great Indo-Muslim political capitals like Delhi, Agra, Lahore, and Jaunpur? Why remove to the village of Sikri at a hard day's march from Agra?[1] Agra and Fatehpur Sikri were in reality joint capitals. For security the bulk of the imperial treasure hoards as well as arsenals and other reserves were kept in Agra fort. The court, harem, and treasury could be quickly removed to Agra for safety.[2]

The newly constructed city bore a similarity to the movable imperial encampment also designed by Akbar. Fatehpur Sikri was an urban form in transition between camp and imperial metropolis. Akbar recreated his camp in stone within the boundaries of Fatehpur Sikri. The facades of the buildings strongly resembled the great wood and canvas structures erected in the imperial encampment. Like the camp, the capital gave the Mughal emperor a disciplined, controlled organism from which to write, rehearse, and play out the drama of imperial rule.

Fatehpur Sikri was also a refuge, a courtly city whose architecture and public spaces were very much an expression of the young ruler's passion for building and design. Here Akbar satisfied those creative, aesthetic impulses typical of the Timurids. Music was already well established under Tansen's leadership. In addition painting, calligra-

1 For a full treatment of Fatehpur Sikri see Michael Brand and Glenn D. Lowry, eds., *Fatehpur Sikri* (Bombay: Marg Publications, 1987).

2 Irfan Habib, "The Economic and Social Setting," in Brand and Lowry, *Fatehpur Sikri*, p. 80.

phy, poetry, history, comparative religion, architecture all flourished in an urbane and sophisticated setting.

AN ISLAMIC CITY

Akbar employed the design and construction of Fatehpur Sikri to symbolize, in those early years, the regime's Islamic foundation. Two nested sacred buildings dominated the city. The great congregational mosque and the tomb (*dargah*) of a widely revered and worshipped Sufi saint were the binary institutions of legal and mystic Indian Islam. The elegant marble tomb housed the remains of Shaikh Salim Chishti (d. 1571) from whom the young ruler frequently sought spiritual advice. Shaikh Salim's blessing and prophecy regarding the birth of Akbar's long-awaited male heir, Sultan Salim, caused the emperor to locate his new capital at the village of Sikri. By placing Shaikh Salim's tomb inside the great mosque, Akbar was able to draw upon the palpable sanctity adhering to it and assimilate this to his own authority.

The emperor encouraged the sons and grandsons of Shaikh Salim to enlist as high-ranking officers in the imperial service rather than to remain at the shrine as heirs to their familial tradition. Incorporation of the Chishti mystical aura into Fatehpur Sikri and its eventual subordination to the Emperor was an essential part of the religiosity Akbar claimed for the regime. It is important to keep in mind, however, that Akbar made his appeal cloaked in the symbols of the broadest, most appealing, form of Sufi devotionalism possible. The Chishtis were esteemed for their austerity and rejection of secular power and influence. It is noteworthy that the young emperor did not choose to so identify himself with the Naqshbandis of Northern India despite his family's long association with that orthodox Central Asian order.

Akbar juxtaposed this appeal with an unambiguous affirmation of the orthodox Muslim foundations of his regime. The great congregational mosque at Fatehpur Sikri is the largest and certainly the dominant building in the city. For nearly a decade after its erection the emperor took an active interest in the operation of the mosque. His devotional acts – under the tutelage of Shaikh Abdul Nabi, the chief jurist of the empire – included sweeping the floor of the mosque and acting as prayer leader.

During this period Akbar gave further evidence of Islamic piety by actively organizing and sponsoring an official pilgrimage to Mecca each year. After 1574 the conquest of Gujarat permitted direct access to the Holy Cities from the west coast port of Surat across the Arabian Sea to Jiddah. The emperor enlarged the pious trust (*waqf*) established by the last Sultan of Gujarat which sent the revenues of several coastal villages as donations to Mecca and Medina. In 1576 the first Mughal pilgrim caravan, under the command of a specially appointed Mughal officer known as the Mir Haj, left Agra for Surat port. There a special pilgrim ship, the *Ilahi* waited. All expenses were paid entirely by the emperor who also sent large sums for charity and several thousand honorific robes of honor for the pious. The first party included Gulbadan Begam, Akbar's aunt, the Empress Salima Sultan Begam and other high-born women. Akbar himself was dissuaded from travelling only by the pleas of Abul Fazl.[3]

The emperor further underscored his piety by travelling on foot from Fatehpur Sikri on an annual royal pilgrimage to the tomb of Khwaja Muin-ud-din Chishti at Ajmer. Regular visits to Ajmer, the strategic site for imperial dominance over Rajasthan, served also to remind the Rajputs of Timurid power. At the beginning of his nineteenth regnal year:[4]

> [Akbar] took the generous-hearted and noble minded prince Sultan Salim, with himself for the circumambulation of the auspicious and heavenly illuminated tomb at Ajmer. When the eye of that fortunate, God-gifted and successful prince fell on the tomb of the great Khwaja, he, following the example of his illustrious father, bowed with great humility to the noble tomb and sacred threshold, and performed the ceremony of circumambulation, and the duty of pilgrimage.

Immediately thereafter followed the ceremony of weighing both ruler and prince against gold and silver and other precious commodities.

We cannot find a clearer statement of the spiritual reference point sought by Akbar for his rule than in this episode. In addition to his own prostration and public worship at the tomb the emperor proclaimed his son Salim's devotion as well. These recurring ceremonies acted out the same devotional message expressed in stone within Fatehpur Sikri. Royal heirs, royal victory, and royal authority flowed from devotion to the Chishti saints.

[3] N. R. Farooqi, "Mughal–Ottoman Relations: A Study of Political and Diplomatic Relations Between Mughal India and the Ottoman Empire, 1556–1748," unpublished Ph.D. dissertation (University of Wisconsin, Madison, 1986), pp. 191–196.

[4] Nizam-ud-din Ahmad, *Tabaqat-i Akbari*, English translation by B. De and Baini Prashad, (Calcutta: Royal Asiatic Society of Bengal, 3 vols., 1927–39) II, 429.

NEW CONQUESTS

Akbar's new capital became headquarters for a new phase of expansion southwest toward Gujarat and the Arabian Sea. The appeal of Gujarat to Akbar, as it was to his father Humayun before him, is not difficult to discern. The coastal region possessed areas of rich agricultural production in its central plain; an impressive output of textiles and other industrial goods; and the busiest seaports of the Indian subcontinent. To link this maritime kingdom with the massive resources of the Indo-Gangetic plain would greatly strengthen Akbar's growing empire.

Akbar could take advantage of Gujarat's political troubles. A weak king, Muzaffar Shah III, had lost control of his kingdom to several parties of Muslim nobles engaged in continuing conflict. The Timurid Mirzas, having found refuge in Gujarat in the past several years, had seized power in the southern portion of the kingdom. The opportunity to put a final end to the sedition of these rebels was appealing. The threat of Christian intervention by sea also existed. The Portuguese in Goa, who already dominated sea traffic in the Arabian Sea, might try to seize the west coast ports if political fragmentation continued. When a Habshi (Abyssinian) noble who headed one of the losing factions invited Akbar to intervene and annex the kingdom, the emperor did not hesitate.

In July, 1572, Akbar occupied Ahmadabad, the capital, and other northern cities and was proclaimed the lawful sovereign of Gujarat in the Friday prayers. The puppet king, Muzaffar Shah, submitted readily as did virtually all the Muslim nobles of the north. By January, 1573, Akbar had driven out the Mirzas who, after offering only token resistance, fled to refuge in the Deccan. The emperor left the new Mughal province in the hands of an imperial governor and returned to Fatehpur Sikri.

Suddenly, within three months, the nobles of Gujarat, disgruntled by their exclusion from imperial service, joined together in an attempt to drive the Mughals out of the kingdom. Husain Mirza retook Cambay, Broach, and Surat, the major ports. Afghan nobles supported by the Rajput ruler of Idar were advancing on the Mughal governor at Ahmadabad. Akbar responded immediately to this crisis by mustering a stripped-down 3,000 man field army. Mounted on the swiftest female camels he and his followers covered the 800 kilometers to Ahmadabad in just eleven days – on a route that caravans required two months to traverse. Akbar's smaller imperial army crushed the rebellion by soundly defeating 15,000 rebels in a bloody cavalry engagement. The victorious emperor, reassured by the death or flight of the rebel leaders, returned to Fatehpur Sikri forty-three days after his departure. The reconquest of Gujarat was the most dramatic episode of Akbar's long career. Speed, decisiveness, and luck were with him. His reputation for invincibility, already rising, swelled even further.

THE DRIVE TO THE EAST: BIHAR AND BENGAL

The Timurid ruler's second major objective lay in Bihar and Bengal where nominally tributary Afghan rulers and nobles still controlled the riverine domains of northeastern India. Akbar could not afford to leave his long-standing enemies, the Afghans, in power in an area so productive and strategic. In 1574, the young Sultan of Bengal, Daud Karrani, repudiated Akbar's nominal sovereignty by having his own name and titles read in the Friday prayers. After a Bengali raid into Mughal territory, Akbar himself led his armies in a difficult siege and assault of the Afghan-held fortress at Patna. The Afghan armies retreated before the Mughal onslaught until Daud was forced to take refuge in Orissa. Akbar returned to Fatehpur Sikri and left command of his armies in the east to his celebrated confidant and revenue minister, Todar Mal.

Todar Mal, commanding the Mughal army in the east, pursued the Afghan king until he forced a battle at Tukarori, near Midnapur. A ferocious elephant charge by the Afghans would have nearly destroyed the Mughal army had not Todar Mal held firm and rallied the left wing. This victory permitted Akbar to formally annex Bengal, Bihar, and Orissa to the Mughal empire, but Daud remained at large, although nominally a Mughal fief holder with lands in Orissa. When the Mughal troops stationed in Bengal suffered epidemic disease and retreated from Bengal, Daud reasserted his control. In 1576 a relief force sent under the command of Khan Jahan, governor of the Punjab, forced a decisive battle at Rajmahal where the Afghans were routed. Daud was finally captured and killed.

Continuing warfare and reverses followed the hard-won Mughal victory in 1576. Bengal remained a region controlled by Afghan nobles and Hindu rajas who deeply resented the Mughal military occupation.

Dwindling numbers of bitter Afghan commanders fought rear-guard actions against the superior Mughal armies. Finally, by the late 1580s virtually all overt resistance ended. Akbar sent Raja Man Singh, one of his most capable Rajput nobles, to set up a regular system of imperial administration in Bengal and Orissa.

CHANGING ROYAL ATTITUDES

The overall cultural and religious climate of sixteenth century India was more open and tolerant of change. Mughal expansion occurred as Indian society and culture was experiencing a richly creative phase. Several centuries of dominant Indo-Muslim power had forced Hindu institutions to adapt to that reality by strengthening popular devotional expression. Generations of Muslim life in north India and the Deccan had gradually shaped accommodation and sympathy to Indian society and even to Hinduism.

In both Hinduism and Islam many mystics, scholars, intellectuals, and more ordinary folk were actively seeking some form of synthesis. Kabir and other poet-saints in the popular devotional *bhakti* tradition of Hinduism offered a middle ground where Ram/Rahim could be worshipped freely in a rejection of the formalism of both religions. Others such as Daud Dayal (1544–1603) shared devotional beliefs and practices with sympathetic Sufis. An avowedly synthetic movement led by Guru Nanak (1469–1539) began in the Punjab. In folk culture there was substantial sharing of customs, ceremonies, and beliefs between ordinary Muslims and Hindus. Such practices as the worship of the smallpox goddess Sitla were often practiced as ardently by Muslims as Hindus in the countryside.

Throughout his residence in Fatehpur Sikri, Akbar engaged in a systematic study and discussion of comparative theology and religion. In 1575, he constructed a large hall to house debates in religion and theology. His personal inquiry into religion grew out of his own disquiet and ongoing spiritual quest. The emperor suffered from a recurring spiritual and personal crisis. At times he was subject to trances which were probably a mild form of epilepsy. Signs of chronic depression were also reported by observers close to him.

At first the debates were confined to issues of Islamic theology, but later, after 1579, participants included learned Jains, Hindu saints, and

Parsi priests. In 1580 the emperor enrolled two Jesuit priests, Aquaviva and Monserrate, who had travelled from Goa at Akbar's invitation to instruct him and his entourage in Christianity.

Akbar's active intellectual role is the more remarkable because he was illiterate. Although brought up in a highly literate family culture, at least four tutors tried and failed to teach the young prince to read. His son Salim, later Jahangir, commented:[5]

My father always associated with the learned of every creed and religion, especially with the Pandits and the learned of India, and although he was illiterate, so much became clear to him through constant intercourse with the learned and wise ... that no one knew him to be illiterate, and he was so acquainted with the niceties of verse and prose compositions that his deficiency was not thought of.

A recent analysis suggests that Akbar was probably dyslexic and thus physically unable to read.[6] Because he was deeply interested in the contents of manuscripts, Akbar developed the practice of having himself read to daily. Possibly because of his affliction he possessed a truly remarkable memory.

Father Monserrate gives a vivid picture of a series of bitter disputations with the ulema at the Mughal court. On these occasions, from the Jesuit viewpoint at least, Akbar was noticeably sympathetic to the Christian point of view and impatient with the inability of the Muslim theologians to argue effectively against them.[7] As his inquiries proceeded Akbar seems to have become less and less enchanted with orthodox Islam and its defenders. His own religious views matured as he interrogated holy men; listened to heated religious disputes; and learned the doctrines of each sect. Increasingly, Akbar moved away from his former devotion to Islam and toward a self-conceived eclectic form of worship focused on light and the sun. In so doing he became more tolerant of non-Muslim practices and less inclined to insist on rigorous enforcement of discriminatory practices aimed at non-Muslims.

[5] Jahangir, *Tuzuk-i Jahangiri* (Delhi, 2 vols. in one, reprint edition, 1968), translated by A. Rogers and edited by H. Beveridge, I, 33.
[6] Ellen Smart, "Akbar, Illiterate Genius," *Kaladarshana* (1981), pp. 99–107.
[7] Monserrate, Antonio, *The Commentary of Father Monserrate, S. J., On his Journey to the Court of Akbar* (London: Oxford University Press, 1922), translated by J. S. Hoyland; annotated by S. N. Banerjee, pp. 50–51.

CROWN VERSUS ULEMA

The young Timurid monarch presided over a predominantly non-Muslim society. By the mid-sixteenth century it was clear that no reasonable prospect existed for large-scale conversion of large numbers of Hindus to Islam. Already deeply immersed in his own speculative inquiries, Akbar faced a familiar political problem: how could he maintain his status as a Muslim ruler worthy of support by the faithful without engaging in such harsh and repressive measures against his Hindu subjects that they were disaffected and rebellious? More importantly, how to elicit active, as opposed to merely passive, political support from non-Muslims? Was the test for full political participation in the imperial system to be the Islamic profession of faith, or could Akbar open a broader, more flexible, notion of the political community of early modern India?

As Akbar's piety and reverence for the leading imperial jurists of the day declined, tension between him and the men learned in the sacred law of Islam, the ulema, grew into a full-blown political conflict. Partly as a result of this struggle, Akbar formulated a new, broad-based political appeal centered on a radically new dynastic ideology. At Fatehpur Sikri the free-thinking emperor and his clutch of radical advisers devised a coherent political doctrine for the empire.

Conflict between the ulema and Akbar fell into several areas. First, the learned men of Islam looked to the Timurid prince to display those qualities of piety and devotion that would serve as a model for the rest of his subjects. Akbar must do all in his power to ensure that Muslims could live a godly life in conformity with the Sharia in a land that could truly be called the *Dar-al Islam.* The piety and zealousness of the ruler, whose every statement and action was scrutinized and reported daily, determined the behavior of his officers and set the tone of the relationship between Islam and the state in Mughal India.

Linked with the above was the question of active leadership and patronage. Would Akbar furnish Muslim theologians and jurists with jobs and grants? The ulema depended upon the state to fund, organize, and manage the mosques, charitable trusts, and seminaries as well as the annual pilgrimage to the Holy Cities. The state relied upon the ulema to staff its law courts and to exercise social and moral leadership in local Islamic communities.

The young emperor became increasingly unsympathetic toward

worldly ulema. Most Mughal theologians and jurists were neither speculative intellectuals nor serious religious thinkers. Many were corrupt and worldly. Maulana Abdullah, the chief patronage officer (sadr) of the empire, possessed a large estate near Lahore. He avoided paying the one-fortieth obligatory charitable tax on property levied on Muslims each year (*zakat*) by the device of assigning the estates to his wife's ownership for a part of each year when the tax came due. When Akbar discovered this deception he was unimpressed by the piety or sincerity of one of his leading ulema.

As his inquiries progressed, Akbar discovered that Muslim learned men held a large proportion of the lands of the empire as tax-exempt religious grants. Many grants were obtained illegally or fraudulently. Large numbers of these holdings, originally dispensed for the lifetime of the beneficiary, had been allowed to transfer illegally to heirs. Furthermore, a sizable number of pious grant-holders were Afghans who had obtained their holdings from the Sur or the Lodi rulers. This was especially true in the Punjab where they formed a majority of grant-holders.

By 1578 Akbar was confident enough to undertake a series of sweeping reforms. He ordered a wholesale inspection and verification of titles for all pious land grants. All those that could not be authenticated were immediately resumed. Thereafter he sharply constricted the area and number of grants and strictly prohibited the practice of unchallenged inheritance. Heirs had to apply for the benefice; their request might be granted or more likely not. But the most bitter blow was to dispense pious grants of land to learned and religious men of all religions – not just Islam. Yogis living in monasteries (*maths*) received lands. Zoroastrian divines (Parsis) obtained lands. Even Brahmin priests enjoyed Akbar's largess.

A second set of issues emerged from tension between freethinking and orthodoxy in medieval Islamic India. The most narrowly fundamental of Islamic orthodox leaders in Akbar's reign shared the view that the Sharia must be rigorously enforced. Flexibility or concessions were weaknesses to be avoided. All those who might be suspected of heresy were to be brutally suppressed. For example, many Sufis or mystics tended to express views in their trances or later recollections of these states that were close to, if not, monist. Most Sufi masters were therefore suspect. Heterodox Shia, whether of the Persian branch or the Ismailis found in the coastal cities of Gujarat, were targets for persecution.

Muslims in India were subject to rising chiliastic emotions as the Islamic millennium – the thousandth year of the Hijra beginning September 27, 1592 – drew closer. A tradition attributed to the Prophet Muhammad that he would only remain in his grave a thousand years and return as the *Mahdi* gained currency. During the fifteenth century a heretical sect based on this tradition emerged. The founder, Sayyid Muhammad Jaunpur (b. 1443) who claimed to be the Mahdi, won large numbers of disciples and followers during his lifetime. Mahdawis, as they were known, were especially strong in Gujarat and western India and seemed to have a special appeal to Afghans of varying stations in life. Sayyid Muhammad rejected the legalism and formalism of the contemporary ulema and of the four schools of law. Instead he prescribed ardent devotion, renunciation, and meditation for his followers. Despite recurring persecution by orthodox ulema, Sayyid Muhammad and his sons and other successors continued to preach and found new circles of followers in Gujarat, Sind, and northern India.[8]

Akbar, who came in direct contact with Mahdawis after his conquest of Gujarat, did not persecute either leaders or followers of this heretical sect. Instead he permitted the Mahdawi saints to explain and defend their doctrines in religious discussions held at court in Fatehpur Sikri.

Third, citing Sharia provisions for treatment of *dhimmis*, the ulema expected to exert direct influence over official policies toward the non-Muslim majority. Faced with the plasticity and resilience of Hinduism, the Mughal ulema rightly feared blurring of boundaries and loss of the community's identity and strength. Therefore, doctrinal purity demanded harsh treatment for idolaters in all spheres of life.

Akbar's conflicts on this question with the Muslim religious establishment began early. In 1563 the young emperor abolished the practice of collecting a heavy tax from Hindu pilgrims when they gathered on festival occasions. In contravention of the Sharia, the emperor also granted non-Muslims permission to repair aging temples or to build new structures. In another controversial measure orders were issued that former Hindus who had been forcibly converted to Islam should be allowed to apostasize and escape the death penalty of the Sharia. He prohibited enslavement of war captives and the common practice of involuntary conversion of non-Muslim slaves.

[8] S. S. A. Rizvi, *Muslim Revivalist Movements in Northern India in the Sixteenth and Seventeenth centuries* (Agra, 1965), pp. 68–134. See also K. A. Nizami, *Akbar and Religion* (Delhi, 1989), pp. 42–51.

The most sweeping policy change, which had a direct impact on nearly all Hindus, occurred in 1579.[9] Akbar abolished the graduated property tax levied exclusively on non-Muslims, the *jiziya*. This was an annual tax imposed on the property of individual non-Muslims, who were legally classified as dhimmis or client groups tolerated and protected by Muslim rulers. State officers, usually ulema, collected sums based upon the wealth or possessions of the individual ratepayer. Only the indigent were exempted from payment. The regressive scale placed a real burden on the poorest taxpayers who paid an annual sum equivalent to a month's wages for an unskilled urban laborer.

The symbolic value of this measure was very great. The jiziya defined the status and public obligations of non-Muslims protected by the Islamic community. Payment entitled dhimmis to a peaceful existence under state protection and exempted them from military service. Terminating this tax implied that the unequal compact between Muslims and non-Muslims was also abolished – hence Akbar's action was bitterly resented by orthodox Muslims.

Other symbolic statements aimed at the political inclusion of non-Muslims. Emperor and courtiers celebrated the most important Hindu festivals such as Diwali, the festival of lights. The emperor adopted the Hindu custom of giving alms to the poor by having himself weighed against gold, silver, grains, and other commodities. Once or twice a year on auspicious dates the proceeds of these ceremonies were distributed to the destitute and needy. An especially dramatic political statement was employment of Rajputs and other high-caste Hindus in critical military/administrative roles (see above). Actions such as these touched some of the deepest sensibilities of members of the Muslim community.

Strains in the relationship between Akbar and the Muslim religious elite came to the fore in 1578. In that year the chief imperial *qazi*, Abdul Nabi, tried a Brahmin accused of insulting the name of Muhammad – a capital offense under the Sharia. Finding him guilty, the imperial qazi sentenced the priest to death. Abdul Nabi carried out the sentence even in the face of Akbar's express disapproval.

Finally, in 1579, Akbar assumed sweeping powers in matters of Islamic doctrine. An imperial edict publicly stated the Mughal emperor's prerogative to be the supreme arbiter of religious affairs within his

[9] Nizami, *Akbar and Religion*, pp. 107–108. Nizami concludes that mention of abolition of the jiziya earlier in 1564 by Abul Fazl in the *Akbar-Nama* is erroneous.

realm – above the body of Muslim religious scholars and jurists. In this edict Akbar stated that if leading scholars disagreed on a point of religious law, the Timurid ruler would decide which opinion would be authoritative and binding upon all Muslims. The edict also sought to claim for Akbar authority as *Khalifa* in preference to the Ottoman Sultan who had claimed that title since seizing control of the Holy Cities in 1517.[10] Under heavy pressure from the throne, the chief judge, the imperial sadr, and several other eminent scholars signed the document before it was published. The only person who signed willingly was Shaikh Mubarak, a distinguished liberal theologian. The declaration was a stunning defeat for the powerful religious hierarchy of the empire.

THE REVOLT OF 1579–1580

Embittered and humiliated, the imperial qazi and sadr took sanctuary in a mosque, and claimed publicly that they had been coerced into signing. Simultaneously a truculent group of imperial officers stationed in the eastern provinces of Bihar and Bengal went into rebellion. Never all that happy with Mughal domination, these fiercely orthodox officers, who counted many Afghans among them, were upset by the recent decree. They were also provoked by tightening administrative controls over the army. A new order commanded that all cavalrymen bring to the muster mounts meeting imperial specifications for size and quality. Once inspected and approved the mounts were to be certified by branding with an imperial mark. This would mean a considerable expense for those commanders whose mounts were deficient.

Mughal nobles of the Central Asian Qaqshals, a Turkish tribal group, led the Bengal rebels. They crossed the Ganges, joined with the Bihar nobles, and defeated the remaining Mughal loyalists in open battle. They captured and killed Shah Muzaffar, the governor of Bengal. The rebel leaders then arranged for a prayer leader to pronounce the name of Mirza Muhammad Hakim of Kabul as the legitimate Muslim ruler of the empire in the Friday congregational prayers. At the same time, the Islamic judge in the city of Jaunpur in the eastern Gangetic plain issued a ruling (*fatwa*) requested by the nobles that enjoined all good Muslims to rise in revolt against Akbar. According to this judgment, the emperor had become an infidel who was hostile to orthodox Islam and should be deposed in favor of his

[10] Nizami, *Akbar and Religion*, pp. 177–178.

half-brother, the king of Kabul. The Afghan aristocracy of Bengal seized this opportunity to join the rebels and fight the Timurid conqueror. Their ongoing resistance thus fused with and gained a new impetus from the revolt of the imperial officers in the east.

Akbar sent a relief army to Bihar under the command of Raja Todar Mal, the imperial financier. The loyalist forces retook Bihar's major forts and cities. He himself brought a large well-equipped army to Kabul and deposed his half-brother. This effectively ended the threat posed by Mirza Muhammad Hakim's claim to the throne. Harsh punitive measures against the Muslim jurists and theologians who had supported the rebels quieted the ideological challenge. Nevertheless, five years elapsed before Mughal field generals were able to reassert their control over west Bengal and put the remaining rebels and their Afghan allies into flight.

At Agra the emperor put a definitive end to further religious opposition by appointing Shaikh Abdul Nabi and Malauna Abdulla as joint leaders of the Haj caravan for 1579. They were to remain in exile at Mecca in order to oversee the orderly distribution of Timurid largess every year. One additional caravan set out for the Hijaz in 1580, but thereafter Akbar, despite a written promise to the Sharif of Mecca, sent no further caravans from India. In this area, as in many others, Akbar's ardent profession of orthodoxy had waned.

AKBAR AS MILITARY COMMANDER

Assigned to tutor Prince Murad, Akbar's second son, the Jesuit priest, Father Antonio Monserrate became a part of the imperial household after his arrival. Present during the lengthy march to Kabul in 1581 he had an unusual opportunity to observe the emperor during a crisis.[11] In his extended Latin report sent back to Rome, Monserrate described and evaluated Akbar's qualities as a war leader.

When news arrived of the revolt in the east and his brother's invasion of the Punjab, Akbar left his mother in charge at Fatehpur Sikri with a garrison of 12,000 cavalry. He sent Raja Todar Mal at the head of a large army to quell the rebellion in Bihar and Bengal. In February, 1581 the emperor "gave instructions for a great quantity of gold and silver and of other stores" to be loaded on camels and elephants, selected a

[5] Monserrate, Antonio, *The Commentary of Father Monserrate, S.J. On his Journey to the Court of Akbar* (London: Oxford University Press, 1922), translated by J. S. Hoyland; annotated by S. N. Banerjee, p. 90.

few of his principal wives and his other daughters, and moved to his "immense white pavilion" in the great camp set up four miles outside the city.[12] The symmetry and disciplined order of the massive encampment "made in the traditional Mongol style" thoroughly impressed Monserrate:[13]

> The ancient custom is that the royal pavilion . . . should be placed in a pleasant open space, if such can be found. On the right are the tents of the King's eldest son and his attendant nobles; these are placed next to the royal pavilion. On the left are those of the second son and his attendants. . . . the most important nobles . . . have their quarters to the right and left in the second line, next to the King's pavilion. Behind these come the rest of the troops in tents clustered as closely as possible round their own officers. To avoid crowding and confusion they are divided into messes, each with its own location. A separate bazaar is established for the King and each of the princes and the great nobles, . . . Those of the King and the princes are very large and very well-stocked, not only with stores of grain and other provisions, but also with all sorts of merchandise, so that these bazaars seem to belong to some wealthy city instead of to a camp. They are always made on one plan, so that anyone who has spent a few days in camp knows his way about the bazaars as well as he does the streets of his own city . . . During the advance for a campaign the artillery is grouped together in front of the camp, opposite the entrance to the royal quarters, in the broadest part of the open ground.

At the center of this great assemblage "every night a flaming torch [was] erected on the top of a tall mast, to act as a guide for stragglers."[14] Despite its size the Mughal encampment was designed to be transported with the entire army on march. The emperor possessed two identical pavilions "which are employed for alternate marches, one being carried on ahead, while he occupies the other."[15]

Similar descriptions of the Great Mughal's encampment became a staple for later observers.[16] Estimates of the size of the imperial camp frequently went as high as 100,000 persons. Precisely replicated at site after site, this huge movable city was visible testimony to the authority and power of the emperor. In this fashion at least, the Turco-Mongol heritage continued to wield a powerful influence over Akbar and his successors.

The discipline and organization of the Mughal army was as

[12] Ibid., p. 75. [13] Ibid., pp. 75–76. [14] Ibid., p. 76. [15] Ibid., p. 77.
[16] M. A. Ansari, "The Encampment of the Great Mughals" in *Islamic Culture*, 37 (1963), 15–24. N. Manucci, *Storia do Mogor or Mogul India* (Calcutta, 4 vols., 1907–8), translated by William Irvine, II, 62–80.

impressive as that of the imperial camp. For this campaign Akbar had mustered 50,000 cavalry, 500 war elephants, and "an almost countless number of infantry."[17] The Jesuit was quick to notice the heterogeneity of the cavalry. Mughal horsemen ranged from Rajputs who typically dismounted their small horses to fight, to Central Asian Turks and Persians who "are most dangerous when they seem to be flying in headlong riot [retreat]."[18] His artillery consisted only of twenty-eight field guns too small for siege work. These were always parked in front of the king's pavilion at each stop.

Marching in a crescent formation with the emperor at the head, the army soon "extended over the breadth of a mile and a half, covering the fields and filling the woods."[19] Despite its size this vast assemblage was kept well supplied and watered. Akbar directed the army toward the foot of the mountains to best afford access to streams for water. Monserrate "was astonished by the cheapness of grain amongst so great a multitude." Royal agents combed the countryside to purchase provisions and to encourage traders to come to the travelling bazaars. Beyond the imperial boundary the emperor sent "heralds" to the petty chiefs and kings along the route with publicly proclaimed promises and threats. If they did not take up arms against the Mughals they would suffer no harm and would be amply rewarded when he returned from his certain victory. If they brought supplies to the camp these could be sold freely, without paying taxes. However, if these local rulers disobeyed him they would be severely punished. Overawed by the size of the army and gratified by Akbar's generosity, all obeyed the emperor "out of self-interest."[20]

Beyond the imperial frontier Akbar sent out 300 scouts who were posted at a distance of eighteen miles from the army in every direction. When approaching narrow defiles the emperor sent out outposts "all around." Consequently, "the army, when on the march, spread itself as freely abroad, in the search for shade and water, and slept as securely at night, as if it had been in its own country."[21] Sappers and miners went on ahead to level roads and to build temporary boat bridges for river crossings. Strict rules forced men and animals to cross the bridges in single file to prevent disaster in mid-span.

Monserrate illustrates Akbar's command of his troops by describing his reaction to an order disobeyed. An officer was sent north along the

[17] Ibid., p. 83. [18] Ibid., p. 85. [19] Ibid., p. 79. [20] Ibid., p. 80.
[21] Ibid., p. 82.

Indus river bank to a particular spot to see if the river could be forded by cavalry. After travelling twenty-five miles, but not reaching the spot named, the officer was told by the local inhabitants that no such ford existed. He returned to report that a bridge must be built across the Indus. When the emperor learned that his scout had stopped short of his destination:[22]

the King ordered him to be seized, dragged to the place which he had told him to go to, bound prostrate on an inflated bag of ox-hide, and launched upon the river. When the report of this was spread through the camp, almost the whole army flocked to the river-side to see this strange sight. The officer was being carried hither and thither in the middle of the river at the mercy of the current. He was weeping, imploring pardon with miserable cries, and trying to move the King to mercy. As he was carried past the royal pavilion, the King gave orders for him to be rescued from the river, entered in the inventories as royal property, exposed for sale in all the bazaars, and finally auctioned as a slave.

The bedraggled offender was bought by one of his friends for eighty pieces of gold and Akbar thereafter pardoned him. Monserrate comments Akbar "showed by this example how much store he set by military discipline and obedience."[23] At the same time, Akbar did not indulge in gratuitous cruelty in this incident. The dramatic impact of this incident was sufficient to make his point.

DYNASTIC IDEOLOGY

From his early youth Akbar displayed an extraordinarily appealing personality. He possessed all the desired qualities of the warrior-hero. He was brave, athletic, generous, and likable. He combined powerful charismatic qualities with exceptionally acute organizational and strategic abilities. Akbar's persona was imposing and attractive beyond the usual hagiography and image-making clinging to any ruler or leader. One of his greatest admirers, his eldest son, Salim, later Jahangir, described his father's appearance in the following terms:[24]

In his august personal appearance he was of middle height, but inclining to be tall; he was of the hue of wheat; his eyes and eyebrows were black, and his complexion rather dark than fair; he was lion bodied [i.e. thin-flanked], with a broad chest, and his hands and arms long. On the left side of his nose he had a fleshy mole, very agreeable in appearance, of the size of half a pea. ... His

[22] Ibid., p. 82–83. [23] Ibid., p. 83. [24] Jahangir, *Tuzuk*, I, 35.

august voice was very loud, and in speaking and explaining had a peculiar richness. In his actions and movements he was not like the people of the world, and the Glory of God manifested itself in him.

Other contemporary descriptions are similar. Monserrate, who first met Akbar when the emperor was thirty-eight, mentioned that "His forehead is bright and open, his eyes so bright and flashing that they seem like a sea shimmering in the sunlight."[25] Monserrate noted that Akbar generally wore uncut hair bound in an Indian turban "as a concession to Indian usages and to please his Indian subjects."[26] The Jesuits were also struck by Akbar's openness:

It is hard to exaggerate how accessible [Akbar] makes himself to all who wish audience of him. For he creates an opportunity almost every day for any of the common people or of the nobles to see him and converse with him; and he endeavors to show himself pleasant spoken and affable rather than severe toward all who come to speak with him.

Akbar's personal qualities enabled him to be as successful as he had been in politics and war. However, in the latter half of his reign, new advisers, themselves attracted to Akbar's persona, began to build a larger ideological structure centered on their master.

In the Fatehpur Sikri years, Abul Fazl's breadth of vision and political acuity brought him to prominence as the leading Timurid ideologue and propagandist. In his new capacity, Akbar's intellectual began to erect a scaffolding for a Timurid dynastic ideology – an edifice aimed at establishing a new legitimacy for Akbar and his successors. In discussions at court, in a wide-ranging official and private correspondence, and in eulogistic poetry Abul Fazl and his brother, the poet Faizi, began to assert Akbar's divinely illumined right to rule lesser human beings.[27] The most systematic expression of this doctrine is found in the *Akbar-Nama*, the voluminous annual recounting of events for forty-seven years of Akbar's reign, with the bulky *Ain-i Akbari* appended as a manual. At the core of this work, permeating every passage, Abul Fazl embedded ultimate legitimacy for Akbar that transcended the accidents of conquest, coup, or succession.

The *Akbar-Nama* portrays Akbar as a superior being, existing closer to God, to true reality. Akbar was the recipient of the hidden light

25 Monserrate, *Commentary*, p. 196. 26 Ibid., p. 197.

27 The discussion following is based upon J. F. Richards, "The Formulation of Imperial Authority Under Akbar and Jahangir" in J. F. Richards, ed., *Kingship and Authority in South Asia* (Madison Wisconsin, South Asian Studies No. 3, 1978), pp. 260–267.

whose ineffable radiance emanating from his brow was perceptible only to superior men. Only an elect group could pierce the veil which guarded the outpouring of light from the Timurid brow. Akbar had esoteric knowledge and authority greater than the recognized interpreters of the Sharia, the *Mujtahid* of the Age, than the most saintly of Sufi masters (*Pirs*) or the eagerly anticipated charismatic savior (*Mahdi*).

The more than fifty paintings illustrating the manuscript now in the Victoria and Albert museum in London (probably the original presented at court) contrast the divine order, harmony, and self-control of the emperor's person with the turgid, struggling disorder of those unwieldy masses of men and beasts surrounding him. The emperor's will calmed and directed the energies of his subjects and all of mankind.

The illuminationist theme is borrowed directly from the Eastern school of Persian Neoplatonic philosophy found in the teachings of Shihabuddin Suhrawardi Maqtul (d. 1191). Suhrawardi argues that all life is given existence by the constant blinding illumination from the East of the Light of Lights or God. All men possess a divine spark, but only the highest of three grades of men are the true theosophists or masters of the age – men such as Suhrawardi himself, Plato, or in Abul Fazl's interpretation, Akbar. A chain of dazzling angels was the means for revealing God's illumination to man. At their head was the Angel Gabriel, identified with the true spirit of the Prophet Muhammad.

Abul Fazl explicitly states the central provisions of this ideology in the introductory passages describing Akbar's ancestry. Beginning with Adam, the ancestor of all men, the eulogist follows the passage of the hidden divine refulgence until it reaches and illumines the spirit and intelligence of Akbar in 1556. From Adam through the Biblical prophets, Abul Fazl traces this illumined descent through the Biblical prophets to Joseph who fathered Turk, ruler of Turkestan. Turk's son Mughal Khan was the first of nine generations of Turco-Mongol kings. The last ruler in the line was defeated and dispersed by an enemy.

The ruler and his tribe retreated in confusion to Mughalistan where they remained in obscurity and seclusion for two millennia. Finally, in a mountain valley far to the east, a most important event occurred: Alanquwa, a Mughal queen married to the king of Mughalistan, became a childless widow when her husband died prematurely. But Alanquwa was a woman of the utmost purity from whose brow the divine light shone. As she lay sleeping in her tent one night, a ray of light miraculously entered her body and impregnated her.

The three brothers, triplets, born of this event were called the Nairun or "light-produced." From the eldest the hidden light passed through nine Turco-Mongol rulers including Chingiz Khan to ultimately reach Amir Timur Gurgan, the great fourteenth-century conqueror. Formal legitimacy for the Timurids began when in April, 1370, Amir Timur crowned himself in Samarkhand. The long narrative descent passes through four generations to Babur, Humayun, and then to Akbar. Humayun was granted a majestic night vision which assured him that "an illustrious successor whose greatness shone from his forelock" would be bestowed upon him. Akbar would be the receptacle for this hidden illumination that had passed from generation to generation.

DISCIPLES AND MANSABDARS

Drawing upon the newly articulated imperial idiom, Akbar and his advisers devised an esoteric means to bind leading nobles to him. In part this appeal emerged naturally from Akbar's own intense spiritual quest that found its fullest expression at Fatehpur Sikri. In the early 1580s the emperor began openly to worship the sun by a set of rituals of his own invention. Four times a day he faced the east and prostrated himself before a sacred fire. Simultaneously, Akbar engaged in abstinence from excessive meat-eating, sexual intercourse, and alcohol consumption. These were all rites and practices much in evidence in the daily world of Hinduism in north India. Worship of the sun and moon with its images of light was easily compatible with the myths of origin and descent central to the ethos of his Rajput nobles.

Shortly thereafter the emperor began to enlist selected members of the nobility as his disciples in association with the worship of sun and light. At noon on Sundays before the sacred fire the emperor presided over an initiation ceremony. Groups of twelve neophytes entered the body of disciples on these occasions. Each initiate swore to accept four degrees of devotion to Akbar: the unhesitating willingness to sacrifice one's life (*jan*), property (*mal*), religion (*din*), and honor (*namus*) in the service of the Master, i.e. Akbar. Muslim initiates signed a declaration agreeing to repudiate the bonds of orthodox Islam and to worship Allah directly, without intermediaries. Throughout the ceremony the neophyte placed his head on Akbar's feet in an extreme form of prostration known as *sijdah*. At the close of the ceremony

Akbar raised up each supplicant, placed a new turban upon his head, and gave him a symbolic representation of the sun embossed on a medallion. Each new disciple also received a tiny portrait of Akbar to wear upon his turban as well as a set of pearl earrings crafted for the occasion.

The number of disciples grew rapidly – to perhaps a majority of the Mughal amirs. Discipleship was an extremely effective means to assimilate a heterogeneous body of nobles and bind them to the throne. Akbar's own charismatic personality and the solemnities of the oaths taken were designed to create a new identity for Mughal amirs. The master–disciple relationship thus established bridged kinship, ethnic, and religious distinctions among the nobles. Oaths bound the disciples to their fellows and committed them to cast aside their former enmities and factional conflict. Even religious beliefs were to be directed to the service and worship of the emperor.

Akbar drew upon several widely accepted institutions for his notion of discipleship and membership in an order. For centuries military slavery in Islamic India, Central Asia, and the Middle East had developed its own norms of behavior. The slave soldier owed obedient submission and profound loyalty to his military commander as long as the latter met minimal standards of good treatment and sympathy for his men. Military slaves in direct service to a royal master felt these obligations even more keenly.

Another model for imperial discipleship was that of the Sufi master (*pir* or Shaikh) with his devotees. The specific terms of this relationship varied from order to order. In general, however, devotees placed the responsibility for their physical and spiritual well-being completely in the hands of their chosen Sufi Shaikh. The latter was to lead them along the upward stages of the mystical path (*tariqa*) to true knowledge of God. As a symbol of complete devotion to their master Sufi disciples put their heads on his feet in exactly the same prostration (sijdah) adopted by Akbar. This latter form of submission to a fellow human being was seen as blasphemous by pious Muslims. Akbar, without question, was deeply influenced by his earlier devotion to the now-dead Shaikh Salim, the famed Chishti saint. The emperor had cast himself in the role of an ardent disciple whenever he made the long pilgrimage to the rocky hillock at Fatehpur Sikri where Salim lived.

Finally, ready at hand was the Indo-Persian model of courtly behavior and submission to the monarch by the nobility. Court ritual with its rigid protocol was designed to evoke feelings of awe, unworthiness, and to emphasize the distance between ruler and even the grandest of his subjects. The discipline of movement, speech, and etiquette demanded in public audiences reinforced obedience to the royal will. Rigid assignment of place – whether closer or further from the throne – graphically demonstrated royal preferment. Command appearances before the throne demanded presentation of a suitable gift. These ranged from 100 gold coins to more valuable jeweled objects or even elephants. Court ritual culminated in the symbolic incorporation of the servant in the body of his royal master. Thus the Mughals, following long precedent, used the device of elaborately ornamented robes of honor, brocaded in gold and silver, as a staple reward for valuable service. The ruler first placed the robes on his own body and then personally draped them on the recipient. The person so favored responded with a ritual gift – usually of gold or silver coin. By these devices the notion of one body in service to the state – ruler and nobles – was promulgated.

LAHORE

In 1585 Akbar transferred his capital to Lahore in the Punjab at the death of his half-brother, Mirza Muhammad Hakim, at Kabul. The Uzbek ruler, Abdullah Khan, who had annexed Badakhshan in 1584, was a possible threat to Kabul. The Uzbeks were subsidizing the Afghan tribes in their continuing defiance of the Mughal regime at Kabul. Akbar immediately sent an army under Raja Man Singh to occupy Kabul and then brought the city and its surrounding districts under direct imperial administration. This task completed, Akbar stayed on in Lahore for thirteen years in a successful effort to clamp imperial Mughal power over the entire northwest.

At Lahore the emperor kept a border watch on Abdullah Khan Uzbek. In 1586 Akbar and the Uzbek Khan negotiated a pact in which Akbar agreed to remain neutral during the Uzbek invasion of Safavid-held Khurasan. In return, Abdullah Khan agreed to refrain from supporting, subsidizing, or offering refuge to the Afghan tribes. Thus freed, Akbar began a series of pacification campaigns directed against the Yusufzais and other tribal rebels. He was also free to round out the empire by annexing Kashmir and Sind, the two remaining kingdoms not fully incorporated into the empire.

An important consideration in this period was the busy overland caravan trade. The overland route from Kabul through the Khyber Pass and Peshawar fed the markets of Lahore with horses from Central Asia, fruits, silks and porcelain (from China), precious metals, and many other valuable commodities. Indian spices, textiles, and other goods travelled outward in a lucrative commerce that sent Indian merchants into the markets of Central Asia and Iran. The Punjab was a major industrial center in which thousands of weavers produced specialized cotton cloth for various markets in Central Asia, the Middle East, and beyond. The scale of this traffic may be judged by the effect of a single accidental fire in Peshawar fort in 1586. The disaster destroyed one thousand camel loads of merchandise belonging to the merchants who had sheltered there when the route was temporarily obstructed.[28]

The caravan trade was vulnerable to banditry or even complete blockage by the Afghan tribes. Keeping trade flowing was a perennial concern for rulers on both sides of the passes. In recent years the powerful Yusufzai tribal group had seized control of Swat and Bajaur and threatened to move further south. The Yusufzai had gained control of the Khyber routes and frequently blocked the roads and plundered caravans.

In late 1585 Akbar marched from Lahore to Attock fort (built by him in 1581). From Attock he sent an army under Zain Khan Koka to subdue the Yusufzai tribal confederation in the valleys of Swat and Bajaur. The emperor pitted Mughal centralized state power against the Yusufzai, the most aggressive and powerful tribal confederation in northern Afghanistan. The Mughals estimated that the confederation numbered 100,000 households in which every male member was armed and battle-ready. Their tribal chiefs had not offered formal submission to the Mughals since Babur received a Yusufzai daughter into his harem in 1519.

The Mughal army forced the submission of many Yusufzai chiefs in Swat and Bajaur. But a relief force on its way to Swat through the difficult mountain terrain met disaster. Split command between a royal favorite, Raja Bir Bar, the court wit, and Zain Khan Koka, an ordinary field general, weakened the usually careful deployment of Akbar's armies. A reckless attack on the Yusufzais exposed the royal army to ambush in the mountain passes. About 8,000 imperial soldiers, includ-

[28] Ahmad, *Tabaqak-i Akbari* (Eng. trans.), II, 602.

ing Raja Bir Bar, were killed in the greatest disaster to Mughal arms in Akbar's reign.

Akbar immediately fielded two new armies to reinvade the Yusufzai lands. Over the next six years, the Mughals contained the Yusufzai in their mountain valleys. The imperialists built and occupied a dozen forts to secure the country and protect the caravan trade. Tribal levies could not withstand Mughal cavalry in the open field; they could not protect their crops or their villages from destruction; nor could the Afghans hold their forts against determined imperial assaults. Akbar's demonstrated ability to clamp firm military control over the turbulent Afghan tribes is an impressive testimonial to the reach of his empire.

In 1585 Akbar dispatched an army north to invade Kashmir when Ali Shah, the current ruler of the Chak dynasty, refused to send his son to the Mughal court. The Kashmiri ruler surrendered immediately, but his son, Yaqub, crowned himself and led a dogged resistance to the imperial armies. Finally, in June, 1589, Akbar himself travelled from Lahore to Srinagar to receive the surrender of Yaqub and his rebel forces. The emperor's visit began the Timurid interest in the beauties of Kashmir and the construction of the numerous royal gardens laid out in that mountain kingdom.

In 1586 Akbar turned his attention to the lower Indus valley. The imperial governor of Multan had failed to secure the capitulation of Jani Bek, the ruler of Thatta (Sind). Akbar responded by sending another large Mughal field army to besiege Sehwan, the river capital on the Indus. Jani Bek mustered a large army and numerous armed river boats to resist. The outnumbered Mughal general defeated the Sind forces in a hard-fought battle on the river. After suffering further defeats, the Sind ruler surrendered and, in 1593, paid homage to Akbar at court in Lahore in person. Jani Bek became a Mughal mansabdar, accepted discipleship under Akbar and was appointed to the governorship of Multan. His former kingdom became the Mughal province of Thatta, divided into three districts under an imperial governor.

The conquest of Sind strengthened Akbar's resolve to retake Qandahar fort and town which had long been in Safavid hands. In 1595 the Persian commandant of Qandahar, having fallen into disgrace with Shah Abbas, defected to the Mughals and surrendered the fortress to a Mughal force. But Shah Abbas chose not to go to war over this provocation.

When the death of Abdullah Khan Uzbek in 1598 eased the threat of invasion from that quarter, Akbar moved his capital once again to Agra – not to Fatehpur Sikri. From Agra he could devote his energies to that most intractable and difficult frontier: the Deccan.

Why did the emperor not return to the delights of Fatehpur Sikri rather than Agra? One reason lay in the increasingly difficult problem posed by his son Salim's rebelliousness. Residence in Agra's more defensible citadel might well have been preferable to the insecurity of Fatehpur Sikri. Relative to the annual income of the empire, the cost of building Fatehpur Sikri, estimated recently at 3.5 million silver rupees, was not consequential. Akbar's desert city was in fact a disposable capital in view of his immense wealth.[29]

These are partial answers, but for a fuller explanation we must look to ideology. Abruptly in 1585 the pilgrimages to Ajmer and veneration of the Chishti saints ended. The emperor did not engage in any public worship at other Sufi tombs. The royal weighing ceremonies were detached from pilgrimage. The silence of the chronicles suggests that Akbar ceased regular worship in the congregational mosque at either Lahore or Agra. He was no longer anxious to display his Islamic piety in public. At Fatehpur Sikri royal heirs, royal victory, and Timurid authority flowed from devotion to Chishti saints properly enclosed within the framework of orthodox Islamic institutions. After 1585, Agra, rather than Fatehpur Sikri was the proper urban setting for the new imperial court.[30]

RETURN TO AGRA

The remaining external frontier lay in the Deccan, the domain of centuries of epic Muslim wars against the infidel. The Deccan landscape, although less hospitable to large-scale military operations than the Indo-Gangetic plain, was certainly less daunting than the mountains of the northwest or the riverine jungles of Assam. Moreover, the existence of large Muslim-ruled kingdoms encouraged the thought of conquest. What the Sultans of Delhi had accomplished surely their heirs, the Timurids, could surpass. Here were five Muslim Sultanates to be ground down and either conquered and annexed or brought under Mughal hegemony: Khandesh, under the Farruqi dynasty; Ahmadnagar, under the Nizam Shahs; Berar under the Imad Shah

29 Habib, "Economic and Social Setting," p. 74, in Brand and Lowry, eds., *Fatehpur Sikri.*
30 Richards, "The Imperial Capital", p. 72.

dynasty; Bijapur, under the Adil Shah rulers, and Golconda, under the Qutb Shahs. (See map 1). Apart from the Sultan of Khandesh, who intermittently paid tribute, none had submitted to the Mughals.

The social landscape, however, was less propitious to Mughal aggression than it might seem. Over the two centuries since the break-up of the Delhi Sultanate, a distinctive Deccan Muslim political culture had evolved in this region. The Muslim elites in each state were predominantly either Shia Persian nobles or Sunni Afghans along with less powerful Indian Muslim converts. Neither of these groups was especially fond of the Timurids – the Afghans least of all.

A further complication lay in the composition of the regional landed aristocracies. Below Khandesh, Rajput domination over the land came to a halt. Instead, in the western Deccan, Marathi-speaking members of the Maratha caste were the heirs of the Yadavas and earlier Hindu kingdoms defeated by the Muslims. In the east, Telugu warriors controlled rural society. The latter could look back to centuries of successful resistance to the Muslims by their forbears in Vijayanagar and its successor states. Gradually, these aristocrats had assimilated to the imposed political order of the Deccan Sultanates. In each case, whether Maratha or Telugu, it is reasonably certain that the thinly populated, largely urban, Muslim elites depended heavily upon an alliance with these rural aristocracies to rule effectively.

The Deccan Sultans imposed few restrictions on the expression of local religious and cultural life. Rarely, if ever, had they demanded conversion to Islam as a condition of high rank in the state. Indeed, Ibrahim Qutb Shah (1550–1580) of Golconda and Ibrahim Adil Shah II (1580–1626) of Bijapur, both engaged in broad-ranging attempts to reduce barriers between Hinduism and Islam within their states in much the same fashion as Akbar in the Mughal dominions. Akbar's new policies and ideological stance might well appeal to the landed aristocracies of both halves of the Deccan, but this linkage was something that would have to be created and sustained by careful statesmanship and administration. The Mughals did not easily or readily obtain the allegiance of either Maratha or Telugu chiefs.

In 1591 Akbar sent embassies to each of the Deccan Sultans to demand submission to Mughal overlordship. On this occasion the ruler of Khandesh sent his daughter to be married to Prince Salim and the Sultans of Bijapur and Golconda sent gifts, but rejected the emperor's demand for formal submission. Burhan Nizam Shah II, the ruler of Ahmadnagar, treated the Mughal envoys with studied brusqueness.

In 1595, while still at Lahore, Akbar ordered an invasion of Ahmadnagar Sultanate – then undergoing a succession crisis after the death of Burhan Nizam Shah II. A large imperial force jointly commanded by Prince Murad (Akbar's second son) and the Khan Khanan, son of Bairam Khan, besieged Ahmadnagar, the royal capital. The Mughals coerced reluctant participation in the imperial army by Raja Ali Khan the ruler of Khandesh. The defending ruler was Chand Sultan, sister of the deceased Sultan and guardian of the infant heir to the throne. The princess held the fortress until a relief army sent by the Sultans of Bijapur and Golconda threatened the imperial armies. A negotiated truce resulted in Mughal withdrawal from Ahmadnagar in return for cession of the province of Berar (the former kingdom annexed earlier by Ahmadnagar) to the Mughal emperor. In 1586 Berar became the first of the Deccan provinces to be brought under direct imperial administration.

Continuing tension and intermittent battles between the Mughals and the defiant Deccan Sultanates marked the next several years. Even the Sultan of Khandesh withdrew to his massive hill fortress at Burhanpur and refused to assist the Mughals. In 1599, Prince Murad, in command of the Mughal Deccan armies, died prematurely from alcoholism. Akbar turned over command in the Deccan to his third son, Daniyal. But in September, 1599, the emperor left Agra at the head of an 80,000 man army for the Deccan to direct operations in person.

Under the emperor's energetic command, Mughal forces stormed the fortress of Ahmadnagar in August, 1600. The Nizam Shahi princess Chand Sultan died at the hands of a dissident mob before the fort fell. Akbar himself led a Mughal army marching into Khandesh. Bahadur, the Sultan of Khandesh, had repudiated his allegiance to the Mughals and had taken refuge in the massive hill fortress of Asirgarh near Burhanpur, capital city of the kingdom. In the last major military command of his life, Akbar directed the siege from his camp at Burhanpur. Relentless Mughal pressure drove Bahadur into face-to-face negotiations with Akbar from which he was not allowed to return to the fortress. Finally, the fort defenders, faced with Mughal capture of two of Asirgarh's outlying citadels, surrendered in early January, 1601.

Khandesh and a large portion of Ahmadnagar joined Berar as new imperial provinces in the Deccan. Akbar assigned the three provinces to Prince Daniyal to administer as the viceroy of the Deccan. On April 11, 1601, the emperor left Burhanpur on the return journey to Agra.

REBELLION OF SALIM

When Akbar departed for the Deccan, he left his eldest son in charge of the capital. In July, 1600, Salim tried unsuccessfully to seize control of Agra fort,[31] and appointed his own officers in the province. There he remained in defiance of his father's orders sent from the Deccan. When Akbar arrived at Agra, Salim marched on the capital with a force of 30,000 horsemen. Akbar sent a stiff letter to him ordering the prince to halt and return to the east where he offered Salim the governorship of Bengal and Orissa. Salim brushed aside this offer, but did return to Allahabad. In May, 1602, he had his name read in the Friday prayers and had coins struck as emperor in his own name.

Akbar recalled his trusted adviser, Abul Fazl, from the Deccan in order to send him to deal with Salim. Fearing the stern presence of Abul Fazl, Salim commissioned Bir Singh, the Bundela raja of Orchha, to intercept Abul Fazl on his return journey. The Bundela raja overpowered the minister's small escort, killed Abul Fazl, and brought his severed head to Allahabad.

The grief-stricken emperor finally was reconciled to his son by his wife Salima Sultan Begam who, along with several of the other noblewomen, acted as peacemaker between the two. Salim appeared at court, with proper deference, was embraced by Akbar, and designated heir-apparent. Thereafter, he returned to Allahabad against his father's wishes and indulged in a period of excessive intake of opium and wine as well as in public displays of cruelty. After the death from alcoholism of Daniyal, Akbar's third son, in 1604, Salim returned to court. In part he was worried by the maneuvering of the partisans of his own son Prince Khusrau. The powerful Raja Man Singh, among others, urged Akbar to set aside Salim's claims in favor of his grandson. After Salim submitted to the emperor, he was confined briefly in the palace in the final episode of this rebellion.

Just under a year later, Akbar fell ill with dysentery, weakened and lay dying. Salim escaped the plots of his enemies in the nobility and

[31] Fort garrisons were under the command of independent officers appointed directly by the emperor and would be unlikely to submit to even a royal prince without express orders.

visited his father who placed the imperial turban on the prince's head and gave him Humayun's sword as heir. During the night of October 25, 1605, Akbar died and was taken to be buried in the mausoleum which he had built for himself at Sikandra, near Agra.

CONCLUSION

When the emperor died in 1605, his legacy was a multi-regional empire, which, in the course of his half-century of rule, had become the dominant power on the Indian subcontinent. Beginning in his adolescent years, Akbar directed a continuing series of remarkable military campaigns in which Mughal armies won victory after victory on the field of battle. No single kingdom or coalition of regional kingdoms could stand against the Mughal armies. Each victory added money, men, and weapons to the imperial armies. Each campaign, battle, and siege was a public event, widely reported and discussed throughout the subcontinent. Year after year, as the Timurid armies proved invincible and as revolts and resistance failed, Akbar's reputation soared. He and his immediate confidants became figures of enormous popular interest. Folk tales about him based on well-known incidents in his life began to circulate. The Mughal emperor acquired an aura of near-divinity and mystery which further reinforced popular perceptions of Mughal infallibility.

After conquest followed annexation. Once-proud rulers were deposed and killed or accepted personal service with the Mughal emperor. Once-independent kingdoms became provinces of the expanding empire. Akbar forcibly unified the collection of regional states in North India into a single, centralized political system. Within this system the Mughal emperor was the single source of political legitimacy and authority. No sultan, raja, or other ruler could devolve legitimate authority without reference to the emperor. All became "landholders" (*zamindars*) in the emperor's eyes, who relied upon a patent of office (*sanad*) to secure their hereditary seats. Military power permitted him to impose a stringent degree of administrative control over each new territory as it came into the empire – and to retain this control despite resistance. The Mughals imposed a new level of public order on the tumultuous society of India.

Akbar deployed overwhelming numbers of heavy cavalry, armored men and horses with bow, lance, and sword, war elephants, musketeers, and artillery. In his many battles and campaigns the Mughal ruler made effective use of the new gunpowder weaponry – more so than his opponents. But gunpowder had become widely available by the mid-sixteenth century. Akbar's string of victories depended upon organizational prowess, not technology. In tracing the sequence of these campaigns, it is important to realize that the Mughal emperor met determined enemies who commanded substantial, well-equipped, well-motivated armies. Most battles were desperate and bloody; the sieges difficult and lengthy. On numerous occasions, Akbar could have been wounded or killed when leading his troopers in battle. Luck and his military skills saved him. The builder of the Mughal empire was undoubtedly a superb military commander in a generally bellicose society.

CHAPTER 3

AUTOCRATIC CENTRALISM

Buoyed by conquest and plunder, Akbar and his advisers built a centralizing administration capable of steady expansion as new provinces were added to the empire. The Mughal emperor presided over a system that moved money, commodities, men, and information freely throughout the empire. The emperor and his advisers were vigorous managers who creatively adapted and responded to changing circumstances. Building on this foundation, Akbar's successors oversaw steady growth in imperial effectiveness, power, and resources throughout the seventeenth century.

Akbar drew upon the rich Persian-derived administrative tradition of the Indo-Muslim states and the hard-edged, extraction-oriented, organizational tradition of the Turkic-Mongol conquest empires from the steppe. Within this context the emperor shaped a vertebrate structure characterized by centralized, hierarchical, bureaucratic offices. Filling these offices were technically qualified officials, functioning within standardized rules and procedures, who generated copious written orders and records. At the apex of this system the emperor acted as a vigorous and informed chief executive.

The first critical step occurred when Akbar allowed the position of chief minister or vakil to lapse and gathered all executive power in his hands. Thereafter he appointed four nearly co-equal central ministers. These officers occasionally came together as an advisory body, but they were in fact independent of each other within their own spheres. Their responsibilities were divided according to the most basic administrative functions as perceived by the emperor: finance and revenue; army and intelligence; the judiciary and religious patronage; and the royal household, with its central workshops, and buildings, and roads, and canals throughout the empire. Any omitted functions were left to the emperor and specially appointed officers. Thus, diplomacy and external affairs, often placed under a minister in charge of the chancery or official correspondence in earlier Muslim states, stayed under the emperor's personal control. These ministers and their higher-ranking assistants and specialized officers were drawn from the body of imperial servants or mansabdars. Each branch maintained a large support staff of clerks, accountants, auditors, messengers, and other functionaries.

The division of functions established at the center was duplicated in the provinces. At each provincial capital a governor, responsible directly to the emperor, shared power with a fiscal officer or *diwan* reporting to the *wazir*; military paymaster and intelligence officer or *bakhshi*, reporting to the central inspector general of the army; and a sadr reporting to the minister for religious and charitable patronage. The governor was responsible for the overall peace, security, and tranquillity of his province. In this capacity he supervised the military intendants or *faujdars* and the commanders of military check points (*thanas*) who were deployed with contingents of heavy cavalry and musketeers throughout each province. The provincial diwan managed imperial revenues, expenditures, and the provincial treasuries. The separation of powers between the governor and diwan was an especially significant operating principle for imperial administration.

THE MUGHAL NOBILITY

Cutting across this bureaucratic structure was another, more diffuse institution. The emperor commanded the services of a body of warrior-aristocrats comprised of the mature royal princes and several hundred amirs (nobles) and higher ranking mansabdars. These officers served as provincial governors or filled other higher administrative positions throughout the empire. Alternatively they were employed as military commanders for armies in the field or as part of the central military. In their military capacity amirs or mansabdars also served as commanders of strategic fortresses reporting directly to the emperor. Paid lavishly, these grandees headed households and troop contingents ranging in size from several hundred to several thousand persons. When transferred from one posting to another, their establishments moved with them. The imperial system depended heavily upon the martial qualities, administrative skills and political and entrepreneurial strengths of this body. From this perspective one might well term the empire a "patrimonial–bureaucratic" system.[1]

Members of this cadre and their privately employed officers and

[1] Stephen P. Blake, "The Patrimonial–Bureaucratic Empire of the Mughals", *Journal of Asian Studies*, 39 (November, 1979), 77–94.

servants carried out other major administrative tasks. Acting as military commanders the nobles recruited, trained, and equipped the bulk of the heavy cavalry which formed the main striking arm of the Timurid armies. They employed bodies of skilled musketeers both mounted and on foot. At its core each military contingent relied on a body of closely related kinsmen and more distantly related lineage mates. Additional manpower was readily recruited by turning to the vast military labor market in northern India and the Deccan. Well trained, professional cavalrymen, infantry, and gunners were available for employers prepared to offer cash.

As recipients of jagirs or salary assignments on the land revenue the nobles filled a critical role in tax collection from the countryside. Amirs and upper mansabdars employed their own staffs to collect the greater part of the massive land tax. Some of this went to pay their own generous salaries, but the greater share went to pay cash salaries to their troopers. The organization of that considerable effort was left up to the nobles themselves. The role of the central administration was confined to inspection, monitoring, and auditing.

As we have seen, Akbar took pains to recruit his nobility from diverse sources. The Mughal nobility became and remained a heterogeneous body of free men, not slaves, who rose as their talents and the emperor's favor permitted. Rajputs, Afghans, Indian Muslims, Arabs, Persians, Uzbeks, Chaghatais were some of the ethnic groups represented. Some nobles were natives of India; many were not. Most were Sunni Muslims; many were either Shi'ite or Hindu in religion. This flow of new recruits helped to prevent the growth of dissident cliques and factions within the nobility. No single ethnic or sectarian group was large enough to challenge the emperor. Instead much of the dynamism of the empire can be traced to newly recruited, capable, energetic men who sought the power, wealth, and high reputation possible in service to the Timurid dynasty in India. The service nobility's entrepreneurial drive and spirit was of inestimable value to Akbar and his successors.

Rewards and incentives rather than force and coercion were Akbar's preferred approach. Mansabdars were free men who enlisted voluntarily in the emperor's service. Most servants, craftsmen, soldiers, professionals, and lesser imperial officers were also free workers who were well-paid for their services. Numerous domestic and personal slaves were employed, but they were outnumbered by free employees.

Apart from harem guards no military slaves served the emperor. The system offered generous money rewards as well as lavish honors and preferments to those who performed well at all levels.

Possessing great wealth and power, these grandees were highly visible public figures. Their personalities, habits, and movements were the topic of endless rumor and speculation. The greatest amirs were objects of empire-wide attention. News of royal favor or disfavor, of illnesses, heirs, marriages, postings, and other information formed the stuff of countless reports that flashed across the empire. Lesser nobles were the objects of local and regional scrutiny. At the upper reaches of imperial society merchants and rival nobles employed spies and agents to obtain reliable information from the entourages of the great men. At the lower levels, in the bazaars and coffee houses of urban India, stories and gossip, often extremely accurate, chronicled the lives of these celebrities. Sexual habits and scandalous behavior were obviously staple fare. Those nobles known to be avaricious, capricious, and cruel were widely condemned for these traits; those known to be munificent, responsible, and humane were praised.

Wherever they were posted, whether at court or in the provinces, the patrimonial households of the nobles were a focal point for aristocratic life and culture. To the extent his resources permitted, each nobleman emulated the style, etiquette, and opulence of the emperor. Each held near-daily audiences or *durbars*, essentially public events, seated on his elevated cushion in the royal style, in which all manner of business was conducted. Officers and staff were publicly commended or rebuked for their performance. Supplicants and visitors, who surmounted the barriers imposed by the nobleman's officers, appeared in front of the great man to seek his favors or good will. As great men do who dispose of vast resources, nobles turned their attention to patronage. Artists and craftsmen found lucrative employment and presented their products to their patron in his audience hall. Noble households were the setting for lavish banquets and other gatherings where the male guests were offered a wide variety of music, dance, poetry, or other entertainments. For some nobles such occasions were the venue for poetry recitations; for some wine and opium were the main attractions.

Noble households were divided into the external, more public areas dominated by men and the interior, secluded space reserved for women. Behind the stone screens of the harem quarters was a domestic world with its celebration of births, marriages, and deaths, religious festivals, and social occasions. The wives, concubines, and female relatives of the master were ranked by seniority, blood ties, and favor in a strictly prescribed hierarchy. Hundreds of female maidservants, often slaves, were employed. The harem was an ordered community with its own decorum and gentility. Ideally, the harem provided a respite, a retreat for the nobleman and his closest male relatives – a retreat of grace, beauty, and order designed to refresh the males of the household.

The Mughal household was also a world of domestic slavery. Numerous male and female slaves were maintained. Their status and tasks varied from the most mundane to those requiring skill, tact, and intelligence. Younger slaves of both sexes were available for discreet sexual services to their masters or mistresses. Slave-eunuchs, usually obtained as castrated young boys from the slave markets of Bengal, moved between the external and internal life of the household. They acted as guards, servants, and often as business agents for high-born women immured in the harem. Mughal noblemen also employed slave-eunuchs as personal confidants and assistants. These favored slave-eunuchs held the utmost confidence of their masters. Not infrequently, despite official and public disapproval, such relationships involved a sexual relationship between master and slave.

In Agra, Delhi, Lahore, Burhanpur, and other major cities, the morphology of urban life was determined by the settlement patterns of the Mughal nobility. The mansions of the higher nobles were the foci for urban quarters as lesser staff and troops built houses and straw huts nearby and vendors of goods and services clustered around a dependable market. Architects and builders found permanent employment in noble entourages. Mughal officers, and, frequently, their women-folk spent large sums of money for the construction of mosques, sarais, and other buildings. Stone bridges and wells were also favorite projects. In nearly every urban center such constructions served as testimonial to the wealth and charitable impulses of these grandees.

The origins of dozens of new towns and villages throughout north India can be traced to investment by Mughal nobles in the facilities for local markets. Seen as an act of public spirit and religious merit, these emporia also served the needs of each nobleman's entourage and increased his earnings from his jagir lands. In a less benign mode, less scrupulous princes or nobles ignored imperial regulations and intervened forcefully in local markets under their jurisdiction. Using the weight of state power they were able to buy up goods at distress prices and sell them at exorbitant monopoly rates. More entrepreneurial nobles invested their money in commercial ventures: financing traders in the long-distance trades overland or by sea. Increasingly nobles began to lease or buy mercantile vessels and try their hand at the highest level of overseas trade.

THE CORPS OF MANSABDARS

All nobles held mansabs; but all mansabdars were not nobles. Generally officers bearing personal decimal ranks of 500 zat or above ranked as nobles during Akbar's reign. By the seventeenth century nobles were officers with personal ranks of 1,000 zat and higher. Nobles and lesser-ranked officers or mansabdars filled a variety of posts, but all were required on occasion to act in a military capacity. All maintained a contingent of mounted armored troopers specified by their suwar rank. In 1595, a total of 1,823 men held mansabs and commanded a minimum of 141,053 followers serving as heavy cavalry with their own horses and equipment.[2] Nobles were also required to support a specified number of war horses, war elephants, and transport animals and carts on a formula based upon their personal rank.[3] This obligation was separate from that specified for their troopers. Toward the end of the reign mansabdars and their followers consumed 82 percent of the total annual budget (81 millions from a total budget of 99 million rupees) of the empire for their pay and allowances.

In their military role mansabdars fell under the jurisdiction of the army minister or *mir bakhshi*. Akbar structured the duties of the office so that the army minister was not chief commander of the Mughal armies. Instead he himself directed overall strategy and assigned field commanders for specific campaigns. The chief bakhshi was responsible for recruitment, recommendations for proper rank and assignment of correct pay and allowances (in cash or assignments on the revenues) for all mansabdars appointed.

The imperial bakhshi stood in open court at the right hand of the emperor. He presented all candidates for appointment, promotion or

[2] Shireen Moosvi, *The Economy of the Mughal Empire c. 1595* (Delhi, 1987), pp. 214–219. Her estimate of the minimum cavalry is given in Appendix 12A. The maximum is 188,070.

[3] K. K. Trivedi, "The Share of Mansabdars in State Revenue Resources: A Study of the Maintenance of Animals", *The Indian Economic and Social History Review*, 24 (1987), 411–421.

commendation in the higher ranks of the mansabdars. The imperial bakhshi's office prepared and recorded written orders of appointment and transfer bearing his ink-stamp imprint which were signed by the emperor. The bakhshi was responsible for inspections of the mansabdars and their troopers, mounts and equipment. His certification was necessary to release cash payments or jagir assignments. Failure to pass inspection meant loss of pay and allowances for any mansabdar.

Each amir headed a cluster of kinsmen, salaried troops, and even slaves. Often, the private officers of higher-ranking mansabdars, although not members of the imperial cadre, held responsible, well-paid, military and administrative positions. Some of the men attached to a nobleman, especially his close relatives, bore ranks and titles as mansabdars obtained directly from the emperor. They, in turn, commanded their own, smaller, clusters of officers and troops. Generally, his entire entourage accompanied the nobleman from post to post. Stripped of dependents and servants they formed one unit of any army in the field.

All cavalry and musketeers commanded by mansabdars were at the disposal of the emperor. All had to meet strict imperial standards. Each officer was required to ensure that his troopers were properly equipped with weapons and chain-link armor. Mounts were to be larger horses of standard Central Asian or Persian breeds – not the scrub mounts of most of the subcontinent. A specified number of the commander's troopers had to bring an additional horse to the muster to serve as a remount. Horses found acceptable were branded on the flank by the imperial mark (*dagh*).

Each mansabdar was free to recruit men of his own ethnicity and religion. Later regulations tended to codify this by stipulating that commanders might not employ more than a fixed proportion of men outside their own group (e.g. Rajputs were to primarily employ Rajputs; Indian Muslims to employ their fellows). Apart from kinsmen, each commander found experienced and proficient troops, whether mounted or foot, available for hire in any sizable town or city. It was up to the mansabdar to negotiate pay and conditions with these men. Salary payments for horsemen were usually stated and paid in cash. The imperial administration calculated the average rate of pay for each horseman at twenty silver rupees per month.[4] But the actual salary

[4] Moosvi, *Economy of the Mughal Empire*, p. 216.

received by the horseman varied according to the bargain struck with his employer.

The dual zat and suwar numerical ranking system formally expressed the uniformity, discipline, and cohesiveness of the corps of mansabdars. In the historical chronicles of the time nobles and higher-ranking mansabdars are invariably identified by their titles and their two-part numerical rank. Ranked nobles became reliable instruments of the imperial will. The emperor personally reviewed all changes in rank, titles, and official postings for all save the lowest ranked officers. Changes in rank could come at any time – without reference to procedure or rules. The sole criterion remained the emperor's favor. Whenever possible, high-ranking officers appeared in person to express submission to the emperor in the public audience hall of palace or camp. Petty mansabdars received written orders in the name of the emperor, relayed through the office of the *mir bakhshi*. Only the emperor could confer and change rank; and no other person held the loyalty of this corporate body.

Written rules and procedures applied to all parts of the empire and to all servants – unless exempted for some special reason. Especially effective was the discipline of daily life at the imperial court, whether at the capital or in the mobile encampment. As that careful observer Antonio Monserrate noticed:[5]

> [I]n order to prevent the great nobles becoming insolent through the unchallenged enjoyment of power, the King summons [them] to court . . . and gives them many imperious commands, as though they were his slaves – commands, moreover, obedience to which ill suits their exalted rank and dignity.

Rigid rituals of submission were acted out daily as the body of imperial officers stood in rows by rank-order in the public audience hall before the seated emperor. Forms of address, titles, and carefully circumscribed speech at court – even in less formal circumstances – constantly conditioned noble behavior. Nobles resident at court shared the responsibility for night and day guard of the emperor and his household. Each week a noble mounted guard in person with troops from his own contingent at the palace or in the encampment. Whether at court or on distant service, all mansabdars worried about their rank, their jagirs, and their favor with the emperor.

[5] Monserrate, *Commentary*.

All officers were subject to assignment in any part of the empire. Akbar's nobles and mansabdars grew accustomed to frequent assignments to far distant provinces punctuated by periods of residence at the capital or at the imperial camp. The Timurid monarch aimed to divorce his imperial elite from local or regional power as much as possible. This was considerably easier to accomplish with the heterogeneous body of foreign recruits to Mughal service. Persian, Arab, Turkish, or Central Asian nobles were necessarily cut off from their native societies. They banded together with fellow countrymen, but had no direct access to home territory. Rajputs, Indian Muslims, and even Afghans (in small, but growing numbers) were a different matter. These men had multiple connections with kinsmen who controlled local domains as zamindars in the provinces. For them a policy that stressed active service outside their native regions was absolutely essential.

SALARY ASSIGNMENTS

The Mughal jagir traces its institutional lineage back to the medieval Islamic iqta or fief in India. Conquering Turkish rulers parcelled out tracts of land of varying size – some as large as a province – to be administered by their nobles and generals as the need arose. These *iqtadars* were responsible for maintaining order and collecting taxes within their domains. After meeting necessary expenses any surplus funds were to be returned to the central treasury. In theory the iqtadars held their fiefs at the pleasure of the ruler. In practice the dynastic shifts and political turmoil permitted iqtas to remain with their holders over generations. Under the Lodis, and to a lesser extent, the Surs, the Afghan nobility held fiefs that permitted them local residence, local resources, and local identities.

Akbar's innovations reversed this trend. Unlike the iqta the jagir of the Mughals separated political and administrative responsibility from rights of tax collection. A mansabdar receiving lands in a salary assignment obtained only the right to collect the taxes assessed on that stipulated area. A jagir might consist of fields in a portion of a village; the entire lands of one or more named villages; or as much as one or even more subdistricts (parganas). The *diwan-i tan* (minister for salaries) matched assessed taxes with the specified salary and allowances of the mansabdar and issued an official jagir document in multiple copies.

Only mansabdars could hold jagirs. All other imperial staff were paid in cash. Receipt of a written assignment permitted a mansabdar to collect the taxes assessed on his lands in quarterly installments each year. Most save the lowest-ranking mansabdars sent personal agents to carry out this task on their behalf.

A jagir-holder possessed only fiscal rights stripped of rights of land-ownership, occupancy, or residence. This was not a fief. It was purely a fiscal instrument designed to meet a narrowly defined end. Only Rajput mansabdars were given more extensive rights of residence and local power within their homelands in Rajasthan. By special dispensation they received patrimonial (termed *watan*) lands as a part of the jagirs assigned them.

In theory the location of a jagir bore little relationship to the official posting or service of the holder. In practice, however, the mature system tended to assign jagirs either within or adjacent to the province of posting. *Jagirdars* frequently held more than one jagir. These were not necessarily contiguous. For example an amir of high rank might receive as many as two dozen separate jagir assignments scattered over several provinces.

The financial ministry further diluted ties between imperial officers and their assigned lands by means of frequent transfers. Deaths, transfers, promotions, and demotions in the imperial cadres necessitated continuing transfer of jagirs. Assigned lands could be transferred from one serving officer to another as often as every two to three years. But the higher ranked jagirdars tended to obtain and hold entire parganas for ten years or even more before transfer.

The financial ministry exerted strict controls over methods and levels of tax collection. Officers of the provincial diwan obtained information from the local intelligence-writer who sent near-daily reports to the provincial capital. They also relied upon complaints and petitions from aggrieved subjects to identify brutal or excessive collection of the revenues. Obviously imperfect, this system did prevent the worst abuses and kept a generally uniform standard for revenue collection in the areas under the regulation system.

The mature system of tax collection and salary payments was one of flexibility and efficiency. Some of the largest tasks of the imperial administration were thereby placed in the hands of the mansabdars themselves who were forced to become capable managers on their own behalf. The system also relied upon private agency in the form of assistance from local moneylenders and currency dealers (*sarrafs*) who often advanced money to mansabdars pending arrival of funds from their jagirs. Local bankers also assisted jagirdars' agents to remit collections by means of private bills of exchange rather than cash shipments. The vast empire of the Timurids rested upon active central control over an essentially decentralized fiscal structure.

THE CENTRAL ARMY

The chief bakhshi generally remained in personal attendance on the emperor. He arranged for the security of the emperor's person, the imperial household, and the palace-fortress. Under Akbar, royal guard troops included over twelve thousand musketeers and several thousand more swordsmen and archers. Four to five thousand gentlemen troopers (*ahadis*) acted as household cavalry for the emperor. The bakhshi was responsible for the system by which nobles on week-long rotation personally commanded their troops on twenty-four hour guard at the emperor's palace or tents in camp.

The bakhshi and his assistants organized the sizable military units directly employed by the emperor. These included artillery men serving the central artillery park; companies of pioneers and sappers; infantry armed with matchlocks; companies of archers; handlers of war elephants and various laborers and porters. Artillery and infantry posted as permanent garrisons to strategic fortresses scattered around the empire were also the responsibility of the bakhshi. All central troops received cash salaries direct from the treasury. The army minister advanced funds against anticipated expenses to nobles designated as field commanders by the emperor. The bakhshi, in concert with the imperial fiscal minister, arranged to send treasure when needed to armies on campaign.

Provincial bakhshis, who were generally higher-ranked, but not noble, officers, conducted inspections to certify fitness for mansabdars and their contingents on duty in that province. Inadequacies turning up in the muster were penalized by partial deductions of pay and allowances, or in the case of jagirs, by claims imposed by the provincial diwan against the delinquent commander's treasury accounts.

The chief bakhshi supervised the corps of public newswriters who sent near-daily reports to provincial bakhshis from every sizable town in the empire. Secret observers reported clandestinely to the provincial bakhshis who forwarded their observations to the center as well. News reports and important official documents travelled rapidly by imperial post. Relays of foot-runners, posted at intervals along the main roads, carried papers rolled up in bamboo containers at a rapid pace around the clock. The emperor received reports from even distant provincial capitals within a few days. The most important news reports were read out daily in the public audience hall. Agents of nobles posted outside the capital or Rajput princes and tributary rulers all assiduously copied these announcements and sent their contents by messenger back to their masters. The empire was connected by a surprisingly rapid information loop for public news.

IMPERIAL FISCAL ADMINISTRATION

Rapid imperial expansion meant that growing revenues from plunder, tribute and taxation poured into the imperial treasuries every year. The imperial finance minister, the wazir or *diwan-i kul*, was responsible for all revenues, the treasury system, the mints and currency, and, directly or indirectly, all expenditures. The first wazir under Akbar was Muzaffar Khan, who had been serving as chief fiscal officer of the imperial household when he became imperial diwan. Towards the latter part of Muzaffar Khan's eight-year term a small group of extraordinarily talented financial officers emerged at Akbar's court. Khwaja Shah Mansur, Mir Fathullah Shirazi, and one Hindu of great ability, Raja Todar Mal, became dominant figures in the Mughal fiscal system. Each served as imperial finance minister for one or more periods, but, more importantly, worked closely with the others to find creative solutions to problems encountered.

When Mir Fathullah Shirazi died Abul Fazl recorded the emperor's mourning for his servant:[6]

> [Akbar] grieved at the departure of this memorial of former sages. He often said that the Mir was his vakil, philosopher, physician, and astronomer, and that no one could understand the amount of his grief for him. "Had he fallen into the hands of the Franks, and they had demanded all my treasures in exchange for him, I should gladly have entered into such a profitable traffic, and have bought that precious jewel cheap."

[6] Abul Fazl, *The Akbar-Nama*, translated by H. Beveridge (Calcutta, 1907–39) III, 848.

This utterance reflects more than conventional panegyric. The emperor's lamentation suggests the intensity with which he and his closest advisers collaborated. It suggests also the high degree of intimacy and emotional involvement between Akbar and his most valued officers at court. We can sense only dimly the exhilaration produced among the architects of the new empire. Much of this intense organizational work occurred in the Fatehpur Sikri years (1571–1584).

Under these men the Indo-Muslim fiscal system inherited by Akbar became a powerful, flexible instrument. Mounting burdens on the central ministry encouraged division of labor in the office. The finance minister himself assumed direct responsibility for the operation and staffing of the central, provincial, and local treasuries. (In his capacity as administrator of the central treasury and mints the minister of the imperial household or *mir saman* reported to the diwan.) Three principal officers served as his direct assistants. The minister of crown revenues (*diwan-i khalisa*) took responsibility for all lands and tax-producing entities whose revenues were reserved for direct deposit in the central treasury. The minister for compensation (diwan-i tan) was responsible for all salary drafts or jagir assignments. Finally, the auditor general commanded a body of auditors who continually monitored and reviewed the records of fiscal transactions.

Akbar's finance ministers took great pains to develop a smoothly functioning pyramidal treasury system. The base was formed by treasuries at the leading towns of larger parganas. At the next level treasuries were located in each provincial capital, and finally central treasuries at the apex of the pyramid. At each level salaried officials – treasurers, accountants, cashkeepers, clerks – presided. The treasuries were more than safety deposit vaults for currency or other valuables. They were vital nodes for the intake, reporting, transfer, and disbursement of funds. Akbar tapped ample reserves and moved funds quickly from his chain of treasuries to support his field armies. On more than one occasion swift dispatch of treasure gave his armies the means and morale for victory. Mughal treasure, effectively deployed, was one of the most potent weapons the emperor possessed. Imperial field commanders were virtually invulnerable to bribery or purchase.

The Mughal system imposed strict accountability on its officials. Treasurers reported their balances in writing every fifteen days and gave written receipts for deposits and demanded written receipts for disbursements. The regime made firm distinctions between private and state funds for all save the emperor. Access to imperial funds was only by written authorization – even for royal princes. Mansabdars obtained cash advances from treasuries, but they had to clear their balances and at times pay interest under the terms of a complicated set of regulations. Their accounts were rigorously audited at death and monies owed the treasury were seized.

The financial administration was run by a cadre of technically proficient officials and clerks. By the sixteenth century Hindu service castes – Khatris, Kayasths, Brahmins, and others – had learned Persian and become indispensable in the operation of government. These caste and family networks came to monopolize the subordinate, but lucrative, positions in all ministries save that of the Muslim sadr. They supplied young recruits to serve as apprentices who already, through training in the family, had been schooled in official Persian terminology, accounting, and reporting methods as well as the difficult chancery script. Generally these Hindu clerks and secretaries were efficient, reliable and loyal.[7]

These family groups, anxious to retain their prosperous circumstances, were the primary means by which the newly forged administrative traditions of the finance ministry were transmitted and refined over time. As the empire added territory, members of these groups formed the cadres that set up regulation fiscal administrations in the conquered kingdoms.

IMPERIAL COINAGE

In 1556 Bairam Khan, acting for his young Timurid charge, struck new Mughal coin in the Indian silver and copper types favored by the defeated Sur dynasty. Bairam Khan adopted the monetary policies of the Surs instead of the Central Asian traditional Timurid style of coinage. By the early 1560s the new regime possessed a fully functioning trimetallic currency: silver, copper, and gold.

Akbar's first silver rupees, similar to the thousands of Sur rupees still in circulation, issued from central mints at Lahore, Delhi and Agra. The new Timurid rupees bore the title "Jalal-ud-din Muhammad Akbar Badshah, Ghazi" on the reverse. The front displayed the Islamic

[7] See John F. Richards, "Norms of Comportment among Imperial Mughal Officials" in Barbara Daly Metcalf ed., *Moral Conduct and Authority* (Berkeley, California: UC Berkeley Press, 1984), pp. 267–281 for a description of Bhimsen, a prominent member of such a service family.

statement of faith "There is no God but Allah and Muhammad is his Messenger" bordered by the names of the four Companions of the Prophet. The legends were struck only in Arabic script, not in the dual Devanagari and Arabic style employed by the Surs.[8] In the public display of his coinage, the young Akbar presented a conservative, Muslim profile.

Akbar's moneyers decided to continue the 21 gram copper *paisa* coins of the Surs, now called *dams*, as the primary issue for ordinary transactions. These coins, bearing only the date of issue and mint name in Persian, were struck at the imperial capital, at mints adjacent to copper mines in Rajasthan or at several towns serving as entrepots for the overland Nepal trade in copper.[9] Shortly after he had asserted his independent rule, in 1562, Akbar revived a gold issue, called a *muhr*, weighing 10.9 grams, based upon the old Delhi Sultanate standard. This marked the first issue of gold coins in Hindustan since the mid-fifteenth century.[10]

In the late 1570s Akbar undertook monetary reforms coinciding with his revenue reforms. In 1577–78 the emperor appointed the mintmaster at Fatehpur Sikri executive officer in charge of all the imperial mints. The well-known calligrapher, Khwaja Abud-us Samad, assumed these new responsibilities.[11] Gold and silver issues were confined to the Fatehpur mint and mints in Punjab, eastern UP, Bihar, Bengal, and Gujarat, to which senior financial officers were sent as mintmasters. For a brief period the emperor and his moneyers flirted with a dramatic style of square coins in a tradition indigenous to western India. In 1580–81 the number of mints striking gold and silver coin was further reduced to two: the mint at Ahmadabad in Gujarat and the Urdu or mint of the imperial camp – the seat of the sovereign. Copper issues continued uninterruptedly from several mint-towns located next to the source of supply of the metal. The intent of these measures was to consolidate imperial control over the minting process.

In 1584 Akbar ordered a new coinage to reflect the ideological and political changes underway in his reign. The new coins bore the single legend: "God is great, splendid is His Glory" (*Allahu akbar jalla jalaluhu*) with the ambiguous play on the emperor's name and titles. The date was stamped with solar, Ilahi years under the new era with the

[8] John S. Deyell, "The Development of Akbar's Currency System and Monetary Integration of the Conquered Kingdoms" in John F. Richards, ed., *The Imperial Monetary System of Mughal India* (Delhi: Oxford University Press, 1987), p. 19.

[9] Ibid., p. 22. [10] Ibid., p. 23. [11] Ibid., p. 30.

old Persian names of the months added. Calligraphy, dies, and stamping all improved visibly on the new coin. Floral decorative touches appeared on the borders. Special issues with portraits of wildlife were struck.[12] In short, the coinage ceased to be indisputably Islamic in its design. The new Ilahi coins, however, remained conservative in reverting to the round shape and customary weights.

Throughout these changes Akbar's minters were careful to maintain a high-quality coinage in each of the three metals. Gold was nearly pure; silver never dropped below 96 percent pure and copper coins remained of high purity. This was a free or open minting system in which anyone willing to pay the prescribed mint charges could bring metal or old or foreign coin to the mint and have it struck. Mints were widely distributed. In 1595 four mints produced gold coins, fourteen produced rupees and forty-two copper coin.

Millions of coin were produced by this system. Minting expenses determined the premium by which coin was valued over bullion – ranging from a high of 10.77 percent for copper to a low of 5.63 percent for silver bullion.[13] Newly minted rupees (*sikka*) circulated at an additional premium of 5 percent over older rupees. Mughal treasuries willingly accepted out-of-date Suri and other coin in payment of taxes, but at a discounted rate that pushed its value down to that of bullion. As a result the huge corpus of Afghan coinage flowed into Akbar's mints, was demonetized, melted down, and reissued as new Timurid coin.

During Akbar's reign the heavy copper dam was the coin of ordinary exchange and the preferred metal in the trimetallic system. Copper coins were issued in enormous quantities. The regime set its land revenue demand in terms of copper dams. Purchasers when acquiring zamindari rights paid for them in copper coin. Prices for ordinary commodities in city markets and wages for laborers, soldiers, and artisans were expressed in copper coin.[14]

Extension of the uniform coinage accompanied imperial conquest. Some newly conquered kingdoms did not immediately adhere to the new standards. Some anomalies were permitted for a transitional

[12] Ibid., pp. 36–37.

[13] Marie Martin, "The Reforms of the Sixteenth Century and Akbar's Administration: Metrological and Monetary Considerations" in J. F. Richards, ed., *The Imperial Monetary System of Mughal India* (Delhi: Oxford University Press, 1987), p. 71.

[14] Irfan Habib, "The Economic and Social Setting" in Michael Brand and Glenn D. Lowry, eds., *Fatehpur Sikri* (Bombay: Marg Publications, 1987), pp. 144–147.

period. But the imperial financiers insisted on a centralized, uniform, monetary system. For any particular type of coin, the design, weight standard, and fabric was identical from one end of the empire to the other. Moreover imperial coins travelled from one end of the empire to the other in rapid fashion. Copper coin found in coin hoards circulated from the heartland of the empire to the frontier in the year of their manufacture. In John Deyell's apt phrase "Mughal currency *had* currency".[15]

Throughout his reign Akbar seized older silver and gold coin found in the treasure hoards of dozens of Indian dynasties. Mughal mintmasters thereby had ample supplies necessary to expand silver and gold currency in normal types. They also cast giant coins and ingots for Akbar's fast-swelling monetary reserve – his central treasure described above.

Paradoxically, although it did not lack for stocks of gold and silver, India produced only minimal amounts of gold from alluvial sources in the northeast. The silver mines of Mewar found in the early sixteenth century were rapidly exhausted. In spite of this disability, unlike contemporary rulers in other parts of the world, Akbar did not have to worry about a trade deficit or bullion famines. Quite the contrary, for the strength of the Indian economy drew a steady stream of precious metals to pay for Indian industrial and agricultural exports. In the medieval and early modern worlds, whatever the available sources of gold and silver, India was the ultimate sink for these metals. When minted, Mughal silver and gold coin did not circulate beyond the Indian subcontinent – not because of inferior quality, but because foreign traders needed Indian coin to pay for exports.

By the latter years of the sixteenth century surging imports of New World silver offered new sources of supply for the Timurid mints. The copper price of silver rose from 48 dams to the rupee early in the reign to as high as 35 dams to the rupee in the late 1580s.[16] The copper price of silver continued to rise throughout the early seventeenth century as new industrial uses for copper in bronze cannon and brass utensils increased its value as well. In succeeding reigns the silver rupee, supported by new fractional *anna* (sixteenth part) coins, replaced the copper dam as a common medium of circulation for most of the empire.

[15] Deyell, "Akbar's Currency System, p. 45.
[16] Habib, "Economic and Social Setting," p. 141.

THE BUDGET OF THE EMPIRE

Akbar's advisers did not have to overcome budget deficits. The imperial reserves of the Mughals – in currency, precious metals, and set and unset gems – swelled during Akbar's half century. In 1605, the imperial treasuries contained gold, silver, copper coin, and uncoined bullion valued at between 139 million to 166 million silver rupees.[17] The mass of set and unset precious stones in the treasury and other precious objects was probably as valuable.

Continued territorial expansion and good management ensured that revenues exceeded expenditures. Plunder from victory swelled the imperial reserves. In 1556 the Mughals at Panipat seized dozens of elephants laden with gold as the wife of the defeated general Hemu tried to flee the battlefield. This was just the first of many such treasures that more than repaid the costs of military conquest. Thereafter additional taxes levied within a more rigorous imperial assessment brought fresh revenue streams into the imperial treasuries. Shireen Moosvi's recent estimate of Akbar's revenues for 1595–96 puts the total at just under four billion copper coins (dams) or the equivalent of 99 million silver rupees per year.[18]

Certain features of this financial reconstruction are immediately apparent. First, an annual surplus of between four and five million rupees was generated late in the reign. Second, expenditures made directly by the emperor were relatively small. The annual expense of the imperial household with its conspicuous display and thousands of dependents was less than five percent of the total budget. The central military establishment, including stables and artillery, as well as the corps of musketeers and ahadis consumed less than 10 percent of the total. Lastly, by far the largest item of expenditure, 81 million rupees, was allotted to the mansabdars. Of this just over half of imperial expenditures, 51 million rupees, supported the cavalry and musketeer contingents of the mansabdars. In other words by far the greater part of this budget was devoted to supporting a massive military establishment.

[17] Moosvi, *Economy of the Mughal Empire*, pp. 198–200.
[18] Moosvi, *Economy of the Mughal Empire*, p. 195. This is the *jama* from the *Ain-i Akbari* revised downward to reflect revenue-free land grants and areas whose revenues were listed but not fully subjugated at this date. It also adjusts for costs of revenue collection to arrive at net revenue realization.

Table 1[19] *Imperial revenue and expenditure, 1595–96*

Income	Millions *dams*	Millions rupees
Effective jama 1595–96	3960.3	99.01
Expenditure: salary bill of mansabdars		
Zat salaries	827.5	20.69
Animal allowance	371.4	9.29
Suwar payment	2038.9	50.97
Total	3237.8	80.95
Central military establishment		
Cavalry and foot	142.9	3.57
Animals/stables	194.0	4.85
Arsenal and armor	22.1	.55
Total	359.0	8.97
Imperial household (including harem/building construction)		
Total	187.4	4.69
Total expenditures	3784.2	94.6
Balance	176.1	4.41
Grand total	3960.3	99.01

IMPERIAL CROWNLANDS

Crownlands (*khalisa*) under the direct administration of the imperial finance minister generated funds that flowed directly to the central treasury. Revenues from these crownlands as well as from a pool of temporarily unassigned jagir lands referred to as *paibaqi* were the mainstay of the center. From these returns the emperor defrayed the costs of his central household, military, diplomacy, and the cash salaries of the lesser mansabdars. Plunder, ceremonial gifts, and escheat from estates of deceased nobles constituted substantial, but irregular, alternative sources of income for the central treasury. A recent estimate for the latter years of Akbar's reign puts khalisa revenues at between 24 and 33 percent of the total assessed revenues.[20]

[19] Adapted from Moosvi, *Economy of the Mughal Empire*, Table 11.5, p. 270.
[20] Moosvi, *Economy of the Mughal Empire*, p. 197.

All remaining revenues were shunted directly to the holders of salary assignments.

The minister of crownlands (diwan-i khalisa) presided over a sophisticated fiscal device. No specific lands adjacent to the capital were demarcated for the khalisa. The Mughal khalisa was instead a fiscal mechanism, a pool of sequestered revenues, that set aside tax collections from designated villages or parganas scattered throughout the empire. Khalisa tracts, usually designated in fertile and untroubled areas, were found in nearly every province of the empire. Cadres of salaried revenue officers directly employed by the minister of crownlands collected crown revenues. The proportion of revenues placed in the crown treasury accounts varied according to the perceived needs of the central treasury. In effect the emperor was awarded a set of jagir assignments, larger than, but comparable to those given great nobles. The emperor's own agents were sent to make collections just as the jagirdars did from their jagirs.

By 1605 Akbar and his advisers had created an autocratic and centralized system. A half-century long territorial build-up brought resources to the center far greater than those available to any regional ruler or provincial governor. The emperor routinely deployed tens of thousands of men, millions of silver rupees, and vast quantities of material throughout his domains. Orders from the emperor or his immediate subordinates flowed outward from the center; written and verbal reports regularly flowed in to the imperial capital. Akbar, the epicenter, actively absorbed reports and issued orders on a daily basis. Relatively quick official communications were essential to centralized power.

Although clearly centered on Akbar, to an outside observer the imperial structures and procedures were complex and confusing. From one perspective the Mughal empire appeared to be a properly bureaucratic system, fully centralized and run by technically proficient bureaucrats moving vast amounts of paper in well-regulated transactions. From another perspective, however, the empire appeared as a series of great patrimonial households dominated at its apex by the massive establishments of the emperor. Akbar drew upon vast revenue to build up his treasure and to support his lavish expenditures on luxurious display. It is equally clear, however, that the great amirs of the empire absorbed a huge proportion of official revenues – monies which were directed, but not directly received by the center. To an unprecedented degree the centralized, autocratic system created by Akbar relied upon private organizational skill, entrepreneurial spirit and energy to carry out the vital tasks of ruling a multi-regional empire. The Timurid empire was both centralized and decentralized, both bureaucratic and patrimonial in its structure and operation.

CHAPTER 4

LAND REVENUE AND RURAL SOCIETY

Despite centuries of Muslim dominance in the Indo-Gangetic plain, Akbar's officials found consolidation of state power incomplete. In the second half of the sixteenth century both force and diplomacy were needed to subdue and pacify rural society. Even within the zone of direct administration, in the most fertile hinterlands of the towns, supposedly inhabited by subjects regulated by a tax system, the Mughals confronted only partially subdued local polities. In more distant regions were barely tributary areas that had been recently settled and colonized by Hindu and Muslim armed warrior-pioneers. Extension of centralized administrative control over these areas would be unprecedented.

In one pargana after another armed, potentially hostile, warrior lineages –Rajputs, Jats, and other locally rooted caste elites – ruled the cultivating peasantry. These local aristocratic lineages and their lineage heads or chiefs dominated individual parganas, or segments of parganas by virtue of conquest, migration and colonization. Parganas in the north were miniature kingdoms containing from as few as twenty to as many as two hundred contiguous villages. These were the primary building blocks of political control in Indian rural society – not individual villages.[1]

Local elites had performed a key role in organizing, financing, and leading peasant-cultivators in a process of jungle-clearing and settlement. Often this expansion required armed battle with indigenous "tribals" or non-Hindu groups who cultivated and settled much less intensively than the newcomers. This same militance that drove agricultural expansion also drove lineage leaders into bloody, treacherous episodes of local warfare. The question for the state was how to channel energies for expansion that would yield increased revenues without permitting internecine warfare in the countryside.

The boundaries of most parganas defined the limits of domination

[1] See Richard Fox, "Rajput 'Clans' and Urban Centers in Northern India," in Richard G. Fox, ed., *Urban India: Society, Space and Image*, and Richard G. Fox, *Kin, Clan, Raja and Rule*, (Berkeley and Los Angeles: University of California Press, 1971).

for each Rajput, Jat, Indian Muslim, or even Afghan lineage. At the center lay a larger village or smallish town in which resided the lineage head. Often this was the original settlement when the lineage forbears had colonized the area. The chief's town found protection behind scrub jungle, bamboo hedges, ditches, mud or stone walls. Within these defenses, the chief or lineage heads built their residences, held miniature court in a rustic aristocratic style and maintained armories, treasuries and lineage temples. The town itself served as a central market place for the pargana. Other lesser towns served as similar headquarters for subordinate chiefs and dependent kinsmen of the petty raja or lineage head.

These chiefs or *zamindars* as the Mughals called them, maintained substantial military forces. A small raja might have under his immediate command a mixed body of several hundred armed kinsmen, slaves, and free, paid retainers. He could also call upon his subordinate lineage mates for troops in an emergency to defend the subdistrict or lineage interests. Zamindari contingents were almost entirely infantry for most local lords could afford few horses or elephants. They were also deficient in artillery. Muskets were available, but the Mughals made every effort to discourage gun-casting or procurement of artillery by local aristocrats.

Zamindars claimed the hereditary right to collect a share of the harvest. They cultivated private land holdings using tenants or laborers in their employ. Generally such lands were exempt from the normal state revenue demand. In addition these chiefs exercised claims to a whole series of taxes and cesses on the peasants, craftsmen and merchants within the pargana. A multitude of market taxes, poll taxes, feudal taxes on production (e.g. an implement or weapon each year from a blacksmith) flowed into their coffers and storehouses each year. Some payments were in coined money; some in kind. Within traditional limits forced labor could be demanded from lesser castes in the pargana.

The Rajput, Jat, Gujar lineage heads and their kinsmen or Afghans or other Indian Muslim lineages retained power partly by weight of numbers, partly by armed belligerence, and partly by the inertia of long custom. In the majority of villages the most powerful and wealthiest peasants were members of the same caste and shared lineage ties with the lineage head at the headquarters town. These village elites cultivated the largest and most fertile tracts within the village.

Untouchable landless laborers, craftsmen, traders, and priests served the dominant caste in an intricate network of hereditary service and exchange relationships.

From the Mughal perspective in 1560 the rural landscape of North India was dotted with principalities of varying size and in varying degrees of subordination and control to the center. Some parganas adjacent to cities were inhabited by peasants lacking strong lineage organization and could be administered on a village by village basis. Most of rural society in North India lay under the tight control of zamindars. By the sixteenth century rural pacification had progressed to the point that no single zamindar or coalition of rural chiefs could withstand the full power of the Muslim state. Preceding Indo-Muslim regimes had begun to fix the boundaries of these tiny kingdoms and to limit internecine warfare among them. Indo-Muslim rulers had begun to determine successions to office by issuing official documents written in Persian and the local language which recognized favored heirs. Only in intervals of political disarray did local lineage elites or petty rajas freely engage in internecine warfare and conquest. Such was the case during the Afghan–Mughal conflicts between 1530 and 1560.

Rarely did local aristocrats engage in larger political ventures. By and large these men, subservient for generations to Indo-Muslim state power, retained foreshortened political horizons. Men like Sher Khan Sur were exceptional. Most local chieftains, whether Hindu or Muslim, did not conceive of or aspire to large-scale state-building.

Nevertheless the relationship between Mughals and their new subjects in the 1560s resembled tribute rather more than taxation. Preceding states had identified and negotiated service agreements with leading lineage members or rajas in each pargana. These local officers, called *chaudhuris* in the north and *deshmukhs* in the Deccan, retained much of their long-standing powers within the pargana in return for making regular monetary payments to central revenue officials. Pargana headmen received a fixed percentage, usually 5 percent, of the total revenues obtained from their subdistrict each year. They also controlled lands exempt from any form of taxation. Lifetime contracts executed in writing as sanads between the local chief and the Indo-Muslim ruler spelled out the terms of this relationship. Each recipient of a grant executed a written bond (*muchalka*) as a guarantee of good performance and paid a fee (pishkash) of six and one-half years' allowances on the revenue in installments to secure this appointment.

At the death of a chaudhuri his son and heir normally obtained a new patent of office from the ruler. The state could, however, depose a pargana headman at any time and replace him with a more satisfactory candidate – usually another kinsman from the dominant lineage and caste in the subdistrict.

The Indo-Muslim state depended upon a local fiscal officer to serve as a counterpart to the chaudhuri. The *qanungo* was a record keeper or accountant whose task was to keep records of villages, land in production and taxes paid each year. He was appointed on terms similar to that of the pargana headmen except that his allowance on the revenue was usually 3 instead of 5 percent and his tax-free lands a smaller allotment than those given the chaudhuri. Qanungos were generally recruited from Hindu higher castes, often Brahmins, especially in the Deccan, but also Khatris, the north Indian trading caste, and Kayasths, the most prominent Hindu secretarial caste in service to Indo-Muslim states. Indian Muslims also assumed this role as they did that of the pargana headman. Occasionally appointments as qanungos or chaudhuri were shared between two or more individuals.

These two positions together constituted a locking device between state and pargana. Through these hybrid offices the ruler extracted revenues, obtained information, and mobilized support from North Indian rural society. In the mid-sixteenth century, however, state access to these miniature polities was limited. By and large these were still tributary relations rather than assessment and collection of taxes. Save for easily accessible parganas the state did not attempt a careful inventory of lands in order to measure agricultural productivity. Instead the annual revenue figure emerged from a bargaining process in which payment only crudely reflected the resources of the pargana. The negotiating skills, truculence, location, and natural defenses of each lineage determined annual payments of revenue.

The state did not penetrate far below the surface of the average parganas prior to the mid-sixteenth century. Strong Muslim sultans managed to freeze pargana boundaries; to reduce the political pretensions of the Hindu zamindars and to restrain inter-lineage warfare and aggression. But in most localities they had little to do with individual village headmen and village elites.

Penetration of the defenses of rural society was the great task for the Mughal administration in the post-1560 period. Imperial administrators worked tirelessly to crack into these hard-shelled structures.

To obtain accurate information and the fullest possible revenues in taxes, rather than negotiated tribute, the empire had to come to terms with armed rural aristocracies. The zamindars were gradually reshaped into a quasi-official service class in the countryside – or they were destroyed.

THE NEW REVENUE SYSTEM

Sher Shah Sur had demonstrated the basic approach that would enable the state to pull greater resources from agricultural production. The Afghan ruler drew upon his personal experience as the revenue administrator of a pargana under the Lodis, and upon the accumulated knowledge of generations of Indo-Muslim revenue collectors dealing with the dense fabric of rural society in North India. In his short-lived package of revenue reforms we find: demand for cash payment from the peasants – not produce rent; cadastral surveys of agricultural land; surveys of crops grown; assessment of land revenue by expected yields; conversion of those anticipated harvest rates to cash values keyed to prevailing market conditions. All data were to be gathered carefully, systematically, and checked at intervals.

Sher Shah perceived that the state in its own interest should assume greater responsibility for encouraging productivity.[2] Those cultivators who reclaimed land from the forest or scrub woodlands for production should be favored with exemptions or reduced tax burdens in the first few years of production on the new lands. Similar incentives should be given for those who sunk wells and increased the cultivable area. Collections should be made systematically and firmly. Measures needed to be taken to ensure reliable handling of funds and strict accountability on the part of officials. A reliable, standardized, high quality coinage must be available. These measures were backed up by flexible armed force effectively deployed. The whole in turn rested upon the ruler's willingness and ability to invest in a major administrative effort in the countryside.

In practice, however, the Sur revenue measures were flawed by excessive uniformity. When Afghan officials tried to fix near-uniform rates of assessment on the harvest across the entire Sur domain, they

[2] See Iqtidar Husain Siddiqi, "The Agrarian System of the Afghans" in *Studies in Islam*, II (January, 1965), 229–253, and Iqtidar Husain Siddiqi, *Afghan Despotism in India* (Aligarh: Three Men Publication, 1969), pp. 136–168.

generated considerable resistance. Converting harvest rates into cash with a single schedule for a large portion of North India simply was impracticable and created enormous inequities. Even within the monotonous reaches of the North Indian plain great differences existed in fertility between localities.

Todar Mal, Akbar's famed Hindu revenue minister, understood and addressed this problem. When he began revamping the Mughal agrarian system in the early 1560s, Todar Mal first pressed to obtain more complete area and production statistics from the subdistrict accountants (qanungos). Officials under his command began to compile lists of minimum and maximum market prices. At the same time Akbar enforced standardization of highly variable customary weights and measures. The imperial yard (*gaz*) set at the equivalent of 31.92 inches helped to establish a uniform unit of land area. The customary *bigah* was fixed at a unit 60 gaz square equivalent (about three-fifths of an acre). The unit of weight for measuring yields, the *man*, was standardized at 51.63 lbs. avoirdupois.

Despite these measures continuing problems remained. Zamindars protested vigorously when imperial officers or mansabdars tried to collect what in their view were exorbitant assessments. The critically important system of salary assignments (jagirs) was faltering. In 1580 Todar Mal began a drastic experiment designed to completely restructure the Mughal agrarian revenue system. The emperor resumed all jagirs or salary assignments for his officers in the North Indian provinces. All lands now fell under the control of treasury officials who would administer them directly.

Todar Mal proceeded to group contiguous subdistricts into revenue circles with similar, shared climate and soil fertility. He placed a revenue officer (*karuri*) in charge of each circle. Under this officer's direction surveying parties moved steadily from pargana to pargana and village to village. They used new bamboo rods with iron joints marked for the imperial yard rather than older hempen ropes that stretched with varying moisture. In the course of five years these survey parties measured and recorded the fields and land holdings of nearly all villages located within that revenue circle.

Other officials, travelling with the survey parties, collected detailed data on average yields and harvests by cultivator and village for the past ten years. They also collected local market prices for all crops, for both the spring and fall harvests, over the same ten year period.

With land measurements, yield and price data in hand the karuri in charge of the revenue circle compiled long, detailed, tables of data. From these tables he was able to calculate a standard assessment for that revenue circle for each crop. This meant that the revenue ministry could demand its appropriate share of each harvest from each field, cultivator, and village in that revenue circle. This demand could be expressed in money terms that bore a realistic relationship to prices paid in local markets. The final assessment was an average struck on the ten-year record of yields and prices for each field and crop. Rice, millets, and wheats were generally assessed at a one-third equivalent of the harvest. Other, more valuable, crops were assessed more lightly, e.g. as low as one-fifth or less for cash crops such as indigo or sugar. Imperial officers assessed fruit trees at so much per tree and cattle at so much per head.

The revenue ministry under Todar Mal established a fresh, accurate revenue assessment to be placed against each village, pargana, revenue circle, district, and province. The new system allowed for variations in agricultural yield between regions. The assessed demand was firmly linked to past average yields and prices. This was, moreover, a cash nexus. The state expressed its demand in copper coin (dams) and expected to be paid in coin. The peasants had to enter the market and sell their produce in order to pay the assessed revenue demand. In future years, revenue officers simply referred to written tables that set out a standard assessment for each crop per bigah or unit of cultivation for that locality. The total assessment for each peasant, village, or pargana could be determined by multiplying the crop rate against the area under cultivation each year.

In the areas of the new "regulation" (*zabt*) assessment imperial officers imposed written demands for tax payment and obtained written acceptances in turn from the village headmen and dominant peasants in each village. The village community remained liable for the entire annual tax assessment and for its prompt payment in four installments. After the initial rigorous survey and establishment of the new system, revenue assessments in North India were only obliquely linked to actual harvests and market prices. In some localities, imperial officers actually sent out survey parties to measure the area under cultivation in various crops twice a year. In others, revenue officers used the established ten-year average with any estimated additions to arrive at the area under cultivation. Whether measured by actual survey or based upon the previous year's total, they multiplied the cropped area by the standard rate per crop to calculate current revenue demand.

After initial establishment of the zabt system pargana accountants annually assembled current data on cultivated area, yields, and prices from the village accountants and their own records. These data were listed as the most recent entry in a register showing returns for the past ten years. The record also showed actual collections for each field, village and the pargana as a whole. Revenue collectors (*amins*) obtained these data to collate with their own records kept at the office of the provincial revenue officer, the diwan. Periodically, the revenue ministry used these ten-year-average data series to revise and update the revenue assessment. Only occasionally, at twenty, thirty year or more intervals, would a systematic land survey and reassessment of a province be judged necessary.

After five years of direct administration and experimentation Akbar was able once again to place the lands of North India with the mansabdars. The jagir system was reestablished with a more accurate base. The state achieved its end. Akbar's treasuries obtained augmented revenues derived from the new assessment (in those lands kept directly under control of the central revenue ministry). His nobles could count on increased revenues to meet their expenses. State revenue demand acted like a giant pump to draw foodgrains and other crops out of the countryside into the towns and cities by a market mechanism. Sale of these foodgrains transferred coin back to the moneylenders and graindealers at a descending series of markets. This supplied funds to offer credit to the peasantry for the next year's cultivation. Obviously, the new system encouraged rapid expansion of the rural to urban grain trade. Graindealers and moneylenders became much more active and visible in the countryside. The Mughal state came much closer than its predecessors to making good its claim for a massive share of rural productivity. A claim of one-third of all foodgrain production and perhaps one-fifth of other crops represented a massive expropriation of rural savings and profits. Much of this sum was collected at the expense of the older claims and perquisites of the zamindars.

A NEWLY DEFINED SOCIAL CLASS

Timurid centralization and rationalization of the land tax system, while certainly impressive, did not inaugurate a full-blown system of direct rural taxation. The new Mughal administration was unable to carry out those drastic measures necessary to place itself in a direct, unimpeded relationship with each producing peasant in the countryside. In order to do so, Mughal forces would have been forced to disarm the dominant chiefs and leading Rajput, Jat, Indian Muslim, Afghan, and other lineages who controlled the land. Effective control might have called for deportation, enslavement, or imprisonment of many of the most determined leaders of local society in North India. These men would have to be replaced by more compliant lineage-mates, or by new cadres imported by the administration. Disarming and subduing regional aristocracies, or converting them into officials was a formidable task that was rarely accomplished by early modern states. The Timurids were not prepared to execute policies more reminiscent of various Ottoman efforts than those characteristic of Indo-Muslim regimes.

Nevertheless, imposition of the zabt system made it possible for the Mughal administration to launch a long-term strategy aimed at eventually reconstituting the rural aristocracy. Under the zabt system, the Mughals cracked the hard cyst of the countryside – the pargana. Imperial revenue officers or agents of mansabdars no longer dealt only with the pargana headmen, or select numbers of village headmen. For the first time a majority of villages included within the Mughal zabt system were placed in direct relationship with revenue officers of the state. The pargana was changing from a miniature tributary kingdom to a petty revenue and administrative unit existing at the convenience of the Mughal empire.

If backed by sufficient force, over time the new regulation system would gradually convert the zamindars to a service class of quasi-officials, dependent upon the state. The new order forcefully appropriated the right to determine that share of his produce to be given up by each peasant. Local lords formerly had paid a species of tribute to the state, when forced to do so, and levied their customary heavy cesses in goods and labor on the peasant. Under the new system they were reduced to receipt of a fixed allowance, usually 10 percent, of the total revenue collected each year. The state more firmly arrogated to itself the right to determine legitimate holders of zamindar's rights. Like the chaudhuri individual zamindars received a written patent of office from the provincial fiscal officer (the diwan). Like the chaudhuri they paid an appointment fee and signed a bond for performance. They were enjoined to increase cultivation and to hand over the stipulated revenue in the required installments for the area under their jurisdiction.

In the refined zabt system, ancient rights of landed dominance obtained by previous generations who colonized, conquered and settled, were transformed into the right to a share of agricultural production. Only those constricted "homelands" personally occupied by the zamindar remained of the unfettered domain held before. These zamindari rights became a form of private property, which, when ratified by the state, could be passed on to heirs and alienated to others. Inheritance recognized by the state conformed to the provisions of both Islamic and Hindu personal law which provided for equal shares to heirs of the same sex. Only chiefs in tributary relationship to the emperor were permitted to keep their patrimonies intact for a single heir. In this attenuated form of property, zamindari claims could be sold or leased to other kinsmen or even to outsiders. Surviving sale and lease documents testify to widespread adoption of the practice – although not to its true intensity or frequency.

Prising open the defenses of local society in the parganas of North India required forceful determination. Armed warrior elites scarcely looked with a kindly eye upon petty revenue officers and survey parties entering their villages. Only the promise of overwhelming force, ruthlessly applied, curbed violent resistance. Imperial faujdars at the head of several hundred mailed cavalry were posted at intervals throughout each province to ensure that the reality of imperial power was not overlooked by those zamindars who might be reluctant to hand over the stipulated revenue proceeds each season.

However necessary, force alone was inadequate. A stable agrarian order required some recognition of the zamindar's interests under a generally accepted notion of legitimate royal authority. Akbar recognized this fact early in his reign and set about trying to elicit the willing cooperation of leading chiefs, lineage elites and other zamindars. The general tone of the new imperial administration was critical. Would compliance be rewarded, or was the new order to be unrelievedly harsh?

Some evidence for the latter approach exists in the detailed archives of the Jat clan (*khap*) Baliyan in Muzaffarnagar District near Delhi. Migrating from the Punjab in the twelfth century, the founders of this clan established the hereditary seat of the clan headman (chaudhuri) at Sisauli village. From this headquarters "territorial expansion, conquest and colonization" of the clan continued until the first decades of the sixteenth century. But "expansion stopped at the establishment of Mughal rule, when law and order were more effectively imposed on northern India."[3] By the late sixteenth century clan members ruled pargana Sisauli numbering the traditional eighty-four villages through their own system of headmen and councils.[4] They were linked to other Jat and non-Jat Hindu lineage groups who met periodically in regional councils (*sarv-khap*).

The record of resolutions preserved in the clan archives shows a pattern of remarkable collective action by a coalition of castes and clans. When state power at Delhi faltered, the allied clan council raised a large militia to mount a defense against banditry. When the Delhi regime was strong, the clan council met to insist on recognition of the legitimate autonomy of the clan councils and to protest excessive and discriminatory taxation such as levies imposed on pilgrims and the jiziya. If relief were not forthcoming, the Jat clans and their allies mustered their militia and threatened outright revolt. In 1490, Sikandar Lodi's administrators chose not to test these resolutions and failed to press their demands according to the clan records.[5] In 1527, when the possibility of resurgent Rajput power was at hand, the allied council sent 25,000 soldiers under the command of the Raja of Dholpur to fight the Mughals. At the battle of Kanua several thousand soldiers from this force were killed.[6]

Suddenly, under Akbar's regime, the tension and conflict found in the allied clan council resolutions stretching across nearly four centuries abated:[7]

> A *sarv-khap* panchayat meeting was held in Shoron [*khap* Baliyan] in 1631 S.B. [A.D. 1574] under the presidentship of Rao Landey Rai of Sisauli village, to consider the changed political conditions in the country resulting from the advent of Mughal rule. Akbar's recent royal proclamation had given full freedom to religious faith and to the *khap* panchayats.

The thousands of persons assembled ratified a series of resolutions which called for royal recognition of each of the eighteen constituent clan councils represented, for freedom to conduct religious affairs, and

[3] M. C. Pradhan, *The Political System of the Jats of Northern India* (Bombay, 1966), p. 95.
[4] Pradhan, *Political System*, Appendix 3, p. 251 lists these villages.
[5] Pradhan, *Political System*, Case 45, pp. 256–257.
[6] Pradhan, *Political System*, Case 47, p. 257.
[7] Pradhan, *Political System*, Appendix 4, Case 48, pp. 257–258.

for the right to have clan officers make revenue collections within the clan areas.

Six years later another allied council meeting passed a resolution to express its appreciation for a recent edict from the Mughal emperor which granted religious freedom and internal autonomy to the clans. The order, preserved in the Baliyan archive, reads:[8]

> By the present *firman* . . ., certain community councils in India which during the reign of the Muslim sultans, before my reign, were charged certain taxes, are now being excused. Each community council has my permission and is free to carry on its traditional functions, in my reign. Both Hindus and Muslims are one in my eyes, so I give freedom [of action] to these councils. They are exempt from the payment of *jazia* [religious tax] and other taxes.
>
> Issued in the reign of emperor of India, Emperor Akbar, 11th Ramzan, 989 Hijri [A.D. 1580]. Mandate issued by grand wazirs, Abul-Fazel and Raja Todar Mal.

Another edict, issued two years earlier, makes similar statements, and is addressed specifically to the two Jat clan chaudhuris of clan Baliyan.[9]

As these exchanges reveal, Akbar made several concessions to the local clans of the upper Doab region between Ganges and Jumna. The councils were to carry on as before without interference. Imposts that the Jats had resisted for centuries were to be waived. In return, however, the clan councils accepted the new revenue system. Measured lands are recorded for all sub-districts in the imperial district of Saharanput which included the lands of the Baliyan and their allied Jat and Gujar clans.[10] They asked for local agency in collection, but did not quarrel with its implementation. In this region at least, imperial policy relied both upon force and conciliation.

In forcing its agrarian system upon the variegated aristocracy of the North Indian plain, the Mughals began to compress and shape a new social class. The latter, despite resistance, found itself becoming more

[8] Pradhan, *Political System*, p. 97. The royal order is reproduced as Mandate No. 1 in a set of plates between pages 96 and 97. Although the seal is indecipherable, the text is accurately translated by the author.

[9] Ibid. The text seems to have been addressed in general to four Jat khaps and one Gujar khap, but the copy preserved is addressed to "Chaudhury Pacchu Mal, Shoron, and Chaudhury Lad Singh, Sisauli."

[10] These figures are recorded in the *Ain-i Akbari* tables under Delhi province. Abul Fazl Allami, *The Ain-i Akbari*, translated by H. S. Jarrett, second edition, corrected and annotated by Jadunath Sarkar (Calcutta, 1949), pp. 296–97.

dependent upon the state for its prosperity and for an essential aspect of its identity.

GENTRY AND TAX-FREE LAND GRANTS

Mughal success in the countryside relied upon the services of numerous local members of what may be termed a gentry class whose interests and activities were both rural and urban. That is, these were men who filled specialized niches in the local economy and administration and whose skills were absolutely essential to the Mughal agrarian order. Among them were members of the literate, trading castes of Hindu India, or in a minority, Muslim traders. These *mahajans* bought grain and other agricultural products for cash from the villages, carried their goods to the nearest market or pargana town, and from there to larger urban markets. Rural traders advanced loans against the harvest to the peasant farmers. In the larger towns various groups of traders were organized into markets whose headman was recognized by the state. These functionaries made regular reports on prices, scarcities, and other relevant market information.

Another source of rural credit was the body of Hindu moneylenders and moneychangers who were active throughout the market towns and larger villages. In addition to lending and converting currencies, they issued discounted bills of exchange for the transfer of funds or for short-term commercial credit. Men drawn from these castes occupied positions as clerks, agents, collectors, and managers at all levels of the local and provincial revenue system. They served as amins or collectors for sub-districts; as clerks for treasuries; as agents for jagirdars; or as qanungos. In this capacity their roles intersected with local Muslim secretarial and trading groups who were their competitors for official posts of this type.

As the imperial revenue system took hold and expanded its reach, the fortunes of this gentry class improved. Although only the outlines of these processes can be discerned, the numbers and resources of the town-based gentry grew steadily in tandem with the prospering market towns. Other forms of imperial patronage contributed to the rise of the gentry class and urban prosperity in this period.

Early on, in Muzaffar Khan's administration, distinction was established between revenue-paying lands and assets and alienated revenue lands and assets. The latter were a means of offering patronage or paying for services by allocating the normal revenues to privileged recipients. Lands given as revenue grants (*madad-i ma'ash*) were often those for which the ruler permitted pious and worthy persons to collect the state's tax revenues for their own support. Previous Indo-Muslim rulers and their nobles had conferred benefits on a primary Muslim clientele of Sufi masters and devotees and worthy and pious members of the ulema. The praises uttered daily for the ruler by this "Army of Prayer" was one of immeasurable, but significant, sources of political support for any ruler in medieval India. Administration of these grants was the primary obligation of the chief ecclesiastical officer, the sadr.

When Akbar began his revenue reforms in the 1570s he discovered many abuses and many grants held by Afghans who were inimical to his regime – especially in the Punjab. The emperor abrogated grants lapsed illegally into hereditary holdings and resumed others that were gained fraudulently. The new policy forced grantees to shift their holdings to selected parganas and districts within the central provinces of North India where these tax-free grants could be better managed and controlled. This new policy was one of the sources of the discontent which culminated in the revolt of 1579 discussed earlier.

Another sore point was Akbar's inclusion of non-Muslim grantees as objects of state largess. More than any previous Indo-Muslim ruler, Akbar conferred madad-i ma'ash grants on many saintly individuals and institutions. Two surviving documents preserved in the Saivite shrine at Jakhbar, sixteen miles from Patankot in the Punjab, confirm this new departure. In the late sixteenth century, as it is today, this institution was the seat of a ruling Mahant (Master) of the Kanphatha sect of Saivite Jogis. A copy of an imperial farman issued in 1581 added fifty bigahs of tax-free land to the parcel of madad-i ma'ash lands obtained ten years earlier in order to compensate for the loss of lands inundated and made useless. Since the Jogi Udant Nath had been "honored with admittance to the imperial court," he obtained confirmation of the earlier largess and the additional lands. In return he was to "remain occupied with praying for the permanence of the Conquering Dynasty while sustaining himself year after year with the entire produce from that (land)."[11] The revenue collectors of the treasury or the jagirdars of that pargana were enjoined to hand over the stipulated lands without hindrance.

[11] B. N. Goswamy and J. S. Grewal, *The Mughals and the Jogis of Jakhbar* (Simla, Indian Institute of Advanced Study, 1967), pp. 51–52.

A second, later, document is an original farman bearing the stamp of Akbar's iron seal (listing his ancestors back to Timur) dated the forty-first regnal year. This order confirms the grant once again, but reduces the amount by eighty bigahs.[12] The same injunctions and formulas to local officers were repeated in this order. The personal attendance of the Jogi leader at the imperial court is consistent with Akbar's interest in interviewing noted spiritual leaders.

In absolute terms such grants provided a living to a substantial number of Muslim and non-Muslim gentry. Moosvi estimates that the overall total largess for twelve provinces amounted at a minimum to 2.2 million rupees each year or the equivalent of 2.38 percent of the total revenues.[13] Moreover the political effect was accentuated by concentration. Outlying provinces – Bengal and Orissa to the east, Kabul and Kashmir to the northwest – did not receive any grants. Over half of the grants were located in the four heartland provinces: Agra, Delhi, Awadh, and Allahabad. And certain parganas within these provinces were favored. The highest percentage of grants seems to have come in four blocks of territory in which there was a high concentration of bigger towns.[14]

The structures created by Akbar and his administration survived with surprisingly little change until the early years of the eighteenth century. Operating jointly, the regulation revenue system and the system of jagirs had a powerful impact on rural society in North India. Imposed and backed by overwhelming Mughal power, this structure intruded beneath the tough defenses of rural life and reshaped the economy, culture, and society of Mughal India.

12 Goswamy and Grewal, *The Mughals and the Jogis*, pp. 59–63.
13 Shireen Moosvi, *Economy of the Mughal Empire, c.1595* (New Delhi: Oxford University Press, 1987), p. 159 and Appendix 1.A.
14 Ibid. 162–165.

CHAPTER 5

JAHANGIR 1605–1627

As Akbar lay ill and dying in 1605, Jahangir, then Prince Salim, nearly lost the throne to Khusrau, his seventeen-year-old eldest son. Raja Man Singh Kachhwaha of Amber and Mirza Aziz Koka (whose daughter was married to the young prince) failed to persuade a majority of the nobles to support this coup. Instead, an opposition party, led by the Sayyids of Baraha, brought Salim safely to the dying emperor, who, before he succumbed, invested the heir with a turban, robes, and Akbar's own dagger. After a week of mourning, Salim mounted the throne in Agra fort, placed the throne on his own head, and took the title Nur-ud-din Jahangir Padshah Ghazi. A confrontation had occurred, but not a war for the succession.

Apparently reconciled to the new regime, Man Singh went to Bengal as the governor, while Khusrau, seemingly restored to favor, resided under semi-confinement at Agra fort. Six months later in April, 1606, Khusrau, on the pretext of visiting Akbar's tomb, fled toward the Punjab with several hundred followers. Quickly assembling an army of 12,000 (paid for from 100,000 rupees seized from an imperial treasure caravan), Khusrau besieged the governor of the Punjab at Lahore. Jahangir, attempted negotiations with his son failing, sent a relief army which engaged the prince outside the city. The short, bloody, battle ended in a rout. Khusrau tried to flee toward Kabul, but the whole countryside was alerted for him through the network of pargana headmen and city provosts. He and his officers were captured when they tried to seize a ferry to cross the Chenab river.

Jahangir, freshly arrived in Lahore, sentenced most of Khusrau's captured followers to impalement before the eyes of their erstwhile leader. The nobles who had led the successful campaign against the rebels obtained increases in rank and new jagirs. To every pargana headman in the lands between the Jhelum and Chenab rivers went tax-free lands for their loyalty in suppressing this revolt.

When Jahangir moved north to Kabul to direct the defense of Qandahar fortress against the Safavids, Khusrau, left under arrest in Lahore, engaged in a plot to kill his father. Four hundred young noblemen and mansabdars swore personal fealty to the prince and received the badge of discipleship in return. An informer revealed the plot to the emperor who swiftly executed several ringleaders and ordered the blinding of his son (who, somewhat later, was able to have his sight partially restored). The maimed Khusrau's more rigorous imprisonment put an end to this succession struggle.

CONSOLIDATION ON THE INTERNAL FRONTIER

Within the formal boundaries of the empire, tightening and deepening imperial domination resumed. For Jahangir, the most irksome internal problem was that of the Rana of Mewar, head of the Sisodia clan of Rajputs at Udaipur who had successfully defied Akbar.[1]

> The real point was that as Rana Amar Singh and his fathers, proud in the strength of their hilly country and their abodes, had never seen or obeyed any of the kings of Hindustan.

One of Jahangir's earliest acts was to send his son Prince Parwaz on campaign against Mewar. This failed in the face of the evasive tactics of the Sisodia ruler as did nearly annual campaigns thereafter. In 1613, Jahangir himself moved from Agra to Ajmer. Equipping his son Prince Khurram with a new army the emperor sent him into the hills of Rajasthan. Khurram set up a series of military checkpoints in the hills at points thought inaccessible by Mughal commanders; sent one after the other columns of cavalry to harry the Rana and his commanders; and made hostages of the families of the most prominent Sisodias. Finally, unable to discourage the grimly determined Mughal prince, Amar Singh capitulated.

The Rana "chose obedience and loyalty" and Jahangir, who "forgave the Rana's offences, and gave a gracious farman . . . impressed with the mark of my auspicious palm."[2] Amar Singh presented himself in person to Khurram and formally submitted. Pleading old age, he asked that his son and heir Karan travel to Jahangir's court and be enrolled as an imperial amir in his place. Delighted by this victory, Jahangir agreed and Khurram returned to a great celebration in Ajmer. The emperor set about wooing his new servant: "As it was necessary to

[1] Jahangir, *Tuzuk-i Jahangiri* (Delhi, 2 vols. in one, reprint edition, 1968) translated by A. Rogers, edited by H. Beveridge, I, 274.
[2] Ibid.

win the heart of Karan, who was of a wild nature and had never seen assemblies and had lived among the hills, I every day showed him some fresh favour."[3] The emperor did indeed lavish expensive gifts, including five elephants, upon the young Sisodia prince; permitted him a private audience in the women's apartments; and even took him on a tiger shoot. Enriched and undoubtedly bedazzled, Karan returned to Mewar with the rank of 5,000 zat 5,000 suwar. In further celebration Jahangir ordered his stone cutters to carve life-sized figures of Amar Singh and Karan Singh. These were placed outside the viewing window of Agra fort where the emperor displayed himself publicly every morning.[4]

The capitulation of the Rana of Mewar signalled that resistance to the Mughal was futile. No mountainous or desert refuge was safe. Proud Rajas such as the Jam of Kathiawar, the remote peninsula in Gujarat, who had never appeared in person at the court of the Sultans of Gujarat or of Akbar, prudently decided to prostrate themselves before Jahangir. No powerful chief could claim long-standing prescriptive rights without a written patent or sanad from the emperor and expect to remain unchallenged.

In hundreds of localities rajas or lineage heads who had experienced only sporadic encounters with Indo-Muslim rulers now found themselves faced by forcible demands for ritual submission and payment of annual tribute. Long-tributary zamindars coped with greater political and economic pressures from imperial officials. If tensions grew too great, various forms of resistance or even outright rebellion occurred. Some negotiation was always possible, but if compromise failed, the outcome was harsh: a punitive expedition in massive force. If fortunate, the offending ruler might retain his life and title; if unfortunate, another claimant to the local *gaddi* would occupy the throne. Or, outright annexation was always an option. With annexation came administration by the usual cadres of imperial officials. Formerly dominant rajas became mere zamindars within their former domains.

SIKH–MUGHAL CONFLICT

During Khusrau's ill-fated coup in 1605, the rebel prince had a brief encounter with Arjun, the fifth Sikh Guru. At Goindwal, one of the

[3] Ibid., p. 277. [4] Ibid., p. 332.

prosperous Sikh towns in the Punjab, Arjun made the mistake of offering his blessing to Khusrau. Jahangir seems to have been consistently hostile to popularly venerated religious figures. In the emperor's memoir he comments:[5]

In Gobindwal, which is on the river Biyah (Beas), there was a Hindu named Arjun, in the garments of sainthood and sanctity, so much so that he had captivated many of the simple-hearted of the Hindus, and even of the ignorant and foolish followers of Islam, by his ways and manners, and they had loudly sounded the drum of his holiness. They called him *Guru* and from all sides stupid people crowded to worship and manifest complete faith in him. For three or four generations (of spiritual successors) they had kept this shop warm. Many times it had occurred to me to put a stop to this vain affair or to bring him into the assembly of the people of Islam.

Simply by making a finger-mark of saffron on Khusrau's brow as an auspicious sign, Arjun suffered a fate similar to most of Khusrau's followers. Jahangir "ordered them to produce him [Arjun] and handed over his houses, dwelling places, and children to Murtaza Khan, and having confiscated his property commanded that he should be put to death."[6] Arjun thereby became the first Sikh martyr to fall before the Mughals.

Arjun's young son, Hargobind, survived to assume his father's role as the sixth Sikh Guru. Partly in reaction to Arjun's persecution, the adolescent Hargobind adopted a new quasi-regal style. He wore two swords, held court, hunted with his retainers and built a fort at Amritsar as if he were a raja or prince. Jahangir, apprised of this, moved to squash the young Sikh leader's pretensions by arresting and imprisoning him in the state prison at Gwalior fort for two years (1609–1611).

Upon his release, Hargobind shifted his household and the central institutions of Sikhism north to the Himalayan foothills. Here, at Bilaspur on the marchlands of Mughal power, the young Sikh leader established his court as a zamindar in circumstances similar to those Rajput rulers who had survived in the hills. A network of supporters continued to send offerings from the plains. The retreat to the hills ended further Mughal persecution of the Guru and his followers in Jahangir's reign.

[5] Jahangir, *Tuzuk*, I, 72. [6] Ibid., p. 73.

RELIGION AND POLITICS

The harshness with which Jahangir treated the Sikh Guru appears to have stemmed more from Arjun's perceived political threat than from hostility to his religious doctrines as such. Religious leaders who cultivated large popular followings suffered persecution; their quietist colleagues did not. Like Akbar, Jahangir sought out eminent holy men like the widely venerated Vaishnava ascetic, Gosain Jadrup of Ujain, whom Akbar had also visited. Several invitations to the imperial court at Agra failed. Finally, in 1616, Jahangir visited the saint at his residence, a hole dug in the side of a hill near Ujain. Emperor and holy man talked for several hours and the emperor returned for later visits over the years. Of his last interview in 1620 Jahangir commented:[7]

> On Monday, the 12th, my desire to see Gosain Jadrup again increased and hastening to his hut, without ceremony, I enjoyed his society. Sublime words were spoken to between us. God Almighty has granted him an unusual grace, a lofty understanding, and excellent nature, and sharp intellectual powers, with a God-given knowledge and a heart free from the attachments of the world, so that putting behind his back the world and all that is in it, he sits content in the corner of solitude and without wants.

Jahangir's meetings with Gosain Jadrup were frequently portrayed by court painters who found the juxtaposition of worldly magnificence and holy renunciation a powerful theme.

A widely-known Muslim religious figure, Shaikh Ahmad Sirhindi did not fare so well with Jahangir. Although he was a dominant figure in the orthodox Naqshbandi Sufi order, which stressed obedience to the Sharia, Sirhindi had adopted a radical, some might even say heretical posture. In what came perilously close to heresy, Sirhindi, while admitting that prophecy had come to an end with Muhammad, the Seal of the Prophets, claimed that certain believers with prophetic proficiency continued to have direct experience of divine inspiration. Sirhindi asserted that he was a present-day manifestation of the Companions of the Prophet who shared in the prophetic qualities of Muhammad.[8] He had direct access without prophetic mediation to

[7] *Tuzuk-i Jahangiri*, translated in Rizvi, *Muslim Revivalist Movements in Northern India in the Sixteenth and Seventeenth Centuries* (Agra, 1965), p. 328.

[8] Yohanan Friedmann, *Shaykh Ahmad Sirhindi: An Outline of His Thought and a Study of His Image in the Eyes of Posterity* (Montreal: McGill-Queen's University Press, 1971), p. 40.

divine inspiration. Sirhindi could therefore offer guidance to the Islamic community. His numerous letters and treatises claimed that in the second millennium of Islam, begun in 1592–93, he would be the "Renewer of the Second Millennium" (*mujaddid-i alf-i thani*). In the second millennium he could help to reverse the downward descent of Islam and the growing separation of the Prophet Muhammad from his community.

Sirhindi wrote hundreds of letters to lay disciples, fellow Naqshbandis, and, on occasion, to Mughal nobles and the emperor. Those letters addressed to Mughal amirs often denounced the participation of Hindus in the regime. Several years of service as a protégé of Abul Fazl at Akbar's court had convinced Sirhindi that the emperor was opposed to the true path of Islam. He hoped for reversal of Akbar's policies and a change in tone under Jahangir. In a few letters Sirhindi called for the humiliation of Hindus and their false religion. Sirhindi vented his deep frustration and anger in bitter comments on the execution of the Guru Arjun – seen as a Hindu – by Jahangir:[9]

> These days the accursed infidel of Goindwal was very fortunately killed. It is a cause of great defeat for the reprobate Hindus. With whatever intention and purpose they are killed, the humiliation of infidels is for the Muslims life itself.

Sirhindi was expressing anger shared by many Muslim learned men. Those theologians, judges, Sufis, and others who relied on state patronage were especially troubled by Akbar's policies. At this point in time a substantial, vocal gentry class of ulema was entrenched in the towns of northern India. Such men were in fact extremely numerous in Shaikh Ahmad's home of Sirhind in the Punjab. Fears for material loss were intermixed with fears for spiritual loss and the weakening of the community of Indian Muslims. There is no question that Shaikh Ahmad articulated and responded to these concerns.

Not all theologians supported Shaikh Ahmad, however. Abd-al Haq Dihlawi, the most respected Muslim scholar of his time, directly challenged Sirhindi's views. In a surviving letter Abd-al Haq denounced Shaikh Ahmad's pridefulness and his claim to "share in the wealth" of the Companions of the Prophet.[10] To claim that no mediation was required between himself and God was disrespectful to the Prophet and heretical.

[9] Translation and text given in Friedmann, *Shaykh Ahmad Sirhindi*, p. 73.
[10] Friedmann, *Shaykh Ahmad Sirhindi*, pp. 88–89.

In 1619 Shaikh Ahmad's growing notoriety and popular following attracted the attention of Jahangir who summoned him to an imperial audience. In his memoirs Jahangir commented that Sirhindi "had spread the net of hypocrisy and deceit," enlisted disciples, and was leading Muslims to false belief and heresy. The emperor was especially incensed by Sirhindi's claim to have surpassed the spiritual stage attained by the rightly-guided Companions of the Prophet.[11] At the audience Shaikh Ahmad was "extremely proud and self-satisfied with all his ignorance."[12] Shaikh Ahmad's arrogance earned him imprisonment in the state prison at Gwalior fort to permit his own confusion and "the excitement of the people" to subside.[13] Released after a year and restored to favor, Shaikh Ahmad travelled with the imperial encampment on Jahangir's tour to the Deccan.

Sirhindi's impact on Indian Islam is controversial. His letters, compiled in three volumes by disciples, continued to be widely read in Mughal and post-Mughal India. After his death in 1624 his followers composed a hagiographic literature that glorified Sirhindi's role as a persecuted champion of Islam. He is portrayed as a leader in the struggle to return the Timurid regime to its proper conduct of the Sharia. His concern for Islamic revivalism and his anti-Hindu sentiments undoubtedly contributed to the sharpening division between the Islamic community and the Hindu community in the seventeenth century.

ENRICHING IMPERIAL CULTURE

Unlike his father, Jahangir was not a great general, a great organizer, or a great builder. Much of his energy was devoted to the courtly culture of the Mughals. The court with its great palace and household and the satellite palaces of the great nobles were glittering ornaments of life in the capital. Court ceremonial and conspicuous display served to impress all those in submission to the Timurid ruler. However, in Jahangir's reign and thereafter, ossifying ceremonial immobilized the principal actors. The emperor especially was encased in a daily round of ceremony. The muffling effect of court life made it more difficult for Jahangir to engage in decisive action in person and more likely that he

11 Rizvi, *Muslim Revivalist Movements*, p. 287 gives a full translation of this passage.
12 Ibid.
13 Ibid.

would delegate active military command. As he lost dynamism, however, the emperor gained in sacral qualities. The aura surrounding his person became more pronounced.

Jahangir did not build a new capital but treated Agra as the imperial center. For extended periods to meet urgent strategic concerns, he moved from Agra to Kabul, Ajmer, or Mandu and the great encampment became temporary imperial headquarters. Jahangir's one attempt to establish a new city near the hills along the Ganges ended because of his illness.[14] Instead the emperor devoted his creative energies to a number of building projects indelibly stamped by his own pronounced aesthetic sensibility.

Notable among these were the great imperial gardens of North India and Kashmir. Charmed by the coolness and ambience of Kashmir, Jahangir made several trips to that mountain valley during the hot seasons on the plains. His urges toward building were consumed in planning and laying out four magnificent outdoor gardens – Shalimar Bagh, Achabal, Vernag, and Nishat Bagh – whose attenuated remains can still be seen today.[15] The use of watercourses, pools, summer pavilions, shade trees and plantings of flowers and shrubs created patterns and designs, which, despite their scale, even today display an appealing delicacy and order.

Jahangir regularly withdrew from the public face of rulership to a more private, circumscribed, arena created by his lavish patronage and inspired connoisseurship. In miniature painting he found a congenial aesthetic form. The emperor was a demanding critic who obtained bold innovation from his painters in techniques of modelling and spatial depth. The talented artists of the imperial workshops painted a wide range of subjects at Jahangir's direction. Studies of animals, flowers, and other natural motifs were painted because of their intrinsic interest to the patron and his immediate circle. Under Jahangir naturalist trends in Mughal painting reached their apogee.[16]

Certainly, for Jahangir, as for Akbar, painting remained a political weapon. Numerous examples of political iconography focused upon the emperor survive. Many paintings from this period – such as that by Abul Hassan showing Jahangir embracing a diminutive Shah Abbas,

[14] Beni Prasad, *History of Jahangir* (London: Oxford University Press, 1922), p. 322.

[15] Sylvia Crowe, et al., *The Gardens of Mughul India* (New Delhi: Vikas Publishing House Pvt Ltd, 1972), pp. 90–120.

[16] Milo Cleveland Beach, *The Grand Mogul: Imperial Painting in India 1600–1660* (Williamstown, Massachusetts: Sterling and Francine Clark Art Institute, 1978), p. 25.

the Safavid ruler, over a globe – display the public face of painting.[17] Nevertheless, Jahangir as patron seems to have been more stimulated by connoisseurship.

Frequent withdrawal to a private sphere of life was partly a reflection of Jahangir's indolence, brought on by his increasing addiction to a potent daily dosage of opium and wine. In a strange, somewhat paradoxical way, Jahangir's passivity strengthened two interfolded motifs within Timurid political culture: the familial claim of the Timurids and especially the descendants of Babur, Humayun, and Akbar to the Mughal throne; and the increasing inviolability of the person of the ruler. Together these two motifs placed a crushing weight upon any challenger or usurper – Timurid or not.

THE ASCENDANCY OF NUR JAHAN

In 1611 Jahangir met, wooed, and married the young widow of a Mughal officer slain in Bengal. Mehrunissa, who was serving in the entourage of one of Akbar's widows, was a classic Persian beauty, thirty years of age. Her father, titled Itimad-ud-daulah, was a high-ranking nobleman at Jahangir's court. The new queen rapidly became Jahangir's favored wife (from among a total of twenty) under the title Nur Jahan or "Light of the World." Nur Jahan's beauty, her great love for the emperor, her strong personality, and her abilities which ranged from fashion design to hunting gave her unusual influence over Jahangir. Her father became the imperial diwan or chief minister. Her brother, Asaf Khan, rose quickly in rank to become one of the leading noblemen at court.

Nur Jahan formed an alliance with Jahangir's second son, Khurram, who, as heir-apparent, held the jagir of Hissar pargana in the Punjab and the right to pitch crimson tents. In 1612 Khurram married Arjumand Banu, later Mumtaz Mahal, the daughter of Asaf Khan. After this marriage, celebrated both by the prince and by Asaf Khan with ostentatious splendor, the alliance was sealed.

Together these four persons – Nur Jahan, her father, Itimad-ud-daulah, her brother, Asaf Khan, and Khurram, the Timurid prince – exerted enormous influence over Jahangir. Imperial rescripts were sometimes issued in Nur Jahan's name. Most startling, however, are the silver rupees minted bearing Jahangir's titles on the obverse and the

[17] Bamber Gascoigne, *The Great Moghuls* (London: Jonathan Cape, 1971), p. 130.

legend "struck in the name of the Queen Begam, Nur Jahan" on the reverse.[18] By adding her name to his coins, Jahangir publicly proclaimed Nur Jahan's sharing of his authority in a prerogative central to Islamic kingship. For over a decade, between 1611 and 1622, Jahangir relied heavily upon advice from Nur Jahan and her colleagues.

Predictably a rival faction left outside the charmed circle of the emperor's favor emerged. Opposition nobles, headed by Mahabat Khan, also an Iranian amir, looked to the blinded Prince Khusrau as a symbol of their resistance to the domination of Jahangir by Nur Jahan's clique. Khusrau universally was seen as a tragic and popular royal figure both by the populace at large and by the royal harem women who resented Nur Jahan's power. Popular opinion also held that he was Jahangir's real favorite instead of the proud overbearing Khurram. The Nur Jahan group waited to claim the throne for Khurram when the emperor died – a not unlikely scenario in view of his excesses.

ROYAL DISCIPLESHIP AND HEREDITARY SERVICE[19]

Jahangir, torn between emulation and rejection of his father, accepted his inherited role as the light-suffused monarch capable of greater knowledge and power than ordinary men. By the emperor's own statement his new title of honor, Nur-ud-din, "light of the faith" linked him with the "great light" the sun.[20]

Jahangir continued to enroll royal disciples from among his nobles and, it would seem, guarded his authority over his disciples more vigorously than Akbar thought necessary. Khwaja Khawand Mahmud, a popular master of the Naqshbandi order, had enrolled a number of nobles as his disciples during Akbar's reign. Much of his appeal consisted of his attachment to the forms and beliefs of orthodox Sunni Islam – consistent with the tenets of the order. Shortly after

[18] H. Nelson Wright, *Coins of the Mughal Emperors of India* (New Delhi: Deep Publications, 1st Indian reprint edition, 1975), p. 93. Originally published by the Asiatic Society of Bengal, *Catalogue of the Coins in the Indian Museum, Calcutta*, III, "Mughal Emperors of India," 1908.

[19] The following section is adapted from J. F. Richards, "The Formulation of Imperial Authority Under Akbar and Jahangir" in Richards, ed., *Kingship and Authority*, pp. 268–277.

[20] Rizvi, *Muslim Revivalist Movements*, p. 221.

Jahangir's accession a high-ranking nobleman complained that Khwaja Khawand Mahmud had pressed him to become his disciple (*murid*) even though the Khwaja knew that he was already the disciple of the emperor. The master responded that he was a disciple of the Holy Law who was enjoined to obey those in authority. Therefore, he, the Khwaja, was himself a murid of the emperor. Only this adroit reply saved the Naqshbandi from the emperor's anger.[21]

Significant direct testimony to continuing royal discipleship comes from the letters and journals of Sir Thomas Roe, ambassador to the Mughal court from King James of England. Roe was in near-daily attendance in the court and camp of Jahangir for nearly three years (1615–1618). He established an affable relationship with the emperor by becoming one of Jahangir's favorite drinking companions.

Like Akbar, Jahangir selected and initiated disciples from among his favored nobles "who [are] worthy of receiving *shast wa shabah*," i.e. the seal or ring and the imperial likeness which were the symbols of discipleship. In his own journal the emperor describes the details of the enrollment ceremony.[22] Roe himself, although he was not aware of the full significance of the event, became a disciple of Jahangir. In August 1616, Jahangir favored the ambassador by enacting, without warning, the ceremony of initiation:[23]

August 17 – I went to visit the King, who, as soone as I came in, called to his woemen and reached out a picture of himselfe sett in gould hanging at a wire gould Chaine, with one pendant foule pearle, which he delivered to Asaph chan, [Asaf Khan, the *wazir*] warning him not to demand any reuerence of mee other than such as I would willingly giue, it beeing the Custome, when soever hee bestowes any thing, the receiuer kneeles downe and putts his head to the groun ... So Asaph Chan came to mee, and I offered to take it in my hand; bet hee made signe to putt of my hatt, and then putt it about my neck, leading mee right before the king. I understood not his purpose, but doubted hee would require the Custome of the Country called *Size-da* [the full prostration or *sijdah* of discipleship]; but I was resolved rather to deliuer up my present. Hee made sign to mee to giue the king thancks, which I did after my owne Custome.

21 Rizvi, *Muslim Revivalist Movements*, p. 184.

22 S. A. A. Rizvi, *Religious and Intellectual History of the Muslims in Akbar's Reign* (New Delhi, 1975), p. 400 quotes the full text of this passage.

23 William Foster, ed., *The Embassy of Sir Thomas Roe to the Court of the Great Mogul, 1615–1619* (London: Hakluyt Society, new series, 2 vols., 1894) I, 244–45.

Roe commented that although the actual money value of his token from the emperor was trifling it was an eagerly sought preferment:[24]

> held for an especiall favour, for that all the great men that weare the kings Image (which none may doe but to whom it is given) receiue noe other than a meddall of gould as bigg as sixpence, with a little chayne of 4 inches to fasten it on their head, which at their own Chardge some sett with stones or garnishe with pendant Pearles.

Selection as a royal disciple was a signal honor. Those who wore the tiny portraits of the emperor were an elect group of imperial servants.

Jahangir in turn behaved as a disciple to the deceased Khwaja Muin-ud-din Chishti whose intercession, he believed, had given him life and Akbar a son and heir. In contrast to his father who seems to have abandoned his own worship of the Chishti saint, Jahangir publicly displayed his veneration. At Ajmer in 1614 the emperor visited the tomb and distributed lavish gifts to the devotees and descendants of the Shaikh. During this residence, Jahangir fell ill with a prolonged fever. After several weeks, the weakened emperor finally went to the mausoleum of the Chishti saint and prayed for health. When his prayers were granted, Jahangir decided that "inasmuch as I was inwardly an ear-bored slave of the Khwaja" he would have holes made in his ears and place a lustrous pearl in each.[25] As soon as the news spread, Jahangir's own disciples and admirers adopted the same fashion and placed pearls in their ears. Jahangir distributed 732 pearls to those officers who had made this gesture. The links of discipleship reached from the Chishti saint, to the emperor, and from there to his own disciples. Timurid and Chishti sanctity were conflated.

AGGRESSION ON THE NORTHEASTERN FRONTIER

Under Jahangir the empire continued to be a war state attuned to aggressive conquest and territorial expansion. In the northeast, after weary campaigns to subdue the Afghans, the Mughals clashed with a new enemy, the Ahoms. This hardy, aggressive, Shan people had been moving from their home in upper Burma slowly down the Brahmaputra valley since about 1400. As they did so, they defeated and assimilated or drove off the indigenous tribal and Hindu peoples of the

[24] Ibid. [25] Jahangir, *Tuzuk*, I, 267.

region. The Ahoms gradually came under Hindu religious and cultural influence as they progressed along the Brahmaputra river.

Ahom determination shaped the limits of Mughal power in the northeast. Unlike many Indian regimes, the Ahoms were not worn down by centuries-long struggles against encroaching Muslim power. Like their opponent they looked back on a history of victorious aggression. Unconstrained by caste, ethnic, or religious barriers, Ahom rulers mobilized virtually all adult male subjects for military service or forced labor when campaigning. They carried on a systematic program of building roads, embankments and irrigation tanks in lands seized and occupied. The Ahom state taxed and organized people by labor levies and produce rather than land in the Indo-Muslim structures. If policy dictated, the Ahom kings forcibly uprooted and moved entire local populations to another habitation. The Mughals found this Southeast Asian style of organization and warfare extremely difficult to combat.

During Jahangir's reign Mughal and Ahom armies battled nearly every year in the riverine and jungly tracts of the northeast. Ahom commanders threw up bamboo stockades, dug traps and pits, and employed their musketeers with great skill. They made surprise night attacks on the Mughal encampments that demoralized and slowed imperial advances. Lahori, the mid-seventeenth century chronicler, recorded the unflattering view of the Ahoms held by the Mughal armies on campaign in this riverine land:[26]

> The inhabitants shave the head and clip off beard and whiskers. They eat every land and water animal. They are very black and loathsome in appearance. The chiefs travel on elephants or country ponies; but the army consists only of foot soldiers. The fleet is large and well fitted out. The soldiers use bows and arrows and matchlocks, but do not come up in courage to the Muhammadan soldiers; though they are very brave in naval engagements. On the march they quickly and dexterously fortify their encampments with mud walls and bamboo palisades, and surround the whole with a ditch.

From sheer necessity the Mughals learned to employ river boats with bow-mounted cannon and matchlockmen as well as cavalry and elephants in the watery reaches of Bengal and Assam.

[26] As cited in E. A. Gait, *A History of Assam*, 3rd revised edition (Calcutta, 2 vols., Thacket Spink, 1963), I, 124.

DISCIPLESHIP ON THE FRONTIER

Younger men, members of a new generation come to maturity since Akbar's death, were inducted into the order of royal disciples. The autobiographical memoir of Ala-ud-din Isfahani, a Persian nobleman known as Mirza Nathan, testifies to the continuing appeal of this institution.[27] In 1607, the youthful Mirza Nathan accompanied his father, Ihtimam Khan, commanding the imperial flotillas of armed river boats, to the eastern frontier. Soon after his arrival in Bengal, Mirza Nathan became seriously ill and lapsed into a fever. On the seventh day of his illness he had an awesome vision. In his feverish sleep "the king of the spiritual and temporal domain" [i.e. Jahangir] appeared and addressed him:[28]

> "O Nathan! Is this the time for a tiger to lie down? Arise, we have granted you security from pain and trouble by our prayers to the Almighty and Omnipresent Lord. Be quick, and placing the foot of manliness and sincerity in your devoted work be a comrade to your great father and be his support."

Nathan awoke fully cured of his fever and convinced of his mission. With the help of his father and Islam Khan Chishti (a member of the Fatehpur Sikri Sufi family), the governor of Bengal, Nathan sent a petition to the emperor describing his holy vision and begging for enlistment as one of the royal disciples. In reply, an imperial messenger returned bearing a tiny portrait of Jahangir "adorned with a genealogical tree" of the Timurid dynasty. Although he was not summoned to court for a personal ceremony, by placing this image in his turban Mirza Nathan openly displayed his devotion and membership in the elect body of disciples.

Mirza Nathan's night vision of the emperor and his eagerness to act upon this occurrence undoubtedly derived from his birth and upbringing within the royal household. When Prince Khurram arrived in Bengal in the course of his rebellion, he referred to the Mirza as "one of the special servants of our Court, ... who was brought up from childhood under our feet."[29] Nathan was in fact a *khanazad* (lit. "son of the house"), which in Jahangir's time seems to have connoted actual

[27] Mirza Nathan, *Baharistan-i Ghaybi*, edited and translated by M. I. Borah (Gauhati, 2 vols., 1936). The *Baharistan-i Ghaybi*, completed by Mirza Nathan in 1632 A.D., contains a full account of his career as a military officer in service on the marches of Mughal expansion in eastern Bengal and Assam during Jahangir's reign.

[28] Nathan, *Baharistan*, I, 17, 74.

[29] Nathan, *Baharistan*, II, 702.

residence in or connections with the imperial household during childhood and adolescence. Later the term took on the wider meaning of hereditary imperial service. This status and whatever preferment it might bring intersected with the institution of discipleship for Nathan.

Sustaining these bonds of discipleship and hereditary family service posed no difficulty in the imperial court or camp. Patrimonial relationships were reaffirmed daily at the array of audiences presided over by the emperor. During the large court audiences formal rituals of authority and submission were enacted by gift exchange: the emperor bestowed offices, titles, increases in rank, as well as honorific clothing, horses, jeweled weapons, or even money. His subordinates invariably made an offering of gold coins or other suitable gifts of value. The most potent of these gifts were full or partial robes of honor worn momentarily by the emperor or brushed across his shoulders. Thomas Roe received from Jahangir "a cloth of gould Cloake of his owne, once or Twice worne, which hee caused to bee put on my back, and I made reverence ..., it is here reputed the highest of fauor to give a garment worne by the prince, or, being New, once layed upon his shoulder."[30] Contact with the sacred person of the emperor was an affirmation of his care and regard for his servants.

How were these personal ties between emperor and disciple sustained, when as in the case of Mirza Nathan, nobles remained on campaign? One tangible means lay in the exchanges necessary for promotion. From his first elevation in rank in 1612 to 500 zat, 250 suwar Mirza Nathan progressed upward until in 1621, as reward for his role in the suppression of a rebellion by a Muslim zamindar, he became an amir at 1,000 zat, 500 suwar. The imperial rescript sent to the Mirza, signed jointly by Jahangir and Nur Jahan, stipulated his new rank and gave the Mirza a new title, Shitab Khan. The new nobleman also received a full robe of honor. To complete the transaction Nathan sent a gift of 42,000 rupees back to the Empress Nur Jahan.[31] All the critical elements of the personal exchange were carried out at a distance.

Other gift exchanges helped to maintain this illusion. On various occasions special imperial envoys delivered a set of soft shawls; a shield sent directly from the hand of the emperor; and two sets of pendant pearl earrings (with their connotations of discipleship). To reciprocate, Nathan organized wild elephant hunts and sent his choicest captives back as personal offerings to the emperor.

[30] Foster, *Embassy*, I, 334. [31] Nathan, *Baharistan*, II, 666.

Mirza Nathan, in common with other imperial officers, occasionally received written orders or farmans bearing the great seal of the Timurid emperor. Such special rescripts were carried from court by one or two imperial macebearers or by royal troopers (ahadis). Protocol on these occasions demanded that the recipient act as if the emperor himself were arriving. The noble rode several miles to greet the messenger; performed the sijdah or full-length court prostration; placed the order on his head and eyes and even kissed it before opening its container.

The emperor used a more dramatic form of communication. A messenger of considerable rank could be sent to recite orders or exhortations verbatim from the lips of the emperor.[32] To end the notorious factiousness of Qasim Khan, governor of Bengal succeeding Islam Khan Chishti, Jahangir sent a revenue officer titled Ibrahim Kalal with written orders of censure for the governor of Bengal, the provincial fiscal officer, the provincial military inspector and paymaster (bakhshi), and the news-writer. When the envoy arrived at the provincial capital, the governor met him, performed the proper obeisances, and received the written farman.

The next morning when the Bengal governor, his three principal officers, and all his leading army commanders were assembled in the audience hall, Ibrahim Kalal solemnly delivered from memory Jahangir's verbal rebuke to each of the four chief officers in turn. Without waiting for a reply he left the audience hall and set out immediately on his return journey.[33] Rituals of obedience and respect were repeatedly enacted even in the absence of the ruler.

EXPANSION IN THE NORTHERN HILLS

To the north, in the Himalayan foothills, the Mughals had an easier time than in Assam. By the 1590s Akbar had established his suzerainty over most of the Rajput rulers whose modest mountain valley kingdoms cordoned the Himalayan foothills from Kashmir to the border of Bengal. Although left internal autonomy, these chiefs were forced to acknowledge the emperor's supremacy, pay annual tribute, send troops for imperial purposes if requisitioned, and send their sons to serve at the imperial court or daughters to enter noble marriages. The Mughal emperor reserved the right to intervene in successions to the ruling seat. A few hill rajas were offered personal service as mansab-

[32] See ibid., II, 307–310 for an example of this practice. [33] Ibid.

dars by the emperor on terms similar to their fellow Rajputs in Rajasthan. Akbar also began the practice of locating faujdars or military governors in the hills to keep the Himalayan princes under surveillance. These officers administered tracts of territory forced from the tributary rajas and annexed as directly administered imperial lands.

The Himalayas permitted passage by traders and nomads over mountain paths, but rendered improbable an armed invasion. The Mughal emperor's main goal here was to extend formal domination to all the petty kings in the region. This could be done without fear of reprisal from a neighboring great power. Jahangir's primary goal in the hills was subjugation of the Raja of Kangra. The latter relied upon the legendary strength of his massive fortress to protect him as it had his ancestors. Mughal operations began as early as 1615 against the capital, but without notable success until finally Prince Khurram took the fortress in 1618. The next year Jahangir travelled in person to celebrate his victory by erecting a mosque in the courtyard of Kangra fort.

RELATIONS WITH PERSIA AND CENTRAL ASIA

The Islamic lands to the northwest of Mughal India – Persia and Central Asia – posed a knotted complex of problems for Akbar's successors. Jahangir was well aware that this region was the source of great danger. From Mahmud of Ghazni to the founder of his own dynasty, raiders and conquerors had marched into North India from the northwest. A fixed aim of Mughal policy was to deflect possible invasion by well-led, massed steppe cavalry. Kabul and Peshawar must be held at all costs, and, if possible, Qandahar and Ghazni. To make matters more difficult, the northwest frontier could only be sealed for very short intervals of great border tension. Rulers on both sides of the frontier profited from the bustling caravan trade.

The symbolic weight of these regions was even more burdensome. Samarkhand was Timur's capital lost to the Shaibanid rulers of the Uzbeks. The latter were inveterate enemies of Babur, the Chaghatai Turks, and his royal descendants. Bukhara, Balkh, and Badakhshan were the lands of Turan that long ago should have been restored to Mughal sovereignty. These regions were also the homeland for the Naqshbandi Sufi order and the ardent Sunni Islam that was part of the Timurid heritage. Jahangir's stated goal was "the conquest of Mawara'a-n-nahr (Transoxania) which was the hereditary kingdom of my ancestors."[34] Central Asian conquest was always an enticing prospect for the Mughals.

Persia in the 1600s presented more difficult problems. Mughal diplomatic relations with Safavid Persia varied with the ideological/political stance adopted by each ruler. Apart from the carefully defined clashes over Qandahar, growing hostility never became unlimited war. Under Shah Abbas the Safavi state, although smaller in territory, population, and resources, readily met any military challenges offered by the Mughal empire. Each state threatened the other by aggressive diplomacy and intervention in neighboring regions. The Safavids were vulnerable in Turan or the Uzbek lands and the Mughals uneasy over the Shi'ite rulers of Golconda in the Deccan.

The Safavids held one grave threat over the Timurids that could not be countered. Persian nobles and administrators, forming one of the largest ethnic groups in the Mughal nobility, kept up close ties with their homeland. Given sufficient encouragement, it was conceivable that Persian mansabdars might revolt, and bring on Safavid intervention. No Indians held similar posts in Safavid Persia.

The Mughals suffered from the long-standing Persian claim of cultural superiority over the colonial Islamic lands in India (or for that matter over Turan). The Timurids accepted this judgment even as they chafed under it. To this imbalance can be added the fierce sectarian bias of the Safavis as ardent Shi'i and their contempt for the Sunni orthodoxy generally accepted by the Timurids. Much to their chagrin, the Mughals owed their survival to the sanctuary provided first Babur, then Humayun by the Safavis. More humiliating than the aid itself was that public adherence to Shi'ite Islam demanded of each by Shah Ismail and Shah Tahmasp.

The complex interaction between Safavis and Timurids was also a product of intimacy. In a strange, and often bizarre, fashion, Safavid and Timurid emperors looked to their opposites for affirmation of their grandeur and worth. In their own eyes, they had no other peers save the Ottoman Sultan. Frequent exchanges of letters, embassies, gifts, and portraits marked what was an extraordinary personal relationship between the two emperors – conducted without ever meeting in person.

Royal attraction and royal competition found tangible expression in the disputed possession of Qandahar fortress, town, and province.

[34] Jahangir, *Tuzuk*, I, 89.

Akbar had recovered Qandahar in 1595 when two Safavid princes defected. As soon as Jahangir became emperor, the Safavid governors of Herat and other border areas organized an abortive assault on Qandahar. After this failure, Shah Abbas patiently ignored this irritant in favor of cultivating warm diplomatic and personal relations with Jahangir.

By 1620, when Jahangir had fallen seriously ill, his queen Nur Jahan, and Prince Khurram (later Shah Jahan) were locked in an intricate struggle for dominance at the Timurid court (see below). Taking advantage of these distractions, Shah Abbas personally led a Persian army against Qandahar in the winter of 1622. Before a relief army could be assembled the ill-prepared 300 man Mughal garrison surrendered and handed Qandahar back to Persian control.

THE DECCAN CAMPAIGNS AND COURT POLITICS

At Akbar's death the Mughals were poised to expand south against the remaining Muslim Sultanates. Khandesh, Berar, and the northernmost portion of Ahmadnagar were firmly under imperial control. Incomplete Mughal assimilation of Ahmadnagar and Akbar's preoccupation with the rebellion of Prince Selim permitted a resistance movement to flare up in that kingdom. Malik Ambar, a "habshi" or Abyssinian military slave officer, established a capital for Sultan Murtaza Nizam Shah (1599–1631) at Khadki (later renamed Aurangabad) fifteen kilometers distant from the great hill-fort at Daulatabad.

Soon after beginning his reign, Jahangir resumed military operations against Ahmadnagar. Unenthusiastic campaigns by a succession of imperial officers produced little result for nearly a decade. Malik Ambar had obtained support from the Jadavs and several other Maratha aristocratic families of the region. Finally, in 1616, the Mughal prince Parwiz commanded a reinforced army that crushed the Ahmadnagar forces in a major battle near Jalna. The imperial armies looted and razed Malik Ambar's capital city at Khadki (or Khirki). Malik Ambar fled to shelter in Daulatabad fort and resumed guerrilla resistance when the Mughals withdrew.

At this juncture the Deccan campaigns became intertwined with the intricate pattern of dynastic politics at the court. When Jahangir ordered Prince Khurram to replace his brother Parwiz in the Deccan,

Khurram refused to set out for the Deccan campaign and leave the only partially disabled Khusrau behind. He and Nur Jahan persuaded Jahangir to transfer custody of Khusrau to Asaf Khan, Nur Jahan's brother. Thus reassured Khurram led a massive army against the dwindling forces of Ahmadnagar. Jahangir travelled in person with his court to Mandu to supervise the operations. Faced with defeat, Malik Ambar offered full control of Berar and Ahmadnagar to the Mughal prince.

The Nur Jahan group reached the height of its power with Khurram's victories in the Deccan and Jahangir's prolonged tour to Mandu and the sea at Gujarat. When, after an absence of five-and-one-half years, the emperor returned to Agra in April, 1619, the political kaleidoscope shifted within a year. Jahangir's health deteriorated to the point that Nur Jahan took active charge of the day-to-day running of the empire. Tensions between Nur Jahan and Khurram rose as the prince looked forward eagerly to his patrimony and acted more and more as a ruling sovereign. In response, in 1620, Nur Jahan arranged a marriage between Shahryar, Jahangir's youngest son, age sixteen, with her daughter Ladili Begam. She would then have a living male heir to the throne under her control when her husband died. The rupture between Nur Jahan and Khurram was complete. This bold action established three royal princes – Khurram, Khusrau, and now Shahryar – as contenders for the throne. Each found noble factions coalescing around them.

Shortly after the emperor's return to Agra, however, unrest in the Deccan flared up again. Malik Ambar renounced the treaty imposed upon his kingdom and encouraged Bijapur and Golconda to send forces to help him drive out the Mughals. Jahangir ordered Khurram to head a relief army, but the prince refused to act unless he could take Khusrau with him. Accordingly, Jahangir reluctantly handed over Khusrau to his brother.

Khurram's dazzling six-month campaign ended with restoration of imperial control in Ahmadnagar and heavy indemnities paid by Bijapur and Golconda. Throughout this period Ahmadnagar was neither fully conquered and annexed, nor neatly assigned tributary status. For at least three decades a common pattern of Deccan diplomacy persisted. Violent resistance to the Mughals alternating with temporary submission was imprinted on the political culture of the Western Deccan. Not least of the participants in this interaction were the leading Maratha captains of the west. They gained autonomy, plunder, and wealth from the inability of the Mughals to impose a definitive political solution in their homeland.

In mid-1621 word arrived at Burhanpur that Jahangir was seriously ill. Khurram had the unfortunate Khusrau secretly killed and then reported his brother's concocted illness and subsequent death to Jahangir. In January 1622, the wazir, Itimad-ud-daulah died suddenly to leave his grieving daughter, Nur Jahan, deprived of his advice and support. Nur Jahan began construction of her father's tomb in a garden along the bank of the Jumna at Agra. Completed six years later, the elegant mausoleum, built of white marble with rich inlaid colored traceries, became one of the architectural treasures of the Mughal period.

THE REBELLION OF PRINCE KHURRAM (SHAH JAHAN)

Suddenly, in March, 1622, while the imperial court was in Kashmir, Shah Abbas besieged and captured Qandahar fort. Despite a direct order, Prince Khurram refused to leave the Deccan to join the relief army unless he were given full command. In the end Jahangir, reacting to Nur Jahan's suggestions, permitted his son to remain in the south and send some of his nobles north. Jahangir appointed the youthful Shahryar commander of the entire Qandahar expedition (with an experienced noble as deputy commander). Some of Khurram's jagir holdings (including Hissar pargana) were transferred to Shahryar. Mahabat Khan, one of the most powerful nobles in the empire returned from Kabul to strengthen the Nur Jahan/Shahryar party.

Convinced that he had lost the political struggle, Khurram rebelled and marched with the Deccan army north from Mandu. Virtually all the amirs and offficers stationed in the Deccan, Malwa, and Gujarat remained loyal to his cause. Mahabat Khan assumed command of the loyalist army which joined battle with the rebel Deccan forces outside Fatehpur Sikri. Suffering a bloody defeat, Khurram retreated back to Malwa. Here he received one million rupees in cash from the provincial treasury of Gujarat to resupply and reman his army. Moving aggressively to Ajmer, Jahangir and Nur Jahan directed the loyalist armies who recovered control of Gujarat and drove Khurram from Malwa. Plagued by desertions from among his officers, Khurram retreated with a small force to Asir, the great hill fortress just outside Burhanpur, the capital of Khandesh, whose commander surrendered to him.

Forced into flight once more, the rebel prince took refuge in Golconda with his family and a dwindling group of followers. Heartened by discreet aid from Abdullah Qutb Shah, Khurram made his way to the northeast through Orissa. A military victory gave him control of Bengal and Bihar. With fresh funds, artillery, horses, and new recruits Khurram placed his forces on river boats and moved upriver on the Ganges. Defeated near Allahabad, Khurram fled toward Bengal where rebellious zamindars forced him south. Leaving his wife and his newly born fourth son, Murad Bakhsh, in the great citadel at Rohtas on the Ganges, Khurram found a strange refuge in the camp of his old adversary Malik Ambar. The latter was engaged in a war with the Sultan of Bijapur and his new ally, the Mughal emperor.

Khurram, at the head of a combined Nizam Shahi and rebel Mughal force, directed a series of assaults on Burhanpur. These failed and the prince fell ill – perhaps due as much to depression as anything else. New negotiations resulted in terms dictated by Nur Jahan. Khurram agreed to remain in the south as governor of the Deccan provinces and to send his two young sons, Dara Shikoh and Aurangzeb, as hostages to the court.

Jahangir and Nur Jahan succeeded in quelling this revolt by the heir-apparent only after several difficult battles and campaigns stretching over thousands of miles. Despite the outcome the most serious weakness of the Timurid system was painfully apparent. Mature royal princes of ability and ambition were a continuing threat to the occupant of the throne and were a continuing focus for factional maneuvering.

MAHABAT KHAN'S COUP

One unexpected result of Khurram's rebellion was the emergence of Prince Parwiz, hitherto seen as a drunken mediocrity, as a serious contender for the succession. Mahabat Khan became Parwiz's backer and manager. Together they threatened Nur Jahan's plans for Shahryar. An open clash came when Nur Jahan called attention to the fact that Mahabat Khan had not obtained the emperor's approval customary for the betrothal of his daughter to a Mughal nobleman. This resulted in the arrest, beating, and imprisonment of Mahabat Khan's prospective son-in-law. The dowry that Mahabat Khan had paid was seized by treasury officials.

In March, 1626, Mahabat Khan chose to confront Nur Jahan and Asaf Khan directly by marching north to the court at the head of four to five thousand Rajput troops. The defiant general reached the imperial camp on the banks of the Jhelum river where he made captive the lightly guarded emperor. Nur Jahan was forced to give herself up to Mahabat Khan. Now in control, Mahabat Khan restored Jahangir to his daily routine as the camp proceeded on its journey. After arriving at Kabul the general, who seems to have had no clearly conceived plan, continued to guard the person of the emperor and to direct imperial business. Nur Jahan and Asaf Khan succeeded in mobilizing anti-Rajput sentiment among the imperial troopers (ahadis), other nobles and the urban population of Kabul. Violent clashes resulted in large numbers of casualties for the Rajputs.

Jahangir, carefully coached by Nur Jahan, acted out a pose of cheerful compliance with the demands of his faithful servant and captor, Mahabat Khan. Supervision of the emperor grew more lax. In June on the return march toward Lahore, near Rohtas fort, the emperor called for a muster and review of his own royal troopers and those of the mansabdars. He asked Mahabat Khan to keep his Rajputs separate. As soon as the royal troopers formed up, Mahabat Khan, recognizing the inevitable, fled the camp to take shelter with Prince Khurram in the Deccan.

Throughout this strange episode it is noteworthy that Mahabat Khan made no attempt to harm the emperor or to replace him on the throne by another Timurid male, or even by himself. Instead, when he first seized Jahangir, Mahabat Khan claimed that he was acting only out of desperation since he feared death or imprisonment from the plots against him. In his desperation he had "boldly and presumptuously thrown myself upon Your Majesty's protection."[35] The Timurid ruler remained a potent symbol of authority to all concerned.

THE END OF THE REIGN

In October, 1626, Prince Parwiz died of the effects of alcoholism at age thirty-eight at Burhanpur in the Deccan. Some suspicions that

[35] Cited in Beni Prasad, *History of Jahangir*, p. 404.

Khurram had hastened the death of his brother were alive at the time. This left only Prince Shahryar, married to a daughter of Nur Jahan and her current favorite, and Prince Khurram as mature candidates for the throne. During the hot weather of 1627 Jahangir had travelled one more time to his beloved Kashmir. Within days Jahangir became seriously ill. The badly enfeebled emperor died October 28, 1627, on the return journey, some distance from Lahore. Neither of his two sons was with him when he died. Shahryar, who suffered from a rare form of leprosy marked by complete hair loss, had been advised to precede the emperor back to the Punjab in the hope that the warm climate of the plain would be curative. Khurram was on duty a thousand miles to the south in the Deccan.

As soon as Jahangir expired, the wazir Asaf Khan, who had long been a quiet partisan of Prince Khurram, acted with unexpected forcefulness and determination to forestall his sister, Nur Jahan's plans for Shahryar. He placed Nur Jahan under close confinement with the body of Jahangir in the camp. He obtained control of Shah Jahan's three young sons who were under her care. The wazir sent an imperial messenger on the thousand mile journey south to bring Khurram back from the Deccan. At the same time Asaf Khan obtained the agreement of a majority of the nobles in the camp to proclaim Dawar Bakhsh, the young son of the deceased Khusrau, emperor. The unfortunate young prince was selected solely as a pawn to be sacrificed in Khurram's interest.

Asaf Khan thereby forced Prince Shahryar, then at Lahore, to fight as a usurper against his cousin. Shahryar used the seven million rupee treasure in Lahore fort to mobilize a large, disheveled, army of hastily assembled mercenaries. He was easily defeated by Asaf Khan just outside Lahore. Captured alive in Lahore fort, Shahryar was made to submit formally to Dawar Bakhsh and then imprisoned and blinded.

Within twenty days imperial runners reached Khurram and the prince started north immediately. Mughal officers along his route presented themselves and received ranks and honors from Khurram, who was seen as the leading contender for the throne. This supposition became a certainty when news of Shahryar's defeat by Asaf Khan intercepted the prince as he crossed the Narmada river. Khurram sent a farman ahead to Asaf Khan who had brought the imperial entourage to Agra asking him to blind, and, if necessary, kill Shahryar, the puppet emperor Dawar Bakhsh, and other mature male Timurid cousins. On

January 19, 1628, Asaf Khan imprisoned Dawar Bakhsh. He then proclaimed Khurram emperor under the title of Shah Jahan by having his name read in the Friday prayers. Two days later, when Shah Jahan's letter arrived, the wazir ordered the execution of Shahryar, Dawar Bakhsh and his brother, and two sons of Prince Daniyal, Jahangir's brother. On January 24, 1628, Shah Jahan entered Agra and was hailed as emperor.

CHAPTER 6
SHAH JAHAN 1628–1658

At his accession, Shah Jahan, the dominant ruler on the subcontinent, controlled vast territories, unmatched military power, and massive wealth. He was heir to an ancient and impeccable royal lineage. The new emperor's pride in these circumstances and in his own strengths was manifest – verging on arrogance by contemporary view. Shah Jahan's confidence was not unfounded. His abilities had been tested over long years of military campaigning, diplomatic negotiation, and political maneuvering. In 1628, at his official coronation, this aggressive, able man assumed the identity for which he had been training all his life. Empire and emperor were well fitted to each other.

Shah Jahan established his capital at Agra in the great fortress built by Akbar. Agra remained the capital until 1648 when the court, army and household moved to the newly completed imperial capital, Shahjahanabad, at Delhi. The spirit and form found in the new capital differed noticeably from that of Fatehpur Sikri. Like the man, Shah Jahan's new city was appropriate to a more formal, more forbidding, and grand monarchy and empire.

KHAN JAHAN LODI

In 1629, Khan Jahan Lodi, an Afghan noble ranked among the highest in the empire at 6000 zat and 6000 suwar, fled Agra and sought refuge with the Nizam Shah ruler of Ahmadnagar in the Deccan. This act of defiance, unprecedented since Akbar's days, was the more sensational because of Khan Jahan Lodi's privileged relationship with Jahangir. It was ominous in that the possibility of a widespread Afghan uprising could not be excluded and could have been the signal for a crisis in the loyalties of the nobility. Khan Jahan, however, rebelled reluctantly, for survival and with little hope of overthrowing his royal master. In many ways his response was a response to a new, less-congenial style of royal authority.

The youthful Khan Jahan Lodi, originally named Pir Khan, had joined Akbar's forces under Raja Man Singh in the last stages of the

Bengal conquest.[1] The personable young Afghan mansabdar quickly became a royal favorite of Prince Daniyal, and, after his death, of Jahangir. Like the emperor Pir Khan was deeply interested in Sufism and mysticism. Retitled Salabat Khan at 3000 zat he was included in the trusted few nobles who met regularly with the emperor in the inner audience chamber of the bath (the *gusalkhana*). The emperor even talked of having his protégé married into the royal family.

Khan Jahan Lodi retained Jahangir's complete confidence even though his accomplishments were minimal. He led a failed Deccan campaign; served as governor of Multan province in the midst of the loss of Qandahar; was recalled to guard Agra fort during the revolt of Prince Khurram; and finally became governor of the Deccan. In the latter capacity he colluded with the Nizam Shah ruler of Ahmadnagar and handed over to him a large tract of the Deccan known as the Balaghat. Just prior to Jahangir's death on Khan Jahan's orders, faujdars and other Mughal officials in this territory gave up their posts to Ahmadnagar officers and retired to Burhanpur. Khan Jahan Lodi was widely reported to have received 300,000 gold *hun* as payment for this notorious transaction.

When Jahangir died Khan Jahan Lodi made the mistake of rebuffing an overture from Shah Jahan for support in the succession. For a time it appeared that he would even resist the new ruler. Finally, however, Khan Jahan Lodi came to court, but remained under a heavy burden of suspicion – in sharp contrast to his role with Jahangir. The emperor asked him to disband part of his followers and some of his jagirs were resumed. After eight months of increasing tension, in October, 1629, Khan Jahan Lodi secretly fled Agra with his family and followers toward the Deccan. Pursued by a party of loyal officers, led by one of the formidable Baraha Sayyids, Khan Jahan survived a desperate battle at the bank of the rain-swollen Chambal river near Dholpur. His two sons, two brothers, son-in-law, and sixty of his retainers were killed and many of his women and dependents were left behind. Aided by Jujhar Singh Bundela, Khan Jahan and his two surviving sons managed to reach the welcoming court of Murtaza II, Nizam Shah and was given command of the Ahmadnagar armies.

Shah Jahan sent three separate armies south and followed them by

[1] Shah Nawaz Khan and 'Abdul Hayy, *The Maathir-ul-Umara* (New Delhi, 1st reprint edition, 1979), edited and translated by H. Beveridge and Baini Prashad, 3 vols., I, 795–804 for his biography.

shifting his court to Burhanpur in early 1630. Over the next year a series of inconclusive clashes followed. Both the Nizam Shahi and Mughal armies looted, burnt and devastated the countryside as they marched. This simply added to the plight of the population who were beginning to suffer from a prolonged drought and dearth. The famine conditions of 1630 would be remembered as the worst for a century or more in the Deccan and Gujarat. Depressed and demoralized, Khan Jahan Lodi proved to be an ineffective commander, and late in 1630 suffered a disastrous defeat. He fled with several hundred horsemen north through Malwa toward the Punjab where he hoped to raise support from the Afghans in that province. Harried by a net of Mughal parties, he was finally trapped and killed. His severed head went south to Shah Jahan who received his trophy in a pleasure boat on the Tapti river at Burhanpur. One of the most dramatic, and potentially serious rebellions by a high-ranking amir was successfully suppressed. Khan Jahan Lodi drew no substantial support from the remainder of the nobility.

RETURN TO AN ISLAMIC POLITICAL CULTURE

Under Shah Jahan, for the first time, the results of an orthodox Muslim reaction to the policies of Akbar and Jahangir had an effect on official policy. Prominent leaders in the Naqshbandiya Sufi order were in the forefront of a widespread revivalist reaction among orthodox Sunni Muslims in India. Prominent charismatic teachers in this order, like Khwaja Baqi Billah (d. 1603) stressed the overwhelming importance of adherence to the Sharia and discouraged extreme forms of mystical devotion among their followers.[2] More controversial figures like Shaikh Ahmad Sirhindi (see Chapter Five) and his sons and disciples took a vigorous anti-Shia, anti-Hindu stance in their adherence to the norms of the Sharia.[3] Obviously concerned to guard the Sunni community against heresy and against the assimilative capacity of Hinduism, the Naqshbandiya Sufis were spokesmen for a broader shift in attitude among Indian Muslims. This was not confined to the Naqshbandiya; the Shattari, Chishti, and other prominent Sufi orders were increasingly affected by revivalist sentiments. Multiple affili-

[2] Sayyid Athar Abbas Rizvi, *A History of Sufism in India* (New Delhi: Munshiram Manoharlal, 1983) II, 185–193.
[3] Ibid., pp. 223–241.

ations and membership in several orders by Sufis and laypersons alike in this period ensured rapid diffusion of attitudes and beliefs among the devout Sunni communities of the empire.

Shah Jahan's attachment to orthodox Islam mirrored a hardening, more formal delineation of Islamic community in the subcontinent. The new emperor's explicitly Islamic idiom was a pronounced departure from the inclusive political appeal made by his father and grandfather. The cumulative effect of these changes on Mughal political culture was substantial. For all pious Muslim rulers the Sharia, as interpreted by one of the four legal schools, was the only acceptable touchstone for official policy. Shah Jahan cautiously began to test Mughal policy against this standard. Some new polities adopted as canonical reversed Akbar's generally liberal treatment of non-Muslims. In 1633, his sixth regnal year, Shah Jahan began to impose the Sharia provisions against construction or repair of churches and temples. When he learned that wealthy Hindus wished to complete construction of several unfinished temples at Benares, he ordered that all recently built temples in the city be torn down.[4] After this initial flurry of destruction only prominent shrines encountered in the course of military campaigns suffered damage.[5]

Shah Jahan celebrated Islamic festivals with an enthusiasm unfamiliar to his predecessors. For example, to mark the birthday celebration (Milad) of the Prophet Muhammad, on September 16, 1633, the emperor staged a pious celebration featuring recitation of the verses of the Koran in the great hall of public audience.[6] Gifts of money were distributed to worthy ulema and Sufis there assembled.[7]

Long-dormant royal interest in the Holy Cities revived. Shah Jahan resumed sponsorship of the annual Haj caravan to the west coast ports under the direction of a Mughal officer, the Mir Haj. Every year two Mughal ships sailing from Gujarat to the Hijaz carried Indian pilgrims whose expenses were met by the state.[8] To fulfill a vow that he had made upon his coronation, Shah Jahan sent two scholars on the Haj laden with Indian goods to be sold for the benefit of the poor in Mecca

[4] E. Bedley and Z. A. Desai, eds., *The Shah Jahan Nama of 'Inayat Khan*, (Delhi, 1990), p. 154. Sri Ram Sharma, *The Religious Policy of the Mughal Emperors* (London: Asia Publishing House, Inc., 2nd edition, 1962), pp. 86–87.

[5] Sharma, *Religious Policy*, pp. 86–87. [6] *'Inayat Khan*, p. 207.

[7] Sharma, *Religious Policy*, p. 81.

[8] N. R. Farooqi, "Mughal-Ottoman Relations: A Study of Political and Diplomatic Relations Between Mughal India and the Ottoman Empire: 1556–1748," unpublished Ph.D thesis, University of Wisconsin, Madison, 1986, p. 208.

and Medina.[9] [10] Eight similar missions followed during his reign.[11] In 1643 the Sharif of Mecca, Zaid bin Muhsin (1631–1666) sent a warmly received diplomatic mission to the Timurid court. In 1650 the head of the earlier mission, Shaikh Abdus Samad, who had been dazzled by the wealth and power of the Mughal court, returned to India and was enrolled as a Mughal mansabdar and made chief judge of the army.[12]

PEACOCK THRONE AND TAJ MAHAL

Shah Jahan's confident sense of Mughal grandeur found creative expression in monumental building at various scales. His first commissioned work, the Peacock Throne, set the tone for a new era of ceremonial display. At his coronation the emperor set aside diamonds and other precious stones worth 10 million rupees for use on the new throne. The empire's most skilled craftsmen labored seven years on the intricate design. Every possible surface was covered with motifs formed by hundreds of beautifully set rubies, emeralds, diamonds, and pearls. Above the canopy was the famed "peacock with elevated tail made of blue sapphires and other colored stones, the body being gold inlaid with precious stones, having a large ruby front of the breast, from whence hangs a pear-shaped pearl of 50 carats . . ."[13] Shah Jahan occupied his new seat in a grand audience in Agra fort in March, 1635.

The Taj Mahal was his second, larger, project – one which has been greatly admired as one of the triumphs of monumental building in world history. On June 17, 1631, Mumtaz Mahal, beloved wife of Shah Jahan, died in childbirth (her fourteenth) at Burhanpur in the Deccan. The emperor was devastated by grief and went into prolonged mourning for her. The dead queen's body was temporarily interred at Burhanpur before being brought to Agra by her son, Prince Shuja. On a plot of land on the bank of the Yamuna river, Mumtaz Mahal was buried. At Shah Jahan's orders, imperial architects and builders began to erect the marble plinth for a tomb over the grave that would be known as the Taj Mahal.

The tomb itself, with its great bulbous dome of white marble flanked

[9] Farooqi, "Mughal-Ottoman Relations," p. 204. [10] Ibid. p. 206.
[11] Ibid. pp. 208–209.
[12] Ibid. p. 208.
[13] Jean Baptiste Tavernier, *Travels in India* (London: Macmillan and Co., 2 vols. 1889) 1, 381–384. The throne itself has not survived its removal from India in 1739 by the Persian invader Nadir Shah.

by four slender minarets, is merely the central feature of a larger walled complex comprising some forty-two acres. An imposing set of gateways and courts offers access to the walled garden with a view of the entrance to the tomb at the far end. The gardens themselves are laid out in a four-part pattern divided off by two intersecting water channels. The entire complex, the product of intense creative effort and great expenditure, required seventeen years to complete.

Shah Jahan did build a mausoleum for his beloved wife. Transcending his grief, however, the tomb-complex affirms the emperor's religious faith in Islam and the centrality of Islam to the Timurid empire. The Taj "was conceived as a vast allegory of the Day of Resurrection, when the dead shall arise and proceed to the place of Judgment beneath the Divine Throne."[14] Every feature of the Taj, from the tiniest detailed embellishment to the largest structural element, forms part of a unified whole designed to support this message.

The gateways and gardens of the Taj are "symbolic replicas of the gateway and gardens of the celestial Paradise."[15] The main entrance represents the gateway by which Muhammad entered Paradise during his miraculous heavenly ascent known as the Mi`raj. The four water channels of the gardens represent the four Rivers of Paradise. The raised marble tank in the center signifies the celestial tank of abundance (Al-Kawthar). The marble tomb itself with its bulbous dome is a replica of the heavenly Throne of God. God sits in this throne above Paradise to tender judgment on the Day of Resurrection. The four minarets can be seen as the four supports of the throne of God referred to in popular medieval cosmology.

The allegory is made explicit by careful placement of lengthy carved inscriptions containing Koranic verses. The design and execution of the inscriptions was the work of Amanat Khan, the imperial calligrapher, who carried out a similar task on Akbar's tomb. The south facade of the main gateway displays the entire Sura 89, "The Daybreak" whose theme is that of the Day of Judgment. In the most awesome imagery, the Sura promises that God will punish the wicked and the thoughtless. Finally, however the Sura ends with God's promise to the faithful:[16]

[14] Wayne E. Begley, "The Myth of the Taj Mahal and a New Theory of Its Symbolic Meaning," *The Art Bulletin*, March, 1979, pp. 7–37.
[15] Ibid., p. 13. [16] Begley, "Taj Mahal," p. 13 and n. 34.

O thou soul at peace,
Return thou unto thy Lord, well-pleased and well Pleasing unto Him!
enter thou among My servants –
And enter thou My Paradise!

The Taj is that paradise. Mumtaz Mahal and, beside her, Shah Jahan lie in graves buried beneath the Throne of God. In the epitaph inscribed on his grave below, Shah Jahan is described as Rizwan, the gatekeeper of Paradise. His was a profound attempt to create an image of God's majesty and power – a profoundly Islamic vision.

A NEW CAPITAL: SHAHJAHANABAD DELHI

In 1639 Shah Jahan launched his most ambitious building project: construction of a new capital. Agra's palace fortress was cramped and the city itself overcrowded. A task force of architects, builders, and astrologers recommended a site just south of Delhi on a bluff overlooking the Yamuna River.[17] Delhi was especially fitting as the old Indo-Muslim center of empire in North India. The author of an early eighteenth century geographical compendium observed, "[Delhi] was always the *dar al-mulk* [seat of the empire] of the great sultans and the center of the circle of Islam [*markaz-i dairah Islam*]."[18] The tombs and monumental buildings of the early conquerors of Hind were to be found there.

Delhi was also a religious center of great sanctity for pious Muslims. The tombs of dozens of revered saints and Sufis could be found in the city and its adjoining countryside. On the death anniversary of each saint, thousands of pilgrims travelled to Delhi to participate in the *urs* festival celebrating his entrance into paradise. Redolent memories of Muslim victory and piety were firmly embedded in the new capital. Akbar had rejected the symbolic associations of Delhi as the redoubt of Muslim conquest; Shah Jahan returned eagerly to these associations.

At an auspicious moment, on April 29, 1639, excavations began.[19] Construction proceeded steadily for nine years. The fort and its buildings consumed 6 million silver rupees in their construction.

[17] Stephen P. Blake, "Cityscape of an Imperial Capital, Shahjahanabad in 1739" in R. E. Frykenberg, *Delhi Through the Ages* (New Delhi: Oxford University Press, 1986), p. 153.
[18] From "Bahjat al-Alam" of Hakim Maharat Khan Isfahani, Persian Manuscript Collection Ethe 729, India Office Library, folio 34a quoted in Blake, "Cityscape," p. 155.
[19] Blake, "Cityscape," p. 155.

Finally, all was ready, and on the auspicious day of April 19, 1648, Shah Jahan formally entered Shahjahanabad and took up residence. Days of grand celebration and royal largess followed as nobles, scholars, and dignitaries assembled under a great canopy of embroidered velvet in the hall of public audience.

Shahjahanabad was a carefully designed courtly city. The emperor placed the great palace fortress, the "Auspicious Fortress' (*Qila Mubarak*) on the river bank at the meeting place of the two major thoroughfares. The fortress, still standing today, with its broad, 60 to 75 ft. high walls of red sandstone forms an uneven octagon nearly two miles in circumference. A stone-faced, water-filled moat protected the land side; the Yamuna river the other.

The southern half of the fort contains the principal palace and an array of living quarters and apartments for the emperor, the harem and household. The largest of these mansions belonged to Jahan Ara Begam, Shah Jahan's favorite daughter. The northern half of the fortress enclosed two large gardens intersected by tanks and water courses. Around the outer walls were offices, storerooms, the mint, and dozens of workshops and the royal stables.

Opposite the fortress on a hillock stood the enormous communal mosque – the Jama Masjid – the largest such mosque in India with space for thousands of worshipers. The Jama Masjid was flanked by a hospital offering free care of the sick and a madrasa or religious school. In its scale and placement the Jama Masjid offered a symbolic counter-weight to the great fortress.

The massive palace-fortress was the terminus for two straight broad thoroughfares which framed the city. From the fort's Lahori gate ran a broad avenue with a covered arcade housing over fifteen hundred shops and porticoes. The avenue and shops were designed and paid for by Jahan Ara Begam, one of Shah Jahan's wives. A branch of the city's canal flowed down the middle of the street. The first of several squares called the *Kotwali Chabutra*, or magistrates' platform, centered on the public area where the city magistrate tried and punished criminals in public. The second great square centered on a large pool. A *sarai* or inn built by Jahan Ara Begam stood at the north end of the square; a *hammam* or public bath at the other. The reflection of the moon by night from the pool gave the square the name Silver or Moonlight square (Chandni Chawk).

The other main thoroughfare extended due south from the Akbarabadi (Agra) gate of the fort over a kilometer to the Akbarabadi gate of the city walls. A branch of the canal flowed down the center of the avenue. Another of Shah Jahan's wives, Nawab Akbarabadi Begam, constructed a double row of shops. Just south of the fort gate Nawab Akbarabadi Begam had designed a broad square. At one end she constructed an imposing mosque, adjacent to it an inn for travelers or sarai, and opposite a public bath.

Within the city walls, framed by the canals and central avenues, the remainder of Shahjahanabad took shape in quarters (*havelis*) defined by the mansions, mosques and gardens of the nobility. The walled and guarded establishment of these grandees included private living quarters for the noble and his harem, his officers and clerks, his slaves, servants, and soldiers. The largest might house 5,000 persons. Around these sites clustered the dwellings of hundreds more traders, servants, and other urban folk dependent upon the great man's largess and patronage.

Shahjahanabad, the emperor's "abode" or "mansion," was a splendid urban creation. Every day the lavish rituals of imperial audiences were imitated on a lesser scale by nobles holding court in their mansions throughout the city. Every day the public rituals of Islamic secular and religous life were enacted in the bazaars, baths, sarais, gardens and mosques of the great city. At its height Shahjahanabad was the pulsating heart of a grand empire.

In addition to these three projects, Shah Jahan kept his architects and builders engaged in a constant series of endeavors throughout his reign. These ranged from Jahangir's mausoleum, completed in 1637, to extensive renovations and additions on Lahore fort, and to Shalimar Garden in Kashmir, completed 1641–2. Shireen Moosvi has estimated that Shah Jahan's expenditure on buildings over his three-decade reign totalled at least 28.9 million rupees.[20] Imposing as is this figure, it was but a small portion of the monies devoted to war and attempted territorial expansion.

CONSOLIDATION ON THE INTERNAL FRONTIER

Under Shah Jahan's vigorous direction the empire continued its expansion. Mughal power realigned political relationships and political

20 Shireen Moosvi, "Expenditure On Buildings Under Shahjahan – A Chapter of Imperial Financial History," *Proceedings of the Indian Historical Congress 46th Session* (Amritsar, 1985), pp. 285–299.

culture in every region of the subcontinent. Even previously remote refuge areas felt the imprint of imperial power.

The small Rajput kingdom of Baglana sitting astride the main route from Surat and the western ports to Burhanpur in the Deccan had been tributary to one Muslim ruler or another for centuries. In 1637, however, Shah Jahan decided on complete annexation. Mughal armies under Prince Aurangzeb easily overran the kingdom. The Baharji, the Raja of Baglana, became an amir of 3,000 zat in Mughal service, but he did not retain his former kingdom as a watan jagir. Instead Baglana was attached to Khandesh province and administered by a Mughal faujdar and representatives of the provincial diwan. The empire began to collect its standard revenues with the aid of deshmukhs and other local notables. The Baharji died soon after the conquest. His son converted to Islam and received the title of Daulatmand Khan, 1,500 zat rank and control of a pargana as a watan jagir in Khandesh province.

In Sind, the northwestern border province straddling the lower Indus river, weak political authority and extremely fragmented tribal polities meant that the Mughals were forced to build an authority structure before they could impose a standardized imperial administration. By Shah Jahan's reign this process was well advanced. Mughal administrators pressed hard against the turbulent horse, cattle, sheep, and camel raising pastoralists of that arid region.[21] From fortified urban bases at Sehwan in the north downriver to Nasapur, and the provincial capital at Thatta in the Indus delta, Shah Jahan's governors and faujdars mounted punitive expeditions against the Baluch and other tribes. Despite occasional setbacks, thousands of tribesmen were killed or sold into slavery. A network of Mughal small forts or *thanas* manned by cavalry and musketeers was established. These policies discouraged raiding and plundering of sedentary cultivators settled near the towns and rendered caravans and river traffic more secure from tribal banditry.

Mughal policy also attempted, with some success, to obtain either taxes or services from the Sind tribesmen. Provincial revenue officials tried to collect revenues from each body of pastoralists on a regular basis. These revenues were demanded in cash, not in animals. If unpaid, a punitive expedition resulted. Occasionally, revenue demands were reduced or eliminated in return for protection of trade or travelers.

[21] Sunita Zaidi, "The Mughal State and Tribes in Seventeenth Century Sind," *The Indian Economic and Social History Review*, 26 (1989), 343–362.

Lineage heads were taken hostage to ensure good behavior on the part of their followers. Many Sind chiefs received payments, honors, and areas as "jagirs" from which they received Mughal support in collecting revenues. Some were even given small mansabs as recognition of their goodwill. Muslim Sufis whose control of tombs and other holy places allowed them to mediate tribal disputes, obtained tax-free land grants and cash allowances to bind them to the imperial cause.

More obscure Rajput houses were subject to new pressures. The Bundelas, a relatively low status clan of Rajputs, had forcibly established a capital at Urchha on the Betwa river in 1531.[22] Over several generations cadet lineages of Bundela Rajputs founded other clan centers in what had come to be known as Bundelkhand. Early in Akbar's reign a Mughal army forced the Bundela ruling house to submit and pay tribute.

In 1595, Bir Singh Dev, a member of the Bundela royal lineage, arranged the assassination of Abul Fazl at Prince Salim's request. On gaining the throne Jahangir intervened to set aside other more likely candidates to place Bir Singh Dev on the Bundela gaddi. Simultaneously, the Bundela ruler became a high ranking Mughal amir and retained control over his kingdom as a watan jagir under terms similar to those of the greatest Rajput nobles. Under these favored circumstances Bir Singh built up a vast fortune and unchallenged domination of Bundelkhand before he died in 1627, the same year as Jahangir.

When Bir Singh's son and heir, Jujhar Singh, presented himself at Shah Jahan's court, the emperor initiated an official enquiry into the estate of the dead Bundela amir. This inquiry may have been prompted by the deceased Raja's vigorous role in the suppression of Shah Jahan's revolt against Jahangir. Alarmed by this prospect Jujhar Singh fled Agra for Urchha without permission. Shah Jahan sent a 34,000 man army in pursuit. The imperial troops devastated the countryside around Urchha before storming the city's fortress. Three thousand Bundela troops died in the battle. Badly defeated, Jujhar Singh abjectly asked for a pardon. Shah Jahan extracted a 1.5 million rupee indemnity, forty war elephants (a regional export), and the annexation of one district to imperial administration. The emperor also insisted that

[22] Kolff refers to the Bundelas as a "spurious" Rajput clan whose members could not intermarry in the larger network of hypergamous Rajput alliances. Dirk H. A. Kolff, *Naukar, Rajput and Sepoy: The Ethnohistory of the Military Labour Market in Hindustan, 1450–1850* (Cambridge: Cambridge University Press, 1990), pp. 120–143.

Jujhar Singh personally serve with his sons and military contingent as a Mughal nobleman in the ongoing Deccan campaigns.

When he finally returned to Urchha in 1634, Jujhar Singh violated imperial rules by leading an illegal raid on his neighboring ruler, the Gond raja, Bhim Narayan. The Bundelas attacked and captured Chauragarh, the ancient town and fortress of the Gonds, killed Bhim Narayan and seized the one million rupee hoard found in the fort. Shah Jahan, acting upon a complaint of the dead raja's son, demanded that Jujhar Singh vacate the lands that he had occupied, return the treasure to the emperor, and pay a fine.

Jujhar Singh's outright defiance of this order inflamed Shah Jahan. He sent another large army under the nominal command of the sixteen-year-old Prince Aurangzeb to invade Bundelkhand. The Mughal troops quickly overran Urchha again and installed a more pliant ruler. Devi Singh Bundela, head of the senior Bundela lineage and a Mughal mansabdar, (whose line had been set aside by Jahangir in favor of Bir Singh Dev) became raja at Urchha.

Mughal cavalry pursued Jujhar Singh, his family and fragments of his army into the forested lands of Chanda, another Central Indian Gond kingdom, which had not yet acknowledged imperial suzerainty. When overtaken by Mughal troops, Jujhar Singh's principal queens were killed by their attendants, but the remaining royal women were sent to join the Mughal harem. Two very young sons and a grandson were converted to Islam. Another older son who refused to convert was killed outright. Jujhar and his eldest son, driven into the jungle, were caught and killed by a party of Gonds.

At Chanda, the Mughal commanders compelled the unfortunate Gond raja to pay a large indemnity and agree to an annual tribute of 80,000 rupees or twenty elephants. At Urchha an intensive search for the Bundela treasure turned up money and precious objects valued at ten million rupees. Shah Jahan himself journeyed to Urchha to see the picturesque waterfalls and hills and palaces of the region. At Urchha, "the Islam-cherishing Emperor demolished the lofty and massive temple of Bir Singh Dev near his palace, and erected a mosque on its site."[23] Aggressive action on the internal frontier in Central India imposed a new, more intense, level of Mughal political domination in Bundelkhand and Gondwana.

[23] Abdul Hamid Lahori, *The Padshah Nama* (Calcutta: Bibliotheca Indica, 2 vols., 1867), I, 121–122. Quoted in Jadunath Sarkar, *History of Aurangzib* (Calcutta, 5 vols., 1912–1924), I, 29.

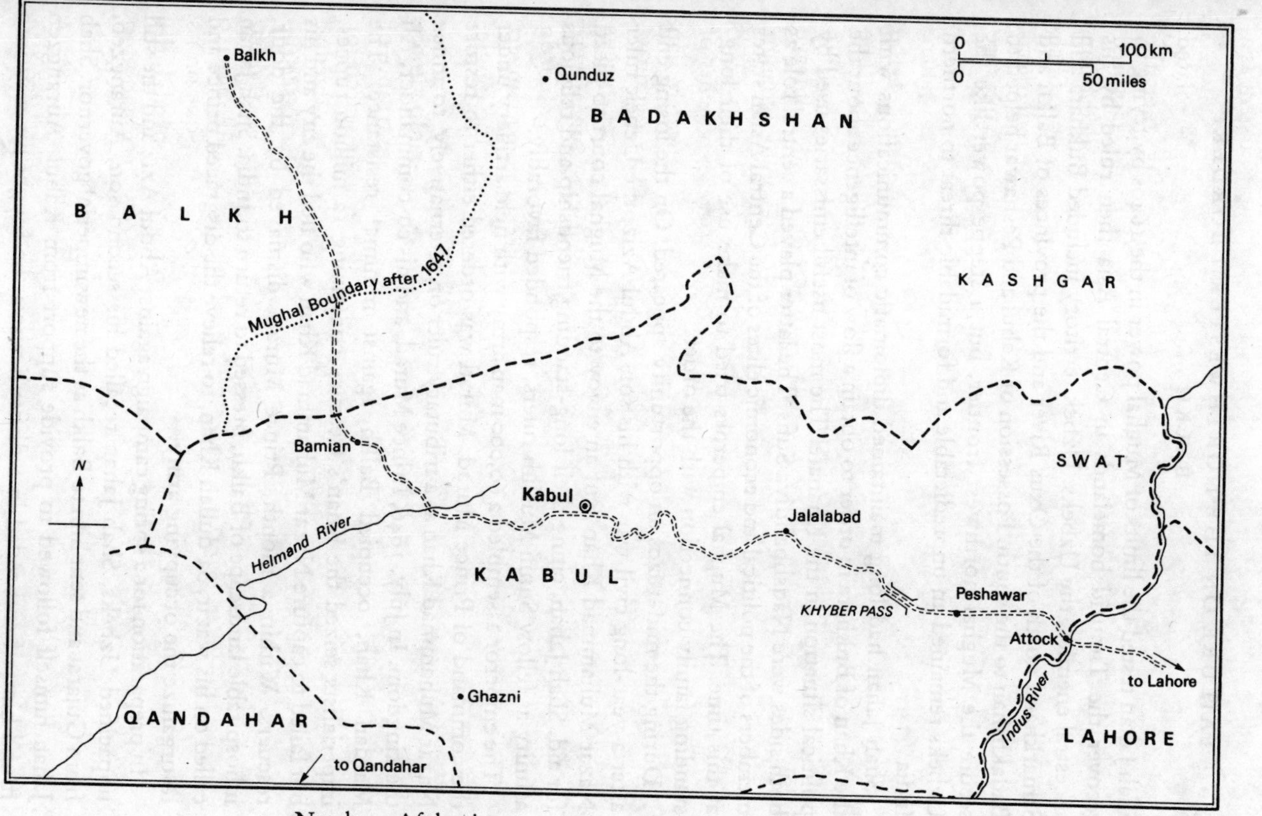

2 Northern Afghanistan
Source: I. Habib, *An atlas of the Mughal Empire* (Delhi, 1982), 1A–B

FAILURE ON THE NORTHWESTERN BORDER: BALKH

Shah Jahan tested the limits of Mughal power in the 1640s by trying to recover the Timurid homelands in Central Asia then ruled by his ancestral enemies, the Uzbeks. Uzbek territory included Bukhara and Samarkhand north of the Oxus River and the provinces of Balkh and Badakhshan to the south. Possession of Kabul and Peshawar helped to secure the Mughal northwest frontier, but a steppe power like the Uzbeks remained an unpredictable and formidable threat to northern India.

Shah Jahan had long maintained diplomatic communications with the Khan of Bukhara in order to obtain a flow of intelligence about the political situation in the Khanate. The most useful emissaries used by both sides were Naqshbandiya Sufis. The latter played a central role as members of the political and economic elites of the Central Asian states at this time. The Mughal emperors tried to make use of their long-standing family connection with the order.

During the mid-1640s an opportunity appeared. On the losing end after a year-long civil war with his son Abdul Aziz, the Uzbek ruler Nazar Muhammad Khan sent an envoy to the Mughal court to plead for aid. Shah Jahan, citing their long-standing friendship and religious affinity as fellow Sunni Muslim rulers, responded favorably.

The emperor assembled a 60,000 man army with field artillery under the command of Prince Murad. Murad was ordered either to restore Nazar Muhammad Khan as a tributary ruler or, alternatively, to annex the kingdom. In July, 1646, Prince Murad, and his co-commander, Ali Mardan Khan, occupied Balkh against minimal resistance. The imperialists seized the Khan's treasury containing 12 million rupees, but failed to capture Nazar Muhammad Khan who fled the city and his rescuers. Within a month, Prince Murad, dismayed by the dour, inhospitable landscape of Balkh, pressed to return to India. Shah Jahan called on his wazir, Sa'dullah Khan, to relieve the disgraced prince and to organize the occupying army.

In preparation for a spring campaign against Abdul Aziz and the still unpacified Uzbeks, Shah Jahan recalled his second son, Aurangzeb, from Gujarat and sent him to Balkh as the new imperial governor. Shah Jahan himself followed to provide support from Kabul. Aurangzeb found himself embroiled in a difficult war as he fought his way into

Balkh. The Uzbeks discovered at considerable cost the effects of the Mughal field artillery and musketeers. But they could outmaneuver the Mughals in fast-moving skirmishes to create a stalemate. During the summer of 1647 the Mughals sat at Balkh and engaged in a protracted series of negotiations with Abdul Aziz at Bukhara.

To its dismay the imperial army discovered that it could not live off the land. In this harsh mountainous land the Mughals found no equivalent to the Indian grain carriers, the *banjaras*, who normally supplied them. Foraging was nearly futile because the generally productive irrigated fruit orchards and grain fields of Balkh were devastated by the war. Under straitened circumstances, Shah Jahan and Aurangzeb negotiated a settlement, not with Abdul Aziz but with his father. Finally, in October, 1647, threatened by the onset of winter, Aurangzeb handed over the city and adjacent districts of Balkh to Nazar Muhammad Khan in exchange for a treaty offering nominal submission to the Mughal emperor. Harassed by Uzbek troops and marauding Turkoman tribesmen, the retreating Mughal army suffered several thousand casualties on the difficult return through snow-bound passes to Kabul.

At the end of two years of sustained effort the Mughal–Uzbek treaty of 1647 extended the imperial frontier north from Kabul by about forty to fifty kilometers. For the remainder, Shah Jahan had to settle for the dubious satisfaction of receiving formal recognition of his sovereignty from Nazar Muhammad Khan at Balkh. At no time did his forces seriously threaten the Uzbek capital at Bukhara or come close to seizure of Samarkhand.

The two-year Uzbek campaign demonstrated the true costs of reasserting Timurid domination over the sparsely populated, impoverished lands in Central Asia. Shah Jahan, by official tally, spent forty million rupees in an attempt to conquer kingdoms whose total annual revenues were no more than several million rupees. The Mughal search for familial vindication in this region crashed against the harsh realities of distance, scanty resources, and determined local resistance. In one sense the Mughal Chaghatais had failed once again to defeat the Uzbeks and Turkomans, their inveterate adversaries.

THE NORTHWEST: QANDAHAR

One of Shah Jahan's fixed goals was recovery of Qandahar fort from his Safavid rival. Finally, in 1638, an opportunity came when the

Persian commander, Ali Mardan Khan, rightly fearing his execution by the capriciously cruel Shah Safi (1629–1642), surrendered Qandahar fortress to the Mughals. Shah Jahan welcomed the distinguished and highly regarded Safavid noble with rank of 5,000 zat and 5,000 suwar and immediate appointment to the governorship of Kashmir.

A decade passed before Shah Abbas II (1642–1666) decided on a major military effort against Qandahar. Taking advantage of Shah Jahan's failure in Balkh, the Safavid armies set out under the young Shah in the winter of 1648. Shah Jahan, although warned of the move, allowed himself to be dissuaded from a relief expedition by his nobles who argued that a winter campaign was unthinkable. The demoralized governor of Qandahar surrendered within two months.

Safavid victory brought an immediate response from the enraged Mughal emperor. Over the next four years, Shah Jahan mounted three major campaigns against Qandahar. Each failed ignominiously. In 1649, moving to Kabul, Shah Jahan organized a 50,000 man army commanded by Sadullah Khan, the wazir, and his most capable son, Aurangzeb. This force reached Qandahar but failed to break the fort's defenses and withdrew before the winter season. Three years later, in 1652, another Mughal army under Aurangzeb also failed to take the fort before winter set in. The Mughals did beat off a Persian relief force in a pitched battle but could not break the fortresses' defenses.

Mughal failure here was partly a measure of the length of the supply line from Kabul, itself at the extremity of the empire. Partly this was a measure of Safavid determination to hold Qandahar. To a considerable extent, however, Mughal siege artillery simply was inadequate to the task. Safavid artillerymen inflicted continuous casualties on the besiegers. The less-accurate Mughal artillery was unable to direct effective covering fire. Many Mughal guns burst with damaging effects when overloaded.

Between April and September, 1653, Shah Jahan made one last attempt to break Qandahar's defenses. He sent his favorite son Dara Shukoh to command a larger siege force. The latter commissioned three specially cast large guns for the task. When they finally arrived, the new siege guns did manage to breach some of the fortress walls, but not in time. Dwindling supplies and the season forced a return to Kabul. Shah Jahan contemplated yet a fourth attempt in 1656, but his advisers persuaded him to abandon the idea. Qandahar remained a Safavid possession until the dynasty itself faltered in the early years of the eighteenth century.

Two attempts to invade Balkh and Badakhshan and three closely spaced sieges of Qandahar consumed Mughal resources and attention for nearly a decade. In the end Shah Jahan failed completely. He did not reach Samarkhand, nor did he retain possession of the gateway to India at Qandahar. The cost was heavy. As the Mughal historian Sadiq reviewed the second Qandahar campaign: "nothing resulted from this expedition except the shedding of blood, the killing of thirty to forty thousand of people, and the expenditure of three crore and fifty lac [35 million] rupees."[24]

NORTH

In the Himalayan foothills Garhwal, a remote Rajput hill state, successfully fought off a Mughal army which tried to impose tributary status in 1635. So badly mauled were the Mughals that it was nearly twenty years before Shah Jahan sent another strongly equipped expedition against Srinagar, the capital. After this army was forced to withdraw, the emperor assembled a 4,000 man force with artillery to march laboriously into the hills and threaten the Garhwal capital. At this point, in 1656, the Raja submitted, agreed to pay tribute and sent his son to serve at the imperial court.[25]

Elsewhere the Mughals did succeed in thrusting beyond the mountain ranges bounding the subcontinent. In the difficult high mountain country north of Kashmir a small Muslim population subsisted in the valleys known as Lesser Tibet or Baltistan. Beneath the shadow of the Balti range the inhabitants extracted modest amounts of gold from the rivers, raised sheep for wool, carried on limited sericulture, and grew fruits, wheat, and barley.[26] The Muslim ruler of Lesser Tibet had given refuge to the last Shia Muslim Chak ruler of Kashmir when that kingdom fell to Akbar's army. The princes of that house occasionally led raids back into Mughal Kashmir. This provocation was the immediate source of Mughal interest in what in their view was a

[24] Muhammad Sadiq, "Shahjahan-Nama," British Museum, Oriental 174. Folio 173a. As translated and quoted in Islam, *Indo-Persian Relations*, 114.

[25] Banarsi Prasad Saksena, *History of Shah Jahan of Delhi* (Allahabad, reprint of 1932 edition, 1973), p. 123. Begley and Desai, eds., *'Inayat Khan*, eighth regnal year, I, 269.

[26] Habib, *An Atlas of the Mughal Empire* (Delhi, 1982), map 3B 35+ 75+ for products of the region.

"barren and impoverished region," which yielded barely 100,000 rupees in revenues to its ruler each year.[27]

In 1634 the Abdal formally acknowledged the Mughal emperor's sovereignty by having Shah Jahan's name read in the khutba or Friday prayers in his capital. When he lapsed in this observance Shah Jahan ordered Zafar Khan, governor of Kashmir to invade Lesser Tibet. In the spring of 1637 Zafar Khan led a Mughal army of 2,000 cavalry and 10,000 infantry 150 miles north in a daring expedition over difficult mountain passes. The army could count on no more than two months of summer weather before the passes were blocked. Because the entire route was virtually uninhabited, the invaders carried all their provisions for the campaign.

When the Mughal army arrived it encountered stiff resistance. The Abdal's armies defended their two principal mountain forts with great stubbornness against sustained assaults by Mughal musketeers and dismounted cavalry. Only after the Mughals overran the forts did the Abdal capitulate. Zafar Khan squeezed an indemnity of one million rupees from the Abdal's treasury, had Shah Jahan's name proclaimed in the Friday prayers and brought the Abdal and one of the Chak princes back to Kashmir as captives.[28] This episode illustrates the extended reach of the emperor and the skill, tenacity, and effectiveness of Mughal military commanders and their troops at their best.

NORTHEAST

In the riverine terrain of the Brahmaputra valley Shah Jahan was content at first to leave the boundary of effective imperial control at Kuch Bihar and Kamrup.[29] At Hajo, capital of Kamrup, a Mughal faujdar guarded the frontier approach to the Brahmaputra valley. Across the frontier, Bali Narayan, brother of the deposed raja of Kamrup, built up a strongly fortified and militarized buffer state at Darrang as a tributary of the Ahom king. Both sides enjoyed the benefits of a brisk trade. Captured elephants, gold from river washings, pepper, and lignum wood were in demand in India and quantities

27 Ibid. 28 Saksena, p. 114.

29 The following is based upon Sudhindra Nath Bhattacharyya, *A History of Mughal North-east Frontier Policy* (Calcutta: Chuckervertty, Chatterjee & Co. Ltd., 1929), pp. 256–286 and S. C. Dutta, *The North-east and the Mughals (1661–1714)* (Delhi: D. K. Publications, 1984), pp. 23–28.

of Indian textiles were readily sold at markets up the Brahmaputra river.

In early 1636, however, slowly building tensions culminated in an Ahom–Mughal war. The conflict was provoked by the murder of a Muslim Assamese trader sent as an emissary to the Ahoms by the Mughals. In the opening episode of the conflict, Bali Narayan and the Ahoms invested Hajo and forced its garrison to surrender. The next year, a Mughal amphibious force sent from Bengal recovered the initiative. At the climactic land and river battle of Burpetah in November, 1637, Mughal cavalry, artillery, muskets, and war-boats destroyed an Ahom army and drove Bali Narayan back to Darrang. The Mughals followed up by administering a sharp defeat to the Ahom river flotilla and seized the river fort of Kajali on the Brahmaputra. The capture and killing of Bali Narayan completed Mughal reoccupation of Kamrup.

The Ahoms responded by sending their full battle fleet and army. In 1638 near Kajali the Ahom army and river fleet drove the Mughals back with severe losses. At this point the Ahom king and Mughal faujdar negotiated a treaty. The Ahoms formally recognized Mughal control of Kamrup and the Mughals agreed to the independent status of the Ahom monarchy. Restoration of the boundaries brought stability in the region for the next two decades. In signing this treaty, Shah Jahan formally conceded the complete independence of the Ahoms. Like the Safavids in the west, the Ahom rulers remained outside the Indian Mughal political system.

THE DECCAN

Shah Jahan, who had been in charge of the Deccan at Jahangir's death, wasted little time in organizing diplomatic and military pressure against the remaining Muslim states of the Deccan. The emperor's pursuit of Khan Jahan Lodi brought a major Mughal campaign against Ahmadnagar in 1630–31 at the height of the great famine. As soon as he obtained the rebel's head, Shah Jahan, then at Burhanpur, renewed the campaign. The Mughal governor of the Deccan, Mahabat Khan, led an army in the successful siege of Daulatabad fort in 1632. This was the final episode in the conquest of Ahmadabad, the western Deccan Sultanate. The young Nizam Shahi prince who had served as a puppet for the Maratha commander, Shahji Bhonsla, became a state prisoner for life in the fortress-prison of Gwalior just south of Agra. Many Ahmadnagar Muslim noblemen and a few Maratha captains entered imperial service. In the territories annexed, an imperial governor, diwan, and other officers imposed standard Mughal revenue and administrative practices in the new province.

Ebullient with this newest triumph, Shah Jahan turned his attention to the two remaining Muslim Sultanates: Bijapur, in the Marathi and Kannada speaking portions of the western Deccan, and Golconda in the Telugu-speaking eastern Deccan. In 1635 the emperor sent a peremptory demand to each Sultan for recognition of Mughal hegemony. Each must strike coins with Timurid titles and have read the emperor's name as ruler in the Friday prayers. Also demanded was payment of annual tribute and the presence of a Mughal diplomatic officer at the Adil Shahi and Qutb Shahi courts.

The Qutb Shah ruler of Golconda quickly complied with these demands. When the Adil Shah did not, Shah Jahan sent three Mughal armies to converge on Bijapur and lay waste the countryside. Faced with certain defeat, the Sultan quickly capitulated. The imposed settlement placed both kingdoms firmly within the Mughal sphere of influence. The southern imperial frontier was thereby stabilized for several decades.

THE SHAPE OF EMPIRE

Shah Jahan's buildings celebrated the expanding territories, growing wealth, and stability of the Mughal empire. In 1647, the historian Abdul Hamid Lahori, closing his enormous chronicle of the first two decades of Shah Jahan's reign, summarized the salient features of Timurid rule.[30] One was simply the sheer size of Shah Jahan's empire. Mughal dominion stretched from Sind in the far northwest to Sylhet on the Brahmaputra and from newly conquered Balkh south to the southern boundary of the Deccan provinces. Twenty-two provinces contained 4,350 parganas – the basic unit of administration. So extensive was the empire that many large parganas in Agra or Lahore provinces generated revenue collections each year of more than one million rupees. This sum, Lahori proudly pointed out, was greater than the total budget for the entire country of Badakhshan.

Secondly Lahori stressed the extent of imperial revenues. The jama

[30] Lahori, *Padshah Nama* II, 709–716.

or assessed annual revenue of the empire was 8,800 million dams – a sharp increase from the 7000 million dams assessed under Jahangir just twenty years before. Lahori attributes part of this increase to growth in population and cultivation under Shah Jahan. Recovery had been especially dramatic in the four provinces of the Deccan and Ahmadabad (Gujarat) which had been desolated by warfare. Recently (after the Mughal victories and Deccan diplomatic settlement of 1636) these regions were restored to their original prosperity.

Thirdly, Lahori extolled the wealth and financial skill of his royal patron. During his fifty-one-year reign Akbar had amassed large amounts of treasure, but Jahangir had expended most of that reserve during his twenty-two-year reign. Shah Jahan had overcome this difficulty and succeeded in bringing great prosperity to the empire. To build up his reserves the emperor stipulated that the imperial khalisa should be set at 1200 million dams equivalent to 30 million rupees. This meant that nearly one-seventh of the annual revenues were funneled directly into the imperial treasury. This was a greater sum than had ever before been made available for the central treasury.

Despite large expenditures on the military and for benefactions, Shah Jahan, since ascending the throne, had accumulated reserves worth 95 million rupees – half in coin and half in jewelry and other valuables. And he had spent 25 million rupees in the construction of grand buildings such as masjids, palaces, forts, tombs, hunting retreats, and gardens in Delhi, Agra, Lahore, Kabul, and other parts of the empire.

Fourth, Lahori stressed the military strength of the empire. Stipendiary cavalrymen numbered 200,000. This figure did not include local troops recruited for revenue collection by faujdars and *amils*. The mansabdars themselves numbered 8,000 horsemen. Seven thousand gentlemen-troopers (ahadis) and mounted musketeers served at court. The remaining 185,000 cavalry comprised the mounted contingents of the princes, the great nobles and other mansabdars. According to regulations promulgated in the ninth regnal year, the number of horsemen mustered was calculated at one-fourth the nominal suwar ranking. The central army counted 40,000 unmounted musketeers, gunners, bombardiers, and rocketeers. From this total, 10,000 foot were posted with the emperor and the remainder stationed in the provinces and forts. Cash salaries paid mounted troops and infantry directly employed by the emperor totalled 640 million dams or 16 million rupees per year. The salaries paid mansabdars for their contingents were set by their assigned ranks.

Lahori's summary implies that the core institutions created by Akbar, which had so successfully driven expansion, were not drastically altered by his son and grandson. Instead, the technicians of empire refined and systematized procedures and policies. The imperial revenue system continued to extract vast sums from the production of Indian agriculturists, craftsmen and traders. Assessed revenues doubled in a half century. In Akbar's fortieth regnal year (1595–96) the total jama was 4061.1 million dams compared to 8,800 million dams in 1647.[31] Part of this increase can be attributed to added territory. Four new Deccan provinces and the kingdom of Baglana added 1,840 million dams to the imperial assessment as did the 180 million dams claimed for the central Asian territories. However a substantial increase in the jama must be attributed to enhancements based upon increased cultivation and production in the older provinces. Mughal revenues were sufficient to enable Shah Jahan to spend lavishly on the military, building and courtly style, while simultaneously adding to his central reserves.

The area covered by the regulation (zabt) revenue system expanded in the first half of the seventeenth century. Detailed records surviving from the late seventeenth century testify to imposition of the standard revenue system in the Deccan provinces. Murshid Quli Khan, diwan of the Deccan provinces under the viceroyalty of Aurangzeb, was the architect of a survey and assessment of the revenue-producing lands in the four Deccan provinces.[32]

To aid recovery after the ravages of war and famine, Murshid Quli Khan set in motion a vigorous program. He recruited headmen and settlers for deserted villages; granted loans for seed and cattle; gave loans to dig wells or build river embankments for irrigation; and he assured the peasantry of continued peace and security. Parties of revenue surveyors and assessors carefully recorded holdings, irrigation facilities, and arable and waste lands. More remote, hilly villages were left to lump-sum payments per plough or allowed to pay the revenue

[31] Total given by Moosvi, *Economy of the Mughal Empire*, p. 194 is slightly higher than the jama given in ch. 3 above.

[32] Jadunath Sarkar, *History of Aurangzib*, I, 189–193; Shah Nawaz Khan and 'Abdul Hayy, *The Maathir-ul-Umara* (New Delhi: 1st reprint edition, 1979), edited and translated by H. Beveridge and Baini Prashad, 3 vols., II, I, 304–309.

by a share of the crops. But the majority of villages underwent a revenue survey and were assessed in cash according to the zabt regulations. Murshid Quli Khan's system formed the basis for all subsequent Deccan revenue assessments – Mughal and Maratha – until the British conquest in the early nineteenth century.

The jagir system retained its central fiscal and military importance, but technical problems developed in matching assessed revenues to the salary needs of the jagirdars. Peasant resistance, bad harvests, and outdated land measurements and assessments all contributed to shortfalls in actual collections from the original assessment figures for each village and pargana. Rather than update the jama figures every year the administration adopted a new expedient. Based upon the ten-yearly record, villages and subdistricts were classified on a "month-scale" to show the ratio of actual collections to assessment. Stable, productive areas, often reserved for the khalisa or princely jagirs, were termed "twelve-monthly" if collections approximated assessments. Those desolated tracts, primarily in the Deccan, with collections at one-fourth of assessed revenues were labelled "four-monthly." In between, other fractional equivalents based on the month-scale were possible. When mansabdars obtained salary assignments rated at less than "twelve-monthly," the numbers of cavalry they were required to recruit and pay were diminished accordingly.[33]

Shah Jahan also dealt with a growing discrepancy between the nominal suwar ranks and the actual contingents mustered by his nobles and mansabdars. In part this occurred because the pay for both zat and suwar ranks was gradually reduced from Akbar's scales. Rather than raise the rate of pay and demand one to one ratios between the numerical rank and actual contingents, Shah Jahan fixed the ratios at less than one. Officers serving in the same province in which they held their jagirs were to muster fully equipped horsemen at one-third of their rank; those serving outside the province in which their jagirs were located were to muster one-fourth the rank; and those sent on distant campaigns, such as to Balkh, were to muster one-fifth.[34] These measures do not imply any weakening of the Mughal military in an absolute sense. Lahori's total of 200,000 armed horsemen for the empire is considerably more than the 147,000 plus cavalrymen

[33] M. Athar Ali, *The Mughal Nobility under Aurangzeb* (Aligarh, 1966), pp. 46–48.
[34] Lahori, *Padshah Nama*, II, 506–507.

supported by Akbar in 1595–6.[35] His figure for the mansabdari contingents relied on the one-fourth formula to arrive at its total.

Shah Jahan's military concerns did not extend to weaponry. Unlike Akbar, who took an intense interest in muskets and cannon, none of his successors paid much attention to technical improvements in firearms. Improved flintlock muskets were very slow to penetrate the Indian military market. Sebastian Manrique, the Franciscan Friar who travelled through India in Shah Jahan's reign, comments that "most of the Mogol militia use bows and arrows. Those who carry fire-arms in their army are matchlock men and people of no rank, known as tufangis. They carry arquebuses, which being poorly made, are, as it were, awkward arms."[36] The emperor and his commanders seem to have been content to employ musketeers recruited from those men readily available in the military labor pool. To a certain extent bowmen were still favored by the Mughals as past of their Central Asian tradition. In any event we notice no thrust toward better weapons or more effective deployment of musketeers.

Artillery was another difficult area. Since Babur first employed field guns at Panipat in 1526, obvious technical progress had occurred. By the time of Shah Jahan the Mughals boasted heavy guns firing balls of sixty to 120 pounds; lighter-weight field guns firing balls of eight to twelve pounds weight; and swivel guns mounted on camels firing a three to five ounce ball.[37] But progress was slow as the Persian and Central Asian campaigns revealed. When stung into action by superior Safavid gunnery, Shah Jahan succeeded in having formidable siege guns cast and transported to Qandahar fort.

Neither the emperor nor his nobles fostered research and development in the science of ordnance. Gunfounding was the province of immigrant Europeans or Ottoman Turks who were largely left to their own devices. Indian techniques for cast-iron were generally backward.[38] The Mughals also relinquished gun-laying skills to a motley cadre of highly paid European and Turkish artillerymen. Some were

[35] Moosvi, *Economy of the Mughal Empire*, lists 1,823 mansabdars in all ranks from ten to 10,000, p. 204; 4,441 gentlemen troopers and 141,053 horsemen mustered by mansabdars, Appendix 12-A, p. 296.

[36] Sebastian Manrique, *Travels of Fray Sebastian Manrique 1629–1643* (Cambridge: Hakluyt Society, 2nd. series, No. 51, 1927), II, 125.

[37] Manucci, *Storia do Mogor or Mogul India* (Calcutta, 4 vols., 1907–8), translated by William Irvine, I, 265–66 and 316.

[38] Tapan Raychaudhuri and Irfan Habib, eds., *The Cambridge Economic History of India* (Cambridge: Cambridge University Press, 1982), I, 293.

well qualified; some were certainly not. No systematic efforts were made to train Indian gunners.

CHANGES IN THE MUGHAL NOBILITY

Lahori closed his history with a listing of the notables of the empire. He mentions a handful of Muslim shaikhs, ulema, physicians, and poets, and avoids any reference to non-Muslims. His primary concern however, is to identify those amirs and mansabdars bearing ranks of 500 zat and above who served Shah Jahan. Since this is one of the very few extant systematic lists of the Mughal nobility, considerable modern scholarly effort has been put into its analysis.

In 1647–8 Lahori named a total of 578 men of whom 133 were deceased and 445 officers were still on active service. He listed each officer by strict numerical rank order to reflect precedence at court and in the esteem of the emperor. Zat rank was usually assigned in increments of 1,000 at the highest level; increments of 500 below 3,000; and by units of 100 below 1,000 zat. Lahori supplies the second suwar or trooper rank, which could not exceed the zat rank, and, if granted, additional "two-horse, three-horse" ranking. The latter conferred greater pay and troop responsibilities on the recipient.

From this list, and other compilations of data on the nobility, it is certain that the corps of mansabdars increased steadily in number and in resources as the empire expanded. Even after adjusting for inflation in rankings, the imperial cadre had nearly doubled from 283 officers at the end of Akbar's reign to 445 in 1647.[39] What had not changed is the extraordinary concentration of power, military command, and wealth in this small contingent of officers. The inner circle of the princes and the great amirs ranked at 2,500 zat and above, some seventy-three men, were truly the fulcrum of empire.

The list begins with the four princes, the sons of Shah Jahan. Dara Shikoh, the eldest son and heir apparent, held the highest rank in the empire at 20,000 zat, 20,000 suwar, 15,000 two–three horse. Shah Shuja, Aurangzeb and Murad Bakhsh are listed in descending order by age and rank. As the accompanying table shows, the four Timurid princes together were entitled to 724 million dams or 8.2 per cent of

[39] M. Athar Ali, *The Apparatus of Empire: Awards of Ranks, Offices and Titles to the Mughal Nobility (1574–1658)* (Delhi: Oxford University Press, 1985), xx.

the current assessed imperial revenues in personal and trooper pay.[40] They mustered 28,000 cavalry troopers with horses and equipment up to official standards – calculated at one-fourth their trooper rank. In general the princes were assigned only the most productive "twelve-month" jagirs in which tax collections approximated assessments every year.

Table 2 *The imperial elite: nobles 2,500 zat and above*[41]

Dams	Zat	(No.)	Suwar	Two–three horse	Troopers ¼ rule
(Millions)					
724	Princes	4	42,000	35,000	28,000
400	7,000	4	21,000	15,000	12,700
88	6,000	2	8,000		2,000
929.7	5,000	15	74,000	23,500	30,250
336.8	4,000	10	29,400		7,350
743.4	3,000	33	66,500	4,500	18,875
87.2	2,500	5	8,500	2,000	3,128
Totals:					
3309.1		73	249,400	80,000	102,303

The four highest ranking nobles in the empire, by comparison, were Ali Mardan Khan, Zafar Jang, Islam Khan, and Sa'adullah Khan who each held 7,000 zat, and 7,000 suwar. All save Sa'adullah Khan held 5,000 two–three horse rank. All were Muslim: two were Iranian in origin, one Turani (of Central Asian descent); and one Indian Muslim. Together they were entitled to 400 million dams or 4.5 percent of the total imperial revenues and mustered 12,700 cavalry troopers.

The seventy-three members of the inner elite received and disbursed 3,309.1 million dams or a staggering 37.6 percent of the entire assessed annual revenues for the empire. They mustered (by the one-fourth rule) 102,303 horsemen for military service. Pay for their personal rank

[40] A. Jan Qaisar, "Distribution of the Revenue Resources of the Mughal Empire Among the Nobility" in *Proceedings, Indian Historical Records Commission*, 1965, 27th session, pp. 237–243.

[41] Calculated from Lahori's listing. An English version of the list is compiled in Athar Ali, *Apparatus*, pp. 212–226.

alone was 643.5 dams or 7.3 percent of total jama`. From these funds and any surplus squeezed from the employment of their mounted contingents, these grandees supported numerous wives, concubines, and slaves; servants, craftsmen; administrators; and musicians, poets, and holy men. They gave lavishly to good works; built on a grand scale and made the requisite gifts to the emperor. Each of these noblemen headed a cluster of other, lesser mansabdars.[42] Often these were sons, nephews, uncles, and other kinsmen who themselves held relatively high rank but who were generally affiliated with and served with their kinsman. Other, non-kin, patron–client ties bound the greater nobles with lesser men.

Table 3 *Mansabdars above 500 zat, 1647–48*[43]

Category	Number	Percentage
Muslims		
Princes	4	.9
Iranis	126	28.4
Turanis	103	23.3
Afghans	26	5.9
Indian Muslims	65	14.7
Other Muslims	29	6.6
Total	353	79.8
Hindus		
Rajputs	73	16.5
Marathas	10	2.3
Other Hindus	7	1.6
Total	90	20.3
Total	443	100.0

Muslim officers constituted four-fifths of the higher mansabdars (see Table 3); Hindus were only one-fifth in number. Muslim nobles of Persian and Central Asian origins (Turanis) continued to predominate

[42] See J. F. Richards, "Norms of Comportment among Imperial Mughal Officers" in Barbara Daly Metcalf, ed., *Moral Conduct and Authority* (Berkeley and Los Angeles: University of California Press, 1984), pp. 260–261 for a later illustration of such clustering in Aurangzeb's reign.

[43] Calculated from Lahori, *Padshah Nama*, II, 715–752.

in numbers and power at all levels of the officer corps. Just over half belonged to these two groupings. (See Table 3). Nevertheless, membership in this elite became more heterogeneous as the Timurids incorporated more indigenous regional aristocracies. This trend had the effect of tying the regime to local society as expansion occurred. Distrusted and sharply limited in number and power for their role in the great struggle for northern India under Akbar and Jahangir, more Afghan officers obtained higher ranks under Shah Jahan. Twenty-six Afghan nobles, just over 5 percent of the total, were listed. These men had direct ties to colonies of Afghan zamindar groups who controlled strategic parganas across northern India from Kabul to Dacca and even more important links with Afghan tribes in the northwest mountain passages.

The two counter-balancing groups originally added by Akbar sustained their positions. Sixty-five indigenous or Indian Muslim officers, including the Sayyids of Baraha, formed just under 15 percent of the total. They too, had close connections with Muslim zamindars in north India.

Seventy-three Rajput officers were slightly more numerous. The highest ranking Rajputs held ranks of 5,000 zat and 5,000 suwar, in the third tier of great nobles below the princes and six nobles of 7,000 and 6,000 rank. They were the heads of the largest Rajput kingdoms: Jaswant Singh, the Rathor Raja of Marwar; Jai Singh the Kachhwaha Raja of Amber; Rana Jagat Singh, the Sisodia Rana of Mewar; and Bethal Das, the Raja of Gaur. Another five Rajputs, including the heads of the Bundela and Hada clans, were included in the great amirs of 2,500 and above. Generally, at this level when the emperor approved succession to the raja's seat, confirmation of rank was automatic. A large portion of jagirs assigned the Rajput heads were given in watan jagir within their own kingdoms. Higher status Rajput officers tended to serve in military roles as field commanders or in quasi-military roles as faujdars. Virtually no Rajputs served as provincial governors, for example. Nor were they employable in administrative posts demanding technical non-military skills.

Less powerful Rajputs either served directly with their master and kinsman or held imperial rank but remained part of the cluster attached to their raja. Combined suwar and two–three horse ranks for the Rajputs in this year puts their required contingents at about 23,500 men from the total mansabdar contingents.[44]

[44] Calculated from Athar Ali, *Apparatus*, pp. 212–226.

The most significant additions were a product of southward expansion. Two groups of officers carried the epithet "Deccani" at the end of their titles. A handful of Muslim nobles formerly in service to one of the Deccan Sultans was now enrolled in the Mughal nobility. Eight men bearing ranks from 4,000 to 1,500 zat were readily merged into the various groups of Muslim nobles.

Ten Maratha officers, ranked from 1,500 to 5,000 zat made the same transition to imperial service. The most successful was Maluji Bhonsla Deccani, who held the rank of 5,000/5,000; his brother Parsuji was ranked at 3,000/2,000. Formerly a high officer in the Ahmadnagar Sultanate, Maluji Bhonsla enlisted in Timurid service along with his two brothers early in Shah Jahan's regime.[45] When Maluji's eldest brother returned to fight the Mughals under Sultan Adil Shah of Bijapur, Maluji and Parsuji were rewarded for remaining loyal. They served actively with their contingents in the siege of Daulatabad fort, the conquest of Baglana, and other campaigns in the Deccan. None obtained major administrative assignments, but were kept in the field. The brothers "always behaved prudently and cleverly and pleased all the governors of the Deccan. Maluji was possessed of some urbanity and gentleness, and ... he was faithful in his friendships." Parsuji was noted for his fondness for Mughal customs in his life style.

Unlike the Rajputs, subordinates and kinsmen of these ten commanders were not favored with direct mansab rank. As a result the Marathas, who remained in private service to their commanders, were more segregated and less fully incorporated into Timurid service than their Rajput peers. Restricted deployment in the Deccan further suggests limited acceptance by the emperor.

Nevertheless, Marathas were a totally new Hindu and zamindar element in the nobility. Even at the end of Akbar's reign no Maratha aristocrats had been accepted into imperial service and only one in Jahangir's reign. Such assimilation was a vital step in creating linkages with local society in the Deccan. This was especially critical in a region where Muslims formed only a tiny minority of the total population.

In the Deccan, unlike North India, the Mughals did not find indigenous Muslim warriors controlling peasants on the land. Throughout the western Deccan tracts, formerly belonging to Ahmadnagar, Mughal officers were struggling to restore stable, contractual relationships with the Maratha intermediaries, the deshmukhs who

[45] Shah Nawaz Khan, *Maathir-ul-Umara*, II, 42–5, translation; text III, 520–24.

controlled the revenues and local power in each subdistrict. If, like the Deccan Sultans, the Timurids could recruit and employ representatives of the Maratha zamindars at the higher reaches of imperial administration, the task of restoring centralized state power in the region would be substantially eased.

"SONS OF THE EMPEROR'S HOUSEHOLD"

The changing composition of the Mughal nobility coincided with changes in the Timurid court culture and the ethos of the nobility. The relationship of the ruler to his elite became less fervent, and more formal – expressed more in the idiom of quasi-kinship than of discipleship. In an early decree immediately after his enthronement, Shah Jahan abolished the extreme prostration (sijdah) for presentation in formal court audiences favored by Akbar and Jahangir. Most pious Muslims thought the sijdah sacrilegious – such extreme submission should be made by the believer only to God Himself. By ending this practice Shah Jahan placated orthodox sentiment and served notice that discipleship with its pledges of fealty and symbols of membership was ended as well.

Jahangir often employed the term *khanazadgi* meaning devoted, familial, hereditary service in his memoirs. Rajputs, Turanis, Iranis, Indian Muslims, and even some Afghan amirs who termed themselves *khanazads* ("born to the house") formed a large component of the nobility, if not quite a majority. All viewed Mughal service and preference within that service as their prerogative. Khanazadgi retained the central values of discipleship: loyalty, devotion, and sacrifice in the emperor's service, but lacked its intensely emotional aspect. From boyhood each khanazad was imbued with a code of aristocratic and military honor. The honor of the warrior was compatible with dignified subordination to the emperor. Buttressing this ethos was the dynastic ideology of the Timurids which still continued to shape and influence the sacreal qualities ascribed to the Mughal emperor.[46]

Khanazads were fully assimilated to the polish and sophistication of Indo-Persian courtly culture in its elaborate Mughal version. The ideal khanazad was dignified, courteous, and well-mannered. He understood the intricate rules for comportment in all social encounters – from the most informal gathering of friends engaged in drinking wine

46 See Richards, "Norms of Comportment among Imperial Mughal Officers".

to the most rigid of grand public ceremonies at court. He valued and often quoted Persian and perhaps Hindustani or Turki poetry, and appreciated Hindustani music, painting, and the other arts nurtured at court.

Punctuating the life and career of each khanazad were moments of personal attention by the emperor. On more formal occasions he received praise, new titles, honors, and promotion in rank in open court. On other occasions worthy officers were favored with intimate meetings in the monarch's less-public audience chambers. Rebukes and punishment were also possible and frequently occurred. But Shah Jahan and his successors were relatively mild and humane in their treatment of their officers. Mughal grandees were not subject to the gratuitous cruelties inflicted by the Safavid rulers. Attendance at court, certainly stressful, was not a daily exposure to physical danger. Attenuated and changed, nevertheless, an emotional bond did persist between emperor and imperial servant.

Cognizant of its value, the emperor nurtured and rewarded khanazadgi. Nobles, on the birth of a son, sent a gift to the emperor with a request that he name the child. The emperor was informed of and gave his approval for the marriage of the children of his nobles. At maturity all sons of an amir were enrolled as mansabdars in the emperor's service. They did not obtain their father's rank and titles, or indeed more than a portion of his estate, but they were marked for promotion and rapid advancement.

Khanazadgi, and the values of hereditary service associated with it, applied to officers serving as diwans or other posts in the fiscal sphere. But skills in finance and bureaucratic management, while necessary, and often rewarded, were certainly seen as lesser attributes compared to those of the commander and soldier. A renowned revenue administrator like Murshid Quli Khan rose only to 3,000/500 at the height of his career. Provincial diwans routinely held lower ranks than did provincial governors or even some city prefects or faujdars. Nevertheless the ethos of service did extend to subordinate officials.

The memoir of Bhimsen Saxena, a Hindu mansabdar from the Kayasth caste, reveals the degree to which the ideal of khanazadgi had permeated the ranks of the technical officers employed in the various administrative posts of the empire. For Bhimsen the Mughal emperor was "the true servant of God and his agent" who tries "to foster peace and prosperity." The "fruits of the empire" were human happiness and well-being. Bhimsen, whose family had an extensive tradition of administrative service to the empire, portrays himself as a khanazad. He saw himself as an indispensable part of the imperial structure without whose humble, but necessary, services the system could not function.

The notion of hereditary familial service combined with assimilation to the Mughal aristocratic life style offered wider application to men of higher and lower ranks and statuses. Khanazadgi, in contrast to discipleship, evoked loyalty and obedience but did not exact expressions of dramatic personal loyalty to a charismatic master. In some ways reversion to hereditary familial service was a reaction to success. Shah Jahan, unlike Akbar, did not have to induce extraordinary effort and unflinching devotion from his nobles. He did expect routine display of courage in battle, the stock in trade of professional soldiers. But success in the nobility also demanded personal affability, attention to ritual and decorum, and those political and organizational skills necessary for grandees everywhere. Those Hindu nobles and commanders willing to adapt to these requirements could gain acceptance.

By mid-century the Mughal empire was expansive, invincible, and wealthy on a scale scarcely dreamed of by the Sultans of Delhi. Shahjahanabad was a fitting new capital for a great empire. Imperial symbolism and ideology was slowly returning to Islamic orthodoxy. By the end of Shah Jahan's reign, however the empire was moving towards its greatest political crisis.

CHAPTER 7

THE WAR OF SUCCESSION

During the last half of Shah Jahan's reign a long-standing political and intellectual conflict in the Mughal empire polarized around the two most able and forceful Mughal princes. The liberal party found an articulate and influential spokesman in the eldest son of Shah Jahan. Prince Dara Shukoh attracted those nobles, imperial officers, scholars, intellectuals, and others who remained committed to Akbar's eclectic ideology and policies. The conservative party found its champion in Shah Jahan's third son. Aurangzeb drew to him Muslim nobles, officers, theologians, official ulema who wished to shift the empire toward a more properly Muslim state in conformity with the Sharia. The latter drew their confidence from an increasingly visible revivalist movement within Indian Islam. By the 1640s and 1650s other major policy issues such as the question of Deccan conquest and Mughal relations with Bijapur and Golconda were drawn into this rivalry.

The two princes emerged as spokesmen in part because of their high rank, status, and patronage they disposed. In reality, however, Dara Shukoh and Aurangzeb were important because of the future. One of Shah Jahan's four sons, all mature men, would win the inevitable struggle for succession and Dara and Aurangzeb were the most likely candidates to prevail. Murad and Shuja, the other two brothers, while competent administrators and generals, were generally seen as weaker candidates for the throne. Neither had adopted such pronounced ideological positions as did Dara or Aurangzeb.

Dara Shukoh remained at court in close personal contact with the emperor. As the favorite and heir-apparent, he greatly influenced the emperor. His greatest ally was his eldest sister the princess Jahan Ara, who served as mistress of the royal household after the death of her mother, Mumtaz Mahal.

In his intellectual curiosity, his open-mindedness, and his mystical interests Dara was in many ways a throwback to his great-grandfather, Akbar. He was an active disciple of Mulla Mir (d. 1635) and Mulla Shah Badakshi (d. 1661) two leading Shaikhs of the Qadiri order of Sufis.[1] In the earliest phase of his mystical studies the prince compiled a hagiography of Sufi saints and a recounting of orthodox mystical beliefs.

Beginning in 1641 the maturing scholar, following the Koranic injunction that no land has been left without prophetic guidance, became convinced that the Vedas and the Upanishads constitute the concealed scripture mentioned in the Koran. He regarded the Upanishads as the ultimate source of all monotheism, including Islam. With the aid of Brahmin scholars in his employ, Dara translated the fifty-two Upanishads into Persian in a work titled *Sirr-i Akbar*. In a subsequent Persian work titled *Majma al-bahrayn* "The Mingling of the Two Oceans," the scholar-prince argued that the essential nature of Hinduism was identical to that of Islam. Using techniques of lexical similarity Dara posited that the cosmologies and mystical practices of Muslim Sufis and those of the Upanishads correspond. For example, *ruh* or "soul" in Islam is equivalent to *atman* in Vedantic Hinduism. The Sufi concept of love is the same as the Hindu notion of *maya* or illusion. Dara had "The Mingling of the Two Oceans" translated into Sanskrit under the title *Samudra Sangam* to make it accessible to Hindu scholars.

The prince only succeeded in persuading most Indian Muslims that he was an apostate who cavalierly ignored the obligatory prayers and other rituals of Islam. Extended discussions with and patronage of three Jesuit priests who formed part of his household confirmed this impression. Conversations with the Hindu Bhakti saint Babalal Vairagi had a similar effect. Although it is likely that Dara remained a convinced monotheist, the appearance of apostasy left him politically vulnerable to attack by the ulema.

Despite his intellectual gifts, Dara Shukoh was a mediocre general and an insensitive leader who failed to strike the right air of authority and sympathy with nobles. The most powerful amirs of the realm were reportedly insulted by his excessive pride and haughtiness.[2]

Aurangzeb, Shah Jahan's third son with Mumtaz Mahal, was of an

1 The following discussion of Dara Shukoh is drawn from Aziz Ahmad, "Dara Shikoh and Aurangzeb" an essay appearing in Aziz Ahmad, *Studies in Islamic Culture in the Indian Environment* (Oxford: Clarendon Press, 1964), pp. 191–200.

2 N. Manucci, *Storia do Mogor or Mogul India* (Calcutta, 4 vols., 1907–8), translated by William Irvine; 1, 221–226 for an account of Dara's flaws and the enemies he made.

entirely different personality. Niccolao Manucci's eyewitness description is apt:[3]

> This prince was very different from the others, being in character very secretive and serious, carrying on his affairs in a hidden way, but most energetically. He was of a melancholy temperament, always busy at something or another, wishing to execute justice and arrive at appropriate decisions. He was extremely anxious to be recognized by the world as a man of wisdom, clever and a lover of the truth. He was moderately liberal, distributing rewards and conferring gifts wherever suitable. But above all, for a long time he pretended to be a faquir (*faqir*), a holy mendicant, by which he renounced the world, gave up all claim to the crown, and was content to pass his life in prayers and mortifications.

Aurangzeb obviously was a man of extreme piety, who punctiliously observed the public rituals of Islam. He did not drink wine or take opium. Engaged in his own spiritual quest, Aurangzeb held long discussions with members of the ulema or shaikhs from the orthodox Naqshbandi order. He avidly read the Koran, treatises on the law, and the works of Al-Ghazzali and other prominent Islamic scholars. But Aurangzeb's piety, as suggested by Manucci, did not interfere with his worldly ambition or continual maneuvering in the high politics of empire.

An experienced military commander and administrator, Aurangzeb served as governor of the Mughal Deccan for eight years; as governor of Gujarat for three years, and then as commander of Mughal armies in the invasion of Balkh and the first two sieges of Qandahar fort. Despite his devoted and able performance in these offices, Aurangzeb's relationship with his father was acrimonious and distant. Shah Jahan, encouraged by Dara Shukoh and Jahan Ara, rebuked his least favourite son frequently, and often unfairly, for a variety of shortcomings. Aurangzeb's principal ally in the imperial household was his elder sister Raushan Ara Begam, the fourth child of Mumntaz Mahal. She sent him a constant flow of information about the emperor and court politics.

In 1652, after the third Qandahar campaign ended ignominiously under Dara's command, Shah Jahan assigned Aurangzeb to administer the Deccan provinces once more. For the next five years polarized tensions in the empire centered on the political struggle between Dara at court and Aurangzeb in the Deccan.

[3] Manucci, *Storia*, I, 229.

CONFLICT OVER THE DECCAN

Shah Jahan sent Aurangzeb to the south enjoined to reform and restore an effective imperial administration. Since Aurangzeb's departure in 1644, a succession of ineffective governors, corrupt officials, destructive military campaigns, and poor agricultural seasons had reduced the productive capacity of the region. Many villages were deserted and areas formerly cultivated were now forested. Every year a shortfall in imperial revenues forced Shah Jahan to send a subsidy to meet the expenses of the Deccan military and administrative establishment.

Under Aurangzeb's capable direction the famed revenue officer Murshid Quli Khan restored order and predictability to the imperial agrarian system (see above). To stimulate cultivation Murshid Quli Khan advanced large loans in Khandesh and Berar for peasants to repair and expand riverine irrigation. In all four provinces he induced energetic men to become headmen and settle abandoned villages by making various tax concessions.[4]

Imperial revenues began to increase, but not enough to compensate for the deficit. Aurangzeb and Shah Jahan wrangled continually over Aurangzeb's request for additional funds to be transferred from Malwa and Gujarat. In an increasingly acrimonious correspondence, Aurangzeb claimed the 800,000 rupee annual tribute from Golconda as well. Caught in his budgetary difficulties Aurangzeb pressed his father for permission to invade and annex the Sultanate of Golconda. Golconda was renowned in the seventeenth century world for its wealth and especially for its rich diamond mines. Shah Jahan, who still bore friendly feelings toward Abdullah Qutb Shah for refuge taken during his own revolt as a prince, ruled out invasion. Undeterred, however, Aurangzeb began a secret exchange of letters with Muhammad Said, Mir Jumla, the Qutb Shahi conqueror of the Karnatak. This initiative brought together two of the most remarkable figures of the seventeenth century.

MUHAMMAD SAID, MIR JUMLA

The tributary status imposed on Bijapur and Golconda in 1636 stabilized the northern frontier of those states and brought a respite from Mughal invasion. A fixed policy aim of the Adil Shahi and Qutb

[4] Jadunath Sarkar, *History of Aurangzib* (Calcutta, 5 vols., 1912–1924), I, 187–194.

Shahi rulers was to prevent by persuasion or bribery an aggressive Mughal forward policy in the Deccan. Their northern frontiers secured by treaty, each ruler was free to expand to the south.

In the southeastern plain and upland area called the Karnatak, political power was fragmented among a number of Telugu and Tamil *nayaks* who were the descendants of the great warrior nobles of Vijayanagara. Bijapur armies under Shahji Bhonsla, now in Adil Shahi service, and other Afghan and Maratha generals forcibly annexed lands from the Palar river, sixty miles south of Madras, to the Kaveri river in the Chola heartland. The latter became a province known as the Bijapur Karnatak. These conquests extended the frontier of Muslim power five hundred kilometers toward the tip of the subcontinent.

In the 1640s large armies from Golconda battered down local resistance and conquered the Karnatak between the Krishna river in the north and the Palar river. This rich, fertile area, also known as the Coromandel coast, was the center of a burgeoning textile industry. Thousands of weavers, dyers, and other craftsmen produced millions of yards of cloth for growing overseas markets.

The architect of this triumph was Muhammad Said, a man of extraordinary talents. Born the son of an oil merchant in Iran, the young Muhammad Said migrated to Golconda in the employ of an Iranian trader. Soon the young entrepreneur obtained a lucrative diamond mining concession at the famed Golconda mines and rapidly became a prominent member of the group of Persian traders and shipowners in Golconda. Domiciled in either Hyderabad or the chief port, Machhilipatnam, these men were closely linked with their fellow Persians in the ruling elite of Golconda and held a commanding position in the kingdom's maritime trade.[5]

By 1634 Muhammad Said, who is credited with unusual organizational skills and personal appeal, had opted for the larger prizes associated with official power in Golconda. Under what has been called a system of "political capitalism" Muslim officials in Golconda at all levels were heavily involved in commerce and shipowning.[6] They used political power to improve their commercial interests by a variety of monopoly devices. Within a short time, Muhammad Said became governor of the port of Machhilipatnam and other coastal territories.

[5] Jagdish Narayan Sarkar, *The Life of Mir Jumla* (Delhi: Rajesh Publications, 2nd. revised edition, 1979), pp. 4–5.

[6] Sinnappah Arasaratnam, *Merchants, Companies, and Commerce on the Coromandel Coast 1650–1740* (Delhi: Oxford University Press, 1986), pp. 225–225.

Retaining these offices under his agents, in 1638 he rose to chief minister of the kingdom and received the title of Mir Jumla.

In his handling of the Karnatak invasion in the early 1640s Mir Jumla proved to be a talented military strategist and diplomat. For ten years (1642–1652) his armies were engaged against the citadels of decentralized Hindu warriors and their troops. His formidable cavalry, infantry and artillery stormed even the most forbidding fortresses of the Hindu nayaks.

By 1652, Mir Jumla governed for Golconda the Hyderabad Karnatak – a kingdom nearly 40,000 square kilometers with annual revenues equivalent to four million rupees a year. His military role added greatly to his wealth. Plunder from looted Hindu temples and diamonds from the newly conquered alluvial diamond workings at Kullur (the richest in the world at the time) swelled his trading capital.[7] Although he sent regular revenue payments north to Hyderabad a large share of the profits from the Golconda style tax farming system remained with him. The agents of Mir Jumla's growing commercial empire were found throughout the markets of the Mughal empire, in Persia, Mocha, Burma, Arakan, and Pegu. In addition to large herds of pack animals employed in the overland trade, Mir Jumla kept at least ten merchant vessels in commission plying between ports in the Bay of Bengal and in the Red Sea.

Perhaps not surprisingly, Mir Jumla ran afoul of his royal master, Abdullah Qutb Shah. Escaping an assassination plot by the Qutb Shah king, Mir Jumla turned to Bijapur and the Mughal empire to negotiate a position for himself and his newly founded domains in another state system.

AURANGZEB AND MIR JUMLA

Always alert to opportunity Aurangzeb opened a correspondence with Mir Jumla. The Deccan governor proposed to Mir Jumla that he hand over the Hyderabad Karnatak to Mughal rule and then attack Golconda from the south while Aurangzeb's armies invaded from the northwest. Mir Jumla accepted Aurangzeb's offer and became a collaborator in a plan to invade Golconda.

When in November, 1655, Abdullah Qutb Shah lost patience with Muhammad Amin, Mir Jumla's boorish son, his envoy at the Gol-

[7] Sarkar, *Mir Jumla*, p. 77.

conda court, and placed him in confinenent; this provided the pretext Aurangzeb needed to move Shah Jahan to action. The emperor enrolled Mir Jumla and his son as high-ranking Mughal amirs and ordered Abdullah Qutb Shah to release Muhammad Amin. Before the Golconda ruler received Shah Jahan's order, however, Aurangzeb had already sent an invading army into Golconda. The Mughal army easily occupied Hyderabad city while the Qutb Shah ruler and his court took refuge in Golconda fort where they were besieged by the Mughal army. Within two months Mir Jumla and his force arrived from the Karnatak to join Aurangzeb,

In the interim, Dara Shukoh and Jahan Ara had been approached at the Delhi court by agents of Abdullah Qutb Shah. The heir-apparent intervened and persuaded Shah Jahan to force Aurangzeb to withdraw. The Qutb Shah ruler would be forced to pay a large war indemnity, lose some border territory and give up a daughter for marriage to Muhammad Sultan, Aurangzeb's son. A peremptory order from the emperor left Aurangzeb, despite his protests, to withdraw.

By mid-year Mir Jumla had brought his entire establishment north to the imperial court at Shahjahanabad. At the unexpected death of the Mughal wazir, Shah Jahan conferred that office upon the newcomer with a one thousand zat increase in rank. Shah Jahan also agreed to treat the entire Hyderabad Karnatak as the jagir of his new minister and to send imperial officers to seize it from Golconda. For the first time Aurangzeb was favored with a powerful friend and advocate who rapidly obtained great influence over Shah Jahan. With this advocate Aurangzeb's policy of imperial aggression won the emperor's approval.

In November, 1656, Muhammad Adil Shah, who had been ill for a decade, died. His eighteen-year-old son, Ali Adil Shah II, faced a factious nobility and rebellious zamindars. Aurangzeb and Mir Jumla had for some time worked up a plan for the invasion of the kingdom as soon as the long-anticipated death of Muhammad Adil Shah occurred. Aurangzeb had been busy in suborning many of the nobles and military commanders in Bijapur service.

Shah Jahan approved an invasion and sent Mir Jumla with troops to assist. In mid-1657, as the Mughal army was poised to take Bijapur, the capital city, Shah Jahan, again urged by Dara Shukoh, ordered Aurangzeb to refrain from a final conquest. Instead he was forced to accept a large war indemnity and cession of the lands occupied to date. The emperor ordered Mir Jumla to return to Delhi. In the midst of Aurangzeb's forced withdrawal, Shah Jahan fell ill in September, 1657. The first act of the great Mughal war of succession had begun.

THE WAR

Shah Jahan's magnificent reign ended in a long-anticipated, convulsive political crisis. When the emperor fell ill, pent-up tensions between the mature Timurid princes exploded into a four-sided war of succession. The war pitted Dara Shukoh, resident at court as the designated heir, against his three younger brothers: Muhammad Shuja, governor of Bengal, Bihar, and Orissa; Aurangzeb, governor of the four Deccan provinces; and Murad Bakhsh, governor of Gujarat and Malwa. All were sons of Mumtaz Mahal and therefore full, rather than half brothers. Despite Shah Jahan's expressed preference for his eldest son, Dara Shukoh, the Timurid appanage system offered no clear precedent for succession.

This was a bloody struggle fought by formidable opponents. Dara, Shuja, Aurangzeb, and Murad battled each other with that intensity and intimacy reserved to brothers with differing personalities. Each prince shared in the Timurid familial charisma and royal authority which gave all an undisputable claim on the throne. Each brother claimed long experience in war, statecraft, and administration and could draw upon the services of extremely able military and administrative staffs. Each commanded a power base, possessed ample treasure and could muster large, well-equipped armies. Only one contender could claim the throne; the others faced the grave.

When Shah Jahan failed to hold daily court audiences the news immediately swept to all parts of the empire. In Delhi the shops remained closed in the bazaars and public anxiety was at a high pitch for several days.[8] Within the palace only Dara, his physicians, his daughter Janan Ara, and a few trusted officers were permitted to see the emperor. Dara quickly assumed command. He seized the agents and spies of his brothers and censored all communications between them and their masters. Shah Jahan's seclusion and Dara's censorship raised speculation that the emperor was either dead or completely helpless. After a month the emperor recovered sufficiently to appear in public.

[8] Manucci, who served Dara Shukoh as a young gunner, gives a full description of the war from the viewpoint of a participant. Manucci, *Storia*, II, 229–386.

Thereafter the depressed and ailing emperor journeyed slowly to Agra to be near his wife's tomb.

In Bengal Prince Muhammad Shuja immediately crowned himself king at Rajmahal and brought his cavalry, artillery, and river flotilla upriver toward Agra. Near Varanasi his forces confronted a defending army sent from Delhi under the command of Prince Sulaiman Shukoh, son of Dara, and Raja Jai Singh. In mid-February, 1658, a well-executed early morning surprise attack routed the Bengal troops. Shuja and his surviving men fled downriver to Monghyr.

To the south, in Gujarat, Murad Bakhsh immediately sent a 6,000 man force to extort a half-million rupee forced loan from the merchants of Surat and to besiege the fort whose commander (appointed independently by the emperor) refused to surrender. Rejecting reports of his father's recovery, on December 5th Murad crowned himself at a public ceremony. In early January Surat fort fell with its treasure and supplies and Murad prepared to march north.

In the Deccan the news reached Aurangzeb just as he was completing peace negotiations with the Sultan of Bijapur after a successful invasion of that kingdom. (see above).[9] Between October and early January of 1658 Aurangzeb tried simultaneously to impose the punitive terms of the peace treaty on Bijapur and to position himself for a run for the throne. In contrast to Shuja and Murad, however, Aurangzeb did not take the irrevocable step of crowning himself. Instead, he engaged in a busy secret correspondence with Murad, and, to a lesser extent, with Shuja. Letters written in cipher encased in bamboo tubes passed from runner to runner over special relay posts newly established between Ahmadabad and Aurangabad. Within a few weeks Aurangzeb and Murad had agreed on a plan for joint action. If they defeated their brothers, Aurangzeb would leave to Murad the Punjab, Afghanistan, Kashmir, and Sind to rule as an independent king and he would rule the remaining territories. Simultaneously, carrying on a wide-ranging correspondence, Aurangzeb induced most of the higher ranking nobles of the Deccan to join him.

In early February 1658, Aurangzeb set his army marching north. He joined forces with Murad at the village of Dharmat on the Ghambira river. Here they met Shah Jahan's army under the command of Jaswant Singh Rathor. In the ensuing battle Aurangzeb's well-

[9] Sarkar, *History of Aurangzib*, II, 278–79.

handled guns and cavalry outfought the imperial army whose survivors fell back on Delhi in disarray.[10]

At Delhi Dara rebuilt a 50,000 man army and awaited his brothers at defensive positions on the Chambal river south of Agra. Aurangzeb outflanked him by finding an unguarded ford. The armies met on a broad plain at the village of Samugarh on the Yamuna near Agra. On 29 May, in the blazing heat of Indian summer, the climactic battle of the succession struggle took place. Aurangzeb's superior tactics and better disciplined artillery and cavalry prevailed against the valor of repeated Rajput cavalry charges. Finally, toward the end of the day, Dara dismounted from his war elephant and fled the field on horseback. A full-scale rout began.

About nine in the evening Dara and a small group of his followers reached his mansion in Agra fort. Unwilling to face his father, he rested a few hours then fled toward Delhi accompanied by his family and a few retainers carrying his treasury.. Aurangzeb occupied Agra city and, when negotiations failed, besieged his father in Agra fort. Deprived of access to water from the river, Shah Jahan surrendered on June 8, 1658 and became his son's prisoner. The vast treasuries and magazines of Agra fort fell into Aurangzeb's hands.

Dara stayed only briefly in Delhi before moving on to Lahore. When Aurangzeb resumed the pursuit, tension between him and Murad grew. Despite warnings, Murad entered his brother's camp for a dinner on 25 June. Here he was disarmed, made captive and quietly sent off to prison along with his son. Aurangzeb enrolled Murad's leaderless soldiery into his service the next day.

Aurangzeb paused in Delhi long enough to crown himself on 21 July in Shalimar gardens with the title of Alamgir or "world-seizer." This action marks the end of the first phase of the war of succession when the outcome was really in doubt. Thereafter Aurangzeb dealt with his brothers from an overwhelmingly strong position.

When Aurangzeb's army crossed the Sutlej river, Dara panicked and fled south down the Indus river with part of Aurangzeb's army in pursuit. At Bhakkar, a river fortification, he abandoned part of his troops, heavy guns, much of a ten-million rupee treasure, and many dependents. Dara fled south with a few retainers to the Arabian Sea where he finally took refuge in Gujarat.

By the end of September Aurangzeb left the tracking of Dara to his

[10] Ibid., pp. 20–25.

officers to meet a new threat: his brother Shuja. Shuja, rejecting Aurangzeb's promises of unthreatened rule in the east, mustered a force of 25,000 cavalry and a flotilla of river boats and marched upriver. In late December Aurangzeb joined his son Muhammad Sultan for battle against Shuja. Despite the last-minute defection of Jaswant Singh Rathor with his Rajput cavalry to Shuja, Aurangzeb's army greatly outnumbered and outgunned the Bengal army. Defeated and routed, Shuja fled with the remnants of his army.

In the interim Dara had regained his courage, acquired funds, recruited a 20,000 man army in Gujarat, and marched north to liberate his father. When he reached Ajmer in Rajasthan the thousands of Rajput warriors promised to his cause by Jaswant Singh Rathor did not appear. Instead, Dara faced a large, well-equipped army commanded by his nemesis, his brother Aurangzeb. In mid-March, 1659, Aurangzeb's army overran Dara's forces in a bloody three-day battle fought in the hills outside Ajmer. Dara survived but fled once again.

On his return to Delhi Aurangzeb felt confident enough to arrange for a properly grand second coronation. On June 5, 1659, at an auspicious time, Aurangzeb sat on the throne in the Hall of Public Audience in the fortress at Shahjahanabad. A reciter read his names and titles as part of the khutba and newly struck coins were distributed. Only the aftermath of the war of succession remained.

Dara, put to flight again, spent the next three months as a wanderer trying to evade capture. From Gujarat, to the Rann of Kutch, to Seistan, to the Bolan Pass, he found little aid or comfort. Finally, he sought assistance from Malik Jiwan, an Afghan chief whose life he had saved from execution in Delhi some years before. His devoted wife, Nadira Banu, a Timurid princess, died of dysentery when they arrived. Dara sent her body off with most of his escort to be interred in Lahore. As soon as he did so, Malik Jiwan arrested Dara and sent word to his pursuers on the Indus.

When Dara Shukoh arrived at Delhi as a prisoner, Aurangzeb first had him paraded in public humiliation through the streets of the city. His appearance and his past generosity aroused much public sympathy. That evening in council Aurangzeb, his sister Raushan Ara, and his advisers, decided on a death sentence. The official ulema condemned Dara to death on grounds of apostasy from Islam and idolatry. On the night of August 30, 1659, two slaves killed Dara and his youngest son Sipihr Shukoh.

There followed a year-and-a-half-long, grim, water-borne campaign in pursuit of Prince Shuja by an imperial army under Mir Jumla. Shuja fought, retreated east and fought until, finally, at Tanda his army was decisively beaten and broken. In early May, 1660, Shuja left Dacca by boat with his family and a few faithful troops to take refuge with the raiding king of Arakan. Here, suspected of a plot against the king, he met his death.

Only Murad Bakhsh remained alive as a captive of Aurangzeb in the state prison at Gwalior fortress. In early 1661 a planned rescue by some of Murad's loyal Mughal officers failed, but he remained a threat. Rather than simply have Murad killed, Aurangzeb arranged a murder accusation. At the start of the war of succession, enraged with the suspicion that the diwan of Gujarat was an adherent of Shah Jahan, Murad had killed his fellow-officer with a spear-thrust. At Aurangzeb's instigation, the diwan's second son demanded justice under the Sharia for his father's death. The qazi of Gwalior fort tried the case and convicted Murad. The son refused to accept payment but asked for retribution. On December 4, 1661, two slaves carried out the execution.

The succession crisis reaffirmed the unity of the empire and the authority of the victorious Timurid monarch. Partition of the empire into two or more appanages did not take place. Division of the empire was a bargaining point, nothing more. The principals knew that whoever acquired the imperial capital and throne would not rest until the partitioned territories – be they in the east or west or south – were recovered. Ultimately the prize was access to a throne ruling a single, unitary empire.

Throughout Mughal India the succession struggle was high public drama. Movements of armies, alliances, battles, and skirmishes, the emperor's health, flights, and in the end, executions – all were of the most intense interest. Rumor and gossip darted across the bazaars of every town and city. Intelligence networks maintained by sarrafs, merchants, Sufi orders, and Hindu maths strained to obtain and transmit timely news. Relays of messengers on foot and horse traversed the roads of the empire. European traders collated and sent back reports to Europe on the crisis. Events thus shared suggest the degree to which the empire had become linked into a unified social system.

The 1658–59 war stretched the resources of a militarized state and society. The crisis disgorged a sizable portion of the great hoarded wealth of the empire found in the provincial and central treasuries and the personal holdings of nobles and officials. Spending on military needs soared as commanders on each side enlisted additional soldiery and bought supplies and munitions. Temporarily, at least, the civil war reversed the flow of revenues and accumulation of reserves. The normal flow of tax collections to the imperial center or to the designated jagir holders virtually dried up in the course of the war.

There were no noticeable or widespread uprisings by zamindars or peasants. Most of the countryside waited and watched for the outcome of events. Aurangzeb's early victories seem to have discouraged direct challenges to the regime. However, local revenue administration functioned but feebly for the duration of the conflict. The revenues of jagirdars and the imperial khalisa dried to a trickle. Agricultural production faltered as well when campaigning armies marched through the countryside. Unfortunately the ravages and dislocation of war were exacerbated by several years of scanty monsoon rains beginning in 1658. Throughout north and central India a general scarcity, amounting to famine conditions in many places, accompanied the political crisis. At Delhi, Agra, and Lahore drought-stricken peasants from the surrounding countryside descended on each city. The emperor and the amirs opened free kitchens to dispense cooked food in each city. Scarcity and the vast influx of dishoarded funds pressed prices to famine levels in the cities.[11]

Timurid royal blood and ample funds were sufficient to recruit equipped, trained soldiers and obtain arms, animals, and military supplies in any part of the subcontinent. When in early 1659, Dara Shukoh arrived at Ahmadabad in Gujarat after his flight from Samugarh, his sympathizer, Shah Nawaz Khan, gave him one million rupees from Murad's treasury. With these funds Dara recruited some 20,000 cavalry and obtained forty artillery pieces within a month's time.[12] Everywhere soldiers and suppliers were fully employed.

By and large allegiances in this war were not determined by broader issues, but by pragmatism or personal loyalties. For the nobles and higher ranking mansabdars allegiance was often determined by the

[11] Shireen Mosvi, "Scarcities, Prices and Exploitation: The Agrarian Crisis, 1658–1670," *Studies in History* 1 (1985), 46–47.
[12] Sarkar, *History of Aurungzib*, II, 164–65.

vicissitudes of imperial posting. The degree of enthusiasm displayed by each noble might be determined by the personal appeal of the prince in question. For officers and men in private employment allegiance was determined by loyalty to one's salt or by lineage or clan loyalties to one's commanders. For those thousands of men in the floating pool of military manpower allegiance was a matter of payment and performance an amalgam of professional pride and the circumstance of battle and campaign.

The succession conflict did bring into the open serious political and religious divisions. At every opportunity Aurangzeb proclaimed his horror at Dara's apostacy from Islam and his idolatry. When Aurangzeb and Murad agreed to act jointly to divide the empire, the public, written statement affirmed that the proposed campaign was not simply a matter of personal power. Instead they had a more lofty aim: "to uproot the bramble of idolatry and infidelity from the realm of Islam and to overwhelm and crush the idolatrous chief [Dara] with his followers and strongholds."[13]

It is doubtful whether Aurangzeb's religious appeal swayed Muslim nobles to support him or caused Hindu nobles to turn against him. What we can assert, however, is that it did make a difference to the empire and its inhabitants which of the four contenders triumphed. Had Shuja or Murad won it is likely that they would have followed Shah Jahan's policies with few dramatic changes. Had Dara won, it is likely that a broader political appeal would have marked his reign. Whether he could have sustained this program in the face of a more conservative climate in both the Muslim and Hindu communities is another question that cannot be answered. Instead, Aurangzeb imposed a narrow, Islamic character on to the political culture of the empire. It was Aurangzeb's insistence on Islamic exclusivity that shaped imperial policy over the next half century.

[13] Sarkar, *History of Aurangzib*, I, 335–337.

CHAPTER 8

IMPERIAL EXPANSION UNDER AURANGZEB 1658–1689

Aurangzeb remained a remarkably vigorous ruler for a half century (1658–1707) before he died at age ninety. During the first twenty years of his reign the emperor kept his capital at Shahjahanabad Delhi. In the next decade the grand encampment became the movable capital of the empire as the emperor campaigned actively in Rajasthan and the Deccan. Throughout the first thirty years of his reign Aurangzeb, who had added "Alamgir" or "world-seizer" to his titles, dedicated himself to fostering a more properly Islamic regime and to aggressive expansion on the empire's frontiers. However, several unrewarding campaigns in the 1660s and 1670s beyond the mountain rim of the subcontinent graphically revealed the harsh costs to further expansion in the north. These campaigns reinforced the emperor's pronounced inclination to move south – to conquer lands long accustomed to Islamic rule.

TESTING THE LIMITS OF EMPIRE: NORTHEAST

To the northeast, Bengal's growing export economy and Muslim settler frontier seemed a likely area for aggressive campaigning. Imperial authority still rested lightly in this region. When Prince Shuja's governorship of Bengal was interrupted by the succession war, zamindars like Prem Narayan, the ruler of Kuch Bihar, rebelled. Simultaneously, Jayadhwaj Sinha, the Ahom king, sent an army to invade and annex Kamrup, the Mughal border district on the Brahmaputra river.[1]

In mid 1660, Aurangzeb, determined to regain control of the northeast, appointed Muhammad Said Mir Jumla, his collaborator in the Deccan, to be governor of Bengal, Bihar, and Orissa. During his first year in office, Mir Jumla restructured the provincial administration, restarted the flow of revenue and generally imposed Mughal authority in all three regions. He shifted the provincial capital from

[1] Irfan Habib, *An Atlas of the Mughal Empire* (Delhi, 1982), maps Assam 13A and 13B display the boundaries of the empire and the Asham or Ahom state in the 1660s.

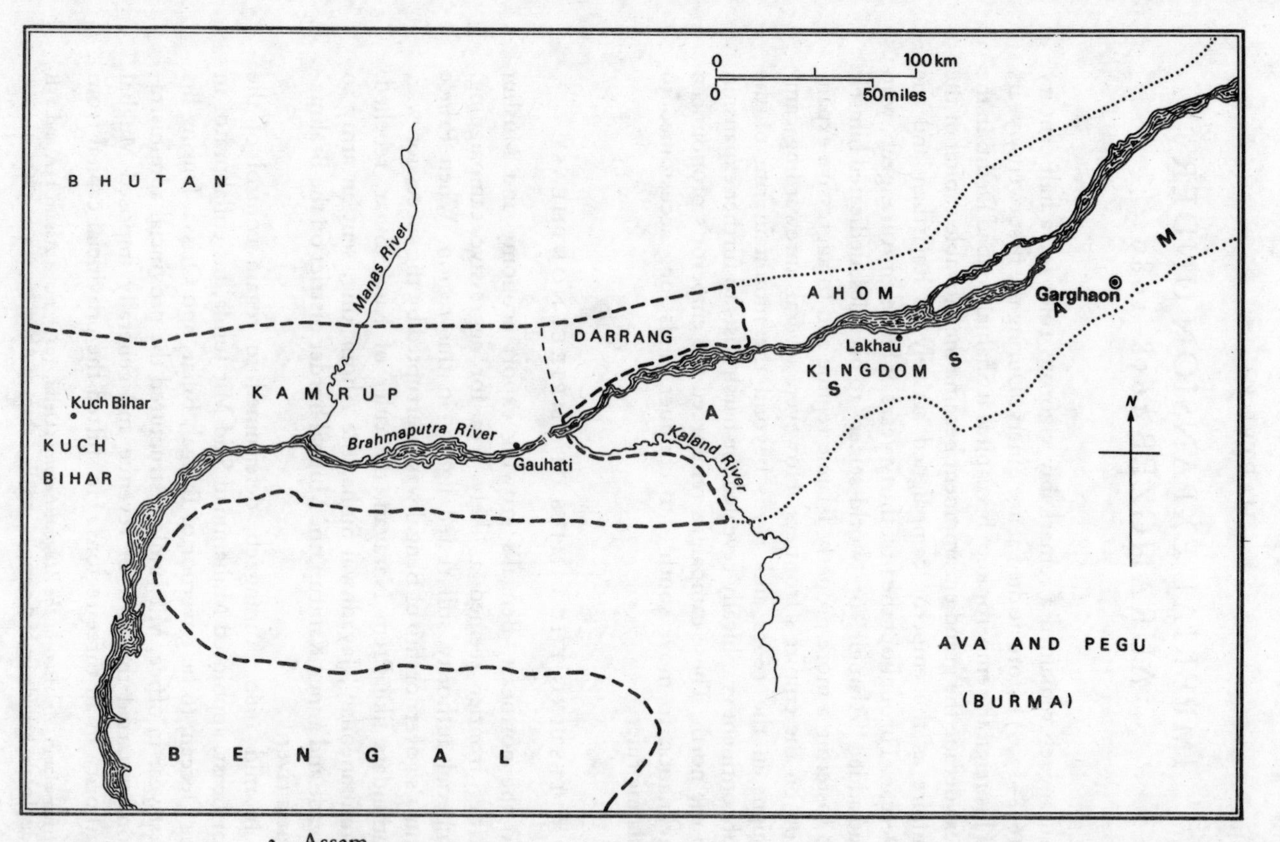

3 Assam
Source: I. Habib, *An atlas of the Mughal Empire* (Delhi, 1982), 13A

Rajmahal east to Dacca, to better reflect the eastward shift in Bengal's population and economy. He also invested heavily in various trading ventures with his own agents and with the European trading companies.[2]

By November, 1661, Mir Jumla was prepared to move to the frontier in "a holy war with the infidels of Assam" according to his official newsreporter.[3] For this venture the Mughal governor assembled a force of 12,000 cavalry, 30,000 foot, and a flotilla of several hundred armed vessels. The latter included ten *ghurabs* or floating batteries carrying fourteen guns which were towed by four rowing boats.[4] Mir Jumla marched directly to Kuch Bihar, entered Kathalbari, the fortified capital, unopposed by the Kuch Bihar ruler who had fled, and annexed the kingdom to the empire. The raja's son, newly converted to Islam, joined the Mughals. The conqueror appointed a temporary faujdar and diwan, changed the name from Kuch Bihar to Alamgirnagar, and set up an imperial mint.

Immediately thereafter the Mughal forces set out for Kamrup. Brushing aside Ahom opposition the Mughals quickly retook Gauhati, the capital of Kamrup. Moving upriver the invaders crippled the Ahom river fleet in a decisive naval battle. By March, 1662 the Mughal army left the fleet and marched inland to seize Garghaon, the capital from which the Ahom ruler and his court had fled. The spoils of war included considerable treasure, hundreds of tons of rice stored in granaries, guns and munitions and dozens of armed river boats.

At this point the rains began and Mir Jumla went into garrison near the capital. The Ahoms cut off the line of Mughal outposts (thanas) leading back to the fleet on the Brahmaputra. Between May and October the Mughal army at the capital and the river fleet at Lakhau survived near-famine conditions, epidemic disease, continuous Ahom attacks, and desertions. When the rains ended supplies and reinforcements permitted the Mughal army to engage the Ahoms once more. Finally in early 1663, the Swargadeo (Heavenly King) and his nobles sued for peace. The Ahom ruler agreed to become a Mughal vassal, to send a daughter with a dowry for marriage to the imperial court, to surrender large amounts of treasure and elephants, and to give up

[2] Jagdish Narayan Sarkar, *The Life of Mir Jumla* (Delhi: Rajesh Publications, 2nd revised edition, 1979), p. 278.
[3] As quoted in Sarkar, *Mir Jumla*, p. 287.
[4] The following description is taken from Sarkar, *Mir Jumla* and Jadunath Sarkar, *History of Aurangzib*, III, 146–182.

extensive territories in Darrang and western districts. Mir Jumla was arranging a phased withdrawal and the administration of the new districts when he became seriously ill and died in March, 1663.

Aurangzeb failed to send another commander of Mir Jumla's stature and abilities to consolidate imperial control of the Brahmaputra valley. Instead, when conflicts over the peace treaty renewed the Mughal–Ahom conflict, successive Ahom kings confronted Mughal faujdars largely unsupported by Delhi. In the end, Gauhati, having changed hands several times, fell under Ahom control in the 1680s and Kamrup was lost permanently to the empire.

The emperor scored an important success on Bengal's coastal frontier. From Chatgaon, a fortified port on the east coast of the Bay of Bengal, the Maghs of Arakan and a community of long-domiciled Portuguese engaged in piracy and slave raiding against the coastal inhabitants of Bengal. Potentially rich deltaic tracts were systematically depopulated as Bengali peasants fled the slave-raiders. In 1664 Shaista Khan, the newly arrived Mughal governor of Bengal, commissioned a flotilla of armed coastal vessels to carry a Mughal assault force against Chatgaon. Shaista Khan formally annexed the Magh headquarters, renamed Islamabad, as a district within Bengal and sent home thousands of freed Bengali slaves. The governor reported to Aurangzeb's query about the new revenues to be gained from the conquest: "In truth, its revenue (*jama*) is the composure (*jamait*) of the minds of the Muslims [with regard to the pirates]. We can easily imagine how fast cultivation will increase in Bengal, now that Magh violence has been put down."[5]

THE INTERNAL FRONTIER: ANNEXATION OF PALAMAU

The remote chiefdom of Palamau (Palaun) was a forested, hilly tract located just south of Bihar between Chota Nagpur and the hills of Central India. Its sparse population engaged in a mixture of sedentary and shifting agriculture in the intermittent valleys of the hills. The Cheros, a tribal people, had retreated to Palamau in the face of rising Rajput power early in the seventeenth century. By the mid 1620s

[5] Quoted in Sarkar, *History of Aurangzib*, III, 212. Sarkar has translated excerpts from the Persian account of Shihabuddin Talish in *Fathiyyah-i-ibriyyah* which describe this campaign. Jadunath Sarkar, *Studies in Mughal India* (Calcutta and Cambridge: M. C. Sarkar and W. Heffer, 1919).

Raja Medini Rai extended the bounds of the Chero domains into Chota Nagpur and the southernmost portions of Bihar province. Friction between the imperial administration and the Cheros grew as the latter raided for cattle in the neighboring Mughal districts.

In 1641, the Mughal governor of Bihar, acting under direct orders from Shah Jahan, led a punitive expedition into Palamau. Faced with this threat, Pratap Rao submitted and paid an indemnity of 80,000 silver rupees. The Mughals annexed Devgaon fort and its environs, one of the three principal fortified towns in the kingdom. Two years later, an attempt by members of Pratap's family to dethrone him permitted the Mughals to intervene. Zabardast Khan, the Mughal field commander, cleared a path through the forest and marched in force from Devgaon to Palamau fort and town. He forced Pratap Rao to surrender in person and sign a tributary agreement. Not content with this, Zabardast Khan carried the Chero Raja back to the governor's audience hall at Patna as a prisoner. At Patna, Pratap Rao accepted a mansab of 1000 zat in service to the emperor, but retained his kingdom as watan jagir in return for an annual tribute of 100,000 rupees.

As the official Mughal estimate of the Palamau Raja's total annual cash revenues was only 250,000 rupees, Mughal tribute soon fell into arrears. Ongoing Chero cattle raids further increased tensions. Shortly after his accession, Aurangzeb ordered Daud Khan Panni, the governor of Bihar, to conquer the chiefdom. In early 1661 Daud Khan, accompanied by several of his faujdars and assisting zamindars, occupied the northernmost forts in Palamau. After the rainy season, he pushed his 6,400 man force directly through the jungle to the capital. The Mughals overwhelmed the defenders in two sharp engagements before storming the walls of the fortress. Pratap Rao fled and lived to rule over a remote corner of his kingdom. Daud Khan Panni appointed a Mughal faujdar to administer the kingdom as a district of Bihar province.

Over two decades, recurring Mughal punitive campaigns brought this small, forested chiefdom firmly into the imperial political system. By this time, the emperor, his advisers, and the governor of Bihar saw little value in political conciliation. The attempt to assimilate Pratap Rao into the cadre of imperial amirs was perfunctory. On the first plausible pretext, Aurangzeb commanded the Bihar governor to lead an army in an assault on the Palamau Raja. A short, bloody, but futile resistance ended with annexation.

TESTING THE LIMITS OF EMPIRE: THE NORTHWEST

The Mughal governor at Kabul ruled over a vast semi-arid mountainous domain on the vulnerable northwestern frontier of the subcontinent. This was a cosmopolitan zone through which a brisk traffic in goods, animals, people, and ideas passed over the Khyber, Bolan and other well-known mountain passes.[6] The inhabitants of the region formed a complex mosaic of lineages and tribal groupings defined by mountain valleys suitable for limited cultivation and grazing. The larger, shared Muslim culture divided into two: that of the dominant Pathans, speaking Pashtun, who were generally tent-dwelling pastoral nomads and traders, and that of the subordinate Tajiks, speaking Persian, who were sedentary cultivators living in mountain villages.

The Pathans were organized into stratified patrilineages formed into named tribes – Yusufzai, Afridi, Wazirs – ruled by tribal councils (*jirgas*) and headed by chiefs or *khans*. In addition to pastoral nomadism the Pathan nomad-traders brought caravans of horses into India and carried Indian goods to Central Asia and Persia. Other Pathans preyed upon the caravans as bandits – or offered protection if bought off by political subsidies. In addition, thousands of Pathans or, as they were known in India, Afghans served as soldiers, traders, and higher-ranking administrators in the Mughal empire and other Indo-Mughal states. Many Afghans had settled into roles as zamindars with varying degrees of wealth and power in pockets of the north Indian countryside. These emigrés kept close contact with their lineage and tribal fellows in the mountains and often sent home remittances.

Control of Kabul and the northwestern border regions was of great strategic concern to the Mughals. When a series of Pathan tribal revolts against Timurid rule broke out Aurangzeb reacted quickly and decisively. In 1667, a Yusufzai chief and self-proclaimed king in the Swat valley led allied Yusufzai lineages in pitched battles against Mughal detachments in Attock and Peshawar. Unrest continued until Muhammad Amin Khan, the imperial *mir bakhshi*, brought a 9,000 man army from Delhi to suppress further resistance.

More serious was the rising of the Afridis in 1672. The Afridi chief

[6] This description is based upon Joseph Arlinghaus, *The Transformation of Afghan Tribal Society: Tribal Expansion, Mughal Imperialism and the Roshaniyya Insurrection 1450–1600* (Durham, NC: Duke University Ph.D dissertation, 1988).

Acmal Khan crowned himself king, struck coins in his own name, declared war against the Mughals and closed the Khyber pass to caravan traffic. The Afridis surprised and massacred an imperial army between Peshawar and Kabul. Other Pathan tribes, including the Khataks under Kush-hal, the celebrated anti-Mughal poet, joined the revolt. The next year the Mughals lost another large army to Afridi ambush in the snowy mountain passes in mid-winter. Finally, in June, 1674, Aurangzeb himself brought another imperial army into the mountains. The emperor sent out well-equipped and supplied columns to open the Khyber and other passes. Another imperial army was ambushed and badly mauled in Bajaur, but the Mughals regained control of the main trade routes. Simultaneously, Aurangzeb offered gold, honors, and other rewards to induce rebel tribal leaders to submit and end the rebellion.

Leaving newly fortified and garrisoned posts behind, Aurangzeb returned tô Delhi by the end of 1675. Thereafter, a new governor at Kabul, Amir Khan, involved himself heavily in Pathan tribal politics and supported factions sympathetic to imperial policies. Lavish subsidies were paid as protection money to keep the passes open. Individual chiefs received frequent payments. Other Pathans were given appointments in Mughal service. Amir Khan proved to be so adroit that no further large tribal rebellions flared up during the two decades he remained as governor at Kabul.

A sympathetic, flexible policy toward loçal warrior aristocracies, if backed by sufficient force, could counteract the tendency toward lineage alliances, monarchy, and state building seen in both the Yusufzai and Afridi revolts. The effort involved in suppressing these risings gave Aurangzeb little incentive to imitate his father's campaigns into Central Asia.

ISLAMIC POLICIES AND IMPERIAL CULTURE

Aurangzeb completed that transformation of Akbar's ideology and inclusive political culture begun by Shah Jahan. The goals of the new Islamic ideologies were simply defined: the Mughal empire must become a Muslim state governed by the precepts of the Sharia for the benefit of the Indian Muslim community. The regime would make every possible effort to encourage conversion of the infidel population. And, failing that, would rule fairly but sternly over the majority population. Increasingly the political culture of the empire would be defined in exclusive Muslim terms.

Aurangzeb's goals for the empire were completely consistent with his own ardent piety as a follower of the Hanafi school. In his later years Aurangzeb exceeded the bounds of normal devotion. Even as emperor he devoted seven years to memorizing the entire Koran.[7] An initial embarrassment, however, was his need to legitimate Shah Jahan's forced deposition and imprisonment. Rebellion against his father placed Aurangzeb in the awkward position of violating both the Sharia and strongly held norms of filial piety for Muslims. In 1659, the emperor sent a richly laden mission to Sharif Zaid, ruler of the holy cities in the Hijaz, to obtain formal recognition. Rebuffed on this occasion, a second mission returned with holy relics sent to celebrate the emperor's ascent to the Timurid throne. Thereafter Aurangzeb was a generous patron of the Holy Places:[8]

> [Aurangzeb] used to send large amounts of money, for some years annually, at others once in two or three years, to the pious men living in retreat in those Holy Cities, and a large number of men in those Holy Places were permanently employed by him on daily stipends to act as his deputies in walking round the Ka'ba, bowing to the Prophet's tomb, reading the two copies of the Quran written by this pious Emperor with his own hand and presented to Medina.

Having placated his own conscience and, to some extent public opinion, Aurangzeb was free to fulfill his Islamic vision of the Mughal empire.

Aurangzeb's zealousness was tempered by highly developed political and diplomatic instincts as with measured speed, he pressed toward his ultimate goal. Aurangzeb retained pride in the Timurid genealogy – but as a descendant of Muslim conquerors, not the heir to a divinely inspired radiance and knowledge. For example, in his eleventh year, the emperor ended as un-Islamic the practice begun by Akbar of appearing on a balcony at sunrise for all who wished to worship or take *darshan* from him.[9] Like his father he turned toward the notion of khanazadgi rather than discipleship to define the ideal relationship

[7] Ibid., p. 314.

[8] Saqi Mustaid Khan, *Maasir-i'Alamgiri*, p. 525 as quoted in N. R. Farooqi, "Mughal–Ottoman Relations: A Study of Political and Diplomatic Relations Between Mughal India and the Ottoman Empire: 1556–1748," unpublished Ph.D dissertation, University of Wisconsin, Madison, 1986, p. 210.

[9] Sarkar, *History of Aurangzib*, III, 89.

with his nobles and imperial officials. Aurangzeb further narrowed the notion of hereditary service by his pronounced preference for Muslim officers.

Aurangzeb's anxiety to conform more strictly to the Sharia closed off several important modes of expression for Mughal political ideology. He ended patronage of the combined art of chronicle writing and book illustration. He stopped the detailed annals of his reign, the *Alamgir-Nama*, after the tenth regnal year. Only privately written, clandestine histories survive. Imperial ateliers were closed and dozens of master painters and their assistants dismissed. Very little monumental building occurred – nothing which would match the gardens of Jahangir or the palaces of Akbar or Shah Jahan. Only properly Islamic forms and idioms were encouraged in the arts. As a result the entire political culture of the empire was narrowed and, in the end, impoverished.

The eclectic, inclusive court culture suffered. Un-Islamic ceremonies were banned as a new moralistic and legalistic tone pervaded court life. Right after his second coronation the emperor abolished celebration of the Iranian New Year or Nauroz festivities at the start of the solar year. In the same year Aurangzeb dismissed the court musicians and ended that imperial patronage responsible for the brilliant development of Hindustani music. Wine-drinking and opium consumption were prohibited. Less-formal socializing between nobles and emperor associated with their use no longer occurred. While this ban probably extended the lives of the emperor and many of his closest intimates (who lived to considerable ages) it did inhibit relations between the emperor and his senior officers. Considering the vital importance of the emperor–noble link in the Mughal system, this was a serious weakness.

Aurangzeb's aesthetic impulses and patronage were confined to the Islamic arts and sciences. His greatest achievement was the legal text known as the *Fatawa-i 'Alamgiri*. When requested, independent jurisconsults gave written opinions, called fatwa, on points of interpretation of the sacred law of Islam. These rulings were often obscure, frequently contradictory, and at times based on weak legal scholarship. Therefore since Aurangzeb aimed at "making the general Muslim public act according to the legal decisions and precedents of the theological scholars (ulema) of the Hanafi school, ... " he commissioned a board of scholars to compile authoritative and reliable rulings in a single work.[10] The *Fatawa-i 'Alamgiri* won rapid acceptance within India and elsewhere in the Islamic world as a guide to correct action for orthodox Muslims.

Other measures directly enhanced the status, power and income of the ulema and the Islamic institutions they served. Under Aurangzeb the fortunes of the ulema returned full circle to what they had been before Akbar stripped them of their influence and power in the 1580s. The chief judge or qazi and the supervisor of pious charity, the sadr, ranking as nobles, were in constant attendance upon the emperor. These men controlled lavish patronage. Appointments to paid employment for supervisors of pious trusts, preachers, judges, and other posts throughout the empire lay in their hands.

Aurangzeb further gratified the ulema by spending liberally to repair and maintain mosques and to support religious charity. His most important concession for the ulema and the larger group of Muslim gentry throughout the empire was in regard to tax-free land grants. Aurangzeb reversed Akbar's policy when in 1672 he resumed all grants held by Hindus. Although not completely enforced in practice, the new policy was a sweeping victory for the Muslim ulema of the empire who could see themselves dividing an increased pool of lands. In 1690 Aurangzeb made all such land grants fully hereditary in another major concession to the ulema.[11]

For many senior nobles, the rise of the theologians and jurists, who generally had limited military and administrative experience, was a disturbing trend. Often ulema were simply greedy and corrupt. Abdul Wahhab Bohra, chief qazi for sixteen years, was notorious for accepting bribes to appoint imperial judges. He retired with a fortune estimated at 3.3 million rupees and other valuables.[12] One of the most outspoken nobles of the period, the Persian amir Mirza Lahrasp, Mahabat Khan, protested against making "sparrows into huntsmen" and relying too heavily on the opinions of the theologians in matters of state.[13]

At his second coronation in 1659, Aurangzeb created a new office, the *muhtasib* or censor, appointed from the ranks of the ulema. This

[10] Saqi Mustaid Khan, *Maasir-i Alamgiri* (Calcutta, 1947), translated by Jadunath Sarkar, p. 315.
[11] Irfan Habib, *The Agrarian System of Mughal India* (London, 1963), p. 311.
[12] Sarkar, *History of Aurangzib*, III, 75.
[13] Athar Ali, *The Mughal Nobility Under Aurangzeb* (Aligarh: Asia Publications, 1966), p. 99.

peculiarly Islamic officer regulated urban markets to prevent disorder and fraud on the public. The muhtasib also enforced Sharia prohibitions against blasphemy, wine-drinking and gambling, and other heretical or idolatrous behavior in public. Previously unknown in Indian Muslim regimes, the muhtasib assumed some of the duties of the indigenous Indian city magistrate, the *kotwal*. Aurangzeb appointed Mulla Auz Wajih, Shah Jahan's former jurisconsult (*mufti*), a prominent Muslim theologian from Samarkhand, chief muhtasib bearing the rank of an amir at Delhi.[14] Other muhtasibs commanding bodies of officers and troops were posted in the major towns and cities of the empire.

ISLAMIC POLICIES AND NON-MUSLIMS

Aurangzeb's revivalism forced him to confront imperial policies toward non-Muslims. His edict of 1669 ordered that all temples recently built or repaired contrary to the Sharia be torn down.[15] Throughout the empire many, although certainly not all, such temples were ruined by official action. The emperor's special targets were the renowned stone temples in the holy cities of Mathura and Varanasi. The great Kesev Rai temple at Mathura built at a cost of over three million rupees by Bir Singh Bundela (responsible for Abul Fazl's death, see above) was pulled down. The golden bejewelled idols were taken to Agra and buried under the steps of Jahan Ara's mosque. A new mosque was erected on the site of the razed temple.[16] Admittedly, this action was an explicit statement of the emperor's view of idolatry; it was also a rebuke to the Bundelas and their troublesome allegiance to the empire (see above). The emperor's message was simultaneously political and religious.

During his reign Aurangzeb issued a stream of discriminatory edicts and regulations. A tax levied on pilgrims travelling to the numerous Hindu shrines and periodic festivals, abolished by Akbar, was reinstated. In 1665 the emperor decreed that Muslims should be taxed at 2.5 percent of value on internal customs duties and Hindus 5 percent. A general edict addressed to provincial governors and revenue officers commanded the dismissal of Hindu officers and their replacement by

[14] Sarkar, *History of Aurangzib*, III, 77.
[15] Sri Ram Sharma, *The Religious Policy of the Mughal Emperors* (London: Asia Publishing House, Inc., 2nd edition, 1962), pp. 130–131.
[16] Ibid., p. 133.

Muslims.[17] Often not fully enforced, these and other measures nevertheless were widely known and disliked by the majority population.[18]

Zealous imperial officers had considerable power to enforce the new edicts, especially among urban non-warrior groups. At Surat in 1669 the qazi terrorized the entire Bania or Hindu merchant community of that city. He pressured several members of the community to convert to Islam and threatened others with forcible conversion unless they paid ransom money. He extorted other sums to prevent defacement of the Hindu temples and shrines in the city. The qazi forcibly circumcised and converted a Bania serving as a Persian writer or clerk, who then killed himself. At this point there was a mass protest: "all the heads of the Banian families of what condition whatsoever departed the Town to the number of 8,000 leaving their wives and children in Surat under charge of their brothers or next of Kinn."[19]

More pragmatic imperial officials failed to support the qazi. And, the emperor himself, if political loyalties were not involved, would compromise. The governor of Surat refused to stop the mass exodus on the grounds that the Banias were the emperor's subjects and "might travel in his country where they pleased." The Banias proceeded to nearby Broach where they remained for three months in defiance of the qazi's threats. They were under the protection of the city prefect of Ahmadabad, who tried to entice the protestors to his city. Finally with the commerce of the port frozen, the Banias agreed to return after receiving letters from the emperor bearing "some assurance of their safety and more freedom in their religion."[20] Aurangzeb also replaced the over-zealous qazi with a more moderate judge.

Aurangzeb announced his most controversial measure in 1679 when he revived the jiziya, a graduated property tax levied on non-Muslims. The court theologians urged this course of action; many of his nobles seem to have argued against it.[21] Cadres of lower ranking mansabdars became special jiziya collectors in cities and towns

[17] S. Moinul Haq, *Khafi Khan's History of Alamgir* (Karachi: Pakistan Historical Society, 1975), translation of Muhammad Hashim Khafi Khan, *Muntakhab-al Lubab*, p. 252.

[18] These measures are given in great detail in Sharma, *Religious Policy*, pp. 142ff.

[19] Sushil Chaudhury, "The Surat Crisis of 1669: A Case Study of Mercantile Protest in Medieval India," *Calcutta Historical Journal, 5 (129–146)*, 1983.

[20] Ibid., p. 140.

[21] N. Manucci, *Storia do Mogor or Mogul India* (Calcutta, 4 vols., 1907–8), translated by William Irvine, II 288.

throughout the empire. In rural areas, the provincial diwans were adding a 4 percent increment to the assessed land revenue each year.[22]

The new tax provoked heated protests in Delhi. Thousands of Hindus from the city and its surrounding districts gathered at the Yamuna river in front of the emperor's balcony on the Delhi fort wall to protest the new tax. When Aurangzeb rode out from the fort to attend weekly prayers at the Jama Masjid:[23]

> ... the Hindus crowded from the gate of the fort to the Jama Masjid in such a large number for imploring redress that the passage of the people was blocked. The money-lenders, cloth-merchants and shopkeepers of the camp Urdu Bazar (Army Market) and all the artisans of the city abandoned their work and assembled on the route of the Emperor ... [Aurangzeb], who was riding on an elephant, could not reach the mosque. Every moment the number of those unlucky people increased. Then he ordered that the majestic elephants should proceed against them. Some of them were killed or trampled under the elephants and horses. For some days, more, they assembled in the same way and requested for remission (of the jiziya). At last they submitted to pay the Jiziyah.

The jiziya collectors generally encountered sullen resistance to payment nearly everywhere – at least initially.

Aurangzeb's ultimate aim was conversion of non-Muslims to Islam. Whenever possible the emperor gave out robes of honor, cash gifts, and promotions to converts.[24] It quickly became known that conversion was a sure way to the emperor's favor. In many disputed successions for hereditary local office Aurangzeb chose candidates who had converted to Islam over their rivals. Pargana headmen and qanungos or recordkeepers were targeted especially for pressure to convert. The message was very clear for all concerned. Shared political community must also be shared religious belief.

THE SIKH MARTYRDOM

Aurangzeb's new policies increased tensions with the still-expanding Sikh community in the Punjab plain and foothills. Before his death Guru Hargobind bypassed the claims of his two living sons to name Hari Rai, son of his prematurely deceased eldest son, as his successor.

22 Sharma, *Religious Policy*, pp. 152–158. 23 Moinul Haq, *Khafi Khan*, pp. 258–59.
24 Sharma has culled a list of the converts from the official newsreports from court. *Religious Policy*, pp. 170–174.

During the great Mughal war of succession, Hari Rai offered support and aid to Dara Shikoh. Consequently, after his victory, Aurangzeb demanded that Hari Rai send his eldest son, Ram Rai to the Mughal court as a hostage. By this time-honored device Aurangzeb aimed to socialize the young Sikh heir to the values and institutions of the Mughal court. Aurangzeb also planned, as he did with many other zamindars, to control the Sikh succession. One faction of the Sikh community supported Ram Rai and favored his candidacy.[25]

The aging and ill Hari Rai rejected the claims of his eldest son and nominated instead a younger son, Hari Krishan, as his successor. The emperor then summoned the Guru and his young heir to Delhi where in 1664 Hari Rai died of natural causes. Before Aurangzeb could determine the succession one faction of the Sikhs elected as their new guru, Tegh Bahadur, the brother of Hari Rai and youngest son of Guru Hargobind.

Generally recognized as the new Sikh leader, Tegh Bahadur spent the next decade in vigorously organizing and proselytizing throughout the Punjab and as far east as Bengal and Assam in North India. It is in this period that substantial numbers of Jats, members of the most numerous cultivating caste group in the Indo-Gangetic plain, began to convert to Sikhism in large numbers. Everywhere Tegh Bahadur travelled large crowds greeted him and his preaching was met with enormous enthusiasm.

By the early 1670s the Sikhs ran foul of Aurangzeb's iconoclastic policies. Imperial officers received orders to demolish Sikh Gurdwaras as well as Hindu temples. At the same time several instances of Muslims being converted to Sikhism by the Guru were reported to Aurangzeb who ordered Tegh Bahadur's arrest. In Agra, the Guru and five companions were captured, arrested and taken to Delhi. There the qazi's court tried and convicted the Sikh leader for blasphemy, sentenced him to death and carried out the execution in November, 1675. After this second martyrdom the annual spring Baisakhi congregation of Sikhs in the hills acclaimed Gobind Singh, the young son of the slain leader, as the new Guru.[26] At one stroke Aurangzeb earned the bitter hatred of thousands of Jat and Khatri Sikhs living in the North Indian plain.

[25] J. S. Grewal and S. S. Bal, *Guru Gobind Singh, A Biographical Study* (Chandigarh: Punjab University, 1967), p. 29.
[26] Grewal and Bal, *Guru Gobind Singh*, pp. 44–47.

THE RAJPUT REBELLION

The most sensitive test for the new militant orthodoxy lay in the emperor's relationship with his Rajput nobles. On the surface the Rajputs had no immediate grounds for complaint. They still formed an influential group within the imperial nobility.[27] Indeed, the highest ranked noble in the empire, was Mirza Raja Jai Singh Kachhwaha of Jaipur (7,000 zat 7,000 suwar) who had been Aurangzeb's most faithful supporter in the war of succession. In 1665 Jai Singh became viceroy of the Deccan provinces, a position usually held by an adult Timurid prince. After 1679 all Rajputs in imperial service were exempt from payment of the jiziya – although their subjects at home were not.

Nevertheless, Rajput nobles as a group were squeezed by what appears to have been deliberate policy. The percentage of Rajput nobles to the total number of nobles dropped noticeably as did their aggregate ranks.[28] The emperor curtailed imperial jagirs assigned outside of Rajasthan and thus reduced the imperial subsidy obtained by these warriors for their barren homeland.[29] The fortunes of the Rajput nobles, who with their followers had for so long been a vital striking arm for the empire, were newly reduced.

Wealth and power derived from imperial service supported and made possible the creation of a locally dominant state structure using the Mughal administrative model within the raja's ancestral domains in Rajasthan. Some lands were directly administered in a form of crownlands or khalisa. The remaining lands were assigned as jagirs to loyal kinsmen or other retainers. The great rajas recruited a service nobility consisting of Rajputs who did not belong to the ruling clan and served as a counter-weight to the claims of equality and brotherhood put forward by the fellow-clansmen of the ruler. Each of these constituencies had a vital interest in increasing the rank, wealth, and status of their Rajput patron.

The death of the ruling raja was a crisis point for all concerned. The Mughal emperor was free to choose any of the raja's sons, or any other close male relative as the new clan head. Normally this choice was made promptly and met no resistance. The various Rajput and

[27] Athar Ali, *Mughal Nobility*, p. 35, Table 2 (a).
[28] Athar Ali, *Mughal Nobility*, pp. 23–24.
[29] Athar Ali, *Mughal Nobility*, p. 100.

non-Rajput factions made the best accommodation they could to the new order.

In the previous reign in 1638, Gaj Singh Rathor, Raja of Marwar in western Rajasthan and Mughal amir, died after an illustrious career while serving at court in Agra. His youngest son, Jaswant Singh Rathor, immediately marched to Agra for his father's cremation. In May, 1638, Shah Jahan, ignoring any claims of Gaj Singh's eldest son then at court, placed the red tika mark of investiture on Jawant Singh's forehead. The emperor gave Jaswant Singh, now Raja, a mansab of 4,000/4,000, a fully decorated robe of honor, a jeweled dagger, a flag, a kettledrum, a war horse, and an elephant.[30] Shah Jahan assigned Jodhpur and four other parganas in Marwar as his jagir. The emperor also named a non-Rathor Rajput as Jaswant Singh's chief fiscal officer (diwan) during his minority. Several days later, Jaswant Singh presented six elephants to the emperor as pishkash. For the next year and a half the young Raja and his Rajput cavalry remained constantly in attendance on the emperor as the latter travelled to Lahore and Peshawar. On several occasions he received further honors and gifts from Shah Jahan. It was only in early February, 1640 that the new Raja returned to Marwar to formally celebrate his accession with his Rathor kinsmen at Jodhpur fort.[31]

Forty years later, in December, 1678, Maharaja Jaswant Singh Rathor died while on duty in near-exile as military commander (*thanadar*) at Jamrud, in Afghanistan. At his death he had no living son as male heir. Two of Jaswant Singh's wives were pregnant and thus spared the funeral pyre.[32] Aurangzeb, upon receiving the news from Jamrud, immediately took the bureaucratic step of formally transferring all of Marwar to the status of imperial crown territories (khalisa). This was not annexation, but simply a measure necessary to reallocate the kingdom in jagirs. The emperor brought his court to the Mughal capital at Ajmer to supervise officials and troops sent to take over the kingdom. When it occupied Jodhpur, the army engaged in considerable temple and idol smashing in the Marwar capital.

[30] V. S. Bhargava, *Marwar and the Mughal Emperors* (Delhi: Munshiram Manoharlal, 1966), pp. 80–81.

[31] Ibid., p. 82.

[32] Unless otherwise noted, the following description of the Rajput war is based upon Sarkar, *Aurangzib*, III, 322–375; V. S. Bhargava, *Marwar and the Mughal Emperors* (Delhi: Munshiram Manoharlal, 1966), pp. 115–166; Robert C. Hallissey, *The Rajput Rebellion Against Aurangzeb* (Columbia and London: University of Missouri Press, 1977); and Moinul Haq, *Khafi Khan*, pp. 263–281.

Returning to Delhi, Aurangzeb invested another Rajput amir, Indra Singh Rathor, son of Jaswant Singh's deceased elder brother, as ruler of Marwar.

The aftermath of these events did not follow the usual script. Rathor dissatisfaction with the Aurangzeb's decisions flared up into a full-scale revolt in Marwar. By investing Indra Singh Rathor, a nephew of Jaswant Singh, the emperor chose to ignore the fact that on the much-delayed return journey from Jamrud to Delhi, the two Rajput queens each bore live sons. The elder boy named Ajit Singh was born to a Sisodia Rajput rani from Mewar. By June 1679, Durgadas Rathor, Jaswant Singh's senior officer, brought his troops and household to the Rathor mansion in Shahjahanabad. At a court audience, Durgadas and the senior Rathor officers pleaded the case for making Ajit Singh, the elder infant, the new ruler of Marwar. Aurangzeb refused but said that he would rear Ajit Singh in the imperial harem and confer the title of raja and noble rank when he came of age. This was conditional, however, on the infant being raised as a Muslim. The Rathor officers, led by Durgadas Rathor, flatly rejected this proposal.

At this point the youngest infant died. Aurangzeb sent an armed detachment under the Delhi magistrate (kotwal) to the Rathor mansion to seize the two Ranis and the surviving heir. Durgadas' refusal to turn over the Raja's widows and son touched off a musketry exchange. As mounted Rajput lances charged the imperial detachment, Durgadas put the Ranis disguised in male clothing on horses and, carrying the infant himself, rode on a desperate flight out of the city. A slave girl with her infant posed as the Rani and remained behind to be captured. Twice parties of Rajputs fell back to sacrifice themselves and slow the pursuit. In the end Durgadas reached Jodhpur with his prizes and entrusted Ajit Singh and his mother to a safe refuge with sympathetic Rathor lineage mates.

Aurangzeb claimed that the slave baby captured was the true Ajit Singh and turned him over to be raised in the harem as a Muslim Rajput prince. In his next move, Aurangzeb sent a Mughal army commanded by Prince Muhammad Akbar, his youngest son, to occupy Marwar. Stubborn, suicidal stands by Rathor defenders did not stop the invaders from seizing Jodhpur. At this point the neighboring Rana of Mewar intervened. The Rana was moved by the pleas of his kinswoman, the Sisodia princess who was the mother of Ajit Singh, and fearful that Mewar would next be invaded. Even the combined

Rajputs, who had no field artillery, could not hold against the main Mughal battle force. By the end of the year the Mughal army had occupied Udaipur, the capital of Mewar. Great and small temples in and around the city fell to the iconoclasm of the Mughals. The Rana and his surviving horsemen retreated to the hills and began a guerrilla campaign.

In early 1680 Aurangzeb returned to Ajmer and left the suppression campaign in the hands of Prince Azam, recalled from the governorship of Bengal, and his two brothers Muazzam and Muhammad Akbar. For nearly a year the Mughals had only mixed success in dealing with the harassing activities of the Rajputs in each kingdom. The death from natural causes of the ruling Rana and the accession of his son, Jai Singh, did not interrupt the resistance. Aurangzeb sent reinforcements and sharply reprimanded each of his sons for lack of success.

AKBAR'S REVOLT

Throughout this period a continuing series of secret Rajput emissaries entreated Prince Akbar to rebel against his father. They argued that Aurangzeb's religious bigotry and his anti-Rajput bias would be the destruction of the empire. With Rajput support, he could seize the throne and reverse these erroneous policies. The Mughal princess Zeb-u-nissa, allied with Akbar, also supported this policy in a copious secret correspondence with her brother. Finally persuaded, on January 1, 1681, Akbar crowned himself emperor and conferred titles on his immediate officers.

Akbar took a full two weeks to lead his combined army 120 miles to Ajmer where Aurangzeb was encamped with only a modest contingent of troops. Akbar's dilatory pace revealed the enormous psychological cost of rebellion against his father's awe-inspiring authority. Finally on 15 January the rebel prince confronted Aurangzeb outside Ajmer. That same evening Prince Muazzam reached his father after a strenuous forced march with troops that doubled the size of Aurangzeb's army.

As usual Aurangzeb was busily engaged in his own form of psychological warfare. A false letter addressed to Akbar praised him for fulfilling the emperor's plot to slaughter the Rajputs between his and Akbar's forces. The document reached Durgadas Rathor who was unable to gain access to the sleeping Timurid prince. Fearing treachery, he and his Rajput horsemen quietly mounted and fled in the night toward Marwar. Most of Akbar's Mughal officers and troopers surrendered to the emperor. The prince could only muster a handful of men from his personal guard to join him in a hasty flight.

Aurangzeb immediately sent Prince Muazzam in pursuit. The Rajputs, who had discovered Aurangzeb's plot, kept Akbar safe in the hills. Finally, after several months Durgadas led the prince by a long evasive route to the court of Shambhaji, the new Maratha ruler. Contemporary opinion held that Prince Muazzam and Khan Jahan Bahadur, the governor of the Deccan provinces, were quietly sympathetic to Akbar and, in fact, did not capture him when they could have done so.[33] Akbar's flight suddenly converted what had been merely an awkward rebellion by the Rathors to a full-blown imperial crisis.

Akbar's defection immediately reduced imperial pressure on the Rajputs. After several months of desultory campaigning the Rana of Mewar agreed to a negotiated peace in which he surrendered three parganas to direct Mughal administration and agreed to permanent payment of the jiziya for Mewar. The Mughal armies withdrew and Aurangzeb sent a robe of honor to recognize Rana Jai Singh's succession to his father's throne.

In Marwar, however, resistance to the Mughals continued for a generation. Aurangzeb left it to the faujdar of Jodhpur to direct punitive campaigns against the rebels. The young fugitive raja Ajit Singh, who was spirited from one refuge to another, remained the symbolic focus of the Rathor guerrilla war. It would be a full twenty years before a settlement was negotiated between the emperor and a now mature Ajit Singh. For this critical period the Timurids lost the services of most Rathor Rajputs.

Whether the rupture with the Rathor and Sisodia clans was avoidable is difficult to assess. Had Aurangzeb been more willing to consider Rajput sensitivities the revolt might not have occurred. Aurangzeb was obviously irritated with Jaswant Singh over his support of Dara in the war of succession and his reported complicity in the escape of Shivaji from Puna (see below). But this should not have interfered with a smooth succession in keeping with Jaswant Singh's own investiture forty years earlier.

Aurangzeb's new emphasis on Islam as a major strand in the political relationship strained the Rajput–Timurid bond. Many Rajputs were deeply disturbed by the new climate as the appeal directed to Prince

[33] Moinul Haq, *Khafi Khan*, pp. 279–280.

Akbar before his revolt suggests. Aurangzeb's attempt to place a Muslim convert on the Marwar gaddi reveals the importance he attached to this issue. Aurangzeb's new hard line did make it more difficult to resolve these issues peacefully. Both Rajput and non-Rajput retainers of Jaswant Singh obviously felt their interests to be jeopardized by the emperor's actions. After the first violent clash, and as the conflict widened to Mewar, opposing idioms of resistance and suppression increasingly found expression in religious imagery. This militant imagery frayed the bond of emotion and interest that tied the Rathors, Sisodias, and other Rajputs to the empire.

CHAPTER 9

THE ECONOMY, SOCIETAL CHANGE, AND INTERNATIONAL TRADE

Aurangzeb's Deccan victories depended as much upon Timurid wealth as his generalship and military skills. After more than a century of conquest and territorial expansion the Mughal emperor possessed enormous resources. From Akbar's annexation of Malwa in 1561 till the fall of Golconda in 1687, every victory generated large amounts of plundered treasure from the hoards of defeated rulers – often sufficient to repay the costs of conquest. Ordinary revenues obtained through taxes on agricultural production and trade poured into the emperor's coffers. In 1689 Aurangzeb had no reason to anticipate revenue shortfalls. Whether for war or for routine costs of administration the empire was self-financing from its own resources.

If a deficit year were to occur the central treasury guarded an enormous hoard of coined and uncoined gold and silver. Millions of rupees in liquid wealth held by several hundred Mughal nobles and higher-ranking mansabdars must also be viewed as a supplementary reserve. Unlike contemporary early modern European kings, the Mughal emperors did not depend upon loans from private financiers to meet routine expenditures or to pay for even the most expensive military campaigns.[1] Military commanders on campaign who needed funds often were authorized to collect large sums from the ordinary holdings of provincial treasuries.

THE REVENUE SYSTEM

At the heart of Mughal finance was the revenue system which taxed agricultural production and urban trade. By its insistence on cash payment, the regime forced foodgrains and other commodities from the countryside to be sold in an ascending hierarchy of markets. Mughal revenue collectors for khalisa lands and collection agents for jagirdars received regular payments in copper and silver coin in installments every year.

[1] J. F. Richards, "Mughal State Finance and the Premodern World Economy," *Comparative Studies in Society and History*, 23 (1981), 285–307.

The state revenue demand more than doubled between Akbar and Aurangzeb. The jama or combined one-tenth urban imposts and nine-tenths land revenue (mal) grew from 5,834.6 million dams in the last years of Akbar's rule to 13,339.9 million dams just after the death of Aurangzeb in 1709.[2] Some of this increase derived from lands added by conquest; some by rising tax demands. In either event the revenues accruing to the emperor and the imperial elite rose substantially over time.

Evaluating this revenue increase is complicated by the secular trend in prices over the seventeenth century. Some economic historians have suggested that a doubling of prices in silver currency occurred in the first sixty years of the century followed by stability until another fifty-year rising trend began in 1700.[3] Therefore, from one perspective, imperial revenues barely kept pace with inflationary trends in silver currency over the long term. More recently Sanjay Subrahmanyam argues that long term price data for the subcontinent in the seventeenth century are both fragmentary and inconclusive: "Overall then, the Indian evidence suggests that price inflation was at best sporadic, and limited to specific regions and specific commodities ..."[4] It is also possible, in view of the scantiness of long term quantitative data, that the silver influx was absorbed for use by an expanding Indian currency system and economy. And that the rate of silver increase was matched by increases in productivity and in the demand for money which slowed or even prevented price inflation.

Nevertheless, for any fiscal administration to adjust upward its assessment decade after decade is a formidable prospect. To attain this degree of success bespeaks a well-run, confident structure capable of responding to changing economic circumstances. Whether Mughal fiscal officers actually noticed and acted upon a long-term upward trend in prices is another question. That they successfully raised taxes is clear.

If the presumed rise in prices did occur and arable lands did grow in area, the total state-imposed burden on agriculture was reduced

[2] Habib, *The Agrarian System of Mughal India* (London, 1963), p. 399.

[3] Irfan Habib, "Monetary System and Prices" in Tapan Raychaudhuri and Irfan Habib, eds., *The Cambridge Economic History of India* (Cambridge: Cambridge University Press, 1982), 2 vols., I, 376.

[4] Sanjay Subrahmanyam, "Precious Metal Flows and Prices in Western and Southern Asia, 1500–1750: Some Comparative and Conjunctural Aspects," *Studies in History*, 7, n.s. (1991), 79–105.

accordingly. That is, the tax load imposed in 1700 fell on more cultivators working a larger arable area than that same tax burden expressed in real terms in 1600. Necessarily, therefore, the same tax demand must have rested more lightly on at least some parts of rural society in this region. Given the provisions of the Mughal revenue regulations favoring lands newly brought into cultivation, pioneering peasant-cultivators or zamindars and their tenants probably benefited disproportionately.

The zabt revenue system gave Mughal administrators a means to impose higher taxes by intensifying imperial control over rural society. Resting firmly on annual collection of data on cultivated area, crops, prices, and collections, the regulation revenue system was a precise tool for taxing agricultural production. When backed by sufficient force, land surveys and data collection permitted the administration to move from tribute-taking or pishkash from local lords to taxation or mal. Under the zabt system each zamindar was reduced to conveying a pre-set tax for each cultivator and village to imperial officials. In some areas the revenue administration could bypass the zamindar and deal directly with dominant peasant-cultivators (*raiyati zamindars*) in individual villages.

Akbar's agrarian order was not a static entity. A succession of imperial diwans extended the territory covered by the regulation system. Between 1595 and the end of the seventeenth century lands surveyed and recorded increased from 201.6 million to 284.8 million bigahs. An undetermined, but probably smaller, part of this increase recorded the extension of cultivation in resurveys of villages and parganas already brought into the system. A larger proportion, however, resulted from incorporating new parganas into the regulation system. In either circumstance, the net growth in measured lands was an impressive organizational feat.

The pattern of change was not uniform. A minority of provinces remained exempt from the new order. The northwestern frontier – Kabul, Thatta – fell outside the regulation agrarian system, as did Kashmir. Similarly, Bengal and Orissa on the northeastern riverine frontier were not subject to measurement. Some provinces showed a decrease in the measured area. Lahore and Multan posted slight declines. Ajmer and Gujarat showed larger reductions.

Nine provinces recorded increases in zabt lands. In these total lands surveyed rose by 110.8 million bigahs. This figure commands our attention. Even extended over the century it implies that the imperial administration planned, executed and recorded surveys for over one million bigahs in an average year. An administrative effort of this magnitude testifies to the tenacity and purposefulness of the Mughal revenue administration. If, in addition, we assume that periodic, fresh surveys were undertaken of previously measured lands. For example, in the mid-1670s Aurangzeb ordered a fresh survey and measurement of Bihar province. Only five of the eight districts were resurveyed before the emperor moved to the Deccan after 1680.[5] Expansion of the zabt system occurred in two regions: Hindustan, the heartland of the empire, and the four older Deccan provinces in the south.

In the course of the seventeenth century the Gangetic plain provinces of Delhi, Bihar, Allahabad and Awadh all showed substantial rises in lands classified as zabt. Agra, if adjusted for the loss of two districts to Delhi, added modestly to the total. In these five provinces land surveyed, measured and assessed rose by 42.3 million bigahs. By 1700 the lands of 181,300 villages were measured – nearly four-fifths the total recorded. In Delhi, Agra, and Allahabad measured villages exceeded 90 percent at the century's end. Clearly, the administration's goal was to obtain saturation coverage of lands in Hindustan.

The assessed revenue demand in the five provinces doubled over one hundred years from 1,784 million to 3,584 million dams. Steady growth in the measured area helped the Mughal state to keep pace with rising agricultural production (and rising prices) over the century. When cultivators cleared new lands and occupied new villages these could be surveyed and recorded for revenue assessment. Similarly, when cultivators turned to more valuable cash crops such as sugarcane or cotton, the revenue system extracted increased returns.

In the Deccan provinces, Khandesh, Aurangabad, Bidar, and Berar listed 60.3 million bigahs of arable under measurement by 1700. From a total of 30,006 villages identified in these provinces, 82 percent (24,637) were subject to measurement.[6] At the end of Akbar's reign, none of the portions of the Deccan under firm Mughal administration contained measured lands. Aurangzeb, who as prince governed the Deccan, commissioned his talented fiscal officer, Murshid Quli Khan, to implement the zabt system in the south. The initial, massive surveying

[5] Muzaffar Alam, "Eastern India in the early eighteenth century crisis," *Indian Economic and Social History Review*, 28, January–March 1991, 62.
[6] Habib, *Agrarian System*, p. 4.

effort took place from 1652 to 1656 during Aurangzeb's second tenure of office. After 1689 the regime faltered in that neither Bijapur nor Golconda (Hyderabad) were subjected to the regulation land revenue system.

The ratio of zabt to unmeasured lands serves as a plausible index of imperial centralization. As the Mughal teams of surveyors and recorders progressed from village to village and pargana to pargana, local Rajput, Afghan or other aristocrats lost power and autonomy. The chaudhuri of a pargana recently surveyed and assessed became a functionary subject to a new level of discipline and control. Great zamindars whose ancestors had paid tribute (pishkash) for generations to Indo-Muslim states now became *mal-wajib zamindars* who collected scheduled revenues in return for tax-free home lands and a fixed percentage of the returns. To retain a semblance of former power, these local leaders could contract to pay the revenue as a *taluqdar* collecting from lesser zamindars for a fee. The latter were frequently retainers or kinsmen now subject to intervening control by the state.

Equipped with detailed, comprehensive data, provincial fiscal officers reduced the negotiable terrain possible for each zamindar. They turned to their schedules of revenue rates and cultivated area tables to settle upon a reasonable demand. Zabt expansion increased the administration's ability to deal directly with village elites. The diwan could better locate and define *raiyati* areas in which village zamindars contracted to pay the stipulated taxes rather than zamindars. Increasing areas in raiyati status enlarged the area in which salary assignments could be freely made to smaller mansabdars. Under the village-wise arrangement smaller officers did not have to worry about the refractory responses of troublesome (*zor-talab*) local aristocrats. The zabt system generally eased the problem of making collections for both agents of the imperial crown lands (the khalisa) or salary assignees (jagirdars).

The system certainly did not hinder, and may have in some ways encouraged, expansion of productive capacity in these regions – especially in higher value cash crops. The diwans used these added revenues partly to strengthen and improve the imperial fiscal structure. Intensified administrative pressure acted to weaken and undercut the dominant social class in the countryside. At the same time peace, order, and new market opportunities, as well as state encouragement, increased the surplus to be shared between producer, middlemen (traders, brokers, moneylenders), zamindars, and the state. The result, by the end of this century, was a rural society entered into a quickening process of change.

THE RURAL ECONOMY

Repressive on occasion, the Mughal revenue system nevertheless did not stifle agricultural investment or inhibit population growth. A recent, conservative estimate by Irfan Habib suggests that the total population of India increased slowly throughout the seventeenth and eighteenth centuries from just under 150 million in 1600 to about 200 millions in 1800.[7] Even recurring periodic heavy mortality from dearth and disease when the monsoon rains failed for two years or more slowed, but did not stop, population growth. The overall trend lay upwards – toward greater human numbers supported by intensifying agricultural production in the countryside.

For the century under review the rural economy of Mughal India prospered. In agriculture the peasantry continued to produce its surplus. If anything, agricultural capacity improved over the long term. Indian peasants in the seventeenth century grew a large number of food and industrial crops efficiently and well. The Mughal revenue system was biassed in favor of higher value cash crops like indigo, cotton, sugar-cane, tree-crops, or opium. State incentives plus rising demand thereby stimulated cash crops grown for the market.

Indian peasants were quick to seize upon profitable new crops. Between 1600 and 1650 two new world crops, tobacco and maize, were widely adopted by cultivators throughout Mughal India.[8] Bengali peasants rapidly learned techniques of mulberry cultivation and sericulture as Bengal became a major silk-producing region for the world.[9] In the eastern Gangetic plain, after the mid-seventeenth century, a rapidly expanding export trade driven by new European trading centers at Patna stimulated expansion of cotton, opium, and sugar as cash crops.[10]

In nearly every region within the Mughal empire the settler frontier of sedentary agriculture moved forward at the expense of pastoralists in the plains or shifting cultivators in wooded areas. To the northeast

[7] Tapan Raychaudhuri and Irfan Habib, eds., *The Cambridge Economic History of India* (Cambridge: Cambridge University Press, 1982), I, 167.
[8] Raychaudhuri and Habib, *Economic History*, p. 217. [9] Ibid., p. 217.
[10] Alam, *Eastern India*, p. 68.

along the terai or foothills of the Himalayas and in eastern Bengal and Assam energetic Muslim peasants reclaimed large tracts from the jungle for wet rice cultivation.[11] To the northwest state revenues in the Punjab doubled in a century. The recently settled, formerly nomadic Hindu, and increasingly, Sikh Jat peasantry vigorously expanded cultivation in the rich river basins of the Punjab. The high fertility of the soil repaid an intensive investment in well-digging to grow wheat, cotton, oil seeds, and other crops. Cash crop demands intensified as market towns sprang up to meet the needs of a booming overland trade in the region.[12]

Fertile soils and relatively easy access to irrigation encouraged rural expansion in the eastern Gangetic plain. In Awadh, Rajputs aggressively settled new lands to expand their zamindari holdings.[13] In Gorakhpur district the extensive forests of Akbar's period gave way to settled agriculture by the early eighteenth century. The administration took special measures to encourage land clearing and settlement. Revenues assessed on Gorakhpur rose 267 percent in that period.[14]

In Bihar in Shah Jahan's reign, the imperial administration bifurcated the old Rohtas district and detached a new district, Shahabad Bhojpur. Partly this change reflected tighter administrative control over the region settled by the Ujjainiya Rajput zamindars in Bhojpur on Bihar's western border. Partly, however, the change reflected considerable expansion of cultivation at the forest frontier – expansion that was actively promoted by the state. A later eighteenth-century account of Shahabad and the origins of its zamindaris states: "most of the zamindaris during the reign of Shahjahan originated in *bankatai* or populating land after clearing forests. Those who did so became zamindars and obtained *nankars* (part of the revenue as zamindari right) for their lifetime. After the death of such zamindars, their sons obtained sanads for the rights held by them on condition of continued service."[15]

ZAMINDARS

In the hundred years elapsed between imposition of Akbar's new revenue system in the 1580s and Aurangzeb's departure for the Deccan

[11] Ibid. 225.
[12] Muzaffar Alam, *The Crisis of Empire in Mughal North India* (Delhi: Oxford University Press, 1986), pp. 139–145.
[13] Ibid., p. 99. [14] Ibid., p. 103. [15] Quoted in Alam, *Crisis of Empire*, pp. 65–66.

in 1680, a composite intermediary social class emerged in outline in the countryside. The growing domain of the zabt system helped to break away the cyst-like defenses of those warriors who dominated each pargana. Local chiefs or lineages no longer could add to their domains by small, vicious, wars against their neighbors. Although still armed and occasionally violent, Mughal zamindars at all levels had to carry out contractually defined tasks for the state or their sanads were not renewed. At the same time buoyant local and regional markets, stimulated by imperial demand, placed new, or at least enhanced, sources of wealth within the reach of every local lord and dominant lineage.

Over time the stability of the Mughal agrarian system strengthened the contractual position of zamindars at all levels. That agreed upon share of the annual land revenue guaranteed to the zamindar by the empire became a form of property that could be sold, inherited and even mortgaged.[16] Obviously, if the rural economy were in crisis – whether from natural calamity or from excessive taxation – there would be no point to a market in such property rights. Numerous seventeenth-century sale deeds for zamindari rights are consistent with a growing rural economy.

Other zamindars contracted for the right to collect the revenue for the state over lands beyond their original zamindari holding. For this service these taluqdars obtained compensation, but they did not possess full rights and the full share of the revenue of a zamindar.[17] Under normal conditions of peace and security this was not an overwhelmingly risky proposition in most districts.

Prosperity and stability benefited smaller village or *khud-kasht zamindars*. Village zamindars were members of the village elite who held ownership rights which permitted them to bequeath, sell or transfer their land. They could not be evicted by revenue officials as long as they paid their share of the village land revenues and continued to cultivate their holdings. These peasants who cultivated their own holdings were also distinguished by ownership of draught cattle and plows.

Village zamindars, acting as a corporate body, jointly managed the financial affairs of the village. They were collectively responsible for

[16] Raychaudhuri and Habib, *Economic History*, pp. 176–77, 246.
[17] Habib, *Agrarian System*, pp. 171–72.

the payment of the land revenue and the village headman came from their number. At the same time they paid revenue at concessionary rates fixed by custom which were less than those paid by tenants or migrant cultivators. These dominant peasants also administered the communal pastures, woodlands, and ponds and other shared resources of the village.[18]

Within the class of khud-kasht cultivators we find considerable evidence of inequality and internal stratification. Data from eastern Rajasthan for the late seventeenth century reveal that the wealthiest peasants, perhaps two to five big men per village, owned six to eight plows and bullock-teams which they let out on share-cropping terms to their less-wealthy fellows.[19] These elite peasants built up profits from investing in cash crops and in extension of cultivation. Often they engaged in moneylending within and without the village.

Detailed testimony from eastern Rajasthan suggests that cultivation was expanding steadily in the late seventeenth century and that the wealthier land-owning peasants put their capital into this effort. Elite peasants universally paid less in revenues than the body of tenant farmer (*pahi*) cultivators in northern India who did not share in the corporate privileges of the village. Often wealthier peasants possessed surplus funds sufficient to lend at interest. They retained profits from expanding arable and the increases in cash crops.

In the 1680s state warfare on local aristocracies receded to be replaced by more routine revenue administration and occasional punitive actions. A slow process of converting Rajputs, Jats, and other local warrior groups into quasi-officials was well underway. Nevertheless, the task remained incomplete. Local zamindars were only partially controlled, disarmed, or displaced by more docile newcomers. A growing cash economy offered them opportunities to profit from both moneylending and cash crops. The Mughal tax demand, while heavy, left substantial assets with zamindars and elite peasants. In accumulating resources, both rural lords and village elites were accumulating the means for defiance – should local rebellion seem feasible.

18 Satish Chandra, "The Structure of Village Society in Northern India" in Satish Chandra, *Medieval India* (Delhi: Orient Longman, 1982), p. 33.

19 Satish Chandra, "Role of the Local Community, the Zamindars and the State in Providing Capital Inputs for the Improvement and Expansion of Cultivation" in Chandra, *Medieval India*, pp. 171–72.

GENTRY AND TOWNS

By the 1680s hundreds of prosperous market towns (*qasbas*) had proliferated in northern India. In each pargana the central town served as principal market for grains sold to meet imperial taxes and as a center for moneylenders and grain traders. The qasbas fostered a growing gentry class. Agents for jagirdars, grain traders, moneylenders, zamindars, retired petty officials, and retired military officers built residences and established households. Many religious figures and other recipients of subsistence grants or tax-free lands (madad-i mash) settled in market towns. Often the grantees amassed wealth and purchased zamindari rights over additional lands.

New towns were often founded or moribund settlements revived by entrepreneurial action. Mughal jagirdars, zamindars, religious figures, or even court eunuchs acted to improve the economic potential of their holdings or, in many cases, for personal renown. Relatively modest funds were required to build a sarai, to dig a well, or to establish a market (*ganj*). In the generally peaceful and buoyant conditions of the Mughal century these efforts flourished. For example the town of Shahjahanpur, now the district town of the same name, resulted from Shah Jahan's grant of fourteen villages to two of his Afghan officers, on condition that they create a settlement and build a fort. The officers imported fellow Afghans from beyond the Indus to settle the town and placed them in quarters according to their lineage and tribal affiliations.[20]

Town life was especially attractive to Muslims who were the dominant group in many north Indian qasbas. Generally, in north India, Muslim gentry benefited substantially from official largess. Aurangzeb's policies aimed at restricting these local tax-free grants to Muslim recipients added appreciably to the fortunes of local town-based Muslim elites in the countryside. Pargana qazis (judges) by the mid to late seventeenth century had become conspicuous in this process.[21] The extent to which many qasbas were Muslim-dominated is revealed in the chronicler's descriptions of the defense mounted against assaults by Banda Bahadur's forces in the Sikh revolt of the early eighteenth century (see below, Chapter 12).

Batala town in the Sutlej–Chenab *doab* northeast of Lahore in the

[20] Raychaudhuri and Habib, *Economic History*, p. 443.
[21] Alam, *Crisis of Empire*, pp. 110–119.

Punjab is typical of such a qasba. Batala was founded on an ancient village mound in 1465 by Ram Dev, a Bhatti Rajput newly converted to Islam, who was the revenue contractor for the Punjab under Sultan Buhlul Lodi's governor. After decades of flooding and warfare, the entire region was depopulated. Ram Dev actively encouraged settlement and reclamation to the point that many villages sprang up around Batala. By the end of the Lodi period Batala had become a pargana headquarters town with a resident revenue collector.[22]

Batala endured several years of warfare and disruption when Babur raided from Kabul into the Lodi-ruled Punjab, but in 1527, the town and its surrounding hinterland was fully incorporated into the new Mughal regime. By the early eighteenth century Batala's population is estimated at between 15,000 and 20,000 persons. Each Muslim occupational or sectarian group or each Hindu caste lived in neighbourhoods (*mohullas*) with well-known names and boundaries. Various functionaries were appointed by the state. Generations of revenue collectors and locally recruited qanungos accepted Mughal appointments. Generations of Muslim qazis, appointed by the provincial sadr, resolved disputes, tried criminals, and protected persons and property in the town.

For nearly 200 years Batala's inhabitants experienced uninterrupted peace until the Sikh attack in 1709. The greater part of the cultivable land surrounding Batala was irrigated by many wells. Later a branch of the Shah Nahr, the canal bringing water to Lahore ordered built by Shah Jahan, carried irrigation water to Batala. Much of the land was intensively cultivated for market gardens by Arain Muslim Rajputs and their tenants. Wheat, raw sugar, and other surplus produce gathered to the town markets was sent on to Lahore. Weavers, dyers, iron-smiths, leatherworkers, carpenters, and other artisans, almost entirely Muslim, were present in Batala in large numbers. Ordinary cotton cloth for *lungis* and other clothing; saddles, shoes and decorated leatherwork, and wood carvings were among the manufactured goods exported. Hindu Khatris, the dominant commercial caste of the Punjab, controlled the commercial life of the town. As many as thirty subcastes of Khatri traders, shopkeepers, and moneylenders owned residential and

[22] The following description of Batala is taken from J. S. Grewal, *In the By-Lanes of History: Some Persian Documents from a Punjab Town* (Simla: Indian Institute of Advanced Study, 1975).

commercial property. Other commercial castes served as sarrafs (moneychangers) and goldsmiths.

The majority population in Batala, however, was Muslim. The town was a vital Islamic center which benefited directly from official patronage. Shamshir Khan, a converted Rajput who was revenue collector of Batala in Akbar's reign, built a large reservoir or tank with an adjoining garden, a mosque, and his own tomb completed in 1588–89. The collector's tomb became a monument to his benevolent activity for Batala Muslims who, if literate, left graffiti in ink on its walls with their names, parentage, and occupations. At the collector's request, Akbar gave lands yielding one hundred thousand dams to the noted Sayyid Muhammad Shah of Bukhar, who used the funds to maintain a large charitable kitchen (*langarkhana*) for residents and travelers.

Royal gifts and grants to the saintly and pious continued in Jahangir and Shah Jahan's reigns. Aurangzeb's long reign saw the construction of a congregational mosque, supported by a fixed allowance set by the emperor. Towards the end of the reign, a Qadiri Sufi master, Muhammad Faziluddin, founded a hospice and a theological college, both of which received revenue free lands from Aurangzeb's successors.

INTERNATIONAL TRADE

During the seventeenth century economic growth in Mughal India was stimulated by the growing importance of a new, external connection: the link between Mughal India and early modern Europe. The northern Europeans – Dutch, English, French, and even Ostenders – organized into joint-stock trading corporations, shunted aside the Portuguese as the dominant naval powers and traders in the Indian Ocean. Each trading concern operated under a royal charter which granted it exclusive national rights to carry out the India trade. The most powerful entities were the Dutch East India Company (founded 1602) and the English East India Company (founded 1600). These proved to be long-lived, highly profitable, long-distance trading corporations. (The French East India Company was a late entrant and suffered erratic management as a royal trading corporation.) These East India Companies created and nurtured a steadily enlarging economic, political and cultural tie with the Indian subcontinent.

East India Company trade exported Mughal India's industrial and processed goods to Europe able to pay for these goods with New World specie. Each region benefited from this exchange. As the century progressed with swelling trade profits came a larger European presence. Profitable trading also encouraged and, in fact, relied upon strong royal support at home. The East India Companies were very much an expression of the national interest of England and Holland.

Under the northern Europeans the scale and range of Indian exports brought directly to Europe increased dramatically. The East India Companies made sharp inroads in black pepper, the Portuguese staple obtained in the pepper-growing regions of the southwestern peninsula. As mass-consumption demands for pepper grew in Europe, EIC imports from India rose accordingly. In 1621 the Directors of the Dutch East India Company put the annual European import of pepper at 7 million lb. of which the Portuguese brought in 1.4 millions and the English and Dutch Companies shared the remaining 5.6 million lb.[23] By 1670 annual imports of both companies combined peaked at 13.5 million lb.[24]

Other Indian commodities such as indigo, grown and processed at Bayana near Agra, and in Gujarat enjoyed a steady and lucrative market in Europe. Relatively fast and inexpensive compared to woad, indigo from India was an important export until cheaper New World sources displaced it in the eighteenth century. Raw silk, produced in mulberry plantations in Kasiambazar and its hinterlands in northern Bengal, became a new source of supply for the silk-weaving industry in Italy and France after 1650. Saltpeter, much in demand for the European munitions industry, also served as a ballast for East India Company ships returning to Europe.

A more significant advance lay in the adoption of Indian textiles as an export commodity. Early in the century the East India Companies had entered the long-established trade in Gujarat and southeastern Coromandel cotton cloths to Indonesia. Profits from this trade helped to offset the costs of spices and the Dutch, already settled at Batavia, had an immediate advantage in this trade. Trial shipments soon created

[23] K. N. Chaudhuri, "Foreign Trade with India" in Raychaudhuri and Habib, eds., *The Cambridge Economic History of India*, I, 399.

[24] K. N. Chaudhuri, *The European Trading World of Asia and the English East India Company 1660–1760* (Cambridge: Cambridge University Press, 1978), Table C.14, p. 529; and Chaudhuri, "Foreign Trade with India," p. 399.

a market for cheaper Indian cotton cloth which undercut woolens and linens for the poorer ends of the market. By the 1620s the English East India Company was selling a quarter million pieces or lengths of Indian cloth at auction in London.[25] Dutch shipments soon rose sharply as sales in Amsterdam grew. By mid-century the comfort and washability of Indian cotton body linen and clothing was widely known in Europe. More costly styles of cotton such as patterned calico and chintz started to penetrate the luxury ends of the market. Indian silk was also much in demand.

Between 1660 and 1689 European demand for Indian textiles soared as prices and demand rose steeply. In 1664 the English East India Company imported 273,746 pieces of cotton cloth from India (approximately 4.2 million sq. meters). The rising trend culminated in 1684 at 1,760,315 pieces (or 26.9 million sq. meters).[26] Dutch imports, although somewhat less, followed a similar trend. The saturated textile market in Europe slumped abruptly in 1689 to be followed by a rising trend at the turn of the eighteenth century.

The return trade from Europe was nearly confined to shipment of precious metals from the New World, or for a time, from Japan. For the entire period, the English could only look to modest sales of broadcloth and woolens, unworked metals such as tin, lead, and copper, and some European luxury goods. The Dutch could offer spices obtained in the Moluccas and Ceylon which had fallen under their control. For both companies, however, purchasing power for Indian commodities rested upon shipments of bullion. In the century after 1660, as textile exports accelerated, the Dutch and English companies together shipped an average of over 34 tons of silver and nearly half a ton of gold every year.[27] In the Mughal dominions imported bullion and coin went directly to the imperial mint to be melted and struck as rupees or gold muhrs. Only then could they be used to pay Indian brokers and traders supplying cloth and other commodities. Often boxes of silver *reales* minted in Peru were transshipped through Amsterdam or London unopened until they reached the Mughal mints at Surat.

[25] Chaudhuri, "Foreign Trade with India," p. 401.
[26] Chaudhuri, *Trading World*, Table C.24, p. 547.
[27] J. F. Richards, ed. *Precious Metals in the Later Medieval and Early Modern World* (Durham NC: Carolina Academic Press, 1983), p. 24. These annual averages were calculated on the century from 1660 to 1760 for both companies.

CREATION OF NEW TRADING CENTERS

In the extreme south of India and in Southeast Asia, the Dutch could freely establish their own fortified trading bases and hope to coerce producers as had the Portuguese. On the Coromandel coast they had little trouble gaining permission from the fragmented Hindu *nayak* kingdoms of the south to establish their own settlement at Pulicat by 1610. Within the territory of the larger, more powerful states of the subcontinent, however, they had to take a different approach. The overall objective was access to Machhilipatnam (Masulipatnam) at the mouth of the Godavari river in the Sultanate of Golconda and Surat, the west coast port in Mughal Gujarat. In 1605 and 1606 a Dutch factor visited Machhilipatnam to negotiate trading entry with the Qutb Shahi ruler of Golconda. This was a prime production area for fine chintz much in demand in Southeast Asian markets. A royal order permitted the Dutch to establish a trading station (factory) at Machhilipatnam port and gave the Dutch a lower export duty. Ten years later, the Dutch received permission to open a permanent factory at Surat.[28]

The English East India Company did not invest in its own settlements in India at first. Instead, in 1611 the English factory at Macchilipatnam was founded; in 1613 a similar trading station became permanent at Surat. In 1615 the Company arranged to have James I send Thomas Roe as a royal ambassador to the court of Jahangir. Roe's success in this mission further solidified the English position at Surat and permitted them to send factors inland to set up trading posts at Agra, Burhanpur, Patna, and other trading centers.

At these trading centers, bodies of Dutch or English factors who were employees of their respective companies sold European goods and purchased supplies of Indian textiles and other export commodities. The trading centers or "factories" were self-sufficient communities of European traders who lived under communal discipline and maintained their own cultural traditions. In the fashion of the time the walled factory compounds served as living quarters and as secure storage for valuable goods. The East India Companies engaged Europeans to serve as armed guards and also hired Indians as well. Larger stations, especially those in the south like Fort St. George, developed early into nearly autonomous city-states.

The Indian trading stations stood at one end of a directly admin-

[28] Chaudhuri, "Foreign Trade with India," p. 388.

istered trading system with London or Amsterdam at the other end. Only two markets existed: the procurement market in each region in India for each commodity and the sales market in Europe for each import. The Companies owned and shipped these goods under their ownership and control throughout. As has often been suggested they were indeed the precursors of the modern multi-national corporation.

The East India Company directors and owners – the Court of Seventeen in Amsterdam and the Court of Proprietors in London – presided over newly evolved complex organizations capable of great efficiency and stability in their operations. Each company employed a system of specialized committees at home for matters like accounts, buying, warehousing, shipping, bullion procurement, and other functions. Through issue of capital stock, loans, and bonds, they mobilized large amounts of short and long-term capital to send in the form of specie to Asia. They kept meticulous accounts which included profit and loss statements for commodities, ship voyages, trading stations and trading seasons.

Practices first perfected by trial and error were codified into decision rules to be applied consistently over time. Company officers organized an intricate shipping schedule to service their far-flung trading stations. Scheduling had to account for close to two years' elapsed time between India and Europe for each trading voyage. All purpose-built EIC ships were either owned outright or leased for the trade and manned by Company staff. All were armed and fully capable of defending themselves against all vessels save European warships.

In Europe the companies stored Indian goods in warehouses and sold them on monopoly terms. In so doing the companies were able to minimize swings in prices and profits. In India, the Dutch and English companies worked very hard to rationalize procurement of Indian goods. Textile produced by individual artisans in sequence – spinners, weavers, dyers, bleachers, and printers – required special efforts at standardization. EIC factors gave out contracts to Indian middlemen/wholesale merchants for delivery of thousands of pieces of cloth of specified quality and style some eight or ten months later. Cash advances committed the merchants and their weavers to deliver the cloth on schedule and acted as a deposit on orders for the producers.

By mid-century the effects of this new trade channel were beginning to be felt in Mughal India. Four coastal zones produced the greater part of textile exports: the area surrounding Surat in Gujarat; the area between Krishna and Godavari in northern Coromandel adjacent to Machhilipatnam; the southern Coromandel between Pulicat and Madras; and the Ganges delta forming a hinterland for the port at Hughli in Bengal.[29] Within each region bullion imports converted to imperial currency paid customs duties, the local expenses of the factors, bribes and presents for officials, and put new income into the hands of weavers and profits into the coffers of Indian wholesalers and brokers.

European activities reached deeply into the countryside in these regions. In northern Coromandel during the latter half of the century, the Dutch at Machhilipatnam expanded their purchases beyond the expensive patterned cloth traditionally exported from the region between the Krishyna and Godavari rivers. They created a new market for plain white cotton cloths or calicoes.[30] The variety known as longcloth or guinees were 35 yard pieces primarily used in the West African slave trade. In the early 1680s the Dutch East India Company purchased 4 to 5 million yards of calicoes each year. Half of these pieces were shipped directly to Holland; half were consigned to Batavia for resale in Southeast Asia. The English factory at Machhilipatnam shipped a like quantity of calicoes for the European market.

The VOC (Verenigde Oostindische Compagnie) placed resident Dutch factors at its head trading station, the port of Machhilipatnam, and three subordinate trading stations inland. These stations were actually markets at which the European factors met twice a year with Telugu merchants of the Komati caste. From June to August they placed orders with cash advances with these middlemen. The Komati wholesalers then executed their contracts with head weavers who controlled the output of dozens of their fellows and who undertook to guarantee delivery of acceptable cloth. Between September and November, the prime sailing season, the Dutch factors received delivery of the woven pieces which had to be checked for general quality, and standardized dimensions and thread count.

In this region the weavers were not concentrated in towns, but rather dispersed in industrial villages scattered throughout the coastal districts. In the eastern portion of the East Godavari delta the Dutch station at the village of Draksharama drew its supplies from a catch-

[29] Chaudhuri, *Trading World*, "India: Main Textile Weaving Areas 1600–1750," p. 244.

[30] The data on northern Coromandel are drawn from Joseph J. Brennig, "The Textile Trade of Seventeenth Century Northern Coromandel: A Study of a Pre-Modern Asian Export Industry" (Madison WI: University of Wisconsin Ph.D. dissertation, 1975).

ment area of sixteen villages. A Dutch census in 1682 revealed that 5,960 households operated 6,930 looms in these sixteen villages for an average of 373 weaving households per village. In the typical northern Coromandel industrial village, weavers, cloth washers, and dyers constituted more than half the households and far outnumbered cultivators.[31] Each household operated by adult male weavers produced between 1,300 and 1,500 yards of cloth per year. At the prices prevailing in the 1680s a weaver paid in cash could purchase foodgrains and meet other subsistence needs and generate a surplus at the end of the year. Head weavers and those with two or more looms did even better.

Cash advances to the weavers travelled down the social hierarchy to reach lower caste women who spun cotton yarn and sold it directly to the weavers. And Dutch advances reached out beyond the region to pay the *banjara* wholesaler/transporters who used thousands of pack bullocks to carry raw cotton to the weaver. The best quality cotton was not grown in northern Coromandel but came from the black cotton tracts of Khandesh and Berar five hundred kilometers to the west. These carriers were given tax-free status by the king of Golconda and later by the Mughals.

There is no question that the East India Companies' activities directly stimulated the economy of each coastal region and the empire as a whole. Bengal offers the most dramatic example of export-stimulated economic growth. After Shah Jahan expelled the Portuguese from their trading station at Hugli in 1631, the way was cleared for Dutch, English, and French merchants to place their factors at that port. Dutch activities in Bengal grew rapidly. In 1663 the VOC imported treasure worth 903,953 florins into Bengal to pay for its purchases; by 1707 treasure imports had increased to 3.2 million florins.[32] The total value of exports followed a similar upward path.[33] From Bengal the Dutch procured growing quantities of saltpeter, shipped primarily to Europe, opium, sold in Indonesia, raw silk divided between Japan and Holland; and woven cotton and silk textiles divided between Europe, Indonesia, and Japan. These were all either enlarged or new markets for Bengal's producers.

A recent analysis concludes that the Dutch trade, which primarily

[31] Brennig, "Textile Trade," p. 292.

[32] Om Prakash, *The Dutch East India Company and the Economy of Bengal 1630–1720* (Princeton: Princeton University Press, 1985), 66–67.

[33] Prakash, *Dutch East India Company*, p. 70.

imported precious metals, caused a real increase in Bengal's output and income. The export surplus was generated by fuller utilization of existing productive capacity and a reallocation of resources to meet European demand. Dutch and English procurement of textiles by the end of the century employed nearly ten percent of the full-time weavers and other workers in the textile sector of Bengal.[34] For Bengal, the growing export market in Europe added another impetus to a steadily enlarging regional economy. This long-term trend, already well underway, continued well into the British colonial period.

Trading company investments in Bengal directly benefited the imperial exchequer and indirectly enhanced the incomes of high-ranking Mughal officers. The stream of silver pouring into Bengal was a mainstay of the copious output of the imperial mints located at Rajmahal, Dacca, Patna, and Balasore.[35] Cash crops like poppy and mulberry flourished. Bengali peasants shifted sizable areas of lands from rice to mulberry in response to market incentives for silk production. Each bigah of land (3/5 acre) in mulberry paid Rs. 3 per year; each bigah in rice paid Rs. 0.75. When in 1706 the Mughal authorities prohibited Dutch trade for nearly a year, provincial revenues suffered as peasants reverted to rice production.[36] The Mughal khalisa (crownlands) received revenues from eleven of the twenty-eight parganas in Bihar which were the primary production areas for saltpeter. A number of amirs, including Asaf Khan, the wazir, held the others in jagir. In the late 1680s VOC factors bought 1,310 tonnes amounting to thirty percent of the total output of refined saltpeter.[37] The crown and prominent nobles held similar interests in the opium tracts in Bihar.[38]

The Mughal empire actively encouraged European trading in Bengal as it did elsewhere. Beginning in the mid-1630s the Dutch obtained from Shah Jahan exemption from payment of transit-tolls (which were the perquisite of local jagir holders) in Bengal.[39] Customs duties, at 3 to 4 percent, remained in force since these were collected by the imperial treasury. A Dutch embassy to Aurangzeb in the early 1660s succeeded in having these privileges continued. The English enjoyed similar

[34] Prakash, *Dutch East India Company*, p. 242.
[35] Om Prakash, "Foreign Merchants and Indian Mints in the Seventeenth and the Early Eighteenth Century," in Richards, ed., *Imperial Monetary System*, p. 171–192.
[36] Prakash, *Dutch East India Company*, p. 238n.
[37] Ibid., pp. 58–60.
[38] Ibid., pp. 57–58
[39] Ibid., p. 42.

concessions. The English as well as the Dutch and French made regular gifts in cash and kind to keep local officials sympathetic to them and to be sure that royal exemptions were obeyed.

Still incomplete, but persuasive evidence exists to argue that the secular trend for Mughal India was that of economic growth and vitality. The state placed few constraints on economic activity. The state delivered numerous services and incentives to foster internal trade at all levels. Even European trading companies were permitted great freedom to drive a steadily growing export trade and to import precious metals. The cultivated area underwent noticeable expansion in a number of provinces. Imperial tax collections rose accordingly. Mughal taxes on agricultural production could be onerous in specific areas and periods, but the overall impression is that neither the level of assessment nor the forms of collection were sufficient to deter continued growth. The question of which classes and groups were the beneficiaries of that growth is yet to be fully answered.

CHAPTER 10

MARATHA INSURGENCY AND MUGHAL CONQUEST IN THE DECCAN

Shortly after Aurangzeb's accession a surprising new source of resistance to Mughal political domination appeared. In the hilly areas of the western Deccan, around Puna, the Maratha leader Shivaji Bhonsla (1627–1680) was carving out a self-sufficient state within the enfeebled shell of the Sultanate of Bijapur. The Bhonsla regime offered a new option for ambitious and aggressive men from both the Maratha warrior caste and literate Maratha Brahmin castes. So successful was Shivaji that by the 1660s he seriously threatened Mughal prestige and domination in the south.

Shivaji was the second son of Shahji Bhonsla, a Maratha general and aristocrat, and Jija Bai, daughter of one of the great Maratha noblemen in the Sultanate of Ahmadnagar. In the early 1630s Shahji had led an ultimately futile attempt to set up a young Nizam Shah ruler as his puppet. When Ahmadnagar was swallowed up by the Timurids, Shahji took service in the Karnatak campaigns of the Sultan of Bijapur. Shahji retained control of his large fief in the western Ghats near Puna. The Sultan of Bijapur had de facto ceded political control of much of the western Ghats to the powerful Maratha chiefs or deshmukhs in that remote area.

Shivaji was raised by Jija Bai, Shahji's estranged wife, at Puna as a rustic Maratha aristocrat. Unlike Shahji's other sons, Shivaji was not indoctrinated into the Persianate high culture of the Bijapur court. At age eighteen Shivaji seized control over his absentee father's estate. He attracted several able young Maratha hill chiefs and their retainers to his service. Partly in response to Bijapur's weak hand and partly in rebellion against his father, Shivaji began to expand his domain in the western hills.

In 1646 the Sultan of Bijapur, Muhammad Adil Shah, fell ill and remained incapacitated for a decade. Shivaji grasped this opportunity to enlarge his power. By the late 1650s the young Maratha leader was independent of Bijapur. He had repudiated the foreshortened political vision of a Maratha deshmukh or rural aristocrat. He was no longer caught within the Indo-Muslim political culture defined by Bijapur.

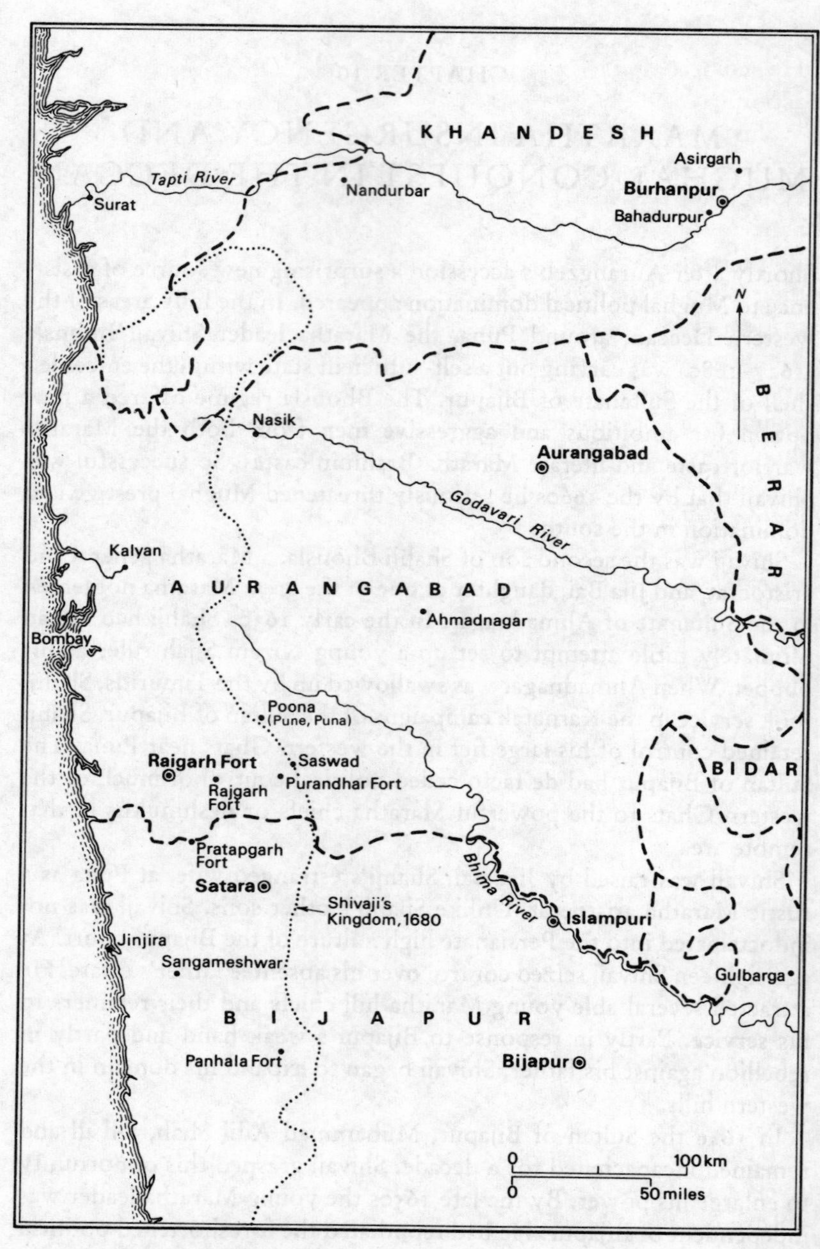

4 The Western Deccan in 1707
Source: I. Habib, *An atlas of the Mughal Empire* (Delhi, 1982), 14A

He had become a ruler free to choose his own affiliations and course of action.

Shivaji's remarkable achievements in these early years are often ignored. With incessant negotiation, threat, and, on occasion, ferociously applied violence, the young Bhonsla chief established dominance over other long-established Maratha deshmukhs in the region. By the same means he took control of nearly forty hill-fortresses from their Bijapur-appointed commanders. These he garrisoned with commanders and troops loyal to him. An impressive cadre of young Maratha warriors and Brahmin administrators organized and ran the army and administration of his growing kingdom. Directly paid infantry and cavalry totalled as many as 10,000 horsemen and 50,000 infantry by the 1660s.

Judicious plunder of government treasure, extortion, and, increasingly, levying of taxes on the populace of the region gave Shivaji sufficient funds to recruit and pay his followers. With these growing resources Shivaji developed a network of interlocking, well-sited and easily defended fortresses in Maharashtra. Rajgarh, designed and built by him, served as the Bhonsla capital. At Pratapgarh, another great mountain keep, he installed a large shrine dedicated to his patron, the goddess Bhawani.

Shivaji extended his domain into the fertile coastal districts of the northern Konkan. His army seized Kalian, a rich trading town, and drove off the officers of the Bijapuri nobleman who held jagirs there. With access to the sea, Shivaji acquired several ships and began to trade with the Persian Gulf and Red Sea. Other armed coastal vessels in his employ sailed on plundering expeditions into the Arabian Sea. He garrisoned several coastal or island fortresses in the Konkan. Throughout this period the youthful raja negotiated with the Portuguese and British for guns, naval supplies, and technical assistance.

In this early phase, Shahji's prominence and influence at the Bijapur court helped to deflect punitive actions against his son. Even in 1649, when the Bijapur Sultan seized and imprisoned Shahji in an attempt to force the general to control his son's activities, powerful friends induced Shahji's release. For several years thereafter Shivaji was relatively quiescent. During Aurangzeb's invasion of 1656, the Sultan was able to call upon his rebel zamindar and send him to plunder Mughal lands as a diversion. This accommodation ended with the death of Sultan Muhammad Adil Shah.

In 1657, the new sultan, Ali Adil Shah, sent Afzal Khan, one of his most capable commanders, with a 10,000 man army to subdue Shivaji. Along the route the Bijapur troops profaned the shrine of Bhawani at Tuljapur as well as several other major Hindu shrines in Maharashtra. After a series of negotiations marked by suspicion on both sides, Afzal Khan persuaded Shivaji to meet to negotiate a settlement with the Sultan. Shivaji and Afzal Khan confronted each other in the Bijapur commander's audience tent on a site near Pratapgarh fort. Within the tent an initial embrace of greeting between the two principals abruptly became a mortal struggle in which Afzal Khan tried to strangle Shivaji. The latter used his concealed iron "tiger claws" to disembowel his larger enemy. At their commander's signal hidden Maratha troops surrounding the site attacked and slaughtered the confused Bijapur soldiery.

Afzal Khan's death and the rout of the Bijapur army was widely celebrated in the Maratha country.[1] The enraged Sultan of Bijapur personally led a new force into the west and reoccupied the southern coastal districts before difficulties elsewhere forced him to retire. The notorious incident ruptured Shivaji's already dubious subordination to the Sultan of Bijapur. As an unattached Maratha chief, he was then forced to come to terms with that Mughal advance that had long enervated the Deccan Sultanates.

CREATION OF AN INSURGENT STATE: SECOND PHASE

During the second phase of his career, between 1660 and 1674, Shivaji wavered between acceptance and repudiation of imperial authority. For the first time the young ruler faced the full weight of Mughal power. In 1660, Shaista Khan, new governor of the Mughal Deccan, swept aside Maratha resistance, occupied Puna and garrisoned the northern portion of Shivaji's territories. After a four month siege and heavy losses, the Mughals captured Chakan, one of Shivaji's hill forts near Puna. The costs of attacking even one of Shivaji's strongly defended hill forts dissuaded Shaista Khan from further sieges. Instead, he deployed flying columns of Mughal cavalry to ravage the country-

[1] Harry A. Acworth, *Ballads of the Marathas*, "The Death of Abdul Khan at the Hands of Shiwaji Maharaha" (London: Longmans Green & Co., 1894).

side. Aurangzeb sent reinforcements including a 10,000 man Rajput force under Jaswant Singh Rathor. Shaista Khan took up residence in the town of Puna itself which served as the central garrison and command post.

On the night of April 5, 1663, Shivaji infiltrated Puna's defenses with 400 of his men. He and a raiding party entered Shaista Khan's mansion, hacked their way to the nobleman's bedchamber and wounded but did not succeed in killing him. Shaista Khan's son, several of his wives, and dozens of his servants and soldiers died in the melee. Shivaji and his troops escaped with only minimal casualties. This exploit delighted the Marathas who celebrated the near-superhuman feats of their hero. Suspicion of pro-Maratha sympathies fell upon Jaswant Singh Rathor whose Rajput troops guarded the outskirts of the city. Shaista Khan, dishonored and humiliated, was recalled and replaced by Prince Muazzam as governor of the Deccan.

A few months later, in January, 1664, Shivaji led 4,000 cavalry on a raid north to Surat, the busiest trading port in western India. The Mughal governor left the unfortified city of 200,000 defenseless and fled to the shelter of Surat fort. Shivaji ignored the fort but spent six days in a leisurely plunder of the town. Among his victims was Baharji Borah, the Ismaili trader reputed to be the richest merchant in the world, whose mansion was virtually destroyed in the search for treasure. Only the Dutch and English merchants, who stubbornly defended their walled compounds with musket fire, escaped the general looting. Finally, Shivaji's troops rode off carrying with them cash and valuables valued at over 10 million rupees. In the aftermath of this raid Shivaji's armed fleet seized Mecca-bound ships and exacted ransoms from the pilgrims on board. His horsemen also raided the outskirts of Aurangabad, capital of the Mughal Deccan while Prince Muazzam, notoriously indolent, did little to stop him. In the same period Shivaji's forces beat back an assault by the Bijapur army and continued to raid freely in that kingdom.

Enraged and disturbed by these insults Aurangzeb sent his most capable general with orders to first destroy Shivaji and thereafter invade and annex Bijapur. Mirza Raja Jai Singh Kachhwaha, a sixty-year-old veteran commander, assembled a large army and relieved Jaswant Singh Rathor at Puna in March, 1665. The dispatches of Jai Singh, preserved by his private secretary, display in almost text-book fashion the skill and resources brought to bear by a high-ranking

Mughal field commander.[2] In a preliminary diplomatic thrust, Jai Singh sent emissaries to Bijapur to warn the Sultan against any effort to combine with Shivaji; agents to the European coastal settlements to insist that they obstruct any sea-borne activity by the Maratha fleet; and Brahmin emissaries to those numerous Maratha deshmukhs who bore long-standing grudges against Shivaji. From the latter he enlisted cadres of Maratha auxiliaries. Promises of high rank and money were made to all of Shivaji's chief officers to undermine their loyalty.

Military operations began immediately. Jai Singh marched due south from Puna, established his base at the town of Saswad, set out outposts, and fought his way to the great hill fortress of Purandhar. For two months the besiegers remorselessly ran trenches, brought up their guns, and assaulted one line of defense after another. Jai Singh sent out cavalry to engage the Marathas and to forage and burn the countryside. Shivaji was unable to relieve the fort or to prevent the devastation of his kingdom. The goddess Bhawani warned him in a dream that he could not successfully oppose a Hindu prince.[3] Demoralized, Shivaji opened negotiations with Jai Singh. Assured of his safety by Jai Singh's sacred oaths, Shivaji, attended only by six Brahmins, came to Jai Singh's audience tent pitched just behind the siege lines.

Convinced that he could not save Purandhar or drive the Mughals out, Shivaji capitulated. Under the treaty of Purandhar Shivaji surrendered twenty-three of his fortresses and the lands they commanded to the empire but retained twelve fortresses and their lands as his estate. He became a vassal of the Mughal emperor, paying tribute, but exempted from personal service as a mansabdar. Instead his young son, Shambhaji, granted the rank of 5,000 zat, would be sent to the imperial court. Finally, Shivaji agreed to lead his troops as part of the Mughal force expected to invade Bijapur. In return he was promised additional lands to be seized from Bijapur. Shivaji surrendered his independence and entered the imperial system as a chief or, in the imperial parlance, a zamindar – the fate of dozens of powerful regional chiefs and kings before him.

Between mid-November, 1665 and February, 1666, Shivaji, with 11,000 troops, accompanied Jai Singh during the abortive Mughal campaign into Bijapur. Before the war concluded in negotiations

[2] Jagadish N. Sarkar, *The Military Despatches of a Seventeenth Century Indian General* (Calcutta: Scientific Book Agency, 1969).

[3] James Grant Duff, *History of the Mahrattas* (New Delhi, 2 vols. in one, reprint edition, 1971), I, 110.

Shivaji allowed himself to be persuaded by Jai Singh to journey northward to the imperial court. Leaving his mother as regent, Shivaji, his son Shambhaji, seven of his principal officers, and 4,000 men left for the north. He was advanced 100,000 rupees for the journey from the imperial Deccan treasury.

At Agra his host and patron was Kumar Ram Singh, Jai Singh's son and his agent at court. On May 12, 1666, the date of Aurangzeb's fiftieth lunar birthday, Shivaji offered gifts of submission and bowed at the foot of the Timurid throne. Aurangzeb made a cursory acknowledgement of his presence but delayed presenting return gifts or other response till later in the ceremony. Shivaji suddenly found himself standing in line behind rows of nobles as the elaborate court audience proceeded. Outraged, Shivaji protested audibly then fell to the floor in a fainting fit. He was hustled out of the audience hall to Kumar Singh's mansion. The suspicious emperor placed Shivaji under house arrest despite his pleas to be allowed to return home, but did permit Shivaji's troops to leave Agra for the Deccan. Aurangzeb refused a private audience and withheld the elephant, jewels, and robe of honor intended for Shivaji.

Feigning illness, Shivaji took to his bed and called for physicians. Over several weeks, he contrived to find a way to escape. This may well have been with the connivance of Kumar Ram Singh or by bribing his guards. Shivaji slipped out of the mansion and was gone far before his absence was discovered and the word sent to Mughal road guards, city prefects, faujdars, and other imperial officers. Arriving safely at Mathura the next day, Shivaji took refuge with a family of Maratha Brahmins who helped to disguise him as a wandering Hindu monk to evade Mughal patrols. Travelling on foot over a long circuitous route to the east he and Shambhaji arrived back at Raigarh in December, 1666.

Aurangzeb, somewhat unexpectedly, failed to send an invading army against Shivaji. Apparently the Yusufzai rising in the northwestern mountains distracted his attention. Two years later, in 1668, Shivaji's frequent petitions to Aurangzeb for pardon were answered. The emperor recognized his title as Raja and restored Chakan fort, but not any of the other twenty-two occupied by the Mughals to Shivaji. Shambhaji, his rank of 5,000 zat restored, went to Prince Muazzam's court at Aurangabad, the Deccan capital, at the head of a thousand Maratha horsemen. The latter were supported by jagirs assigned in

Berar province. Shambhaji and Prince Muazzam formed a congenial bond during the two years in which the young Maratha heir served the Mughals.

Soon however, a rupture occurred. Mughal treasury officers tried to recover from Shambhaji's jagirs the 100,000 rupees Shivaji had drawn for expenses on his trip to Agra. Incensed, Shivaji recalled his son and seized a number of his former strongholds. Mughal retribution was hindered by internecine conflicts between Prince Muazzam and his most powerful subordinate, the Afghan nobleman Dilir Khan. The latter accused the prince of collusion with Shivaji in a plot to seize the throne. The crisis was eventually resolved and Muazzam exonerated, but the immediate pressure on Shivaji lifted.

In October, 1670, Shivaji assembled a 15,000 man army and marched north toward Surat. The Mughal governor offered only nominal resistance at the city walls (recently erected by Aurangzeb's order) and the Marathas plundered the city again. After several days of looting the raiders carried off cash and goods worth over six and a half million rupees – less than before. Trade at Surat went into decline for the next several years as it became clear that the empire was no longer able to defend its most lucrative ocean port.[4] After further raiding in Mughal Khandesh, Shivaji fought a pitched battle with a 5,000 man Mughal army before returning to Raigarh.

For the next four years Shivaji's Marathas raided and plundered to the northeast in Khandesh in Mughal territory and southeast into Kanara in Bijapur lands. Both Bijapur and imperial armies pursued the raiders and often engaged them, but with mixed success. Shivaji's commanders discovered that they could meet Mughal armies in the field on equal terms. The weight of Mughal heavy cavalry and field artillery were canceled out by greater mobility and higher morale on the part of the Maratha troops.

CREATION OF AN INSURGENT STATE: THE MONARCHY

Buoyed by these victories and by the ever-increasing flow of plunder and taxation coming into his coffers, Shivaji took a momentous step. In June, 1674, he had himself crowned as an independent Hindu

[4] M. N. Pearson, "Shivaji and the Decline of the Mughal Empire," *Journal of Asian Studies*, 35 (1976), 221–235.

monarch.[5] Many months of preparation preceded the ceremony. Shivaji immersed himself in a period of intense prayer and worship at a number of temples and shrines. In the meantime his Brahmin advisers persuaded Gagga Bhatta of Varanasi, the foremost Hindu theologian of his day, to declare that Shivaji was not a mere Shudra of the Maratha caste, but a lapsed Kshatriya, a Rajput, whose ancestors could be traced back to the solar line of the Ranas of Mewar. Gagga Bhatta travelled to the Maratha capital where he first purified Shivaji and then invested him with the sacred threat and Vedic verses of the twice-born castes.

On June 6, 1674, after a night of fasting, Shivaji underwent the Sanskritic royal consecration (*abisheka*) ceremony. Seated on a gold stool with his wife, Sorya Bai, beside him he was bathed with Ganges water poured from gold jugs. After changing to a royal scarlet robe, he then sat upon a newly built, gold-covered throne. To the accompaniment of Brahminical chants and artillery salvos, Gagga Bhatta raised the royal umbrella over his head and hailed him as Siva Chhatrapati. Thereafter followed lavish gifts to thousands of Brahmins, officials and other dignitaries and a royal procession through the streets of the city. The entire ceremony was estimated to have cost five million rupees.

Shivaji's coronation, widely reported throughout the subcontinent, was one of the most important political acts of the seventeenth century. Within his kingdom's borders the coronation ceremony impressed his legitimate authority over even the oldest of Maratha aristocratic houses. Beyond his borders it established the Bhonsla ruler and his descendants as a ruling house the equal of any other. More startling, however, was the fact that for the first time in generations a regional monarch claimed royal authority without reference to the Timurid emperor. With this dramatic act Shivaji, unlike his father, asserted his independence from Indo-Muslim authority and political culture. In an avowedly revivalist ceremony he created a militantly Hindu monarchy. The new ruler was a *Chhatrapati*; not a *Padshah*. Insurgency against Mughal rule had acquired a new rallying point.

THE QUTB SHAH/BHONSLA ALLIANCE

Within two years the new monarch revealed a bold new strategy. Shivaji first negotiated a truce with the badly harassed Mughal gover-

[5] The coronation ceremony is described in detail in Jadunath Sarkar, *Shivaji and His Times* (Calcutta: M. C. Sarkar & Sons, Sixth edition, revised and enlarged, 1961), pp. 201–215.

nor of the Deccan provinces. Then he agreed to a defensive alliance against the Mughals with Madanna Pandit, the Telugu Brahmin who was chief minister of the kingdom of Golconda. Under the terms of this agreement Golconda, the wealthiest and most stable of the Deccan states, agreed to an annual subsidy to support Shivaji's campaigns against the Timurids. Thus encouraged, in January, 1677, Shivaji led a 60,000 man army eastward to Hyderabad, the capital of Golconda. Here he held a series of meetings with Abul Hasan, the Qutb Shah Sultan and Madanna Pandit, along with his brother Akkanna, the commander in chief of the Qutb Shah army. In these meetings the two rulers negotiated a military alliance aimed at conquest and joint annexation of the lands of the Bijapur Karnatak. This wealthy, prosperous area along the southeastern Coromandel coast was currently ruled by nearly independent Bijapur governors or by tributary rulers. The latter included Shivaji's half brother, Vyankoji Bhonsla, who had carved out a kingdom around Tanjore on the Kaveri river. The Qutb Shah Sultan, heavily influenced by his two Brahmin officers, agreed to supply a large monthly cash subsidy and an auxiliary five thousand man force with artillery to accompany the Marathas.

En route to the Karnatak, Shivaji left his army at Anantapur, and made a pilgrimage to the famous Siva temple of Shri Shaila on the Krishna river. At this sacred site the royal worshiper spent ten days in devotion before the image of Siva's consort. At one point Shivaji tried to commit suicide in front of the goddess, but was restrained by his attendants. On departing, he gave funds sufficient to build a bathing *ghat* on the river, a monastery, and a guesthouse for pilgrims.[6]

A year-long campaign sufficed for the Maratha ruler to take possession of Jinji and Vellore, the two commanding bastions of the Bijapur Karnatak. Vellore surrendered only after a fourteen month siege. Victory permitted Shivaji's officers to occupy and annex territory yielding revenues of two million gold hun per year. In Tanjore, however, his half-brother Vyankoji rejected Shivaji's claim for half their patrimony, defended that position with his army and eventually paid Shivaji 600,000 rupees to be left undisturbed. Shivaji proved unwilling to give up any portion of his new possessions to Golconda. But this sticking point did not terminate the defensive alliance between him and the Qutb Shah.

[6] Sarkar, *Shivaji*, pp. 291–292.

DYNASTIC SUCCESSION

Upon his return to Raigarh in early 1678, Shivaji faced the problem of contriving an orderly succession to the Bhonsla throne. The Maratha ruler and his council of ministers formally proposed a division of the kingdom between his two sons to take place after Shivaji's death. Rajaram, the youngest, would receive the home territories to rule; and Shambhaji, then a turbulent youth of nineteen, would be given the newly acquired lands in Mysore and Jinji.

Shambhaji's publicly expressed dissatisfaction with this arrangement became widely known. Dilir Khan, the Mughal governor of the Deccan, wrote secret letters to the young prince offering Mughal aid to win his patrimony if he agreed to an alliance. In December 1678, Shambhaji, in disgrace for the rape of a respectable Brahmin woman, escaped his father's surveillance and fled. Accompanied by his presumably forgiving wife Yesu Bai he rode to the camp of Dilir Khan on the border of Bijapur. When notified, the delighted Aurangzeb made the young fugitive prince a Mughal noble with the title of Raja and seven thousand zat – an extremely high rank.

For nearly a year Shambhaji served with Dilir Khan in a series of campaigns against the combined forces of Bijapur and Shivaji. The gradual dissolution of central political authority in the Sultanate encouraged intervention by both the Mughals and Shivaji. Shambhaji, however, became increasingly disillusioned and unhappy with his Mughal associates. In November, 1679, Shambhaji and Yesu Bai, responding to frequent overtures, returned to the Bhonsla court.

During this interval Shivaji issued a long public letter to the Emperor Aurangzeb which eloquently rebuked him for reversing the wise policy of Akbar and Jahangir by imposing the jiziya on Hindus. Shivaji chided Aurangzeb for adding the hardship of this tax to his already over-burdened subjects. And, he pointed out that in the Koran God is styled Lord of all men, not simply of Muslims and that both Muslim and Hindu worshipped God in their own way.[7]

Shivaji returned from a great plundering raid into Mughal territories in Khandesh and Aurangabad to meet his repentant son. In late March, 1680, the Bhonsla ruler, whose health had been declining for some time, developed fever and dysentery which ended a few days later in his death at age fifty-three.

[7] Sarkar, *Shivaji*, pp. 320–323.

Three days after Shivaji's death, his eldest wife Sorya Bai proclaimed her son, Rajaram, king at Raigarh fort. Shambhaji rejected this and openly assumed regal powers. Quickly gaining overwhelming support among the Maratha officers, he occupied the capital at Raigarh without resistance. The deposed Rajaram was unharmed, but his mother and about two hundred of her followers were executed. Shambhaji carried out a full-blown coronation in February of 1681 to fully legitimize his role as Shivaji's successor. The Bhonsla dynasty had survived its first test: one of Shivaji's sons became undisputed ruler of the Maratha kingdom.

THE LEGACY

Shivaji's legacy included a compact unitary state. Within the western Ghats and the littoral districts of the Konkan, Shivaji constructed an effective civil administration supported by a firmly controlled network of scores of massive hill-fortresses and strongly sited island coastal strongholds. His insistence on strict discipline and accountability, on cash payments rather than fiefs, and efficient, uncluttered organization greatly impressed contemporary observers. He also made surprisingly effective use of access to the sea for trading and plundering from his coastal ports. Shivaji's unexcelled strategic and diplomatic skills – based firmly upon timely access to information – were also widely admired and feared. In this respect he was a worthy match for Aurangzeb, his greatest enemy.

Shivaji's successes shaped a new mode of aggressive political and military action against the Indo-Muslim powers. Reassertion of imperial Mughal power against the Deccan Sultanates in the 1650s created circumstances favorable to Shivaji's rise in the western Deccan. His insurgent state gained resources and confidence as it challenged imperial might. By the early 1660s the Maratha had adopted a new style of wide-ranging predatory raiding into Mughal and Bijapur lands. By the 1670s Maratha forces in Baglana seriously constricted, if they did not cut off altogether, the important overland caravan routes running from Surat to Burhanpur in Khandesh. The raids produced a steady flow of plunder or, in later years, extorted payments in return for immunity. The latter was often expressed as *chauth*, the 25 percent of the revenue traditionally left to zamindars by Indo-Muslim states in Gujarat and Khandesh. It was the annual profits from raiding beyond his borders that sustained the home territories. Shivaji could pay and pay well because he tapped the productive resources of a much larger, and more productive catchment area surrounding the western Ghats.

The unitary state died quickly. But the tradition of aggressive Maratha predation against the empire continued unabated. Once released, the organizational and martial energies of the hill Marathas surged outward into the wider world of the Mughal Deccan. No longer merely zamindars engaged in petty local skirmishes or hired captains employed by Muslim Sultans, Maratha commanders raided and conquered in the name of the Bhonsla dynasty. Timurid officers in the Deccan encountered a new, unsettling type of resistance – a resistance that could not be swept aside by the usual repertoire of Mughal diplomatic and military tactics. Mughal administrators found themselves ruling lands devastated and disrupted by incessant Maratha raiding and plundering. Maratha deshmukhs could look to a powerfully appealing alternative to submission to the empire.

THE MOVE TO THE DECCAN

In the desert outside Ajmer, Prince Muhammad Akbar came very close to dethroning Aurangzeb in one quick stroke. In exile at the Bhonsla court, he posed a less immediate, but no less serious, threat to Aurangzeb. Akbar's familial charisma as a Timurid prince gave him a potent political appeal. Akbar could become the catalyst for an alliance between Shambhaji, Abul Hasan Qutb Shah, the ruler of Golconda, and even Sikandar Adil Shah, the young king of Bijapur. Since the wealthiest and most powerful Muslim kingdom, Golconda, was now under the effective domination of two Telugu Brahmins and the aggressive Maratha kingdom was an avowedly resurgent state, restored Hindu domination of the Deccan was not such a far-fetched possibility. Especially worrisome was the continuing factionalism and weakness of Sultan Sikandar Adil Shah's regime in Bijapur. If Akbar were to ride north at the head of combined Maratha/Sultanate armies would the rebellious Rajputs of Marwar and Mewar hesitate to join them? And, if the balance of power began to shift how long would it be before other Mughal nobles transferred their allegiance to a younger, more vigorous sovereign?

Akbar also posed a larger challenge to those policies most deeply cherished by his father. Partly by circumstance and partly by personal inclination Akbar became a rallying point for those unhappy with Aurangzeb's treatment of non-Muslims and especially with his reimposition of the jiziya. Many nobles were dismayed by the rising power of the Muslim ulema and the constricting of the open political culture of Akbar and Jahangir. These views converged with a growing uneasiness over Aurangzeb's unrelenting aggressive posture in the Deccan. Accommodation with Bijapur and Golconda and the new Maratha state seemed the better course to many of Aurangzeb's nobles. Just as Dara Shukoh was symbol and spokesman for similar policies a generation earlier, so Akbar became a focal point for opposition in the 1680s. The costs of Aurangzeb's policies were starting to become apparent to those within the inner circles of the empire and to external observers as well. To Aurangzeb, therefore, the danger posed by Akbar's presence in the Deccan was grave and required immediate action.

Hard on the news that Akbar had proclaimed himself emperor, in late January, 1681, Shambhaji led 20,000 Maratha horsemen deep into Khandesh. At Bahadurpur, a prosperous trading suburb of Burhanpur, the raiders seized the Mughal jiziya collector and leisurely plundered the town for three days. Due to the large numbers of bankers and traders who lived in the town, Bahadurpur had "a large quantity of precious metals and every kind of merchandise belonging to the seven climes, huge quantities of other goods from every sea port, valued at lakhs [hundreds of thousands] of rupees ... stored in its shops."[8] Shambhaji, in contrast to his father's practice, condoned casual rape and violence by his troops. The reduced Mughal garrison of Burhanpur remained penned up in the citadel as the raiders burnt, looted, raped and tortured. The Marathas "plundered lakhs of rupees in cash from the bankers and merchants of every Purah [quarter], and set fire to them. Some men of noble birth killed their women and received martyrdom as they fell in fighting ..."[9]

As Shambhaji's army withdrew toward Baglana, Khan Jahan Bahadur, the governor of the Deccan provinces, missed intercepting the Marathas by just a few kilometers. Popular rumor had it that Khan Jahan Bahadur had been bribed by emissaries from Shambhaji to avoid contact with the Marathas. Public outrage was great. Plundering on

[8] S. Moinul Haq, *Khafi Khan's History of Alamgir* (Karachi: Pakistan Historical Society, 1975), p. 277.
[9] Ibid.

this scale would jeopardize the long-distance overland trade and exchange for which Burhanpur was such a critical node. But the protest to the Mughal emperor took a narrower, more sectarian view:[10]

The learned and pious persons [i.e. the ulema] and the nobles of Burhanpur, sent a petition to the Court describing the domination of the infidels, the destruction of the property and honor of the Muslims and the discontinuance of the *Jum'ah* prayers in future.

For the dominant notables of Burhanpur, Shambhaji's raid was not simply an outrage against public order, but it was a blow directed against the Muslim community by an infidel. If the Mughal empire could not safeguard Muslim lives and property, the Friday congregational prayers could not include Aurangzeb's titles as ruler.

Stung by this appeal and dismayed by his son's rebellion Aurangzeb marched south as soon as he concluded a peace with Mewar. From north India Aurangzeb brought the entire central army directly under his command; those of the three remaining princes, and the contingents of his best generals. Accompanying the army was the imperial harem and household and the central administration with its attendants, clerks, and officers. Tens of thousands of artillerymen, musketeers, and pioneers; artists and craftsmen; clerks and scribes; physicians, artists, and musicians, and a staggering array of servants and menials marched in their allotted places and sheltered within or beside the great encampment every night. A well-organized bazaar with its traders and their dependents trailed the official establishment.

For the first time since his reign began the emperor committed his full resources to stabilize the southern frontier of the empire. This momentous decision shifted the center of imperial power from Shahjahanabad south to the tented, movable, capital in the Deccan.

Despite the high drama of Akbar's flight and Aurangzeb's pursuit a curious stalemate marked the next several years. Shambhaji had prevaricated and avoided a joint military thrust north to restore Akbar to the throne. Akbar became increasingly frustrated as Shambhaji ignored his pleas for joint action. Caution, indecision, or fear prevented Shambhaji from a bold assault on one of the Mughal armies in the Deccan. Akbar argued that victory in such an encounter would clear the way for a victorious march to Delhi. Instead, Shambhaji diverted his attention to the coast where for four years he engaged in two

[10] Ibid., p. 279.

furious little wars: first with the Siddis of Janjira (a small piratical maritime state tributary to the Mughals) and the English East India Company at Bombay, and second with the Portuguese at Goa. Each conflict ended in weary stalemate. Dispirited, Akbar made several attempts to charter or build a ship that would take him to refuge in Persia.

Aurangzeb positioned strong defensive forces at a number of strategic points in the Mughal Deccan to fend off Maratha raids. For the next four years he sent two or more field armies into the Maratha kingdom every year. One after the other his commanders found that they could maneuver freely, plunder and burn villages and towns, and return. Mughal commanders found it too expensive to assault the dozens of hill and island fortresses of the kingdom. Shambhaji relied upon his father's decentralized network of strongpoints to shelter much of his population and to resist all but the most determined imperial sieges. Nor were they able to draw Shambhaji to a main force battle that would decide victory or defeat. In short, the emperor could discourage Shambhaji from following Akbar to a northern filibuster by keeping up steady military pressure on his home territories. He could discourage large scale Maratha raiding in the Mughal Deccan by keeping sizable armies in the field. But total conquest of the Maratha kingdom demanded a much greater commitment of imperial resources and determination than Aurangzeb had previously thought necessary.

CONQUEST OF THE DECCAN

Frustrated in his Maratha campaigns, Aurangzeb turned to a goal which had long eluded him: the final conquest of the two Deccan Sultanates. His first target was Bijapur. The youthful Sultan, Sikandar Adil Shah, continued to offer clandestine military aid to Shambhaji despite Mughal pressure. In the early months of 1685 a Mughal army of nearly 80,000 men, commanded by Prince Azam and Prince Shah Alam, laid siege to the massive city walls of Bijapur. For fifteen months Sikandar Adil Shah commanded the 30,000 man garrison in a stubborn defense against Mughal trenches and artillery. The Mughals held on despite dearth in the countryside and pestilence and near-starvation in the imperial lines. Aurangzeb countered threatened reinforcements from Golconda by sending Prince Shah Alam to invade that kingdom. Finally, in September, 1685, when Mughal trenches reached the fort walls, Sikandar Adil Shah surrendered his much-depleted garrison.

Aurangzeb annexed Bijapur as a province within the Mughal empire. The deposed Sultan was kept under confinement in the imperial encampment. Most of the leading Afghan and Indian Muslim nobles of Bijapur who had survived were assimilated into the Mughal nobility. The emperor appointed a governor, a provincial fiscal officer, faujdars, and fortress commanders so that a standard Mughal provincial administration could be created in the new province.

Golconda was next. In 1685, during the siege of Bijapur, Aurangzeb had sent a large army under Prince Shah Alam to invade Golconda. The invaders fought their way past numerous Qutb Shah cavalry to the vicinity of Hyderabad. Qutb Shah resistance collapsed when Mir Muhammad Ibrahim, a Persian noble commanding the defenders, defected to the Mughals. Abul Hasan Qutb Shah, the royal household, military, and thousands of panic-stricken residents of Hyderabad fled to the great fortress of Golconda several kilometers outside the city. Before the Mughals entered Hyderabad the urban mob looted and raped indiscriminately as all order in the city broke down.

Negotiations began immediately between Abul Hasan Qutb Shah, penned up in Golconda fort, and Prince Shah Alam, commanding the occupying army in Hyderabad and Aurangzeb, near Bijapur. The helpless Sultan agreed to dismiss his two Brahmin ministers, to pay a huge war indemnity, and to cede some border territory to the Mughals. Before Abul Hasan could remove Madanna and Akkanna from office, however, a Muslim court faction arranged the murder of the two Brahmins by a party of armed palace slaves. Rustam Rao, their nephew and a high-ranking military commander, and numerous other Telugu Brahmins and their servants were also slain. The conspirators sent the severed heads of the hated Brahmins directly to Aurangzeb. Thus satisfied, the Mughal army withdrew to Bijapur.

After the fall of Bijapur, Aurangzeb spent a week in devotion at the Gulbarga tomb of Shaikh Sayyid Muhammad Gesu Daraz, one of the most revered Sufi saints in the Deccan. In mid-January, 1687, Aurangzeb led his grand army directly toward Hyderabad. Abul Hasan and his court and army once again retreated to Golconda fort. The Mughals completely invested the four mile length of the outer wall of the massive stronghold. Aurangzeb pressed the siege stubbornly against a well-supplied, well-armed, garrison. Two mines driven under the walls exploded prematurely and killed several thousand imperial troops. Aurangzeb issued a proclamation annexing the entire kingdom of Golconda, which was largely under Mughal control.

The end came by betrayal. An opened gateway permitted a surprise assault on September 21, 1687. Taken captive, Abul Hasan joined his colleague Sikandar Adil Shah in the imperial encampment. The fabled treasury of the Qutb Shahs, now depleted, yielded gold and silver coins valued at over sixty million rupees along with vast quantities of jewelry, gold and silver utensils, and other valuables.[11]

Aurangzeb repeatedly stated that he could not forgive the willingness of both Sultans to ally themselves with the perfidious infidels. In response to the plea of a deputation of Muslim ulema from Bijapur who asked him how he could justify making war on fellow Muslims, Aurangzeb replied that the Sultan had sheltered and assisted Shambhaji who harassed Muslims everywhere. The same stern judgment applied to Abul Hasan who had committed the additional crime of handing over control of his state to his two Brahmin ministers. During the Golconda siege Aurangzeb appointed a muhtasib in Hyderabad with orders to demolish Hindu temples, build mosques, and put down all forbidden deviations from proper Islamic practice.

Aurangzeb's zealousness even began to arouse resistance among his strongest supporters. The chief sadr, Qazi Abdullah, begged the emperor to accept Abul Hasan's capitulation after the sack of Hyderabad and allow him to renew Golconda's tributary status. Other senior ulema protested the continued assaults on fellow Muslims.

As in most policy issues, resistance centered on Prince Shah Alam who was widely known to favor a conciliatory attitude toward both Deccan Sultans. At Bijapur Shah Alam negotiated secretly with Sikandar Adil Shah to arrange a surrender in return for concessions. Aurangzeb, discovering this, sharply rebuked his son and pressed ahead with the siege. When at the Golconda siege, Shah Alam opened similar negotiations with Abul Hasan Qutb Shah, Aurangzeb swiftly arrested Shah Alam and confined him, his wife and four sons in the imperial encampment. This proved to be a captivity lasting seven years. Any possibility of an informed discussion of Deccan policy among the imperial elite vanished. If even theologians and princes were stifled, then ordinary nobles could hope for little.

[11] Moinul Haq, *Khafi Khan*, p. 366.

With the fall of the two Deccan Sultanates, Aurangzeb then turned his attention to the Marathas. His son Akbar was no longer a threat. Unsupported by Shambhaji, the rebel prince and a few dozen followers chartered a ship for Persia where they obtained refuge at the Safavid court. During this period Shambhaji was preoccupied with internal politics and not with external raiding. His harsh ruling style, offensive womanizing, and erratic administration had aroused the Maratha deshmukhs to great hostility. By popular report he spent considerable time in drinking and debauching instead of on state business.

Right after the fall of Golconda fort Aurangzeb sent one of his amirs on a special mission. Muqarrab Khan, a Golconda nobleman of recognized ability, had deserted to the Mughals in return for appointment as a Mughal noble. Muqarrab Khan was to lead his 25,000 cavalry to the Maratha kingdom. Ostensibly he was to besiege Panhala fort, but his real task was to hunt down Shambhaji. Late in 1688, Mughal spies discovered that Shambhaji was relaxing in the gardens and mansions of his pleasure palace at Sangameshwar, in the hills thirty-five kilometers northeast of Ratnagiri. Muqarrab Khan immediately made a forced march across the western Ghats and captured both Shambhaji and his Brahmin chief minister alive.

The two captives were brought to the imperial encampment beside the Bhima river. Shambhaji, although a monarch, was not treated with the dignity permitted the Bijapur and Golconda rulers. Dressed as buffoons he and his minister were presented to Aurangzeb who knelt in thanksgiving prayer. During interrogation by Mughal officers, Shambhaji sealed his fate by insulting both the emperor and the Prophet Muhammad. A panel of ulema sentenced him to death for having slain and captured good Muslims. After a fortnight of torture, Shambhaji and his companion were hacked to death and the pieces thrown to the dogs.

In 1689 Aurangzeb had surmounted the crisis created by Akbar's rebellion seven years earlier. His son was a refugee at the Safavid court. Bijapur, Golconda, and the Maratha state were safely conquered and annexed. Everywhere Mughal power was triumphant. The new acquisitions added 221,107 square miles to the empire – an increase of over one-quarter. Four new provinces were added: Bijapur and the Bijapur Karnatak, and Hyderabad and the Hyderabad Karnatak. The Maratha lands were divided between Aurangzeb province in the north and Bijapur in the south. The Mughal frontier in the south was now coterminous with the farthest extent of Indian Muslim domination on the subcontinent.

CHAPTER 11

THE DECCAN WARS

Aurangzeb's triple victory – Bijapur, Golconda, and the Maratha kingdom – should have been the prelude to a new era of peace, prosperity, and political stability in the Deccan and southern India. With the exception of the Tamil regions of the Golconda and Bijapur Karnatak, but recently conquered in the 1640s, the western Deccan of the Marathas and the eastern Deccan of the Telugus had long been accustomed to Indo-Muslim rule. After a brief period of overseeing initial arrangements, the emperor would lead his grand encampment and central army triumphantly north back to Shahjahanabad. As they had dozens of times in the past cadres of imperial administrators could assume those powers exercised by their defeated counterparts in each of the three kingdoms. Surplus revenues from the new provinces would flow northward to enrich treasuries in Delhi and Agra. Instead, the reverse occurred. Aurangzeb remained in the Deccan, year after year, fighting an endless war and hoping to reverse a descending spiral of public order and imperial power in that region.

The insurgent Maratha state did not die with Shambhaji. His younger brother Rajaram, hastily crowned, fled to the extreme south to take refuge in Jinji fortress. Maratha officers left in the north directed an intensifying campaign of predatory raiding against the Mughals. Imperial officials faced enormous difficulties in defending their districts and in collecting revenues.

Grimly determined to stamp out this rebellion, Aurangzeb made the great imperial encampment his capital. For six years the emperor's camp occupied several sites between Puna and the city of Bijapur. In 1695, he selected a permanent location at Brahmapuri, renamed Islampuri, on the southeast bank of the Bhima river. At this site Aurangzeb lived uninterruptedly under tents for nearly five years. In 1699 the emperor ordered Islampuri to be completely walled round with earthen defenses. He placed Asad Khan, his chief minister (wazir) in charge of the court, the emperor's household and those of his nobles. Departing the encampment, Aurangzeb led his weary army in a strenuous six-year-long campaign against the hill-fortresses of

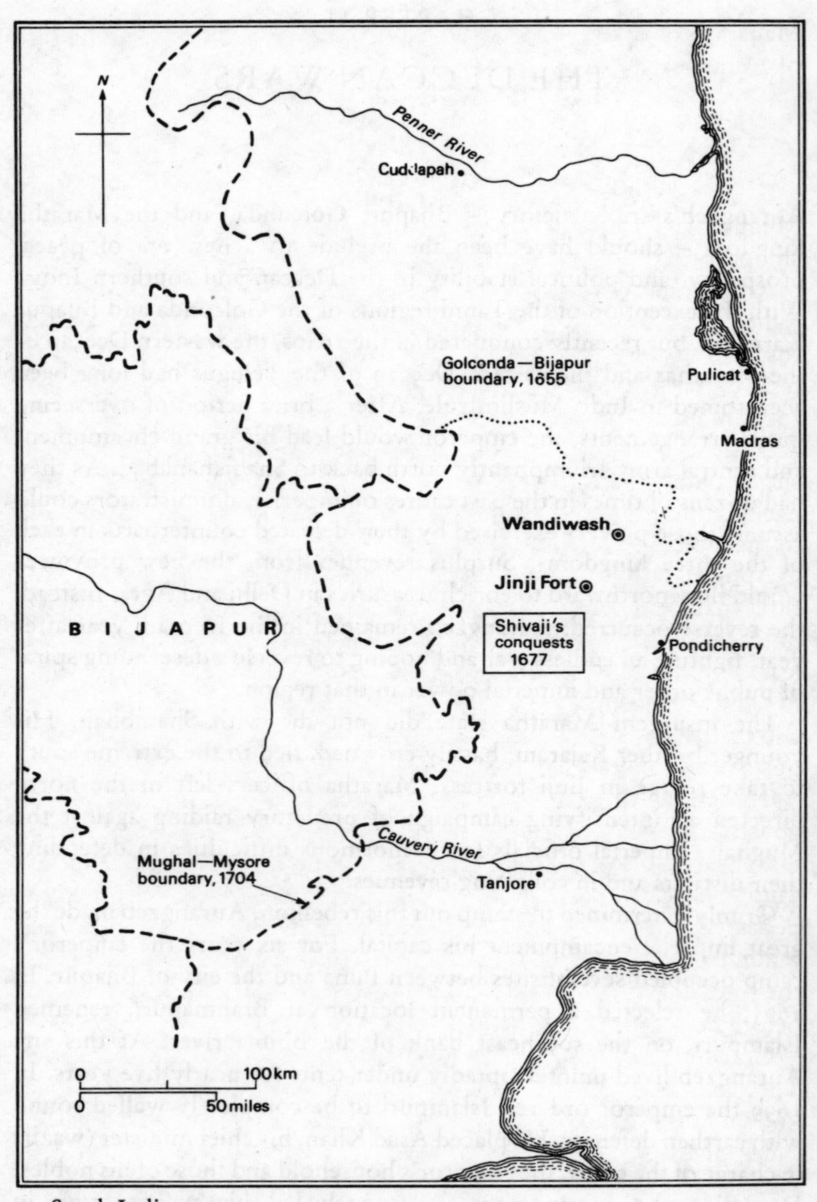

5 South India, 1707
Source: I. Habib, *An atlas of the Mughal Empire* (Delhi, 1982), 16A

Maharashtra. Finally, gravely ill and worn out, he retreated to the city of Ahmadnagar for a year before he died in early 1707.

THE EASTERN DECCAN UNDER MUGHAL RULE: 1687–1700

Mughal annexation and administration of Golconda proceeded smoothly in the years immediately after the conquest. For the majority of Golconda's population, absorption by the Mughals did not mean radical changes in their lives and fortunes. After the fall of Golconda fort and capture of the king, little further resistance occurred. At a festive grand audience held in Golconda fortress, the emperor gave robes of honor, promotions, and other rewards to his two sons, Prince Azam and Bidar Bakht, and the amirs who had participated in the siege. Soon thereafter imperial officials began inventorying and packing the enormous treasure of the Qutb Shahs for shipment north to the imperial vaults in Delhi.

Abul Hasan was not killed, but languished as a state captive. His three daughters were placed in honorable marriages with Mughal nobles. His adoptive son, Abdullah, and other male relatives and at least twenty-four Muslim nobles (largely of Turco-Persian descent) became Mughal nobles.[1] Other mid-level Muslim functionaries, artists and craftsmen, and military officers were offered and accepted similar posts in the imperial administration as lower-ranking mansabdars.

The Hindu officials of Golconda fared less well. Several Brahmin governors still in office did not reemerge as Mughal grandees, but disappeared into obscurity. Those Telugu nayaks recruited by the Qutb Shahs from the Kamma, Valama, Kapu, and Razu warrior-peasant castes, who served as military commanders, found themselves redundant after 1687. Only one officer, Yacham Na'ir, who served in the Karnatak with Mughal field armies at Kinji, became a Mughal amir before he was beheaded for treason by his new employer.[2]

Golconda had been annexed and retitled *Dar-al Jihad*, Hyderabad. The lands to the south were detached to form a separate province known as the Hyderabad Karnatak. In 1688 Aurangzeb transferred a cadre of experienced Mughal officers into the new provinces. The

[1] This discussion of post-conquest Golconda is drawn from J. F. Richards, *Mughal Administration in Golconda* (Oxford: Clarendon Press, 1975), pp. 52–214.

[2] See J. F. Richards, "The Hyderabad Karnatak, 1687–1707" in *Modern Asian Studies*, IX (1975), 241–260.

Mughal governor, Jan Sipar Khan, and his son Rustam Dil Khan, were Irani amirs, of long familial service. Nine mansabdars and their contingents were stationed as faujdars or military intendants across Hyderabad. Twelve mansabdars assumed independent command of the greatest fortresses in the former kingdom. A similar clutch of officers took charge of the newly constituted Hyderabad Karnatak.

Before conquest the ongoing alliance between the Bhonsla rulers and Golconda had ensured that the eastern Deccan was free from Maratha raids. This immunity ended with Mughal annexation. Between 1688 and 1692, the Marathas made several sweeping long-distance plundering raids into Hyderabad. Maratha raiding bands generally outnumbered the provincial detachments of Jan Sipar Khan. The latter did little to confront or drive off these invaders. The Marathas held up traders on the roads and freely entered the smaller market towns to plunder, but did not engage in a full-scale assault or siege on either Hyderabad or Machhilipatnam, the major coastal port. After 1692, the Mughal siege of Jinji to the far south diverted Maratha attention from Hyderabad.

Despite the weak Mughal response, few, if any, of the local Telugu warrior aristocrats either joined or supported the Marathas. The nayaks did not share in the insurgent tradition of the Maratha Bhonslas of the western Deccan.

In spite of occasional Maratha incursions, the new regime wasted little time in adapting the Golconda revenue system to Mughal practice. A technically competent mansabdar, Muhammad Shafi, became the first Mughal diwan or provincial fiscal officer of Hyderabad. The new diwan negotiated written agreements with the Telugu warrior chiefs who had served the Golconda state as pargana headmen and Brahmins who served as local accountants throughout the new province. Almost immediately taxes began to flow into the provincial treasury.

A systematic review revealed the pre-conquest revenues for Hyderabad proper to be 13.7 million rupees per year and that for the Karnatak 8.3 millions. A full-scale regulation survey and reassessment zabt of the new lands was not done. Instead, the Mughals left the old Qutb Shah totals intact since these alone added 12 percent to the overall revenues of the empire. The only new burden imposed was the capitation tax on non-Muslims, jiziya which returned about a million rupees per year. Additional revenues – and occasionally a spectacular diamond – came from the famed Golconda diamond mines in the Karnatak whose operation was now an imperial, rather than a Qutb Shah, monopoly.

The regime imposed the imperial monetary system on Golconda. The diwan established a central mint at Hyderabad and subordinate mints in the major trading centers to strike copper, silver, and gold currency. The eastern Deccan began to shift toward a silver standard in place of the older Deccani gold standard based upon the gold hun or pagoda.

MARATHA INSURGENCY: THE STRUGGLE FOR JINJI

To the west, in Bijapur, the central state had been wracked by factional struggles and a weak monarchy for nearly two decades. The entire political structure of the western Deccan was in disarray and required systematic reconstruction by the Mughals. This Aurangzeb attempted to do. Just as he did with Golconda the emperor sent reliable nobles and mansabdars to serve as provincial governor, faujdars, and fortress commanders and their troops. A diwan and his staff restored Bijapur's revenue system. Jagirs were assigned to support them. Unfortunately, establishing political ties between the new regime and Bijapur's zamindars in the countryside was far from easy. The Maratha deshmukhs of Bijapur faced a more treacherous political context than that presented to their Telugu counterparts in the east. Bhonsla power and authority still challenged that of the Timurids.

Immediately after receiving the news of Shambhaji's capture the senior commanders at Raigarh fort, the Maratha capital, turned to Shambhaji's younger brother Rajaram instead of his young son. In February, 1689, they conducted a hasty coronation ceremony for Rajaram, the third Bhonsla ruler. When, within days a Mughal army arrived and besieged the capital, Rajaram secretly fled. The Mughals did capture Shambhaji's principal queen, Yesu Bai and her nine-year-old son Shahuji, the putative heir to the Bhonsla throne. Three other royal wives and four other children were taken as well.[3] Aurangzeb decided to raise Shambhaji's heir as a member of his own household within the red canvas screen marking his living quarters and harem (*gulalbar*). The emperor kept his young captive strictly confined, but

[3] Jadunath, Sarkar, *History of Aurangzib* (Calcutta, 5 vols., 1912–1924), v, 203–207.

well-treated, and free of pressure to convert to Islam. Shahuji was to be raised as a Maratha princling who was also a khanazad.

The Bhonsla monarchy had a competing claimant who was free of Mughal control. Shahuji's uncle, Rajaram, fled disguised as a Hindu religious mendicant (*yogi*), accompanied only by a few of his closest officers. The small band made its way 800 kilometers on foot to Jinji, the enormous triple hill-fortress, on the southeastern coast. Here a Maratha governor still controlled part of the Bhonsla domains on the southern boundary of the Bijapur Karnatik.

For the next eight years the southeastern coast became a principal arena for the Mughal–Maratha struggle.[4] At Jinji, Rajaram took full charge of the Maratha districts still under Bhonsla control and encouraged a general uprising against Mughal authority in the Karnatak districts. Aurangzeb sent Zulfikar Khan, the son of his chief minister, south with a sizeable army in pursuit of Rajaram.

The siege of Jinji lasted until the fortress finally fell to a Mughal assault in 1698. Throughout the siege the emperor kept a large army supplied with treasure, fresh troops, and military supplies. The supply line stretched from the imperial encampment near Bijapur, through Cuddapah as a base, to the Mughal siege camp outside Jinji. Rajaram obtained substantial assistance from his cousin, Shahji II, the Raja of Tanjavur. More important were reinforcements from the Bhonsla kingdom. As Maratha raiding bands grew in size and confidence in the Deccan they periodically were recalled to attack the Mughals in the Karnatak.

Prince Kam Bakhsh, the emperors' youngest (and dearest) son, and the imperial wazir, Asad Khan, joined Zulfikar Khan with another large army as the siege ended its first year. Despite these reinforcements, the imperial army was still unable to completely cut off the stubbornly defended fort. At the end of the second year, two celebrated Maratha generals, Dhana Singh Jadev and Santa Ghorpare, commanding an army of 30,000 horsemen, arrived from the Deccan. These troops, after capturing and holding for ransom the local Mughal faujdar, severed all supply and communication links for the besieging army. Plentiful foodstuffs carried cheaply in bulk by the active coasting trade had supplied the besiegers from the European ports at

[4] The following is largely based on Sarkar, *History of Aurangzib*, v, 50–109; and G. T. Kulkarni, *The Mughal–Maratha Relations: Twenty-Five Fateful Years (1682–1707)* (Pune: Deccan College Post-Graduate Research Institute, Department of History, 1983).

Madras and Negapatnam. This flow ended. All communication and funds from the emperor's camp were also cut.

At this point a familiar scenario played out. Persuaded by false rumors that Aurangzeb had died, Prince Kam Bakhsh secretly tried to arrange a peace settlement with Rajaram. He also plotted to take over supreme command of the Mughal army in preparation for the inevitable war of succession. The wazir and Zulfikar Khan, finding the Mughal position untenable, had already burst their cannon and begun to withdraw from the siege lines when they learned of the plot. They arrested Kam Bakhsh and made a fighting withdrawal fifty kilometers north to Wandiwash, a Mughal-held fortress. Finally a strong relief force with supplies and letters arrived from the north.

In the second phase of the Jinji campaign, Asad Khan returned to the imperial court with Kam Bakhsh. At the court, Aurangzeb reluctantly received the errant prince at an informal audience in the harem. He did so at the plea of his daughter, Zinat-un-nissa, who was a partisan of Kam Bakhsh. The emperor uncharacteristically forgave his youngest son his transgressions at the siege and did not confine him to the camp.

For the next four years, Zulfikar Khan used Wandiwash as a base to engage in a forcible restoration of Mughal authority in the area around Jinji. A campaign against Tanjuvar forced Shahji II to pay tribute and to agree temporarily, at least, to stop supplying aid to Rajaram. Aurangzeb sent men and treasure to support Zulfikar Khan, but long periods frequently intervened between shipments. Often short of funds, Zulfikar Khan foraged and exacted taxes and tribute in practices little different from the Maratha armies. The unfortunate inhabitants of the southeastern coastal districts found themselves in a continuing war zone. Many refugees took shelter in the fortified European city-states of the coast.

Zulfikar Khan's next foray against Jinji in 1694–95 was so half-hearted that popular opinion had it that the Mughal general was in collusion with Rajaram. It was rumored that Zulfikar Khan, anticipating Aurangzeb's death from old age, planned to carve out an independent kingdom for himself on the southern coast during the war of succession.

Aurangzeb rejected overtures from Rajaram for a negotiated settlement and, in 1697, finally ordered Zulfikar Khan to an all-out assault on Rajaram. Forced into action, the Mughal army scaled a wall and took the lower citadels and fought their way through to the highest citadel in the fortress. Apparently warned by Zulfikar Khan, according to rumor at least, Rajaram hastily fled Jinji just before the final assault. When the much-reduced garrison of the citadel capitulated in February, 1698, the Mughals captured unharmed four of Rajaram's queens, three sons, and two daughters who were sent to Aurangzeb's grand encampment to join Shahuji.

WAR IN THE DECCAN 1689–1698

In the Maratha homeland Raigarh and most of the Maratha forts were quickly taken and manned by Mughal garrisons.[5] From Jinji, Rajaram sent a stream of letters, robes of honor and golden bangles to his remaining fortress commanders, other officers and to deshmukhs throughout the Maratha Kingdom. He urged them to reject Mughal authority and to ravage and plunder imperial territory.

Maratha resistance to the Mughals in the western Deccan took on a decentralized character which proved to be extraordinarily effective. Santa Ghorpare, Shana Singh Jadev, and several other of the most able, battle-tested Maratha commanders rapidly built up armies that often swelled to 30,000 men. Their troops were minimally armored Maratha light horsemen with lances, swords, and occasionally muskets. Nearly equal in numbers were large contingents of "Karnataki" musketeers renowned for their marksmanship. Except for the rainy season, each Maratha band campaigned continuously in raids or battles with the Mughals.

Deprived of Bhonsla funding, these commanders plundered or exacted a form of protection levy called chauth from each locality. Chauth or one-quarter was the customary share the zamindar retained from the land revenue in Gujarat and the western Deccan. The Maratha captains demanded chauth from village or pargana headmen, or from the town notables as an option to being raided. Regular payment of this levy, computed on the established Mughal assessment (jama) provided steady support for the irregular Maratha raiding forces. Such an arrangement became, in effect, a rudimentary revenue system albeit shared with Mughal authorities.

Individual Maratha horsemen were no match for determined Mughal cavalrymen whose chain-link armor, lances, muskets, and

[5] Description based on Sarkar, *History of Aurangzib*, v, 20–49, 110–137; and Kalkarni, *Mughal–Maratha Relations*, pp. 135–166.

heavy battle horses made them formidable fighting units. In larger battles, Mughal heavy cavalry supported by effective field artillery was superior to the Maratha horsemen. But in mobility, leadership, supplies, and certainly in morale, Maratha irregulars were the equal of imperial troops. Able commanders like Santa Ghorpare outmaneuvered and captured several high-ranking Mughal noblemen with many of their troops. The luckless amirs paid high ransoms from their own resources for their eventual freedom.[6]

Throughout the Jinji siege, Maratha commanders alternated between expeditions to the south to assist Rajaram and spells of campaigning in the western Deccan. An extraordinarily effective Mughal faujdar, Matabar Khan, succeeded in taking the Maratha hill forts in the Konkan, the fertile coastal strip, in 1689–90.[7] Thereafter, Matabar Khan successfully beat off Maratha raiders until his death in 1704. But in the interior districts of the Maratha homeland, in Bijapur, and in Khandesh, the Mughal imperial troops did not succeed in stopping the raiders. Maratha mobility, decentralized authority, and a steadily growing system of parallel or shadow government prevented Aurangzeb from devising an effective strategy to contain the insurgents.

THE FINAL DECCAN CAMPAIGN, 1698–1707

After his escape from Jinji, Rajaram returned unscathed to the Maratha homeland and set up his court and residence in Satara, a strong hill fort. Within the imperial encampment at Islampuri, Aurangzeb received his news with dismay and made a momentous decision:[8]

> As the reports of the enemy's daring raids and ravages in the Imperial territories and his increasing strength were being received successively, the Emperor resolved to start jihad against them and to capture the forts which were places of their refuge and thus to uproot entirely those accursed people.

At the age of eighty-one Aurangzeb declared a holy war against the Marathas. He took personal command of the grand army in a continuing assault on the hill fortresses of Maharashtra. The princes, all

[6] S. Moinul Haq, *Khafi Khan's History of Alamgir* (Karachi: Pakistan Historical Society, 1975), p. 414.
[7] Sarkar, *History of Aurangzib*, v, 138–158.
[8] Moinul Haq, *Khafi Khan*, p. 453. Khafi Khan, *Muntakhab al-Lubub* (Calcutta: Asiatic Society of Bengal, Bibliotheca Indica, 1874), Part II, 459. Khafi Khan uses the term *jihad* in the text.

senior officers and nobles were ordered to leave their families and households at Islampuri, now walled round, and set out on campaign.[9] His first target was the fort of Vasantgarh to be followed by Satara.

Rajaram left Satara to lead a large Maratha field army on a devastating campaign into Khandesh and Berar. In the latter province he planned to join forces with the Gond raja of Deogarh, now in rebellion against the Mughals. Mughal spies gave Aurangzeb information soon enough for him to send Prince Bidar Bakht with a large army to intercept Rajaram. Near Ahmadnagar a bloody battle resulted in a decisive defeat for the Marathas. Rajaram survived to lead his remaining troops in a running flight to safety to Singugarh fort. A few months later, the third Bhonsla ruler became seriously ill and died March 2, 1700.

Since December, 1699, Aurangzeb was deeply engaged in the investment and siege of Satara fortress, the Maratha capital. Ignoring all difficulties Aurangzeb pressed forward with an attempted mining of the fortress. Finally, in mid-April when the mines blew a breach in the walls, the assault failed. The first mine explosion burst outward killing 2,000 Mughal troops waiting to attack. After news arrived of Rajaram's death, Subhanji, the Maratha fort commander, surrendered on terms. Subhanji and his officers and relatives were taken into Mughal service.

With scarcely a pause, the emperor led his army directly to the attack against the nearby Parligarh fortress. Six weeks into the siege, the Maratha fort commander surrendered the fort in return for his life and a large monetary payment. Aurangzeb placed a garrison in the fort and then led the Mughal grand army into a well-deserved rest for the rainy season.

Shortly after Rajaram's death, his senior widow, Tara Bai, successfully maneuvered to place her four-year-old son, Shambhaji II, on the throne. Tara Bai was to act as regent. In this capacity she made a peace overture to Aurangzeb who was encamped before Satara fortress.[10] The Maratha queen proposed formal submission to Mughal authority. She offered to cede Satara, Panhala, and five other of the most imposing hill fortresses, and to send 5,000 Maratha horsemen to serve the governor of the Deccan. In return her son would be recognized as the Maratha ruler, given the rank of 7,000 zat as a Mughal amir, and

[9] Sarkar, *History of Aurangzib*, v, 159–235 and Kulkarni, *Mughal–Maratha Relations*, pp. 169–259.

[10] Sarkar, *History of Aurangzib*, v, 136.

exempted from personal service at the imperial court as his great-grandfather Shivaji had been. Tarabai also stipulated that Shambhaji II should be made the *sardeshmukh* or head deshmukh of the Mughal Deccan provinces. In effect, this was a new position which would have given the Maratha ruler 10 percent of the imperial revenues in return for his assistance in revenue collection and maintenance of order. The proposal would have Shahji become simultaneously a Mughal nobleman and the dominant zamindar of the entire Deccan. If consummated, this proposal would have reinserted the Bhonsla monarchy within the structure of Timurid authority at two levels. Aurangzeb, distrustful as ever, rejected Tara Bai's proposal outright, and put all his attention into his campaign against the hill-fortresses.

Between 1700 and 1705 another eleven strongholds fell to the imperial armies – among them those offered up by Tara Bai. Aurangzeb personally led his weary army into the field after each rainy season and commanded most of the sieges himself. In most instances the emperor resorted to bribery to persuade the Maratha commanders to surrender on terms. Large Maratha armies hovered, harassed and sometimes defeated Mughal cavalry beyond the imperial lines. They were never sufficiently strong to defeat the Mughal grand army in a fixed battle or to drive off Aurangzeb's besieging forces. Aurangzeb took heavy losses in men and animals every year from battle casualties and disease. He drafted levies of troops from provincial governors around the empire; called for drafts of horses from Kabul and Surat; and received regular shipments of treasure from the north.

During this last phase, Aurangzeb maintained two highly mobile, aggressive, field armies. Each was headed by experienced noblemen who regularly pursued and defeated even the strongest Maratha forces. The first battle group was commanded by Zulfikar Khan Nusrat Jang, returned from his victory at Jinji in the south, along with Daud Khan Panni, a former Bijapur officer of Afghan descent, and two Rajputs, Dalpat Rao Bundela and Ram Singh Hara. In 1701–02 Zulfikar Khan's troops fought nineteen major battles with the Marathas in a six-month-long campaign of constant movement.[11] After 1702 Zulfikar Khan was appointed bakhshi of the empire and worked more closely with his father Asad Khan, the imperial wazir. He and his commanders

[11] V. G. Khobrekar, ed., English translation of *Tarik-i Dilkasha* (Bombay: Govt. of Maharashtra, 1972), p. 233.

alternated between service at the sieges and forays to pursue the Maratha raiders. These troops frequently escorted treasure caravans from North India and goods caravans from Burhanpur to the imperial encampment.

The Turani nobleman Ghazi-ud-din Khan Firuz Jang commanded the second battle group. Surrounding him was a familial cluster consisting of his sons Chin Qilich Khan, Hamid Khan and Rahim-ud-din Khan, and a cousin, Muhammad Amin Khan, with their followers. Firuz Jang served as governor of Berar and took an active role in the defense against Maratha incursions from that province. Each amir and subordinate officer in these two groups took great pride in keeping his cavalry contingents at full strength.

On at least two occasions the emperor half-heartedly experimented with negotiations that would make use of Shahuji Bhonsla, the Maratha prince who was still a captive in the imperial encampment. Now mature, the 21 year-old Shahuji had a claim to the Maratha throne fully as strong as that of Rajaram's young son.

In 1703, Aurangzeb first offered freedom to Shahuji Bhonsla in return for converting to Islam. When he refused, Aurangzeb tried to arrange a settlement with the leading Maratha generals. He recruited Raibhan Bhonsla, son of Vyankoji, Shivaji's brother who had been Raja of Tanjavur, into Mughal service as a high-ranking amir. Raibhan was to act as an intermediary between Shahuji and the Maratha generals. Shahuji would be released to become ruler of the Marathas and given the right of collecting chauth or 25 percent of the Mughal revenues for the Deccan. The negotiations failed due to mistrust on both sides. The emperor feared Maratha trickery. The Marathas themselves had not all that much to gain by making a settlement. In 1706, the year before he died, the emperor again tried to arrange a peace by offering again to release Shahuji. This also fell through.

PARALLEL GOVERNMENT IN THE WESTERN DECCAN

Aurangzeb's final campaigns further weakened imperial authority elsewhere in the Deccan provinces. Declining personal and corporate security hurt productivity in trade and agriculture. These problems were heightened by the failure of monsoon rains throughout the Deccan in 1702–04. The entire region was hit by the scarcity and soaring prices of famine conditions. The usual outbreak of plague and other epidemic disease added to mortality figures.

Rebuffed in her diplomatic initiative, Tara Bai immediately shaped an energetic military response. The Mughal historian Khafi Khan reported that:[12]

[Tara Bai] started an endeavour to ravage Imperial territories. She engaged herself in arranging and posting her forces in the six [provinces] of the Deccan up to the frontiers of ... Malwa, with the object of ravaging the territories and in winning the loyalty of her officers in a way that all the efforts and the conquests of the forts by 'Alamgir failed to keep them in proper check; until the end of her regime the rebellions of Marhatas continued to gain strength every day.

Under Tara Bai's aggressive policies, Maratha attacks resumed in the east as well. In 1702, an enormous army estimated at 50,000 horse and foot attacked and looted Hyderabad city. The Mughal governor simply took refuge in his fortified mansion.[13] In 1704, in the midst of general dearth and scarcity, the Marathas paused to plunder Hyderabad city before ranging as far as Machhilipatnam on the coast. Some Telugu zamindars joined the invaders or plundered on their own. Most did neither, but waited for the intruders to leave. Other ruthless, ambitious men, who were not zamindars, took advantage of the dislocation caused by the raids to attract armed followers and plunder on their own.[14]

Long-distance caravan trade out of Hyderabad city to Gujarat or northern India was shut down completely between 1702 and 1704.[15] The main artery leading from Hyderabad to Machhilipatnam was blocked as well. Caught in a cycle of disorder and dearth, peasants and zamindars no longer paid Mughal revenues to the dismay of Mughal jagirdars.[16]

Imperial authority in the western Deccan faced a different and, ultimately, a graver threat. In the 1699 campaign just prior to his death, Rajaram and his leading commanders marched confidently into Khandesh and Berar. Instead of raiding, they demanded regular payment of 25 percent of the imperial revenues for chauth and an additional 10

[12] Moinual Haq, *Khafi Khan*, p. 508. [13] Richards, *Mughal Administration*, p. 218.

[14] Richards, *Mughal Administration*, pp. 219–220; and J. F. Richards with Velchuru Narayana Ras, "Banditry in Mughal India: Historical and Folk Perceptions," *The Indian Economic and Social History Review*, 17 (1980), 95–120.

[15] Ibid,. pp. 225–229. [16] Ibid., p. 221.

percent based upon the fiction that the Maratha ruler was the hereditary head deshmukh of all the Deccan provinces. This was no longer a simple plundering expedition:[17]

> All who submitted to the payment of [Rajaram's] demands were protected, and the Mughal garrisons that remained passive spectators were not molested, but such as made unsuccessful opposition were put to the sword. On this occasion the Mahrattas were more systematic in their exactions than they before had been; where they could not obtain ready money they took promissory notes from the Patells [village headmen] . . .

Tara Bai regularized these arrangements to create a dual or parallel administrative structure. For each province she appointed a Maratha commander as governor, who headed a field army of seven or eight thousand horsemen. The governor built a small fortress to use as his headquarters and deployed collectors to receive payments of chauth and sardeshmukhi in various parts of the province. If chauth were not paid because of opposition from imperial faujdars or from local zamindars still loyal to the Mughals, the governor "rushed to their help and surrounded and plundered that place."[18] The governor also deputed officers to guard the main routes. Any merchants who wished to travel safely had to pay a fixed sum per cart or laden pack bullock. The Maratha road tax was set at an amount three to four times that which the Mughals levied on merchants. In some villages headmen who were Maratha sympathizers had constructed small forts. With the aid of Marathas they resisted the Mughals when they came to collect the revenues.

Mughal governors and faujdars and many zamindars still remained stubbornly opposed to the Marathas. But a growing number of zamindars, town notables, and village headmen had openly sided with the raiders. In 1702, when a Mughal field army under Nusrat Jang appeared in Khandesh and Berar, the Maratha governors assembled 60,000 horsemen with the aid of zamindari levies.[19] As this process of slow permeation occurred, the frontier line of Maratha raids moved north. The Marathas crossed the Narmada river, the traditional boundary between the Deccan and north India, in 1700. Soon they were mounting raids in force into Gujarat (Ahmadabad) and Malwa provinces.

[17] James Grant Duff, *History of the Mahrattas*, as quoted in John F. Richards, "Official Revenues and Money Flows in a Mughal Province," in John F. Richards, ed. *The Imperial Monetary System, of Mughal India* (Delhi: Oxford University Press, 1987), p. 222.

[18] Moinul Haq, *Khafi Khan*, p. 508.

[19] Khobrekar, *Dilkasha*, p. 228.

RISING EUROPEAN POLITICAL POWER

Slowly, decade after decade, as the Timurid regime was embroiled in the Deccan wars, the English, Dutch, and French East Indian Companies developed the capacity to challenge the authority of the Mughal emperor and to negotiate with imperial authorities from a position of growing strength. To some extent European confidence grew out of improved information and experience in dealing with the Mughals as well as a carefully nurtured constituency of sympathetic Mughal officials. But much more was involved. The East India Companies were always conscious of their superiority at sea. Indian shipping of any sort was vulnerable to seizure by well-armed Dutch, English, or French merchant vessels. In extremities, the East India Companies could carry out a naval blockade of any of the Mughal ports. Or, they could seize Indian vessels at sea as reprisals for maltreatment on the subcontinent.

Along the coasts, wherever gaps in strong indigenous state power occurred, the European trading companies built autonomous city-states similar to Portuguese Goa. As early as the 1620s the English factors at Surat had urged that Bombay island and its magnificent natural harbor, then virtually unused, be acquired from the Portuguese and used to build a secure base for their operations. Finally after prolonged negotiations the East India Company Court of Directors received the grant of Bombay as part of a marriage settlement between Charles II of England and Catharine of Aragon.[20] For three decades successive governors of Bombay encouraged trade and settlement and built up the defenses of the island.

In 1689–90 the autonomy of Bombay was severely tested. Due to a miscalculation by John Child, the governor of Bombay, the English East India Company became involved in a brief war with the Mughals. Child was a leading spokesman for a more aggressive English policy in India. Troubled by unauthorized English private traders operating in India, Child tried to put pressure upon the imperial authorities at Surat to stop their trading. East India Company vessels captured and held eighty Indian vessels sailing to Surat. Aurangzeb, angered by this, stopped all English trade and ordered his local officers to seize all English trading missions. At Hughli, in Bengal, the English factors fled

[20] M. D. David, *History of Bombay, 1661–1708* (Bombay: University of Bombay, 1973), p. 26.

down the river to a site which became the town of Calcutta. At Bombay, the Mughals ordered the Abyssinian sea lord, the Siddi, who was tributary to the Mughal emperor, to attack Bombay. The Siddi's troops succeeded in occupying most of the island, but did not capture the city and its citadel. In the end frantic negotiations and offers to pay reparations by the English ended the imbroglio.

Over the next few decades Bombay's defenses became more formidable and its population and trade grew steadily. Strong traditions of internal order, religious toleration, modest customs and other taxes, and other inducements brought thousands of migrants to Bombay. By the early eighteenth century, Bombay had begun to challenge Surat's role as the leading port of trade for western India.[21]

Along the southeastern coast of India, in the Hyderabad and Bijapur Karnataks, an area marked by fragmented and shifting political authority, the three East India Companies founded and nurtured several enclaves. By the 1680s these city-states served as the headquarters to their respective companies for trading activity to the north in Golconda. The Dutch controlled the port of Pulicat and protected it with the guns of Fort Geldria. Forty kilometers to the south the English had built a busy port on the open roadstead at Madras protected by Fort St. George. Still further south the French occupied Pondicherry, another bustling trade center, protected by state-of-the art fortifications and a French garrison.

At the Mughal conquest of Golconda, the French and Dutch factors came to terms with Aurangzeb and obtained permission to trade in Golconda's former territories much as before. Madras was threatened with Mughal attack in 1689–90, but pressing needs for support in the campaign against the Marathas at Jinji diverted the attention of Mughal commanders. Madras supplied munitions, foodgrains, and even gunners to the Mughal army besieging the Maratha fortress.[22] Pondicherry and Madras flourished as thousands of migrants fled to seek the security offered by these enclaves in the midst of devastating warfare in the region. By the turn of the century the former sheltered some 60,000 inhabitants and the latter well over 100,000.

By the 1690s the Mughal emperor began to pay considerably more

[21] Ashin Das Gupta, *Indian Merchants and the Decline of Surat c. 1700–1750* (Wiesbaden: Franz Steiner Verlag, 1979), pp. 7–8.

[22] J. F. Richards, "European City-States on the Coromandel Coast" in P. M. Joshi and M. A. Nayeem, eds., *Studies in the Foreign Relations of India* (Hyderabad: Government of Andhra Pradesh, State Archives, 1975), p. 511.

attention to the East India Companies. The main issue was that of uncontrolled European piracy in the Indian Ocean for which the emperor tried to hold the East India Companies responsible. Tensions soared over the capture of the *Ganj-i Sawai*, the largest vessel in the Surat mercantile fleet. Every year, protected by its eighty guns, this great vessel transported high status pilgrims to Mecca and then travelled to Mokha to trade in Indian goods. In 1695 the ship was returning to Surat from Mokha with a full load of passengers and treasure worth 5.2 million rupees. Off the Indian coast Henry Bridgeman on the ship *Fancy* and another pirate ship attacked, dismasted, and boarded the *Ganj-i Sawai* against feeble resistance. For three days the pirates raped the women and plundered the ship. When the vessel finally reached Surat public outrage was very great. The Surat governor occupied the East India Company factory and jailed all the occupants. The atrocities committed against high-born Muslim women and against pilgrims returning from the Haj were deeply felt and blamed on the English.[23]

At this point in time the emperor's attention was drawn to the English minting of rupees at Bombay. These were coins adhering to Mughal standards for fineness and weight but bearing the insignia of the English monarch on them. When some of the survivors of the pirate attack and some of the offending rupees were exhibited in open court, Aurangzeb authorized an attack on Bombay by the Mughal tributary, the coastal chieftain, Siddi Yaqut Khan and his fleet. This attack faltered against the fortifications of Bombay.

Piracy persisted despite protests of innocence and promises by the Dutch and English to help in its suppression. In 1702 Aurangzeb reacted to the depredations of European pirates by interdicting all trade with the Dutch, English, and French companies in the empire. The Mughal faujdar of the Hyderabad Karnatak, Daud Khan Panni, an amir who was a confidant of Zulfikar Khan, took the opportunity to demand payment of large arrears of presumed revenue from the English at Madras. He also announced that his officers would inventory and survey the East India Company lands in and around the city and send troops to occupy the unfortified Indian quarter of Madras. The British resisted and a siege ensued. Continuing negotiations ended with the lifting of the siege after three months. Daud Khan Panni received a large monetary payment from the English and in return

[23] Sarkar, *History of Aurangzib*, v, 343–351.

publicly proclaimed the independence and autonomy of Madras.[24] Pondicherry, under the governorship of François Martin, survived a similar set of threats to make a similar settlement with the faujdar.[25]

Mughal failure to seize Bombay and Madras was a direct result of Aurangzeb's overwhelming preoccupation with the Maratha problem. The emperor was unwilling and increasingly unable to bring sufficient military weight to bear to occupy these ports. After Aurangzeb's death none of his immediate successors was prepared to pursue the matter. Bombay and Madras continued to flourish as autonomous trading centers in the years that Surat and Machhilipatnam were in decline.

THE IMPERIAL ELITE IN THE DECCAN WARS

The never-ending Deccan war battered at the cohesion and morale of the imperial elite. Long-serving Mughal amirs and mansabdars became disillusioned with imperial service. Aurangzeb's military impotence in the Deccan was more obvious every passing year. The hardships and danger of life in the imperial encampment in the Deccan continued without relief. Maratha raiders rode boldly close to the encampment and cut off supplies of foodgrains during the sieges. As Bhimsen, who wrote from personal experience, commented:[26]

> Ever since His Majesty had come to the throne, he had not lived in the city, and adopted all these wars and hardships of travel, that the inmates of his camp, sick of long separation, summoned their families to the camp and passed their time; a new generation was thus born (in the camp).

After 1689 the Mughal elite divided into those men committed to service in the Deccan and those fortunate enough to be deputed elsewhere. As Bhimsen's passage suggests, nobles in the Deccan rarely left it. Whereas officers who proved to be reliable and competent on provincial assignment in the north tended to remain.

Aurangzeb undercut that critical process by which the responsible officers of the empire received rewards and reprimands directly from the throne. Amirs posted to the north rarely participated in the ceremonial enactment of the emperor's authority at court audiences. Those officers in the Deccan who did attend audiences in the emperor's camp were forced to confront the dissonance between the still-grand

[24] Richards, "European City-States," p. 516. [25] Ibid., p. 512.
[26] Khobrekar, *Dilkasha*, p. 233.

ceremonies within the encampment and the hollowness of imperial power without.

In an unprecedented development, many Mughal mansabdars in the Deccan routinely shirked their duty as warriors. Governors and faujdars in every province often kept their troops safely locked up in their forts rather than challenge large bodies of Maratha raiders. Aurangzeb increasingly failed to punish or even admonish those officers who failed to engage the enemy.

By its length and inconclusiveness, the Deccan war fostered considerable interaction between Mughal and Maratha commanders. Many Mughal officers spent time in Maratha camps waiting for ransom payments to be made. Some Maratha commanders had been in imperial service. Violent, bloody battles certainly occurred, but an equal, if not greater, number of clashes were avoided by intense unofficial negotiation and clandestine agreements. Increasingly anxious for their future in Aurangzeb's waning years, many imperial governors and faujdars negotiated immunities for themselves, their followers and the areas they administered or their jagir lands. Some offered outright payments in cash; others offered services.

Part of the reluctance to do battle displayed by a growing number of Mughal commanders can be traced to deficiencies in their contingents. Increasingly Mughal mansabdars in the Deccan failed to maintain the full number of properly mounted and armed cavalrymen stipulated by imperial regulations. So widespread was this abuse and so inept were the imperial inspections that it became a commonplace observation in every bazaar.

Aurangzeb contributed to demoralization by inflating Mughal ranks and honors. At the fall of Bijapur and Golconda, Aurangzeb enrolled sixty-four Muslim nobles from those states as high-ranking amirs. Thirty-two of these "Deccani" nobles as they were termed, were given ranks of 5,000 zat or more. They constituted 40 percent of all nobles with the highest ranks.[27] Although most were able warriors and administrators and fully fluent in the shared Indo-Persian courtly culture of India, they still encountered considerable resentment from Mughal nobles who were khanazads.

Marathas, appointed for political reasons by Aurangzeb, constituted the other category of Deccani nobles. In the last half of the reign,

[27] M. Athar Ali, *The Apparatus of Empire: Awards of Ranks, Offices and Titles to the Mughal Nobility 1574–1658* (Delhi: Oxford University Press), pp. 26–27.

ninety-six Marathas were enrolled as Mughal amirs.[28] They comprised 16.7 percent of the total nobility. Most (sixty-two) were ranked below 3,000 zat in contrast to the Deccani Muslims. Nevertheless this was a large and unsettling element to force into the Mughal nobility. Some Marathas enlisted with the Mughals out of enmity against the Bhonsla dynasty.[29] Kanhoji Shirke, who had been badly treated by Shambhaji, joined Mughal service with his family members and rose to the rank of 6,000 zat. Others, driven by expediency, vacillated in their allegiances. Virtually all the Maratha nobles were employed as auxiliary field commanders with their troops and proved to be of doubtful reliability. Ranks and honors bestowed upon the Marathas as political rewards were viewed with great cynicism by the long-serving Mughal nobles in the Deccan.

Aurangzeb was not in a position to devise a new "Maratha policy" similar to Akbar's "Rajput policy" a century earlier. Neither his personality or his reputation for piety lent themselves to a warm welcome for Maratha chiefs. Few, if any, of these Maratha commanders had a substantial exposure to Indo-Persian high culture, or indeed, could communicate freely in Persian. For them to be assimilated fully into the imperial elite required a systematic, conscious effort that Aurangzeb was certainly not prepared to make. Nothing analagous to the political marriages arranged between the Rajputs and Timurid house seemed feasible for improving relations with the Marathas. At best, the emperor could hope that the years invested in nurturing and socializing the young Shahu might be rewarded by placing him on the Bhonsla throne. And, as long as other descendants of Shivaji occupied that throne, the Mughals had difficulty in matching incentives for raiding and plundering offered by the insurgents.

Accommodating Deccani Muslim and Maratha nobles put strains on imperial resources. Khanazads serving in the Deccan complained bitterly about an emerging shortage of jagirs:[30]

> At last, things reached such a state that the whole country was assigned to the new recruits from the Deccan and their agents, through bribery, obtained the choicest (jagirs) yielding the highest revenue for the Deccanis, and it was plain for all to see that the ranks and numbers of the new and unknown mansabdars went on increasing while the mansabs of the old mansabdars went on declining.

[28] Athar Ali, *Apparatus*, pp. 29–30. [29] Sarkar, *History of Aurangzib*, v, pp. 207–213.
[30] Abul Fazl Mamuri, *Tarikh-i Aurangzeb*, ff. 156b–157a, translated excerpt from Athar Ali, *Mughal Nobility*, p. 29.

The number of claimants for jagirs began to exceed the lands in the temporary pool (paibaqi) awaiting assignment.[31]

The most obvious response to this situation would have been to assign productive lands in Golconda and Bijapur to jagirdars. Instead, Aurangzeb appears to have made a deliberate policy decision to favor the needs of the central treasury over those of mansabdars claiming their pay. Most of the lands in Hyderabad province, formerly Golconda, were kept in khalisa earmarked for the central treasury. Other lands stayed in the temporary pool of lands for extended periods of time.[32] Similar policies seem to have prevailed in Bijapur and the Maratha lands.

The shortfall in jagirs in the Deccan proved to be more than an artifically created problem. As the Deccan wars continued the Maratha style of predatory raiding and Mughal reprisals drove greater and greater numbers of peasants off the land. Burnt villages and towns and butchered traders and caravans hindered production. Embittered men joined the Marathas or groups of bandits as public order declined.[33] Under these conditions jagirdars holding lands in the Deccan provinces found it more difficult to collect even reduced revenues. Mughal officers clashed with one another over access to those tracts of land where revenues could be reliably collected. By the early 1700s many Mughal officers in the south suffered real impoverishment as they failed to obtain paying jagirs.

Doubt, uncertainty, and frustration led to widespread unhappiness with Aurangzeb's policies. At the highest levels of the nobility, one group of nobles aligned themselves with Zulfikar Khan Nusrat Jang and his father the wazir, Asad Khan, at the head of a mixed coterie of nobles (see above). These men favored some form of negotiated settlement with the Marathas that would end the drain of imperial resources in the Deccan. Zulfikar Khan was directly involved in several offers and counter-offers between Aurangzeb and the Bhonsla rulers. Despite his aggressive military role, Zulfikar Khan remained in continual contact with his adversaries throughout this period.

Others supported Ghazi-ud-din Firuz Jang and his son Chin Qilich Khan, who headed a family group of Turani Muslim amirs. One

31 Athar Ali, *The Mughal Nobility under Aurangzeb* (Aligarh, 1966), pp. 92–94.
32 J. F. Richards, *Mughal Administration in Golconda* (Oxford: Clarendon Press, 1975), pp. 157–162.
33 For details of these years in Hyderabad province see Richards, *Mughal Administration*, pp. 215–235.

member of the group, Muhammad Amin Khan, had served as chief religious officer (sadr) briefly for Aurangzeb. Members of this faction insisted on a hard line. They felt that the full weight of imperial military power should be brought to bear on the Marathas to end the war and that no settlement was possible with these infidels.[34]

All of these men shared two or more decades of Deccan service. All were deeply involved in trying to stabilize imperial rule in the south. They might differ over the means, but the end was unarguable. Aurangzeb's prolonged stay in the Deccan had succeeded in turning imperial priorities upside down for the officers who surrounded him in his last years. The Deccan, not the north, was the center of their universe.

THE NORTHERN PROVINCES

After 1680 imperial administration in the north was subordinated to the emperor's involvement in the south. Aurangzeb kept up a brisk exchange of reports and orders between himself and his administrators and commanders in the north but his absence demanded careful management. On the whole, by using his sons and grandsons and his most capable nobles, the emperor kept intact imperial institutions and order in the northern plains. Crises did occur and were dealt with efficiently. Diversion of the empire's core military to the south did make the frontiers, revenues, and supply lines vulnerable to disruption.

To the northwest, the Afghan revolts of the 1670s had shown the importance of firm, personalized, and flexible imperial policies. Amir Khan, an extremely able Shi'ite Irani officer, assumed the governorship of Kabul at the close of the Afghan campaigns. For twenty years, Amir Khan's shrewd interventions into the internal politics and rivalries of the Yusufzais, Afridis, and other Afghan lineages kept the northwest relatively peaceful. In large measure this stability was secured by large subsidies paid in cash from the Kabul treasury to various chiefs and factions. The caravan trade continued to move large quantities of goods across the mountain passes with little interference.

In 1698, when Amir Khan died, his wife Sahibji, an aristocratic Mughal woman who had advised him closely, assumed full charge of the frontier administration for nearly two years. Finally Aurangzeb's

[34] Athar Ali, *Mughal Nobility*, pp. 106–111; Satish Chandra, *Parties and Politics at the Mughal Court*, (New Delhi: People's Publishing House, 2nd. edn., 1972), pp. 1–10.

new governor, his son Prince Shah Alam, arrived at Kabul. Only then did the much-admired noblewoman return to the south, send on Amir Khan's sons to court for appointments, and then proceed on a pilgrimage to Mecca.[35] The prince kept a firm hand on the frontier until his father's death in 1707.

On the northeastern frontier, along the Brahmaputra, Gadadhar Singh, a new, vigorous monarch of the Hindu Ahom kingdom, ascended the throne in 1681. At a conference of his nobles in 1682 the Ahom ruler set out his plans to retake Gauhati and to force the Mughals back down the river. The Ahom flotillas drove back the Mughal frontier posts (thanas) and engaged Mansur Khan, the faujdar, at an island garrison in the river opposite Gauhati. At the battle of Itakhuli, in September, 1682, the Ahom forces chased the defeated Mughals nearly one hundred kilometers back to the Manas river. The Manas then became the Mughal–Ahom boundary until the British occupation.[36] War booty taken from the discomfited Mughals included much treasure, war boats, arms, munitions, and elephants.

Itakhuli was the last main force battle to occur between the two powers in the northeast. Thereafter Gadadhar Singh and his son and successor Rudra Singh (1696–1714) devoted their energies to consolidation of royal power under a newly proclaimed form of officially sponsored *Sakti* Hinduism. Mughal expansion in the northeast had ground to a standstill, and the Ahom rulers had become so confident that by the end of Aurangzeb's reign they were preparing to invade Mughal Bengal.

Aurangzeb was dependent upon peace and order in the north to supply surplus revenues to pay for his incessant campaigning. Bengal, which regularly delivered a large surplus of revenues over expenditures, was a matter of special concern. In 1696–97 a dramatic revolt underscored the difficulties of absentee rule from the Deccan. Ibrahim Khan, the governor of Bengal, faltered badly in responding to a serious revolt. Sova Singh, a zamindar of Midnapur district in the far southwest corner of Bengal, had allied himself with Rahim Khan, leader of those Afghan zamindars in Orissa who were discontented with Mughal rule. The allied rebel forces killed Raja Krishna Ram, the

35 Shah Nawaz Khan and Abdul Hayy, *The Maathir-ul-Umara* (New Delhi, 1st reprint edition, 1979), edited and translated by H. Beveridge and Baini Prashad, 3 vols., I, pp. 246–253.

36 S. C. Dutta, *The North East and the Mughals (1661–1714)* (Delhi: D. K. Publications, 1984), pp. 154–156.

Khatri revenue collector of the district, seized his family and treasure, and occupied Burdwan town. The rebels then routed the Mughal faujdar in western Bengal and Rahim Khan, the Afghan chief, led troops to occupy Nadia and Murshidabad. Ibrahim Khan remained inactive at Dacca while that portion of Bengal west of the Ganges was left for plunder by the increasing numbers of rebels.

At that juncture, the daughter of Raja Krishna Ram killed Sova Singh with a dagger when he tried to assault her. Rahim Khan, the new leader, titled himself Rahim Shah to proclaim his regal aspirations. His rapidly growing force had reached 10,000 horse and five to six times as many infantry. Aurangzeb dismissed Ibrahim Khan from his post, appointed his own grandson, the Timurid prince Azim-ud-din to the governorship, and ordered Zabardast Khan, son of the dismissed Bengal governor, to take the field immediately. Zabardast Khan, using his cavalry and field artillery effectively, drove the rebels into retreat for the rainy season. By early 1698 Prince Azim-ud-din arrived and confronted Rahim Shah and his revived rebel force near Burdwan. In a brief, hard-fought battle the imperial troops killed Rahim Shah and crushed the rebellion.

Aurangzeb's main concern was to restore the Bengal revenues which had plummeted during the revolt and not revived under the management of his grandson. Azim-ud-din was fully engaged in sequestering all possible revenues to himself and his followers in Bengal as he prepared for the war of succession soon to come. Regular surplus funds shipped from Bengal to the Deccan faltered. In 1701, Aurangzeb selected one of his most capable financial officers to become chief fiscal officer of Bengal. Kartalab Khan was a young Brahmin slave purchased by a prominent Irani Mughal officer, Haji Shafi Ibrahimi, who served Aurangzeb as diwan of the Deccan provinces. Converted to Islam, the young boy was treated as a son by his patron and painstakingly trained in the clerical and fiscal arts necessary for Mughal service.[37] In 1701 Kartalab Khan transferred from Hyderabad, where he served as diwan, to Dacca where he became imperial diwan of Bengal and Orissa.

The new diwan, who, in the Mughal system, held nearly equal and independent powers from the governor, immediately took fiscal control away from Prince Azim-ud-din. He discovered after compiling an up-to-date revenue roll for Bengal that the crown revenues had

[37] Abdul Karim, *Murshid Quli Khan and His Times* (Dacca: Asiatic Society of Pakistan, 1963), pp. 15–26.

dwindled, the jagirdars were appropriating more than their stipulated salaries, and that only the relatively small customs duties found their way to the provincial treasury. Embezzlement of revenues by imperial officers was pervasive. Kartalab Khan increased the khalisa lands by confiscating some jagirs and by transferring others from Bengal to less productive areas in Orissa. He employed a number of Hindu subordinate revenue officers, largely Khatris from the Punjab, to take charge of various parts of the province on farming terms. That is, they put up security bonds for the assigned collections in their area and were paid a percentage of the proceeds.[38]

Rigorous attention to receipts and brutal imprisonment and torture for defaulting zamindars, chaudhuris, or other local officials and for the collectors themselves brought fast results. Kartalab Khan was so successful that in the first year he generated a ten million rupee surplus. In 1702, the diwan sent this treasure south to fill Aurangzeb's nearly empty treasury. By this time the prince's jealousy and rage had grown to the point that he tried to have Kartalab Khan killed. The diwan survived the attempt and shifted his offices from Dacca to Makhsudabad, a trading center on the Ganges, where he had been appointed faujdar as an additional charge. When reports of the fracas reached Aurangzeb, the emperor reprimanded his grandson and forced the prince to leave Bengal and take up residence at Patna in Bihar as provincial governor.

Azim-ud-din retained the absentee governorship of Bengal, but Kartalab Khan was left the most powerful imperial officer in the province. The young Brahmin slave boy was fast becoming an imperial grandee. In 1703, the Bengal diwan travelled to Aurangzeb's court in the Deccan and presented another large remittance and his accounts as well as lavish gifts for his sovereign and superiors. At that audience, Aurangzeb gave his favored officer a full robe of honor, a kettledrum, a standard, a promotion to 2,000 zat and 1,000 suwar, and a new title: Murshid Quli Khan. The title was a direct reference to the deceased Murshid Quli Khan who had carried out the Deccan revenue settlement some fifty years earlier. Aurangzeb permitted Murshid Quli Khan to rename his headquarters Murshidabad and to open an imperial mint in that city. Murshid Quli Khan also assumed the duties of governor of Orissa (removed from Azim-ud-din), and faujdar of

[38] Jadunath Sarkar, ed., *History of Bengal: Muslim Period 1200–1757*, (Patna, 1973), pp. 408–410.

Sylhet, Midnapur, Burdwan, and Cuttack in Orissa. On his return he also became diwan of Bihar. The emperor permitted Murshid Quli Khan to select his own deputies for these posts. And, in 1704, fourteen members of his adoptive kin from Iran arrived in Bengal and were given mansabs and postings under him. Murshid Quli Khan remained in office and kept up annual shipments of treasure to Aurangzeb and his successors in Delhi for over two decades. In so doing, he became the *de facto* ruler of Bengal as the imperial structure collapsed.

REVOLT OF THE JATS NEAR AGRA

Aurangzeb relied upon the great royal road running from Delhi to Agra, through Dholpur, and past the great prison-fortress at Gwalior to Burhanpur as the central conduit for fresh treasure, supplies, animals, and troops. Unfortunately this route passed through the Chambal river ravine country and other stretches of more desolate hills and forests. Year after year as the rich traffic along this route expanded, the temptation for banditry and plundering grew accordingly.

In the districts of Kol (present-day Aligarh), Agra, and Sahar, straddling the Yamuna river, Jat peasants and zamindars proved to be especially troublesome.[39] In 1685, Rajaram, a Jat zamindar at Sinsini, eighty kilometers west of Agra, strengthened a strongly defended fortress of hardened mud. Shielded by difficult terrain and bamboo/scrub forests these forts could beat off all but the most determined assaults. Already refusing to pay the revenue, Rajaram led his Jat clansmen to plunder traffic on the royal road. They even attempted to enter Sikandra to despoil Akbar's tomb, but were driven back by the faujdar. Soon the overland route to the Deccan was virtually closed. Even great nobles travelling with their entourages were not safe. In 1686, a Turani amir, Aghar Khan, who was marching from Kabul to Bijapur with his troops and household, tried to pursue the Jats who had plundered his baggage train. Outside the Jat fort he was killed along with his son-in-law and eighty of his followers. In the face of this palpable threat imperial revenue collectors and other officials either fled the districts or remained penned up in the towns.

In late 1687, Aurangzeb sent Bidar Bakht, his young grandson, north with troops to suppress the Jats. In the interim the newly appointed governor of the Punjab, Mahabat Khan, a former Hyder-

[39] Sarkar, *History of Aurangzib*, v, 296–303.

abad officer, had encamped near Sikandra on the Yumuna river. The Jats boldly attacked his camp in force and only retired after losing four hundred casualties.

Rajaram's Jats outmaneuvered the local imperial forces and occupied Sikandra where they succeeded in looting Akbar's tomb. According to Manucci:[40]

Already angered by the demands of the governors and faujdars for revenue, a great number of them [Jats] assembled and marched to the mausoleum of that great conqueror Akbar. Against him living they could effect nothing; they therefore wreaked vengeance on his sepulchre. They began their pillage by breaking in the great gates of bronze which it had, robbing the valuable precious stones and plates ... of gold and silver, and destroying what they were not able to carry away. Dragging out the bones of Akbar, they threw them angrily into the fire and burnt them.

Whether the Jats actually seized Akbar's remains, the desecration of the tomb was as Manucci puts it "the greatest affront possible to the house and lineage of Taimur-i lang (Timur]." After this incident Rajaram, the Jat leader, was killed by a Mughal musketeer in a subsequent clash, but the Jat stronghold at Sinsini was untouched.

Aurangzeb responded to these events by commissioning the young Raja Bishun Singh Kachhwaha of Amber (Jaipur) as faujdar of Mathura and as jagirdar of Sinsini, the Jat stronghold. The new commander and his Rajput troops marched directly to the Jat stronghold and besieged it. After a four-month siege, the Mughal troops laid a mine successfully, opened a breach, and stormed the small fort. Fifteen hundred Jat defenders died; nearly a thousand imperial troops were killed or wounded. Another small fortress at Sogar fell to the Mughals. By January, 1691 the Jat revolt around Agra was temporarily suppressed.

The Kachhwaha raja was given extensive holdings in jagir over the Jat territories and asked to restore normal administration. This he was unable to do and intermittent Jat resistance continued over the next fifteen years. After a brief interval, Churaman Jat, a nephew of the dead Rajaram, who proved to be exceedingly able, emerged as new militant leader who resisted any revenue demands. The Jat peasantry displayed a remarkable solidarity with their caste-fellows who were zamindars. In the Kol, Agra, and Sahar districts, a region stretching over approxi-

40 Manucci, *Storia do Mogor or Mogul India* (Calcutta, 4 vols., 1907–8), translated by William Irvine, II, 320.

mately forty parganas, village patels and the dominant elites in each village actively supported Churaman Jat with men and material.[41]

Churaman Jat also joined forces with Rajput zamindars from the Naruka, Kilanot, and Chauhan clans, in nearby Alwar, Ajmer, and Ranthambor districts. The Rajputs were trying to resist the Kachhwaha Raja's attempts to displace them from their holdings in favor of his own clan members. The rebel zamindars did not share caste identity with most of the peasants in these districts and did not enjoy anything near the same support that the Jats did. In many areas Rajputs were violating imperial regulations by trying to extend their limited lands to control peasant villages free of zamindar control. Nevertheless a united front against the Mughals and against the Kachhwaha regime successfully denied revenues and any sort of control over these districts in the remainder of Aurangzeb's regime.

Despite his advancing age, Aurangzeb was an active, energetic chief officer of the Mughal empire in the last eighteen years of his reign. The centralized structures of the empire continued to function. But Aurangzeb's long absence from the North Indian heartland of the empire and his obsession with the endless Deccan war strained imperial institutions and resources. Pouring treasure and manpower into the south prolonged rather than ended the war with the Marathas. A policy debate was muted. Thoroughly intimidated by their indomitable father, Aurangzeb's sons found neither the means nor the courage to challenge the emperor's plans. After 1689, in both newly conquered and older Deccan provinces public order, political stability, and agricultural and industrial production were in a descending spiral.

[41] R. P. Rana, "Agrarian Revolts in Northern India during the Late 17th and Early 18th Century," *The Indian Economic and Social History Review* 28 (1981), 287–326.

CHAPTER 12

IMPERIAL DECLINE AND COLLAPSE, 1707–1720

Aurangzeb died March 3, 1707, in his encampment at Ahmadnagar in the Deccan. In a written will the emperor made a futile attempt to divide the empire between his three living sons. Instead, the usual war of succession, so long delayed, broke out almost immediately. At the imperial encampment, Prince Azam Shah, supported by the imperial wazir, Asad Khan, adopted royal titles, struck coins and marched north toward Agra. At the frontier fortress of Jamrud, in the Hindu Kush, his elder brother Muazzam received the news of his father's death twenty days later. Imperial messengers had averaged seventy miles per day to bring the dispatches over 1,400 miles.[1] Muazzam, who had been preparing his army for the inevitable war for well over a year, began a forced march south to Agra.

At a site just north of Lahore, Muazzam declared his accession to the throne and took the title of Bahadur Shah. By June 1st the newly crowned emperor occupied Delhi. By June 12 he arrived at Agra where he met his son Prince Muhammad Azim, who had marched from Bengal and took possession of Agra fort and the central treasury. The imperial reserves at Agra proved to be little depleted by the Deccan wars. Bahadur Shah's officers found coined and uncoined gold and silver totalling 240 million rupees – considerably greater than Akbar's reserves at his death.[2] Muhammad Azim brought additional funds from the Bengal treasury which further strengthened his father's cause.

In mid-June, 1707, the two contenders met just south of Agra at Jajau, near Samugarh, the site of the climactic battle between Aurangzeb and Dara Shukoh. At Jajau, Azam Shah and his two sons were killed on the battlefield and his troops routed. On the victor's return to Agra all nobles who made submission were welcomed and given appropriate postings.

While Bahadur Shah was preoccupied with the Rajputs during 1707 (see below), news arrived that his brother, Muhammad Kam Bakhsh,

[1] The description of the war of succession is drawn from William Irvine, *Later Mughals* (New Delhi: Oriental Books Reprint Corporation, 1971), 2 vols. in one; 1, 1–66.

[2] J. F. Richards, "Mughal State Finance and the Premodern World Economy", *Comparative Studies in Society and History*, 23, (1981), 293.

had crowned himself as an independent ruler at Bijapur. In response to this direct challenge, by May, 1708, Bahadur Shah marched south with an army of over 300,000 men. Prolonged negotiations with an increasingly despairing and unstable Kam Bakhsh ultimately failed. Outside Hyderabad in January, 1709, Bahadur Shah's troops encircled Kam Bakhsh who was left with but a remnant of his army. He and his two sons were killed in the clash that followed.

No sharp ideological cleavage divided Bahadur Shah from either of his brothers and the new emperor was quick to pardon and accept any nobles who had supported his dead rivals. Despite the problems of Aurangzeb's last years, the empire passed, seemingly intact, to his son and successor. Nevertheless, Bahadur Shah, who was considerably more moderate in his approach to doctrinal purity, was still hampered by the aftereffects of Aurangzeb's unremitting insistence on Islam as the only touchstone for loyalty. He never formally abolished the jiziya, but the effort to collect the tax became ineffectual and dispirited.

A serious financial crisis faced the new emperor. Revenue collections in the Deccan were squeezed by Maratha activity. In the northern provinces revenues interrupted by the 1707–1709 war did not regain their assessed level. The main source of funds remained Bengal. Treasure carts and bills of exchange continued to arrive at the capital from Dacca. Failure to assign fully productive jagirs strained the loyalties and reduced the effectiveness of members of the nobility and the corps of mansabdars. The regime's inability to keep order in the countryside undercut long-standing agreements between the state and the zamindars. If the state could not fulfill its obligations, local aristocrats were not inclined to pay the land revenue. These strains in the imperial fabric found expression in the most important political crises to occupy Bahadur Shah: disaffection of the Rajputs, growing militancy among the Sikhs and Jats in the north, and continuing Maratha insurgency in the south.

RAJPUTS AND JATS

Since his dramatic escape in infancy, Ajit Singh, the Rathor prince, had survived to become the acknowledged ruler of Marwar and holder of a 3,500/3,000 rank as a reluctant Mughal amir. Ajit Singh took advantage of the death of Aurangzeb, his life-long enemy, to drive the Mughal occupation force from Jodhpur and take full possession of his capital.

He destroyed those mosques erected since the Mughal occupation and forbade Islamic prayers in the city.[3] After the climactic battle at Jajau, Ajit Singh failed to acknowledge Bahadur Shah's authority. In this continuing defiance he was reportedly supported by his contemporary, Jai Singh Kachhwaha of Amber, who had first aligned himself with the Azam Shah then deserted him at the climactic battle, and by the young Rana Amar Singh Sisodia, who ruled Mewar from Udaipur.

Bahadur Shah personally commanded a large royal army which, by January 1708, occupied Amber, the Kachhwaha capital. The emperor conferred the Kachhwaha gaddi on Jai Singh's brother, Vijai Singh, who had actively served Bahadur Shah earlier. However, a Mughal faujdar and his troops continued to garrison the city after the royal army marched on. The Udaipur Rana averted Mughal invasion by sending an envoy with lavish gifts while he and his family fled to the sanctuary of the Mewar hills.

Mughal troops easily brushed aside Ajit Singh's clansmen and seized Jodhpur, capital of Marwar. Shortly thereafter, Ajit Singh surrendered and appeared in person before Bahadur Shah's durbar. The emperor restored noble rank to Ajit Singh, granted him the title of Maharaja, and gave generous mansabs to two of his sons. For his part, Ajit Singh had to swallow the indignity of having an imperial qazi and mufti placed on duty in Jodhpur. These officers were "to rebuild the mosques, destroy the idol-temples, enforce the provisions of the Shariʿat about the summons to prayer and the killing of cows, to appoint magistrates and to commission officers to collect jiziyah."[4] Mughal occupation of both Jodhpur and Amber was a further tightening of imperial domination over Rajasthan.

Ajit Singh Rathor and Jai Singh Kachhwaha, forced to accompany the distrustful emperor on his Deccan campaign against Kam Bakhsh, managed to effect their escape and return to Rajasthan. With assistance from the Rana of Mewar each rebel prince recovered control of his capital. Together they joined forces to besiege the Mughal redoubt at Ajmer, but were repulsed by the imperial faujdar. In a conciliatory measure supported by many nobles, the emperor affirmed the mansabs of the errant rajas, but refused to grant them their capitals under the watan jagir arrangement. Whether or not to negotiate a further

[3] Satish Chandra, *Parties and Politics at the Mughal Court 1707–1740* (New Delhi: People's Publishing House, 2nd. ed., 1972), p. 29.
[4] *Khafi Khan*, pp. 606–607 quoted in Chandra, *Parties and Politics*, p. 33.

reconciliation with the Rajputs or to brutally suppress them was a matter of intense debate among the emperor's advisers and nobles. In the end the question was resolved by the Sikh revolt at the close of 1709. A hurriedly cobbled agreement gave Ajit Singh and Jai Singh their homelands and capitals as watan jagirs and six months leave to return to their kingdom.

This hasty compromise did not entirely restore the Rathors and Kachhwahas to the fully committed, zealous warriors for the Timurid cause that they had once been. A consistent, firm, but sympathetic policy was necessary to return the emperor–Rajput relationship to its former intensity. Unfortunately, Bahadur Shah and his successors were never given the opportunity to rebuild this imperial asset.

THE SIKH REBELLION

The tenth Sikh Guru, Govind Singh, who had supported Bahadur Shah in the war of succession, joined the royal entourage as the emperor marched to confront Kam Bakhsh in the Deccan. Govind Singh's mission was to obtain redress against Wazir Khan, the faujdar of Sirhind whose brutal execution of Govind Singh's two youngest sons was the latest Mughal-inspired Sikh martyrdom. Despairing of justice, the Guru sent an emissary back to the Punjab to bring the Jat peasantry to revolt against tyranny if his mission failed. That emissary, Lachman Das, an ascetic renamed Banda or the "slave" of Govind Singh, was armed with the Guru's standard and kettledrum. While Banda and a small band of followers paused at Delhi, news of Govind Singh's assassination reached the capital. The most plausible explanation for the assault is that the young Pathan assassins were hirelings of Wazir Khan who was threatened by Govind's accusations. Just before he died Govind Singh informed his followers that he was the last of the line of true Gurus and that henceforth they were to look upon the *Granth Sahib* or holy book as their true and constant guide.[5]

Banda immediately began to assemble hundreds of Sikhs at his camp under the dead Guru's standard. In what rapidly became a millenial resistance movement, he preached sermons, gave benedictions, welcomed converts to Sikhism, and freely gave out any offerings he received. Banda issued proclamations offering refuge to anyone

[5] Khushwant Singh, *A History of the Sikhs* (Princeton: Princeton University Press, 1963), 2 vols., I, 95.

"threatened by thieves, dacoits or highway robbers, troubled by Mohammedan bigots, or in any way subjected to injustice or ill-treatment."[6] Banda's primary appeal lay in those parts of the sub-Himalayan interfluvial zones in the Punjab and Delhi provinces where formerly pastoralist, recently settled, Jat peasants, anxious for recognition, responded to Banda's egalitarian appeal. They, and numerous lower-caste or untouchables – scavengers, leather workers – travelled to Banda's camp, converted, and took the name Singh as members of the Khalsa.[7] All were prepared to fight for the new faith.

In November, 1709, Banda's army stormed, leveled, and massacred Samana, a prosperous, Muslim-dominated Punjab town. A half dozen Punjab towns shared a similar fate before the Sikhs reached Sirhind where they aimed to revenge themselves on Wazir Khan. After a winter of preparation on both sides, in May, 1710, Banda led thousands of badly armed peasants against Wazir Khan's artillery, Mughal cavalry and cohorts of volunteer Muslim *ghazis*. Despite their lack of firearms, or horses, the Sikh army overran the Mughals and killed most of them in desperate hand-to-hand fighting. Two days later the Sikhs stormed Sirhind, massacred those inhabitants who did not hastily convert to Sikhism, looted the city and destroyed the buildings. After Sirhind, Banda adopted the title of padshah, started a new calendar and issued coins bearing the names of Gurus Nanak and Govind. Each coin displayed the cauldron of the Sikh communal kitchen and the sword of the Khalsa. By this time, in the style of a millennial leader, Banda was reputed to deflect bullets from their course and protect his men from swords and spears by his spells.

In the next few months, Banda's armies had overrun the Punjab plain between the Yamuna river to the Ravi and beyond. Only Lahore, Delhi, and a few Afghan towns held out:[8]

> For eight or nine months, and from two or three days march from Delhi to the environs of Lahore, all the towns and places of note were pillaged by these unclean wretches, and trodden under foot and destroyed. Men in countless numbers were slain, the whole country was wasted, and mosques and tombs were razed.

Bahadur Shah hurried north to the Punjab to organize a fastmoving drive against the rebels. By the end of 1710 Mughal commanders had

[6] Singh, *Sikhs*, 1, 103.

[7] Muzaffar Alam, *The Crisis of Empire in Mughal North India* (Delhi: Oxford University Press, 1986), pp. 144–145.

[8] Khafi Khan quoted in Singh, *Sikhs*, 1, 109 n.

pushed Banda's peasant forces from the plain to Mukhlisgarh, a fortified refuge in the hills. Banda escaped capture in the final assault and remained free to rally new followers in another attack on the Punjab plains in early 1711. Bahadur Shah moved to Lahore in order to better command the campaign, but remained frustrated as Banda stayed at large. In February, 1712, Bahadur Shah died of natural causes and a new war of succession immediately broke out.

The Sikh rebellion was a dramatic testimonial to severe disaffection in the provinces of north India. For well-equipped Mughal troops to be routed by ill-armed peasant infantry was a shocking and nearly unprecedented development. Only a religious appeal rooted in class hatred could so galvanize these disparate bands of rebels. Banda's millennial message focussed long-standing peasant and lower-caste grievances against the regime and its allies, the qazis and other prosperous Muslim gentry who were grant-holders under the regime and Afghan, Rajput, and other non-Jat zamindars. In the savage battles fought over several years, Muslim solidarity typified by the emergence of armed ghazis was an important element in the resistance to the Sikhs. The Muslim populations of the Punjab towns fought desperately to save themselves. Banda, on the other hand, appealed to the Sikh version of martyrs for the faith who would be protected in battle by his own extraordinary powers. The Muslim chroniclers all decry the ascendance of low-caste or even untouchable Hindus to positions of power under the Sikh regime.

Imperial forces under Bahadur Shah swept the Sikh armies from the plains back into the hills. But they had less success in squelching what had become strong guerrilla movements resting on wide popular support. Unlike the Rajput zamindars of the plains, many of the Rajput hill chiefs were secretly in sympathy with any resistance against Mughal power and supplied Banda with information, material and refuge when needed.[9] Only in 1715, in Farrukhsiyar's reign, was the Punjab governor able to surround Banda and his followers in his hill fortress. After an eight month siege, the Mughals captured Banda and his starving garrison alive. Gory public executions followed of Banda, the self-proclaimed ruler, and hundreds of his followers.

[9] Alam, *Crisis of Empire*, pp. 155–164.

THE MARATHAS IN THE DECCAN

In October, 1707, in the confusion surrounding Aurangzeb's demise, an important event occurred. Prince Azam Shah permitted Shahuji, the son of Shambhaji Bhonsla, to leave the imperial encampment where he had been confined since infancy. The young Maratha prince was free to seize leadership of the badly disunited Maratha chiefs and generals. He was pitted against Tara Bai, the widow of Rajaram (d. 1701) who claimed the Bhonsla throne on behalf of Rajaram's son Sivaji II. By releasing Shahuji, Prince Azam opted for a conciliatory policy with the Marathas. Aurangzeb's endless war had failed.

If Shahuji could ascend the Bhonsla throne with Mughal support, he would be the first Maratha ruler thoroughly socialized into imperial culture. Aurangzeb had treated Shahuji with warmth and generosity in the hope that he could be useful in the future. Shahuji was not forced to convert to Islam, and was given proper Brahminical instruction in the Hindu faith. His attitudes toward the Timurid empire were considerably more sympathetic than most Marathas. In the last phase of the war of succession Bahadur Shah conferred high Mughal rank upon the freed Bhonsla prince and obtained the services of Nimaji Sindhia with a large Maratha contingent for the campaign against Kam Bakhsh.

The question of a Deccan settlement arose immediately after the death of Kam Bakhsh. Zulfikar Khan, who had survived the war of succession by deserting to Bahadur Shah at a critical moment in the battle of Jajau, became absentee governor of the Deccan provinces as well as head bakhshi of the empire. Daud Khan Panni served as Zulfikar Khan's deputy in the south with his headquarters at Aurangabad. Continuing to favor a soft line with the Marathas, Zulfikar Khan wasted little time in presenting Shahuji's emissary to Bahadur Shah with a proposed settlement. Shahuji asked that he be made head deshmukh of the Deccan provinces with an allowance of 10 percent of the imperial revenues. He should have authority to divert an additional 25 percent of the Deccan revenues as chauth. In return Shahuji would restore order and prosperity to the war-ravaged provinces. Simultaneously, a counter-proposal came via Munim Khan, Bahadur Shah's wazir and rival of Zulfikar Khan. An emissary from Tara Bai asked only for a 10 percent share of the imperial revenues and appointment as head deshmukh of the Deccan. She too offered to put down insurgency and renew prosperity.

Formally at least, both offers, if accepted, placed the Bhonsla ruler in a subservient position to the Mughal emperor by seeking appointment as a deshmukh and zamindar. Shahuji and Tara Bai thereby hoped to strengthen their claim to sovereign power over the splintered Maratha chiefs and armies. Shivaji had founded his dynasty on rejection of imperial authority; his two descendants were seeking that recognition by the emperor as local rulers.

In the end Bahadur Shah equivocated and granted a sanad as head deshmukh to each claimant but did not concede the collection of chauth. This non-policy simply incited the two Maratha factions to fight for supremacy – a policy that could only be damaging to imperial territories.

During the last two years of Bahadur Shah's reign massive Maratha armies only loosely tied to either Shahuji or Tara Bai raided and plundered in all the Mughal provinces in the south and ventured as far north as Malwa. So devastating were these raids and so ineffectual the Mughal defense that Daud Khan Panni, Zulfikar Khan's deputy in the Deccan, negotiated a private agreement with Shahuji to turn over to the Bhonsla prince the full 35 percent of revenues he had requested from the emperor. In return Shahuji agreed to restrain the freebooting Maratha chieftains and restore order. This essentially temporary and private agreement did little to help Shahuji bring the numerous Maratha chieftains under his effective authority. During Bahadur Shah's reign the umbrella of imperial authority in the Deccan became even more bedraggled and tattered than it had been in Aurangzeb's last campaigns against the Maratha hill forts.

THE WAR OF SUCCESSION

In early January 1712, Bahadur Shah, then in his seventieth year, lay dying at Lahore. As was his invariable custom, he occupied the tents of the great imperial encampment rather than the royal quarters in Lahore fortress. Unlike his father, Bahadur Shah kept his four mature sons in close attendance on him, rather than permitting them to build regional power bases as provincial governors. Each prince remained alert with his troops in his own tented encampment on the outskirts of the city. The leading contender for the throne was Bahadur Shah's second son, Prince Azim-ush-Shan, who had accumulated a vast fortune as governor of Bengal and Bihar 1695–1706, commanded a large army, and had come to be his father's chief adviser. In a new departure, however, his opposition centered on an amir, Zulfikar Khan, who as chief bakhshi of the empire and viceroy of the Deccan, was the most powerful noble at Bahadur Shah's court.

Prior to Bahadur Shah's demise, Zulfikar Khan negotiated an unusual agreement with the three remaining princes – each of whom viewed his chances of survival as nearly nil. Zulfikar Khan proposed that the three princes combine against their half-brother. If victorious, they would divide the empire: Jahandar Shah was to become emperor of Hindustan, Rafi-ush Shan to rule the northwest from Kabul, and Jahan Shah to take the Deccan. Zulfikar Khan would become the imperial wazir residing at Delhi whose deputies would act as chief ministers at the courts of each of the other brothers. This proposal, solemnly sworn on a Koran, centered symbolic unity upon the eldest prince, Jahandar Shah, whose titles would appear on a common coinage. Effective rule however, would fall to Zulfikar Khan as wazir.

The battle for power erupted even before the emperor died on January 12, 1712. In a three month struggle at Lahore, the most powerful nobleman in the empire out-generaled and defeated the most powerful prince. Azim-ush Shan died caught in quicksand in the Ravi river trying to flee the victorious allied forces. Not surprisingly, Zulfikar Khan then shifted his support to Jahandar Shah, probably the most pliable of the three princes. Within a month he had defeated and killed Rafi-ush Shan and Jahan Shah. On March 29, 1712, Jahandar Shah enthroned himself as emperor on the field of battle outside Lahore.

The new emperor found that he could not reward his long-standing confidant and assistant, his foster brother Kokaltash Khan, who was pushed to one side. Instead, Zulfikar Khan became wazir with the unprecedented rank of 10,000/10,000. His deputy, Daud Khan Panni, remained in charge as viceroy of the Deccan. Zulfikar Khan's private fiscal officer, Sabha Chand, became diwan of the imperial khalisa.

After the coronation, Zulfikar Khan actively persecuted dozens of those nobles who had supported the dead princes. Most were imprisoned in Delhi and their property confiscated. Two amirs, however, were publicly executed. This is the first time that nobles on the losing side were punished. In the past, only the royal contenders and their progeny were killed and their property seized. New distortions in the system marked this second succession struggle to occur within five years.

JAHANDAR SHAH, 1712–1713

Jahandar Shah moved his capital back from Lahore to occupy the fortress and palace at Shahjahanabad Delhi. This should have strengthened the new emperor's authority. Instead, in the few brief months of his reign the strongest aspects of Mughal centralized power suffered dramatic, debilitating changes – changes that would have to be corrected rapidly if the empire was to survive. First, the long-standing power and authority of the Timurid monarchy itself was weakened. The new wazir, by virtue of his role in the succession struggle, his reputation, and his political and military resources, assumed the executive direction of the empire. Zulfikar Khan, not the emperor, decided on appointments and imperial policy. For the first time since Akbar's early years, the Timurid occupant of the throne had allowed day to day authority to slip into the hands of an overmighty minister.

It was Zulfikar Khan who, consistent with his long-standing posture, pressed forward with a broad policy of conciliation for the emperor to promulgate. First, only nine days after the coronation, jiziya was abolished. Second, important concessions to the Rajputs followed. Ajit Singh Rathor received an enhanced rank, the title of Maharaja, and appointment as governor of Gujarat. Jai Singh Kachhwaha was given the same rank, the title of Mirza Raja, and governorship of Malwa. Other territorial additions to their hereditary domains brought an enthusiastic response from the two former rebels. Third, as a partial solution to the Maratha problem, the emperor granted a mid-level noble rank, the title of Anup Singh, and the deshmukhi of Hyderabad province to Shivaji II, the son of Tara Bai and Rajaram. This was an attempt to divide the Maratha domains between Shahu and his cousin and to bring each figure into the Mughal system as a formally recognized feudatory.[10]

Unable to challenge Zulfikar Khan's authority directly, Jahandar Shah resorted to conspiring with Kokaltash Khan and his clique to undermine the wazir's position.[11] This further inflamed factional resistance to Zulfikar Khan and damaged the emperor's reputation.

By his own behavior Jahandar Shah lowered the dignity of the monarchy. After his accession the emperor raised his favorite concubine, Lal Kunwar, to the status of a queen. The new queen was the

[10] Chandra, *Parties and Politics*, pp. 74–75.
[11] Chandra, *Parties and Politics*, pp. 67–82, forcefully makes this argument.

daughter of a well-known court musician who, despite his talent, shared the demeaning status accorded all musicians by Mughal aristocratic culture. Lal Kunwar was widely disliked for her origins and her influence over the emperor. She and Jahandar Shah violated decorum by their display of drunkenness and amorousness. Royal frivolousness disturbed many at court as Lal Kunwar and the emperor devoted much time and energy to planning and arranging for lavish, expensive public festivals. Thrice-monthly city-wide illuminations at Delhi became excessively expensive. Unearned honors, ranks and titles given Lal Kunwar's father and brothers further offended the nobles and their followers.

The fast-slipping authority of the emperor coincided with a severe administrative and fiscal crisis. The shortage of productive jagir lands begun in Aurangzeb's reign did not abate but continued to plague the corps of mansabdars. At the same time the divergence between the true income from jagirs and that assigned on paper became wider. Inflated ranks given by Bahadur Shah and Jahandar Shah after each political struggle simply added to the demand placed on shrinking resources.

The meticulous procedures of the zabt revenue system unraveled in the scramble to secure even partial revenues from the North Indian countryside. Zulfikar Khan and his officials ignored widespread violations of imperial regulations. Officials at all levels became open to bribes and various forms of peculation. Middlemen seized the opportunity to make their fortunes. Everywhere revenue farming became the practice. In place of carefully calculated assessments based on relative fertility and market prices, officials of the khalisa and agents of jagirdars settled for bids made by private revenue farmers. The sharply discounted revenues were collected immediately from the successful tax bidders and their bankers.

The signs of imperial fiscal bankruptcy were obvious. Jahadar Shah's own troops remained unpaid from the time of his accession. The only revenues that could be counted upon with any certainty were the regular shipments of treasure from Bengal. Prices of foodgrains, vegetable oils, and other commodities rose to new heights as supplies dwindled in the markets of Agra and Delhi. When revenue collections no longer arrived at the capital, the stimulus for urban sales of foodgrains declined. Regional and local economies absorbed the flow of taxes, produce, and loans upon which the Mughal revenue system was based.

A SUCCESSFUL COUP, 1713

Farrukhsiyar, the second son of the slain Prince Azim-ush Shan, began marching from his post as governor of Bengal when the war of succession began. Hearing of his father's defeat and death, Farrukhsiyar, after vacillating, crowned himself at Patna as a contender for the throne. Virtually his only prominent supporters were two brothers: Sayyid Husain Ali Baraha, who owed his position as governor of Bihar to Azim-ush Shan, and his brother, Sayyid Abdullah Khan Baraha, who benefited from the same patronage to become governor of Allahabad.

The Sayyid brothers looked to their kinsmen in the Baraha clan settled on the upper Doab region between the Ganges and Yamuna for their strength. The Barahas could field several thousand fighting men marked by their conspicuous bravery, kinship solidarity, and loyalty to the Timurid house. As Indian Muslims settled on the land tied into four linked patrilineages, they closely resembled Rajputs in their dual ties to locality and empire. They could recall the family tradition in which their ancestors were key players in the struggle to put Prince Salim, later Jahangir on the throne (see above). In return for Baraha support in what was a risky, even foolhardy, venture, Farrukhsiyar promised the brothers appointments as wazir and mir bakhshi, the two highest ranking posts available if he prevailed.

In November, 1712, Jahandar Shah's son, Prince Azz-ud-din, and two of the emperor's chief officers, all inexperienced in military affairs, led a large army to try to stop the rebel advance from the east. Near Allahabad, the prince and his advisers, uncertain of their troops, broke and fled before giving battle. In the aftermath of this rout, more nobles and zamindars brought troops to align themselves with Farrukhsiyar. At Delhi, Jahandar Shah and Zulfikar Khan tried frantically to muster an army to meet the advancing rebels. The biggest problem was lack of money. The last imperial reserves had been consumed in organizing the large army sent east with Prince Azz-ud-din. The unpaid royal soldiery refused to march without pay. In desperation, Jahandar Shah's officers broke up gold and silver vessels from the palace, passed out immensely valuable jewels and jeweled articles from the treasuries, and even ripped gold and silver from the walls and ceilings of the palace to meet this emergency. From these frenzied actions the bankruptcy of the Timurids was painfully apparent.

Finally in early December, Jahandar Shah and Zulfikar Khan set out toward Agra at the head of 40,000 cavalry, as many musketeers and bowmen, and artillery. The emperor's top commanders were faction ridden and demoralized. Newly recruited forces from Chin Qilich Khan and several Turani nobles, who had been out of favor since Aurangzeb's reign, were regarded with considerable (and justified) suspicion by Jahandar Shah's commanders. In mid-January, 1713, the two armies met at Agra in a desperately fought day-long battle. As agreed, the Turani contingents under Chin Qilich Khan betrayed Jahandar Shah and stood by without fighting. Before the battle was concluded Jahandar Shah dismounted the royal elephant and fled with Lal Kunwar into Agra. Hurriedly they set out as isolated fugitives to Delhi. In the aftermath of the battle, Zulfikar Khan also retreated with his surviving troops towards Delhi.

FIRST PHASE OF THE POLITICAL STRUGGLE, 1713–1715

At Agra Farrukhsiyar installed himself in Jahandar Shah's duplicate set of royal tents, and caused his name and titles to be read in the Friday prayers at the great public mosque. As the new emperor marched toward Delhi he appointed Sayyid Abdullah Khan to be wazir or chief fiscal officer of the empire, and his brother Sayyid Hussain Ali Khan, still recovering from battlefield wounds, as chief bakhshi of the empire.

At Delhi, Jahandar Shah had sought refuge with Zulfikar Khan. The latter imprisoned his former sovereign and offered to hand Jahandar Shah over to Farrukhsiyar's officers. When Farrukhsiyar arrived at the capital, he greeted an unsuspecting Zulfikar Khan effusively and warmly in an audience before leaving him to be brutally slain by a body of royal slaves. That same day Farrukhsiyar ordered the execution of Jahandar Shah who had been confined with Lal Kunwar in Delhi fort. Lal Kunwar was sent to that portion of the palace where widows and families of deceased emperors resided. Several other nobles and higher-ranking administrators were executed. To add to the general sense of insecurity, these slayings were carried out under the guise of normal, even cordial, audiences with the emperor or his highest officers. Suddenly the victims were seized and knifed or strangled by palace slaves. Farrukhsiyar completed this initial purge by ordering the three most capable Timurid princes, including his own twelve-year-old brother, blinded and confined in the state prison in Delhi fort.

Still fearful for his throne, Farrukhsiyar, urged on by a court party of nobles dependent upon him, soon began conspiring to destroy the Sayyid brothers. The larger issue concerned the extent to which the wazir or the Timurid ruler would be the effective ruler of the empire. The emperor's plotting launched a desperate struggle between Farrukhsiyar and his two leading nobles. Between 1713 and 1719 the factional struggle at court was the single dominant political fact in the empire. Virtually all other policies and reforms were sacrificed to this conflict. Neither party could assemble enough military power and political support to readily destroy the other. Instead, the vital link between emperor and noble, which shaped the solidarity of the Mughal elite, was further shredded over the next six years.

Tension between emperor and wazir was especially harmful in trying to formulate policy toward the Rajputs and Marathas. All the leading Rajput rajas sent letters of submission and felicitation to Farrukhsiyar, but refused to appear in person at a court audience. Trying to divide the Rajputs, Farrukhsiyar offered the governorship of neighboring Malwa to Jai Singh Kachhwaha, who accepted and left for his post. Appointment to the distant province of Thatta (Sind) was flatly rejected by Ajit Singh Rathor.

In response Farrukhsiyar sent Sayyid Husain Ali Baraha in command of a large army to bring Ajit Singh back to court. As he departed, the emperor sent secret letters to Ajit Singh promising him imperial favor if he were to defeat and kill Husain Ali Khan. Ajit Singh opted to come to terms with the Sayyids rather than the emperor. In the course of a four-month campaign, more movable negotiations than battle, Ajit Singh and Husain Ali Khan agreed on a treaty. The raja promised to give his daughter in marriage to the emperor; to send his son Abhai Singh to court to serve as a Mughal noble, and to come himself when summoned. He also paid tribute and agreed to accept the governorship of Thatta. In a secret codicil, Husain Ali Khan promised that as soon as Ajit Singh had shown public compliance by marching toward Thatta, he would be reappointed governor of Gujarat. This was a first step in an emerging alliance between the Rathor ruler and the Sayyid brothers.

Upon Husain Ali Khan's return to the capital in mid-1714, the court struggle broke out into the open. Conflicts over appointments and maladministration by the wazir's deputy, Ratan Chand, flared up.

Farrukhsiyar diverted funds so that two of his courtiers, Khan-i Dauran and Mir Jumla, could assemble troops sufficient to attack the Sayyids. For their part, the Sayyids could not muster enough men from among their own kinsmen and dependents to prevail over the emperor. Considerable evidence exists that they were reluctant to violate long-standing norms of deference to the Timurid ruler – even if they had put Farrukhsiyar on the throne.

In mid-1714, Abdullah and Husain Ali Khan, fully aware of the emperor's plans, retired to their mansions in Delhi surrounded by the nearly ten thousand Baraha kinsmen and troops they commanded. From this redoubt they sent letters asking the emperor to allow them to retire from imperial service. Farrukhsiyar, fearing rebellion if they did so, tried to appoint a new wazir, but none of the emperor's intimates were willing to confront the formidable Sayyids in direct combat in the streets of Delhi. Months of protracted negotiations between two armed camps finally produced a compromise. The emperor agreed to send Mir Jumla, his favorite seen as most hostile to the Sayyids, to Bihar as provincial governor. In return Husain Ali Khan would give up his post as mir bakhshi of the empire and take up the governorship of the Deccan provinces in person. The emperor's man Khan-i Dauran became imperial bakhshi. Abdullah Khan would remain in Delhi as wazir.

In May, 1715, Husain Ali Khan left for the Deccan. Husain Ali Khan carried with him several concessions wrung out of the emperor. The new Deccan governor carried the grand seal which gave him full authority to appoint and dismiss all office holders and to assign jagirs in the Deccan. In an unprecedented measure, Husain Ali Khan was given full authority to appoint, transfer and dismiss the commandants of the great fortresses. Prior to this all Timurid rulers had jealously guarded this power to provide a counterweight against overambitious provincial officials.

Shortly after sending Husain Ali Khan to the Deccan, Farrukhsiyar transferred Daud Khan Panni from the governorship of Gujarat to Khandesh, one of the six provinces under the Deccan administration. In a secret dispatch, the emperor ordered Daud Khan Panni to attack and, if possible, kill Husain Ali Khan. If he were successful Daud Khan would become governor of the Deccan provinces. Instead, in a battle fought near Burhanpur, Husain Ali Khan easily defeated and killed Daud Khan Panni who had only a small cavalry force. Among the latter's captured effects were the secret communications from Farrukhsiyar.

SECOND PHASE OF THE POLITICAL STRUGGLE, 1715–1718

Immediately after the settlement, however, in Delhi there was a brief thaw. In December, 1715, the emperor celebrated his long-agreed marriage to the daughter of Ajit Singh Rathor, in an attempt to settle the long smoldering problem of Rajput loyalty. Sayyid Abdullah Khan participated fully in the elaborate ceremonies surrounding this great public event.

News of Daud Khan Panni's death and the emperor's treachery soon restored mutual hostility. Emperor and wazir continued in a frustrating stalemate over the next two years. The political climate of the capital remained tense and suspicious. Farrukhsiyar busied himself in several abortive plots to seize Abdullah Khan. The emperor fixed upon one noble after another as possible victors over Abdullah Khan and as putative wazirs. None could be persuaded to risk an armed showdown with Sayyid Abdullah Khan given the unreliable nature of the emperor's support. The wazir looked to his own security by keeping thousands of his Baraha kinsmen on armed alert. When he attended the daily audience he was accompanied through the streets of Delhi by three to four thousand armed cavalry.

The financial crisis deepened. Abdullah Khan's diwan, Ratan Chand, leased all revenues to the highest bidders. Even the khalisa (crownlands) were leased out to those collectors who submitted the best bids. Ratan Chand extracted a lease in writing and payment in advance from the collector's backers. Small to middling ranked mansabdars found it impossible to collect revenues from their assigned lands. The treasury began cash payments of fifty rupees monthly for many of these men. Even these payments were late and often not fully made. Larger jagirdars could only manage by obtaining heavily discounted payments from revenue farmers or their bankers. Their best opportunity for realizing funds was to obtain a jagir assignment uninterruptedly near their home territories. Under conditions of financial stringency, the emperor even tried briefly to revive collection of the jiziya – a measure which aroused intense opposition from Ratan Chand and other Hindu officers serving in the administration.

In this period the emperor started to lose credibility with even his most loyal supporters. Even day to day administration in Delhi deteriorated. Violent affrays in the streets by frustrated and fearful armed men became common daily fare. Increasingly Mughal nobles had to look to their own armed strength and their diplomatic and political skills for sheer survival, not simply for the emperor's preferment as in past reigns.

Despite the final suppression of the Sikh revolt and the public execution of Banda and his followers in Delhi in mid-1716, other localized resistance flared up. The Jats in and around Delhi and Agra had been armed and turbulent since the last years of Aurangzeb. During the battles of the 1708–09 war of succession, their leader, Churaman Jat, assembled large numbers of his kinsmen to pillage arms, money and other goods from both sides in the struggle. From Bahadur Shah he obtained forgiveness in the form of rank and titles as a Mughal amir. During the 1712–13 battles, the Jats once again looted and pillaged each side equally. In an effort to stop Jat robbery of merchants and travelers along the royal high road from Agra to Delhi, the imperial wazir made Churaman official road guard responsible for keeping order on that stretch of road. This appointment simply gave him an imperial mandate to plunder.

The emperor pressured Jai Singh Kachhwaha to lead a punitive campaign against the Jats. A large, primarily Rajput, imperial army cut its way through the surrounding jungle and invested Thun, the Jat fortress. The siege dragged on for twenty months against the well-supplied and armed garrison. Jat robbery and rural guerrilla action outside the fortress increased during the siege. In the end Abdullah Khan negotiated a settlement over Jai Singh's head. Churaman paid a substantial indemnity, gave a bribe to the wazir, surrendered his fortresses and agreed to serve wherever he was posted.

Meanwhile in the Deccan, Husain Ali Khan rejected Daud Khan Panni's pact with the Marathas which gave them over a third of imperial revenues in return for keeping order. As a result Maratha raiding and indecisive open warfare continued. Husain Ali Khan's difficulties were compounded by letters sent from the emperor to Shahuji Bhonsla and other Maratha chiefs urging them to oppose the Deccan governor's forces. Maratha armies were steadily seizing full control of more and more territory in the northern Deccan. In the south the Deccan governor's authority in Bijapur, Hyderabad, and the two Karnataka provinces were virtually nil.

Under these dismaying conditions, the Sayyid brothers changed their policy to try and enlist the Marathas as their allies. Husain Ali Khan began negotiations with Shahuji in mid-1717 and finally arrived at a formal treaty in February, 1718. The boldness with which this treaty conceded Mughal failure and Maratha success is startling. The Sayyid brothers were prepared to admit Shahuji and the Marathas into partnership in the southern empire in return for their political and military support in the struggle at the center. The new agreement gave Shahuji unchallenged authority over Shivaji's original *swaraj* lands in Maharashtra and coastal Konkan and, in addition, ceded recent Maratha conquests in Berar, Gondwana, and Karnatak. A critical concession was the right to employ Maratha agents to collect the 35 percent share of imperial revenues from chauth and sardeshmukhi throughout the six provinces of the Deccan. In return Shahuji agreed to pay tribute of one million rupees and to maintain fifteen thousand Maratha troopers to be placed at the disposal of Husain Ali Khan. Shahuji also agreed to keep order and to refrain from levying duties or taxes beyond those in the imperial assessment. When Farrukhsiyar refused to ratify this agreement, Shahuji simply acted as if the treaty were formalized and proceeded to send his collectors out and attach a 10,000 man cavalry force to Husain Ali Khan.

THE FINAL CRISIS

By mid-1718 the enmity between emperor and minister, barely concealed beneath rigid Mughal norms of court civility and decorum, erupted as the balance of power began tilting toward the Sayyids. When the emperor made several appointments to the Deccan provinces in violation of the earlier agreement, the wazir simply voided them. Enraged, the emperor engaged in abortive plots to kill Abdullah Khan before he appealed to the three most powerful noblemen left in the empire. Ajit Singh Rathor, the Turani nobleman, Nizam-ul Mulk from Moradabad, and Sarbuland Khan from Bihar brought a total of 70,000 or more troops into Delhi. By his temporizing and equivocation, the emperor alienated all three amirs. They either left the capital or aligned themselves with the wazir. Toward the end of 1718 the emperor could count on only Jai Singh Kachhwaha and his 20,000 Rajputs. The standoff continued until the end of the year.

Earlier Abdullah Khan had written to his brother, Husain Ali Khan, asking him to return in force from the Deccan. In October Husain Ali left Burhanpur for the march north at the head of 15,000 cavalry, 10,000 matchlockmen, and artillery. He was joined by Balaji Vishwanath, Shahuji's Peshwa or chief minister, who brought 10,000 Maratha horsemen (paid a rupee a day from the Mughal treasury). The public reason for return, contrary to the emperor's orders, was that Shahuji had offered an important exchange proposal. The Bhonsla ruler requested that his mother Yesu Bai and his younger brother, who had been held captive at the Mughal court since 1689, be released. In exchange he handed over the son of Akbar, the deceased Mughal rebel prince. Husain Ali Khan must bring the boy to Delhi in person. The supposed Timurid prince was in fact an imposter, the son of a Qazi who bore a resemblance to the Timurids. Husain Ali Khan supplied him with a scarlet tent, robes, and a crown as well as appropriate attendants on the march. The threat, plain for all to see, was that Farrukhsiyar could be readily deposed in favor of this claimant to the Timurid throne.

In February, 1719, Husain Ali Khan entered Delhi with his drums beating and standards flying in defiance of imperial etiquette. Farrukhsiyar, anxious to conciliate the Sayyid brothers, agreed to dismiss all royal officers commanding Delhi fort and all officers who controlled access to court audiences. The emperor also dismissed Jai Singh Kachhwaha, who departed reluctantly from the capital at the head of his mounted Rajputs. When Farrukhsiyar delayed giving up control of the palace-fortress, Abdullah Khan met him in person in the audience hall. An angry and abusive exchange between emperor and minister occurred in which all decorum was lost and all the anger and fear of years of conflict released. The wazir stormed out of the audience and Farrukhsiyar retreated to the women's apartments in the palace. Abdullah Khan then turned out all the imperial guards and seized control of the fort and palace.

That night rumors as to the events in the palace spread throughout the city. The emperor refused to come out of the women's quarters where he was guarded by armed female slaves. The next day, on 28 February, several nobles and military commanders still loyal to Farrukhsiyar marched at the head of their troops toward the fortress. En route they clashed with the Maratha horsemen of Husain Ali Khan.

Unprepared for street fighting nearly 2,000 Marathas were killed and stripped of their clothes and weapons by a mob of bazaar dwellers and unpaid soldiery.

Threatened with the urban mob and the Rajputs of Jai Singh who were only a few miles distant, the Sayyid brothers opted for direct action. They could not reasonably depose Farrukhsiyar and replace him by one of themselves – the sentiments for a Timurid ruler were still too deeply embedded. But they could depose Farrukhsiyar and replace him with a pliable young prince. First they tried unsuccessfully to seize Prince Bidar Dil, son of Bidar Bakht, who was regarded as the most able of the Timurid princes. But he, fearful of being killed, remained in hiding. In the end Abdullah Khan settled on Prince Rafi-ud-darjat, son of Rafi-ush-shan and grandson of Bahadur Shah, as the candidate. The startled youth was seated on the Peacock Throne and proclaimed emperor.

An armed party burst into the women's quarters, captured Farrukhsiyar, and brought the deposed ruler to the wazir. Abdullah Khan found in his own pen case a needle used for applying collyrium to his eyes and ordered the emperor thrown down and blinded immediately. Farrukhsiyar was then imprisoned in the fort. Public announcement of the new emperor ended the riots outside the fort. Two months later, the Sayyid brothers had Farrukhsiyar strangled in his prison cell and buried in a crypt in Humayun's tomb.

SAYYID RULE, 1719–1720

The Sayyid brothers assumed stringent control over the new puppet emperor. Rafi-ud-darjat was guarded day and night by a select group of Baraha soldiers. All court audiences were played out to a script prepared by the wazir. In June, the ill-fated Timurid ruler died of tuberculosis. His brother, Raji-ud-daulah, fell victim to the same disease within weeks of replacing his brother on the throne. Finally, the Sayyids settled on the eighteen-year-old Prince Roshan Akhtar, son of Jahan Shah and grandson of Bahadur Shah. Roshan Akhtar, titled Muhammad Shah, became the new Timurid ruler in September, 1719.

Under the Sayyids, imperial policy turned toward inclusive policies. Imperial seals confirmed the treaty with Shahuji and the satisfied Marathas left Delhi to return to the Deccan. They tried to conciliate Ajit Singh Rathor by allowing his widowed daughter, who had converted to Islam for the marriage to Farrukhsiyar, to renounce Islam and return to her father at Jodhpur. This was the first time a Rajput princess had been allowed to leave the imperial harem and return home. This concession aroused great indignation among the Muslims of the capital. Formal concessions were made to Churaman Jat as well.

However, the Sayyids were not able to command the full loyalty of a demoralized and dispirited imperial nobility. Opponents found a leader in the Turani amir Nizam-ul Mulk who was given the governorship of Malwa. Released from the closest forms of surveillance, the young emperor had sent a plea to Nizam-ul Mulk to free him from his Sayyid captors. When the Sayyids tried abruptly to transfer him from Malwa the Nizam marched against Delhi. In his appeal for noble support, the Nizam deplored the ruin of the Timurid house and the monarchy; he protested that the Sayyids were intent on ruining all the old Irani and Turani families of the empire; and that they were following a disastrous pro-Hindu policy. The Nizam drew to him all those Irani and Turani commanders who were appalled by the deposition and slaying of Farrukhsiyar. They were especially dubious about full power in the empire going to a group of Indian Muslims, no matter how illustrious their familial service to the Timurids. From one perspective this split could also be seen as a division between foreign, more cosmopolitan officers and locally rooted cadres comprised of Indian Muslims, Rajputs, Marathas, and Jats.

In August, 1720, the Nizam won a key battle at Shakarkhedla in the Deccan against a combined Maratha/Sayyid army. A successful plot secured the assassination of Husain Ali Khan while he was marching toward the Deccan with the emperor in his camp. Muhammad Shah then joined the insurgents in a campaign against Abdullah Khan. The latter was defeated and captured outside Delhi in November, 1720. After two months in captivity Abdullah Khan was executed.

THE NORTHERN PROVINCES

Between 1707 and the accession of Muhammad Shah in 1720, instability at court had its impact in every part of the empire. The carefully divided jurisdictions of governors, fiscal officers, faujdars, bakhshis (army paymasters and intelligence officers), and jagirdars blurred, and in some provinces, disappeared. Imperial orders which in the past had been executed unquestioningly were now ignored. Both public and secret news reports sent to the center declined in frequency and in quality. The regulations of the zabt revenue system elided into more or less open revenue farming. Jagirdars found that to collect their stipulated revenues from local authorities they had to assume full military and police powers over their holdings. Tax collections diminished and became erratic in most provinces due to local resistance. The level of internal violence undoubtedly increased in nearly every locality as zamindars and peasants rebelled.

Weakened central authority in confused times created new opportunities for aggrandizement by provincial officers. During the first three decades of the eighteenth century, strong protodynastic figures developed nascent regional kingdoms in several northern provinces. Under regional authority political conditions stabilized. These rajas, governors, or diwans, putative rulers, intensified revenue collections, suppressed zamindari rebellions, and reorganized their administrations, all with the aim of strengthening their powers while still paying lip service to the emperor's authority. The northern provinces were edging toward stability within a loosened, decentralized imperial structure.

In Rajasthan, the leading Rajput amirs energetically subverted the intricate imperial administrative controls imposed on that province. Under existing arrangements the entire province fell under the control of the imperial revenue administration headquartered at Ajmer, the seat of the governor. Lands were assigned routinely as jagirs or retained in khalisa for the central treasury. Only the relatively limited home domains or watan jagirs of the rajas were left in their control. After settlement of the second Rajput war in 1708 (described above) the Rajputs devoted considerable effort to extending their watan or home territories in an attempt to build near-autonomous regional kingdoms.

Jai Singh Sawai, the Kachhwaha head of Amber, used two methods to peacefully gain control of lands adjacent to Amber. First, his agents at court lobbied for and obtained temporary, regulation jagirs to support his pay claims.[12] Second, Jai Singh's agents actively offered written contracts by which they undertook to pay a fixed proportion of the official revenues for non-Rajput officers given jagirs in eastern Rajasthan. Lesser Rajput thakurs of various clans were then given revenue farming contracts to produce the money each year. For Mughal officers, beset by the factional conflict of Farrukhsiyar's reign,

12 Satya Prakash Gupta, *The Agrarian System of Eastern Rajasthan* (c.1650–c.1750), (Delhi: Manohar, 1986), pp. 1–37.

even discounted revenues paid regularly were preferable to the expense of trying to collect revenues from turbulent Rajput bhumiyas. Those jagirdars who tried to collect their own revenues in this region found their agents hindered and harassed by Kachhwaha officers.

As Farrukhsiyar's authority weakened, Jai Singh simply assumed permanent powers over all his jagirs and revenue farms. By 1726, the six parganas adjacent to Amber had been absorbed into Sawai Amber as the core territory of the new eighteenth century state.[13] Six other contiguous subdistricts had been enlarged and added to the total. For the first time since Bharamall negotiated his daughter's marriage to Akbar in the 1560s the Mughal emperor no longer controlled the lands and revenues of eastern Rajasthan.

Some provinces experienced greater instability than others. For the thirteen year period, Awadh in the eastern Gangetic plain had a total of fifteen governors, some completely absentee. In response to disorder in Awadh later governors were given unprecedented powers, notably over the fiscal and revenue institutions managed by the provincial diwan. By 1714, the amir Chabele Ram, accepted the Awadh governorship on condition that one of his relatives become diwan.[14] When the Sayyids appointed Girdhar Bahadur as governor in 1719 the new governor, who had been in revolt, named the province he wanted, demanded to be made diwan, and obtained an unprecedented appointment as faujdar for the entire province.[15] In 1722, a dominant proto-dynastic figure emerged. By that time there was ample precedent for Burhan al-Mulk, the founder of the kingdom of Awadh, to bundle all administrative authority in the province into his own grasp and to beat down resistance from the zamindars.

In Awadh the majority of zamindars, whether Rajput or Afghan, were engaged in widespread defiance of Mughal authority and revenue demands. The Bais Rajputs of Baiswara, who had been turbulent since the last years of Aurangzeb's reign, united under the banner of a single war leader and fought the Awadh governor in a three day battle at their central fortress. Temporarily beaten, they were forced to submit, but by mid-1715 they had launched another coordinated uprising. Once again Chabele Ram, the Awadh governor, defeated and dispersed the rebels. Afghan zamindars in Lucknow district remained in armed resistance to the governor and faujdar throughout 1714. The same year

[13] Ibid., p. 26. [14] Alam, *Crisis of Empire*, pp. 64–65.
[15] Alam, *Crisis of Empire*, p. 69.

virtually all the Rajput chiefs in Awadh district itself were in revolt.[16] Lacking sufficient direction and support from Delhi, the governor was unable to muster overwhelming military strength to put an end to the risings.

Despite seizure of revenue powers by later governors, collections from Awadh were erratic and modest at best. Most of the lands in the province were allocated to jagirdars, many of whom were stationed outside the province. Local resistance made it difficult, and in some instances impossible, to collect the stated assessment. In Farrukhsiyar's reign the Sayyid brothers began to assign jagirs in Awadh to Indian Muslim officers native to the province.[17] The lands assigned were located in the home territories of each officer who received the assignment as watan jagir. An additional number of his kinsmen and private officers also received jagirs adjacent to his. These jagirdars were expected to keep the assignments for extended periods and to use their local kinship and patronage ties to build strength sufficient to collect revenues from the zamindars and peasants. The end result was to begin the process of converting jagirs in Awadh to fiefs held in perpetuity.

The administrative and political circumstances in Bengal and Orissa were different. Under Murshid Quli Khan, the efficient fiscal officer appointed by Aurangzeb, the two provinces were marked by stability and order after 1707. Reappointed diwan (after a two year transfer) by Bahadur Shah, Murshid Quli Khan resumed his post in 1710 with a new rank of 2,000 zat.[18]

In 1712, when Prince Farrukhsiyar was preparing to make his bid for the throne, he demanded the accumulated revenues of Bengal and Orissa. Murshid Quli Khan refused pointblank on the grounds that the prince was not yet emperor and had no legitimate claim to the funds. Farrukhsiyar sent a 3,000 man force to bring back the treasure or Murshid Quli Khan's head. In a lengthy battle outside the plain at Murshidabad, the stubborn diwan's troops killed Farrukhsiyar's general and routed his army. When in early 1713, Farrukhsiyar crowned himself at Delhi, Murshid Quli Khan sent the Bengal surpluses to him without delay and was confirmed in his position.[19] Farrukhsiyar also made Murshid Quli Khan deputy governor of

[16] Alam, *Crisis of Empire*, pp. 96–97. [17] Ibid., pp. 124–129.

[18] Abdul Karim, *Murshid Quli Khan and His Times* (Dacca: Asiatic Society of Pakistan, 1963), pp. 29–30.

[19] Jadunath Sarkar, *History of Bengal: Muslim Period 1200–1757* (Patna, 1973), I, 407.

Bengal (acting for the emperor's infant son) and governor of Orissa.[20] In 1717, to retain his support, Farrukhsiyar promoted Murshid Quli Khan to governor of Bengal.

Murshid Quli Khan's success was based on imperial loyalty and obedience in his accustomed role of careful fiscal manager. Throughout the twists of deadly factional politics at the center, Murshid Quli Khan retained his grip on Bengal by faithfully sending Bengal revenues to a cash-starved monarch. Between 1712 and his death in 1727 during the reign of Muhammad Shah, Murshid Quli Khan sent an average of 10.5 million rupees per year to Delhi. These constituted the revenues of crownlands, tribute from zamindars, and miscellaneous funds for both Bengal and Orissa – all meticulously accounted for.[21]

Whether this annual drain harmed the economy of Bengal is difficult to determine. Internal peace and increased cultivation and trade were pushing expansion of the Bengal frontier to the east and the sea. Shipping ten million or so rupees in carts each year certainly put a strain on the provincial money supply. Ample imports of New World silver by the Dutch and English trading companies were converted immediately to new coin at the provincial mint. Whether severe methods of collection from intermediaries caused oppression of the peasantry is also difficult to decide. It is doubtful if Murshid Quli Khan's total revenue demands were proportionately any greater than they had been under earlier administrations. Past surplus funds had gone to enrich a succession of seventeenth century Bengal governors.

Although he used force ruthlessly and effectively when necessary, Murshid Quli Khan pared down his provincial army to 2,000 horsemen and 4,000 infantry.[22] No serious external threats menaced Bengal and Orissa during his administration. Nearly all the official revenues were shipped to the emperor. Murshid Quli Khan kept expenses to a minimum remarked upon by his contemporaries. His personal fortune, although large – six million rupees at his death – was not excessive.

Paradoxically, however, as the center weakened, the Bengal governor became more autonomous. More Bengali Hindu officers found

20 Karim, *Murshid Quli Khan*, p. 48.
21 Karim, *Murshid Quli Khan*, p. 85 n. Based on a total of 165.1 million rupees for fifteen years and nine months. This was from the fifth year of Bahadur Shah to the ninth year of Muhammad Shah.
22 Sarkar, *History of Bengal*, I, 412.

employment in his administration and joined the relatives of Murshid Quli Khan and those North Indian officers who had already followed him to Murshidabad. By 1727 his son-in-law Shuja-ud-din Muhammad Khan, then serving as deputy governor of Orissa, simply seized control of the two provinces in defiance of Murshid Quli Khan's wishes in what amounted to a coup. The new administration was duly ratified by the emperor, Muhammad Shah. By this time Bengal and Orissa had become a regional state paying tribute to the Mughal ruler in Delhi.

THE DECCAN

Virtual paralysis in Delhi eroded provincial administration in the Deccan as it did in the north. In the western Deccan, however, no strong, dominant governor emerged. Instead, Maratha raids enfeebled Mughal administration in Khandesh, Aurangabad, Berar, and Bijapur. Bereft of support from the emperor, provincial governors and their cadres either accommodated, sheltered in their fortified capitals, or fled outright. The Maratha style of repeated raiding and plundering followed by more formal tribute taking (chauth) was damaging and disruptive. In the aftermath of Maratha raids, dispossessed peasants and defeated soldiery turned to banditry in large numbers. Roiling conflict and confused claims and counter claims between Maratha intruders and Mughal authorities ruined many formerly prosperous areas. In Khandesh province the process of sorting out the dual shares of Mughal jagirdars and Maratha chiefs and their revenue collectors took years to resolve. Revenues remained low and were often paid in kind. Many villages were deserted by the 1720s.[23]

Insecurity and disorder accompanying this conflict was especially damaging to the long-distance overland trade. Hard hit were those cities, like Surat, that had been the busiest entrepots of that trade. In 1716, the Dutch East India Company was forced to close its trading station in Agra because it was impossible to buy Bayano indigo or specialized textiles and ship the goods reliably overland to Surat. Caravans organized by private merchants, even though protected by hired guards, could no longer travel safely from Agra to Surat.

[23] Stewart Gordon and John F. Richards, "Kinship and Pargana in eighteenth century Khandesh," *The Indian Economic and Social History Review*, 22 (1985), 384; and Richards, *Monetary System*, pp. 223–224.

Zamindars leading armed bands of peasants threatened and attacked even strongly armed parties headed by Mughal officials. It was not uncommon for bands of 5,000 men of whom 2,000 were carrying muskets to be reported.[24] If these local rebels did not succeed, groups of Maratha horsemen were likely to intercept caravans.

After 1707, Indian and European merchants at Surat could not obtain adequate supplies of textiles, indigo or other export commodities from their normal production areas. They could not profitably transship imports like Mocha coffee or Indonesian spices to their normal markets. The cost of bills of exchange between Agra and Surat shot up to as high as 12 percent for a transaction that had formerly cost 1 to 2 percent.[25] For a time production within Gujarat helped to meet some of this demand, as the Dutch opened new trading stations in Ahmadabad and Broach. Textile prices rose and supplies dwindled in Gujarat as a reflection of rising insecurity from Maratha raids in the province.

The money supply of the formerly prosperous port dried up. The imperial mint shut down for several years and numerous moneychangers went bankrupt.[26] After 1710 it became difficult to obtain cash for imported goods. Declining exports reduced bullion imports sharply at Surat. A drain of silver coin in payments to the imperial armies in the Deccan continued with no compensating payments in return.

By the end of Farrukhsiyar's reign, Surat, the principal Mughal west coast port, was cut off from its empire-wide trading hinterland and reduced to trafficking with a regional hinterland no greater than the boundaries of Gujarat. The relative security of British-controlled Bombay made it a rival port and entrepot rapidly surpassing Surat in importance.

The lands of the eastern Deccan suffered the same conditions as those in the west under Bahadur Shah and his immediate successors. Maratha raiding, banditry, and devastation were commonplace in Hyderabad province between 1707 and 1713.[27] In 1708, the capable, long-serving governor of Hyderabad, Rustam Dil Khan, was killed by Prince Muhammad Kam Bakhsh in a clash over access to the provincial

24 Gupta, *Indian Merchants and the Decline of Surat*, pp. 140–143 for the journey of the last Dutch trader to leave Agra in 1716.

25 Ibid., p. 152.

26 Ibid.

27 J. F. Richards, *Mughal Administration in Golconda* (Oxford: Clarendon Press, 1975), pp. 264–305.

treasuries. Over the next few years three successive governors were unable to cope with widespread disorder, insolvency, and army mutinies. Finally, in 1713 a new governor appointed by Farrukhsiyar arrived in Hyderabad. This was a turning point for regional political life.

Both capable and determined, Mubariz Khan at once set about restoring order. He hammered any Maratha raiders and drove them decisively beyond his borders. At the head of several thousand Mughal heavy cavalry Mubariz Khan rode in repeated punitive raids against rebellious Telugu zamindars, bandit chiefs, and renegade Mughal commanders.

In 1715, Mubariz Khan made an accommodation with Sayyid Husain Ali Khan, sent by Farrukhsiyar to be governor of the Deccan with powers of appointment for all provincial officers. At Aurangabad, Mubariz Khan aligned himself with the Sayyids and obtained reappointment to his post in Hyderabad. At this meeting, Husain Ali Khan appointed his new adherent provincial diwan as well as governor and authorized Mubariz Khan's son to become commander of Golconda fort, the leading bastion of the province. These were both formerly independent assignments made by the emperor. After this meeting Mubariz Khan ignored the provisions of the 1717 treaty which conceded 35 percent of imperial revenues to be collected by Maratha-appointed agents. In the eastern Deccan these provisions did not apply. The Marathas were blocked from setting up a dual administrative structure in the eastern Deccan.

Mubariz Khan also ignored his obligations to the emperor. He made few, token payments to the central treasury from the Hyderabad revenues. He freely confiscated the khalisa crown parganas in Hyderabad and sent his own agents to collect the revenues. Virtually all official appointments or transfers to and from Hyderabad ceased after 1713. The governor filled important provincial offices with his six sons, his uncle, his trusted slave-eunuch, and other members of his entourage. This became a system of regional officials, recruited within Hyderabad.

By the end of Farrukhsiyar's reign, Mubariz Khan restored the authority exercised over the province by the governor or earlier by the Qutb Shah rulers. Relative peace and order permitted revenue collection and greater stability for the inhabitants of the province. In so doing the imperial governor in reality became a regional king – not because he was disloyal, but rather because he had little choice. The emperor and the imperial wazir offered little support or encouragement to distant governors. Had the throne recovered power and strength it is likely that Mubariz Khan could once more have been brought into a revived empire. It did not, and in 1724, the Nizam-ul Mulk, who was trying to establish his own independent domain in the Deccan, defeated and killed Mubariz Khan at the battle of Shakarkhedla.

For over a decade, instability and weakness caused by the bitter conflicts over the throne wrenched at imperial authority and efficiency. Revenues plummeted and the entire imperial structure entered a downward spiral. Perhaps if a strong Timurid monarch or, for that matter, a charismatic nobleman capable of founding a new dynasty, had occupied the throne, this descent might have been checked in the 1720s. Certainly, as the examples of both Murshid Quli Khan in Bengal and Mubariz Khan in Hyderabad illustrate, the habits and beliefs in imperial service could have been resurrected among Mughal nobles and technocrats. Instead, during Muhammad Shah's lengthy reign, the empire slipped into a loosely knit group of regional successor states.

CONCLUSION

During his half-century-long reign from 1556 to 1605, Akbar's repeated victories enabled him to build a multi-regional empire from the territories of defeated kingdoms. He and his advisers devised innovative and durable centralized institutions. But dynamic expansion did not end with Akbar's death. Instead, the Mughal empire continued to expand and to deepen its administrative control from 1556 until 1689.

Imperial dynamism was at its core military. The Mughal empire was a war-state. The dynasty and nobles were warriors governed by an aggressively martial ethos. By far the greater proportion of the state's resources was devoted to war and preparation for war. Every year Mughal troops were engaged in active campaigning against foreign enemies or domestic rebels. The Mughal emperors made little apology for attacks on neighboring states and needed still less by way of provocation. In common with all imperial rulers, they regarded adjoining states as either tributaries or enemies – no other category was possible.

To the north it was only when Mughal arms reached the extremities of the Indian subcontinent that the limits of expansion were established. Beyond the subcontinent the physical and social landscape together presented overwhelming obstacles. In the mountainous zones of the north Mughal armies found themselves precariously extended on their supply lines. They had difficulties foraging for firewood and fodder for their animals and could not rely upon the Indian grain merchants who supplied their needs when campaigning in the subcontinent. The Mughals encountered strong resistance mounted by formidable rulers and peoples who were not assimilated into the Indo-Muslim political system and who were not especially impressed by Mughal imperial might.

To the south the empire expanded slowly, but steadily. The physical terrain, although often difficult, did not stop military operations. Society in the Deccan and further south was well-instructed in the brutal truths of Indo-Muslim power. In these regions however,

Mughal diplomatic pressures weakened the centralized control of the Deccan states. As a result Mughal generals and administrators found it difficult to conquer and rule regions in which political power was fragmented. Imperial policies also failed to fully adapt to the differing cultures and social structures of the dominant Maratha, Telugu, Kannada, and Tamil landed aristocracies. Conquest and political control became a time-consuming, and often frustrating task. It is in the south after 1689 that Mughal expansion faltered and ended.

The sea blocked expansion to east and west. Mughal military power was land-based – not maritime. Unlike their contemporaries, the Ottoman Turks, the Timurid emperors never considered or pursued expansion by sea. The culture of seafaring was completely foreign to the Mughal elite. They were more than willing to invest in trade by sea and even own seafaring vessels, but this interest did not extend to placing themselves on board anything so unpleasant as a sea-going vessel. Pilgrims travelling to the holy cities for the annual Haj were the only exceptions to this rule.

Intermittent internal warfare was also characteristic of the Mughal empire. Numerous kingdoms and chiefdoms not subject to direct administration by Mughal governors existed in the less accessible and fertile regions of the empire. Formal submission, payment of annual tribute, and the supply of troops or war elephants to the emperor sufficed initially to keep these rulers on their ancestral seats. The impetus for consolidation, for conquest on the internal frontiers of the empire was difficult to restrain. By and large tributary kings engaged in a constant political battle to survive. Lapsed payment of tribute brought warnings and a punitive campaign with the ever-present possibility of full-blown annexation to direct administration.

After conquest and annexation an imperial peace prevailed. The Mughal empire sustained a relatively high level of public order. Towns and cities and their immediate hinterlands were generally free of organized predatory violence. The main roads were secure for traders and travelers. Mughal military governors (faujdars) city magistrates, or road commanders (*rahdars*) vigorously pursued and punished bandits and rebels. Elsewhere, like Europe in the same period, there were areas in the hills or the infamous sandy ravines of the Chambal river valley where the king's writ ran weakly, if at all. Travelers ventured there at their peril.

In the countryside Mughal dynamism found expression in an

ongoing struggle with the lords of the land, or in Mughal parlance the zamindars. Imperial officials combined threat and reward to induce local warrior aristocrats or village lords to assist in the collection of imperial revenues. At times force was necessary. In some areas especially belligerent zamindars rebelled periodically and awaited the arrival of imperial troops with some zest. More frequently negotiation and persuasion sufficed for compliance.

The Mughal revenue system was engaged in a continuing campaign of political socialization. Its aim was to transform armed, often-truculent, parochial warrior-aristocrats, into quasi-officials. By entangling local aristocracies in the revenue system imperial officials were also engaging the zamindars, even remotely, in a broadly shared imperial culture. For over a century this effort continued with notable success. As new lands came into the empire or tributary kingdoms were annexed, time-tested devices were employed to assimilate the local aristocracy and dominant peasant groups to the demands of the revenue system. After 1689, however, administrative momentum dwindled. The inability of Mughal officials to maintain the imperial peace in the Deccan provinces had its effect. Loss of morale and a sense of direction beset local officers elsewhere in the empire. Those zamindars who had been brought into a wider system in the course of a century were now confronted with new prospects and new hazards.

Imperial expansion and consolidation before 1689 drew part of its dynamic energy from a radical political orientation put forward by the emperor Akbar. In his formulation the interests of the dynasty and the state were given precedence over narrowly defined interests of Islam in India. In a marked departure from previous practice active participation in the imperial system was open to non-Muslims as well as Muslims. In every way possible the emperor tried to make the imperial system inclusive rather than exclusive.

Despite large-scale conversions and immigration, Islam remained a minority religion in every region of the subcontinent. The resilience of Hindu caste-defined society made further mass conversions unlikely. In the sixteenth century, Indo-Muslim rulers faced a political dilemma. If they restricted the higher levels of political and military service to Muslims, they drew from a very narrow base of support. If they opened recruitment to all persons of talent and substance, there would be a strong reaction from the orthodox Muslim establishment. Akbar made a determined effort to break out of that dilemma by creating a new dynastic ideology that would appeal to his subjects of all religions and statuses.

Akbar's centralized empire successfully tapped into the rising productivity of the Indian economy in the early modern period. New world economic linkages were an important stimulus to economic activity. Portuguese trading in the Indian Ocean increased, rather than decreased, the overall demand for Indian goods and services. Flows of New World specie came pouring into the subcontinent – in a lesser portion through Goa and in a much greater stream through the normal sea and overland routes to India. Akbar's state seized upon these abundant supplies of gold and silver to fashion its currency and to fill its treasuries. With the conquest of Gujarat in 1574 the Timurid empire became a coastal state with access to the new inflows of precious metals. In Gujarat could also be found the industrial production of cloth which could pay for these imports. Gold and silver were an indispensable resource as the empire expanded.

The imperial economy expanded in tandem with centralized state power in Mughal India. Although hard quantitative evidence is scanty, the qualitative evidence suggests that the Mughal empire stimulated economic growth. State revenue and consumption demands encouraged and shaped the growth of India's varied and lively regional and subcontinental markets. Imperial insistence on payment of the land revenue in official coin forced the sale of food grains and other crops to local grain dealers who then responded to consumption demands for the towns and cities. The consumption demands of several million persons dependent upon state salaries or largess fostered markets for a vast range of manufactured and processed goods.

In more specialized areas the emperors routinely looked to private markets and entrepreneurial activity to meet official needs. Some luxury goods and staple commodities were produced in the large household establishments of the emperor and nobles, but most goods and services were supplied from the private sector. Continuing military operations fostered a peripatetic bazaar sector geared to supplying food grains and other essentials to Mughal armies on the march. The emperors and their military commanders relied upon cash payments to mobilize troops at whatever location, numbers, skill, and equipment they needed. Similarly, for large-scale building projects, they would obtain cadres of highly skilled workers in ample numbers at any location.

In general imperial integration seems to have fostered the growth of inter-regional trade and linkages. Much of this trade was in luxury goods, but not all. During the Mughal period provinces with food surpluses, such as Bengal, sent these goods to food-deficit areas like Gujarat by means of the active coastal shipping industry. The empire taxed overland and maritime trade, but at a modest, and generally predictable level. Increased security from banditry and arbitrary confiscation offset the costs of customs and other duties imposed.

WORLD CONNECTIONS

After Vasco da Gama's voyage around Africa, India's pepper and other spices and cotton textiles drew first Iberian, then Northern European traders to the subcontinent armed with plentiful supplies of gold and silver from the New World. Self-sufficient in most products and commodities save for precious metals, India eagerly accepted gold and silver as payment for a rising export to Europe. By 1600 the Dutch and English East India Companies had begun to exploit the commercial potential of the Cape route direct to South and Southeast Asia. This new sea link carried steadily expanding cargoes between Mughal India and Europe. European textile demand stimulated Indian cloth production throughout the subcontinent. Despite frequent strains, the interests of both the Mughal empire and that of the East India Companies were well served by this new connection. Beyond the economic effects, what were the cultural impacts of this change in Europe and Mughal India?

By the first decades of the eighteenth century hundreds of European traders, seamen, diplomats, and adventurers had endured the long sea voyage to India. These men, and a few women, traversed the length and breadth of the subcontinent. Many were employed by Indians; more Indians were employed by them. Despite the lengthy delays, letters were exchanged regularly between India and Europe. Those who returned gave first hand accounts of India to those at home. Numerous collections of letters and travel accounts were published and disseminated widely amongst the reading public of Europe. From this proliferating literature, Europeans obtained a detailed picture of early modern Mughal India.

What of the return traffic? What sort of information did Mughal India receive about Europe? The most direct answer is, very little.

Despite regular shipping between Indian and European ports, no Indians other than a few seamen made the voyage. Traveler's accounts and letters describing Europe to a Mughal public simply do not exist.

Europeans could travel freely in Mughal India because state and society were so remarkably indifferent. In China at the same period all foreigners were tightly controlled by imperial officers. Japan during the Tokugawa period excluded all Europeans from the islands. Only a handful of Dutch traders were permitted a tiny enclave at Dakshima from which they could carry on trade. By contrast, Mughal India was completely permeable to foreign visitors. Society, rather than the state, placed barriers against intruders in India's compartmentalized society. After they had paid customs duties, all foreigners were free to travel anywhere and to remain as long as they wished. This resulted in a network of Europeans domiciled in every major town on the subcontinent.

Emigrés of higher status or ability occasionally developed friendships with Mughal officers or Indian merchants, but the impact of these relationships was minimal. Indians displayed little interest in European culture or society. As we have seen Akbar's interest in Christianity moved him to entertain Jesuit missionaries at his court – a practice engaged in by his more inquiring descendants until the death of Dara Shukoh. After Akbar, however, none of the Mughal emperors had any appreciable interest in Europe. Jahangir, Shah Jahan, and Aurangzeb all admitted envoys from the trading companies or their rulers, and displayed an intense interest in the types of presentations and gifts offered. Beyond this little notice was taken. In the historical writing of the period these curious foreigners were largely ignored – despite their depiction in paintings of the Mughal court.

The Europeans carried with them a variety of technological advances. Some techniques and devices were widely accepted, used, and indigenous adaptations produced. For example, the use of the capstan (a wheel and axle on a vertical axis) for hauling heavy objects was adopted for launching ships at some ports.[1] Some techniques and devices were adopted but not produced locally. The use of hand-driven pumps to move standing water from boats was a technique readily accepted by Indian shipmasters in the seventeenth century. But there is no evidence of indigenous manufacture. Some innovations were seen

[1] Ahsan Jan Qaisar, *The Indian Response to European Technology and Culture (A.D. 1498–1707)* (Delhi: Oxford University Press, 1982), p. 33.

purely as a curiosity in spite of widespread practical application in Europe. Telescopes were used regularly as navigational aids and for long-distance observation in warfare in Europe. Examples were presented to various Indian dignitaries but elicited no usage or production.[2] European mechanical clocks and watches used routinely by Europeans in India were ignored by Indian society.[3]

The question of technology transfer in regard to firearms is complex. The casting of cannon and manufacture of muskets was apparently a matter of routine and the technical skills and materials to accomplish this were widely available. Despite its importance, Mughal histories and other surviving documentation have little to say about the technical side of weaponry. Those armorers, smiths and other technicians who actually cast cannon or fabricated muskets were mute. We have frustratingly little direct information about the production and distribution of firearms in Mughal India.

Some innovations were adopted and diffused widely. Animal-borne swivel guns became a routine feature of Mughal warfare. These were guns with stocks often two or more meters in length which fired a ball perhaps 10–12 cm. in diameter.[4] Other developments such as the flint-lock musket widely used in Europe in the 1620s, lagged. Adoption of this device in Mughal India was much slower. For most of the century the matchlock or arquebus was the dominant weapon.[5] Use and manufacture were two different spheres. Pistols were known and used on a wide basis in seventeenth century Mughal India, but were not commonly manufactured in India.[6]

The apparent indifference of the Mughal elites to improved weaponry is striking. Official interest in weaponry was occasional and haphazard at best. As usual Akbar was exceptional in that he took a keen interest in trying to improve the quality of muskets. He kept a special collection of muskets and tested them himself for their firing qualities. After Akbar only occasional references to the technical side of weapons occur. Mughal artillery was certainly far superior to anything that could be deployed by regional rulers, tributaries, or by zamindars. Within the subcontinent the combined effect of Mughal artillery and well-handled heavy cavalry continued to be decisive. But

[2] Ibid., p. 35. [3] Ibid., p. 66.
[4] Surviving specimens may be seen in various museums or in the collections of forts such as that at Golconda outside of Hyderabad.
[5] Qaisar, *Indian Response*, p. 52. [6] Ibid., p. 54.

the Mughals may well have started to fall behind other contemporary powers in the seventeenth century.

The emperor and his nobles employed a polyglot group of European soldiers and adventurers as artillerymen. In the last half of the seventeenth century European gunners, who were often deserters from the East India Company ships and garrisons, had a virtual monopoly on gunners' positions. By falling back on this expedient, the military elites of Mughal India essentially abdicated any responsibility for technical improvements in gunnery. They left these matters up to small cadres of foreign specialists – most of whom had only the most rudimentary training and but limited experience.

By the early years of the eighteenth century Mughal India was not keeping pace with Europe in field artillery. For example, in 1701, William Norris, the English ambassador to Aurangzeb's court, finally obtained an audience with the emperor who was then engaged in the siege of Panhala fort near Kolhapur. So impressed was the Mughal chief of artillery with twelve light brass field guns that Norris brought in his entourage that the English ambassador was forced to offer them to the emperor at the court audience.[7] Norris also supplied six gunners to operate the guns in the siege. Even allowing for Mughal disorganization in Aurangzeb's last years, the gap between the artillery of early modern Europe and that of India was widening. Later in the century the Maratha, Mysore, and Mughal successor states made strenuous and largely successful efforts to overcome this disadvantage in their wars with the British.

Perhaps the most puzzling cultural divide was to be found in differing approaches to writing and literacy. In common with much of the early modern Islamic world, Mughal India did not adopt movable type printing. The Portuguese operated a printing press with movable metal type at Goa in the 1550s. Religious tracts in various south Indian languages were printed from fonts of Romanized script.[8] Akbar acquired a large number of printed European books for his library from the Jesuit missionaries. In 1606 the Jesuits showed Jahangir a copy of the Gospels printed in the Arabic script to verify that this was possible.[9] Nevertheless, despite this exposure, none of the emperors, intellectuals, or nobles showed any interest in printing. This is

[7] H. H. Das, *The Norris Embassy to Aurangzib* (Calcutta, 1959), pp. 293–94.
[8] Qaisar, *Indian Response*, p. 58.
[9] Ibid., p. 60.

especially surprising in view of the enormous mass of written materials required to operate the imperial administration. Widespread adoption of mechanical printing only began in Bengal under British colonial rule.

Mughal civilization was far more outward looking than Tokugawa Japan. Certainly the emperor and the imperial elite were informed about its neighboring countries and regions. Elite and popular attention was fixed primarily on the Islamic world to the west and especially on the Ottomans and Safavids. The Mughal emperors, measuring their success by wealth, victory, and grandeur, saw little to interest them in the politics and culture of Europe.

REVERSALS AND DECLINE

It was only after Aurangzeb annexed the Sultanates of Bijapur and Golconda that the forward momentum of victory and centralized control slowed and reversed. The three decades from 1689 to the end of Farrukhsiyar's reign in 1719 saw the deterioration and, in the end, the destruction of the centralized imperial system. An empire accustomed to never-ending expansion and victory could not adjust to losses and defeats. No longer confident and unassailable, the emperor, the princes, and the nobility of the empire struggled with shrinking resources, loss of control, and growing disorder. Aurangzeb's rigid and imperceptive policies, especially in the Deccan, failed to respond to the growing crisis.

Under Aurangzeb imperial policy reverted to the militance of Indo-Muslim frontier expansion. Under Aurangzeb political loyalty was increasingly seen as sectarian loyalty. Only Muslims could participate fully in the Timurid empire. Religious sentiment did translate in complex and meaningful ways into political responses in Mughal India.

High level policy debate – never a strong point within the system – was pallid and ineffectual. Unlike contemporary Ottoman practice, we find no examples of clearly stated memorials to the throne, written by high-ranking officers, that questioned the costs of Aurangzeb's Deccan war. When such debate did occur, during the great sieges of Bijapur, Golconda, and Jinji, the princes were the locus. And, unfortunately, their role as loyal opposition encountered Aurangzeb's fear and suspicion of his sons. Opposition or independent negotiation with the enemy was viewed as treasonous.

Between 1707 and 1720 the centralized structure of empire broke apart. Four wracking, bitter, wars of succession occurred in this thirteen-year period. The bureaucratic edifice manned by skilled technical staff lost its efficiency and probity. The two central institutions managed by that bureaucracy – the zabt revenue system and the assignment of jagirs – degenerated to caricatures. The revenue system slid into tax farming and those jagirs assigned rapidly became local fiefs. Mughal officers maneuvered successfully to have jagirs assigned to their home localities and to keep the same assignments for extended periods.

This rapid collapse could have been an inevitable result of a "jagir crisis," that is the widening gap between the salary demands of the mansabdars and revenue-yielding lands sufficient to meet those needs. Was it this crucial link between rural society, the regulation land tax system, and the military elites which faltered? Was the jagir crisis symptomatic of a mismatch between the ever-rising resource demands of the state and the capacity of Indian society to meet those demands? Irfan Habib has taken this view.

In the well-known last chapter of his 1963 book, Habib argues that official revenue policy – driven by ever-expanding imperial expenses – appropriated the entire surplus produced by the peasantry. The jagir system itself inevitably drove up the revenue demand as time passed. This flaw did not show up in the nominal assessment, which increased roughly in tandem with prices, but rather in the behavior of the individual jagirdar. The latter, who held his lands for no more than three or four years before transfer, maintained no long-term interest in their prosperity. Hence each jagirdar's need for money encouraged him to "sanction any act of oppression that conferred an immediate benefit upon him, even if it ruined the peasantry and so destroyed the revenue-paying capacity of that area for all time."[10] Cultivation fell off as oppression increased and peasants left the land because they could not survive. Responding to this cycle zamindars squeezed between the jagirdars and the peasantry entered into armed revolts at the head of their rural dependents. In support of this argument Habib refers to the protracted revolts of the Jats and Sikhs. The most devastating zamindari rebellion flared up in the Maratha resistance in the Deccan.

This powerful interpretation has colored virtually all recent popular

[10] Irfan Habib, *The Agrarian System of Mughal India* (London: Asia Publishing House, 1963), p. 320.

writing and most scholarly views of the Mughal empire. In recent years critics have become more vocal. Examination of post-conquest imperial policies in Golconda suggests that policy choices had a bearing on the severity of the jagir crisis. Aurangzeb seems to have decided to retain many productive tracts in Golconda and also in Bijapur under direct crown control. Thereby jagirdars serving in the Deccan were denied access to the new resources obtained by conquest and annexation.[11] Other critics have pointed out difficulties in firmly identifying the links between oppressive jagirdars, agrarian resistance and imperial decline. Checks against abuse were built into the system. A plausible case can be made that agricultural production was increasing, not decreasing, and that peasants were not fleeing the land, but expanding the cultivated area. It is difficult to accept the notion that the imperial system itself either stifled or stagnated economic growth and social change. Quite the reverse. Evidence for a prosperous town gentry, well-to-do peasants, and a substantial commercial and trading community abounds.

As Satish Chandra has pointed out transfers of jagirs for large holders may have not been as frequent as we have previously thought and many nobles may have held on to their lands for ten years or more. "In fact, not frequent transfers but the decay of the practice of periodic transfers of jagirs during the eighteenth century made the jagirs hereditary, and led to the further strengthening of the zamindars as a class."[12] In short, the jagir crisis, while certainly serious, was not the central reason for imperial decline.

The revolts in northern India occurred partly because of inattentive and weak administration in those years when Aurangzeb was preoccupied in the Deccan. From one perspective, at least, the shortage of productive jagir lands can be located in official policy and in the devastation and dislocation wrought by the Deccan wars. Thereafter a series of political crises caused by struggles over the throne rapidly weakened the integrity of non-hereditary salary assignments and the regulation land tax system.

Was there a structural disjuncture between Mughal state and society that led to long-term, unremedied, structural weaknesses? Two linkages were essential for centralized Mughal authority. These were the ties of emotion and interest that bound the nobility to the throne and

[11] See Richards, *Mughal Administration*, for a full discussion of this issue.
[12] Satish Chandra, *Medieval India* (Delhi: Orient Longmans, 1982), p. 73.

those contractual ties buttressed by self-interest that linked the rural warrior aristocracies to the empire. For nobles and zamindars the aim was similar: to convert armed warrior aristocrats into dependable imperial servants. Mughal expansion and dynamic growth was the impetus for a slow, but steady socialization and transformation of each group. Retreat on the frontiers, confusion, and loss of confidence halted this process.

Both linkages came under intense strain in the years between 1689 and 1720. Factional conflict, sinking at times to bitter fighting in the streets of Delhi, severely tested the loyalties of the nobility. Nobles and mansabdars discovered that personal ties to the emperor were attenuated as the factional struggle proceeded. The emperor was less and less able to deploy and control amirs to meet imperial needs. Nobles managed their households, revenue collection, troops, and their assigned tasks to best serve perceived needs for survival – not royal favor and preference. In the provinces, impeccably loyal governors and diwans ignored regulations and taboos. To survive they shaped regional systems of power and authority which became Mughal successor states. Even a consummate technician like Murshid Quli Khan became a regional ruler in Bengal and Orissa despite his manifest loyalty to the Timurid throne.

These problems were most severe with the two major groups of Hindu nobles. Aurangzeb proved unable to repair his relationship with the Rajputs. Long-term trends within Rajasthan, such as the steadily centralizing authority and power of the great Rajput noble houses, may have demanded alterations in the Rajput–Timurid relationship. Since the Rajput war of 1679 the Mughal empire had suffered from the growing alienation of this important segment of the Mughal nobility. Aurangzeb and his immediate successors were unable to restore a relationship of affection, trust and dependence between the ruler and Rajput amirs. What proved to be half-hearted attempts at conciliation and reincorporation failed.

Equally devastating was Timurid failure to incorporate Maratha rulers and commanders in the western Deccan as full participants in the governance of the empire. Crucial opportunities to enlist Maratha loyalties were lost. Those Marathas who accepted imperial mansabs were used primarily as troop commanders in the Deccan and were not rotated in service elsewhere in the empire. In the east, apart from one or two unhappy exceptions, no Telugu aristocrats were recruited as nobles and military commanders. The regime's preoccupation with the Marathas prevented any attempt to incorporate this numerous and able warrior group into the imperial elite.

The later Timurid regime did not succeed in converting armed zamindars into disarmed quasi-officials who would reliably carry out imperial policy. Instead, by the second decade of the eighteenth century, widespread violent resistance by zamindars occurred in every region of North India as well as in the Deccan. The Sikh, Beas Rajput, and Jat resistance are only three examples of widespread violence in the countryside. That intrusion into the hard-shelled pargana structures of the country begun by Akbar with the zabt system faltered during the Deccan wars. Across North India thousands of zamindars discovered that contractual agreements (sanads) made with the Mughal emperor possessed dwindling worth. The regime was failing to guarantee zamindari rights and failing to enforce zamindari obligations in the countryside.

In the south the Mughals failed to reconstitute the agrarian system of the western Deccan. Decades of Mughal campaigns and diplomatic pressures on Ahmadnagar, Khandesh, and Bijapur weakened authority structures in the Muslim Sultanates of the western Deccan to the point that they could not retain the services and loyalties of Maratha deshmukhs and other landholders in the countryside. Inclusion in the emerging Bhonsla structure became a viable alternative to many, but not all, Maratha zamindars. In the eastern Deccan under the Sultanate of Golconda, the state retained coherent authority in the countryside over the Telugu aristocracy. After conquest the Telugu nayaks did not join the Marathas in rebellion and remained relatively quiescent under the new regime.

Widespread violent resistance directed against the Timurid regime by zamindars and peasants can be explained simply as a predictable response to weakened imperial power. Oppressed and burdened by Mughal revenue demands local zamindars and peasants at the first opportunity joined in resisting the demands of the centralizing state. The difficulty with this analysis is that the secular trend between Akbar's reforms in the 1580s to 1700 or thereabouts suggests that, although occasional episodes of brutal oppression can be identified, most zamindars and peasants were prospering. With the exception of war-torn regions in the Deccan, generally agricultural production seems to have increased and the area under cultivation grew steadily.

Agricultural growth responded directly to expanding markets driven by the state's revenue demands and by the demand impulses generated by new export markets. Networks of trading towns (qasbas) and larger villages grew more dense. These were inhabited by increasingly well-to-do traders and moneylenders like the Khatris in the Punjab.

Under these circumstances cooperation with the regime could pay real dividends. The state by its contractual relationships with zamindars and elite peasants (often referred to as "village zamindars") provided guarantees of security and stability. A market in the sale and lease of zamindars' rights emerged. Consequently peaceful aggrandizement began to supplant the aggression, colonization, and settlement of warrior/peasant lineages formerly engaged in miniature local warfare. Documented sales of zamindar rights supply powerful evidence that the centralizing Timurid regime successfully intervened in the arrangement and distribution of local power.

Why then these revolts under the later Mughals? One answer is that the very success of the Timurid agrarian system brought about important changes in rural society. These changes required, but did not receive, recognition and adjustment by the regime. Under Shah Jahan and Aurangzeb sizable numbers of Muslim ulema and their dependents were given tax-free grants of land. Royal patronage provided the umbrella under which grant recipients took up residence in market towns or in larger villages. Returns from untaxed lands as well as frequent engagement in the trading life of these towns brought prosperity to a burgeoning class of Muslim gentry. In addition to tax-free lands they also enjoyed freedom from the burden of jiziya. If from these bases Muslim, or even Hindu trading groups, took the opportunity to obtain zamindari rights, their interests would inevitably clash with those of the zamindars. The current evidence, though sketchy, suggests a real cleavage between Muslim gentry ranks and those of the Jat peasantry in the Sikh rebellion, for example.

Rising production and monetization of the rural economy put more resources at the disposal of both zamindars and peasants. Many successful local lineages, like the Beas Rajputs, growing in numbers, wished to expand their domains. If the Mughal agrarian order continued strong and resilient, these groups could have used their profits to purchase or lease added rights in neighboring lands. Such expansion would have been an important step in demilitarizing these warrior lineages. On the other hand, if the state's local control slackened as it did in Aurangzeb's later years, prosperous zamindars could count on greater resources – money and men – by which to annex new lands with time-honored violent methods. Possessing ample funds they could obtain the services of non-kinsmen from the local military labor market. For such warrior elites the constraints of expansion by purchase may well have been irksome and the violent tactics of men of honor preferable.

As yet unexamined is the extent to which local zamindars had slowly gained a military advantage vis-a-vis imperial forces. The growing popularity of improved muskets and greater proficiency in their use should have been advantageous to zamindars who relied primarily on foot soldiery. Better-equipped, more numerous, and better drilled musketeers might even the balance with imperial heavy cavalry. Certainly the Mughals themselves increasingly hired professional, specialized bodies of musketeers available for service from eastern Hindustan (Buxaris) and other localities in the subcontinent.[13] If local elites could use their financial strength to hire large numbers of competent musketeers, they could have reduced the tactical disparity between themselves and Mughal contingents.

Mughal intervention in rural Indian society, initially highly effective, hesitated at a critical juncture. If the agrarian system had remained intact, its effect would have been to slowly demilitarize cadres of local warrior aristocrats.[14] Instead the long-term effect was to increase the confidence and the resources of the zamindars and to encourage conflict with more prominent gentry and trading groups. Perhaps the empire was not sufficiently flexible to deal with social change that its new order itself had helped to bring about. The Timurids failed to incorporate zamindars into the political life and culture of the Mughal empire nor did they have the resources and will to forcefully disarm and demilitarize these bellicose warrior groups in the countryside. Only their successors, the British, who were constructing a rapidly modernizing colonial state, were able to reach that goal after decades of remorseless military campaigns.

When the empire began to decline signs of economic decline in the subcontinental economy are noticeable. Growing disorder brought on by unchecked raiding and plundering in the Deccan did inhibit

[13] Dirk H. A. Kolff, *Naukar, Rajput and Sepoy* (Cambridge: Cambridge University Press, 1990), pp. 159–176.

[14] Barrington Moore, in his *Social Origins of Dictatorship and Democracy* (Boston, 1956), first articulated this vital point in a comparative assessment.

economic activity. But in many regions, growth continued at a steady pace. The structural break-up of empire in the early eighteenth century did not necessarily force the complete dissolution of the inter-regional imperial economy. Instead, those forces for change already present responded to new incentives and growth continued.

By the first decade of Muhammad Shah's reign, money, information, orders, and men no longer moved from capital to province and from province to province at the emperor's command. After 1720 the formerly centralized empire continued as a loosely knit collection of regional kingdoms, whose rulers, although styling themselves imperial governors, offered only token tribute and service to the Mughal emperor at Delhi. The Marathas, headquartered at Poona, were organizing a counter-empire, one less rigid, more flexible than the Mughal empire. The symbols and aura of Timurid authority continued to fascinate the hardened Indian and European politicians and generals of eighteenth century India. The Mughal empire was fast becoming merely the empty shell of its formerly grand structure.

GLOSSARY

abisheka	the Brahminical coronation ceremony for Hindu rulers.
ahadis	cadre of high-status cavalrymen employed directly by the Mughal emperor.
amil	agents in charge of revenue collection.
amin	a revenue officer charged with revenue collection.
amir	a Mughal officer of high status and rank, a nobleman.
anna	one-sixteenth part of a rupee.
bakhshi	a military paymaster also in charge of military inspections and intelligence gathering.
bankatai	populating land after clearing the forests.
banjara	itinerant traders employing thousands of pack oxen to transport salt, foodgrains, and other bulk commodities.
bek	a Central Asian or Turkish term for a man of high status and rank.
bhaibamdh	a Rajput patrilineage claiming shared descent up to six or more generations.
bhakti	popular devotional Hinduism centered on poet saints and their followers.
bhumiya	warriors of the land, less powerful retainers of a Rajput thakur or chief.
bigah	unit of land area standardized by imperial decree at approximately three-fifths of an acre.
chabutra	the raised platform found in city squares used for public executions and punishments.
chaudhuri	in North India quasi-official recognized as the headman of a pargana by the imperial authorities.
chauth	traditional one-fourth portion of the land revenues claimed by zamindars and later the Marathas in western India.
chhatrapati	Sanskrit term for all-conquering ruler.
dagh	a distinctive brand placed on the flank of horses meeting imperial standards.
dam	Mughal copper coin valued at one-fortieth of a rupee.
Dar-al Islam	the abode or land of legitimate Islamic rule and practice.
Dar-al Jihad	the land of war or unbelief.
darshan	personal worship of a god.

deshmukh in the Deccan a quasi-official recognized as the headman of a pargana by the imperial authorities.

dharma variable rights and duties associated with different castes in the Hindu social order.

dhimmis those non-Muslim peoples treated by Islamic rulers as dependent communities with fixed rights and obligations.

din religion.

diwan a fiscal or revenue officer within the Mughal administration.

diwan-i khalisa officer in charge of all lands and revenue producing units administered directly by the emperor.

diwan-i kul also wazir or chief imperial fiscal minister.

diwan-i tan Mughal minister in charge of salaries and perquisites for mansabdars.

doab land lying between two rivers.

durbar a public audience held by an official or ruler.

farman a formal, written, edict issued by the Mughal emperor under his personal seal.

fath nama the victory proclamation issued by a Muslim ruler.

fatwa a public ruling on a point of law issued upon request by a Muslim jurist or mufti.

faujdar a Mughal officer given military and executive responsibility in a fixed area.

gaddi Hindi term for the low cushioned seat of a ruler.

ganj a grain market.

gaz imperial measure of length roughly equivalent to a meter.

ghat literally a step; used to refer to the bathing steps at a river.

ghazi an armed warrior fighting for the faith of Islam.

ghurab a shallow draft war boat carrying cannon for use in rivers and estuaries.

gulalbar the screened-off living quarters and harem of the Mughal emperor in camp.

gusulkhana the personal bathing room, of the Mughal emperor, used for secret conferences with senior officers.

hammam a public bath.

haveli the quarters or urban areas surrounding noble mansions.

hun a gold coin circulating in the Deccan and South India.

iqta provinces or other regions ruled in the name of medieval Indo-Muslim rulers by nobles or other officers.

jagirdar holder of revenue-producing lands assigned for salary, i.e. a jagir.

jagir — temporary fiscal right conferred by the Mughal emperor to collect the land tax from a specified village, pargana, or large area.
jama — total revenues or revenue demand.
jan — life or spirit
jauhar — killing of female dependents in a last rite of defeated Rajput warriors who then seek a suicidal death in battle.
jihad — striving on behalf of the Islamic faith in the conflict with unbelievers.
jirga — an Afghan tribal council.
jiziya — an annual tax levied on protected non-Muslim communities by Islamic rulers.
karuri — a revenue official under Akbar.
khalifa — the caliph or the secular successor to the Prophet Muhammad who assumes leadership of the entire Muslim world.
khalisa — lands or other entities producing revenue directly for the emperor and the central treasury.
khan — a Turkish and Central Asian honorific term for chief or nobleman.
khanazad — "son of the house", an officer boasting hereditary family service to the Mughal emperor.
khap — an extended patrilineal Jat clan.
khud-kasht zamindar — smaller zamindars dominant within villages.
khutba — prayers which acknowledge the legitimate ruler of the kingdom uttered at the time of the weekly congregational Friday prayers.
kotwal — a city magistrate.
langarkhana — the Sikh charitable kitchen at which all comers are fed.
lungi — cotton cloth used as a men's loincloth.
madad-i mash — tax-free lands given to pious or otherwise worthy recipients as charity.
madrasa — school or seminary offering instruction in Islamic jurisprudence, theology, philosophy and similar topics.
mahajan — traders in grain and other commodities.
mahdi — Muslim belief that the Prophet Muhammad will return as the savior of Islam or mahdi.
mal — property and goods.
mal — term for revenues obtained from the land tax.
mal-wajib zamindar — a landholder who collected specified revenues for the Mughals in return for tax-free lands and a percentage of his collections.
man — imperial unit of weight.

mansab rank, status and position denoted by numerical rank and title.
mansabdari of or pertaining to mansabdars.
mansabdar officer holding a specified numerical rank and title awarded by the Mughal emperor.
maths centers or hospices for Hindu orders of monks.
mir bakhshi a high-ranking officer reporting directly to the emperor in charge of military pay, inspections, recruitment, and intelligence.
mir saman officer in charge of the royal household, palaces, treasuries, mints and royal construction projects.
mohulla a town quarter or neighborhood.
muchalka a bond drawn up to assure good performance.
mufti a Muslim jurist who issues public decisions on legal matters.
muhr Mughal gold coin.
muhtasib Islamic official appointed to enforce the Sharia and to regulate markets and commerce.
mujtahid interpreter of the Holy Law of Islam.
murid disciple who has sworn devotion to a Sufi master or to the Mughal emperor.
namus the honor of the warrior.
nankar that portion of the revenue alloted zamindars for their services.
nayak local king or chief in South India.
padshah Persian term for emperor or great king.
pahi tenant farmers in Rajasthan.
paibaqi unassigned jagir lands managed temporarily by the diwan-i khalisa.
paisa copper coin of the Sur dynasty.
pargana a small, named and bounded, rural administrative area containing between ten to over one hundred villages and one or more larger towns.
pir a Sufi saint or master.
pishkash tribute paid in money or goods to a superior.
qanungo quasi-official recognized by the imperial administration as the keeper of revenue records for a pargana or district in North India.
qasba a town, frequently applied to rural market towns.
qazi a judge charged with upholding the holy law of Islam and carrying out numerous civil functions.
rahdar military commander assigned the task of road security.
raiyati peasant held, not zamindari.
raiyat Mughal term for peasants or rural subjects.

reale	a Spanish silver coin minted in the New World revenues in lieu of pay and perquisites.
sabat	a covered approach way, often a trench, constructed to allow an assault on a besieged fortress.
sadr	Muslim head of religious patronage for the Mughal emperor.
sakti	worship of the energies of Kali or Devi, the great destructive female goddesses in Hinduism.
sanad	a written document or order conferring office or privileges.
sarai	a public inn run for the benefit of travelers.
sardeshmukh	chief of the deshmukhs within a province or region.
sardeshmukhi	that ten percent of the revenue allocated to the chief deshmukh or a region.
sarkar	a named territorial and administrative unit between the pargana and province.
sarrafs	moneychangers and purveyors of short-term commercial credit in Mughal India.
shaikh(s)	leader or head of a Sufi order or hospice.
shast-wa shabah	imperial seal and miniature portrait.
sijdah	the extreme form of ceremonial prostration favored by Sufi disciples before their masters and adapted by Akbar for his court.
sikka	newly-minted coins circulating at a premium.
suwar	numerical ranking denoting the number of armed heavy cavalrymen each Mughal officer was required to bring to the muster.
swaraj	refers to the original Maratha homelands under Shivaji.
taluqdar	a zamindar who collected land revenues from his fellow zamindars in return for a commission from the imperial revenue ministry.
tariqa	the mystical path followed by all Sufis and other mystics in search of God.
thakur	North Indian term for master or lord; used commonly by Rajput and Jat castes.
thana	a fortified military frontier checkpoint.
thanadar	commander of a military border post.
tika	the vermilion mark placed on the forehead of a Rajput ruler.
ulema	men learned in the Sharia or Holy Law of Islam and the Islamic subjects of higher learning.
urs	the anniversary of the death of a revered saint.
vakil	deputy or assistant, chief minister in Akbar's early years.
waqf	a trust for religious and charitable purposes founded by a Muslim.

watan	ancestral lands held in the family of a Maratha chief or warrior.
watan jagir	ancestral holdings assigned in jagir to Rajput Mughal officers.
wazir	chief fiscal minister for the Mughal emperor.
zabt	the mature system of land tax assessment and collection under the Mughals.
zakat	obligatory tax levied on the property of Muslims every year for charitable purposes.
zamindars	landlords or landholders who controlled the peasantry directly.
zat	personal numerical rank held by a Mughal officer.

BIBLIOGRAPHIC ESSAY

GENERAL HISTORIES

The short narrative account of the Mughals in *The Oxford History of India* (Oxford, 3rd edition, 1958) is helpful for a quick overview. R. C. Majumdar, ed., *The History and Culture of the Indian People, The Mughul Empire*, although detailed, has a decidedly anti-Muslim bias. More readable, with superb illustrations, is Bamber Gascoigne's *The Great Moghuls* (London, 1971). Another popular narrative is Waldemar Hansen, *The Peacock Throne* (New York, 1972). A number of regional or provincial histories cover the entire Mughal period. Among these are Jadunath Sarkar, ed., *History of Bengal: Muslim Period 1200–1757* (Patna, 1973) and B. C. Ray, *Orissa Under the Mughals* (Calcutta, 1981).

BABUR, HUMAYUN, AND SHER SHAH

Babur's own memoir can be read in the A. S. Beveridge translation of his *Babur-Nama* (New Delhi, reprint edition, 1970). Stephen Dale discusses the intensely personal nature of this memoir in "Steppe Humanism: The Autobiographical Writings of Zahir al-Din Muhammad Babur, 1483–1530," *International Journal of Middle East Studies* 22 (1990), 37–58. The most recent full biography is Mohibbul Hasan, *Babur, Founder of the Mughal Empire in India* (Delhi, 1985). Still lacking is a first-rate study that places Babur intelligibly in both his Central Asian and North Indian worlds. Humayun's reign is covered in Ishwari Prasad, *The Life and Times of Humayun* (Calcutta, 1955). Gulbadan Begam, in her memoirs, *The History of Humayun* (London, 1902), translated by A. Beveridge offers a noblewoman's perspective on the dynasty and India. Thomas W. Lentz and Glenn D. Lowry, *Timur and the Princely Vision* (Los Angeles, 1989) argue that Timur and his successors refined a coherent aesthetic designed to buttress and support political domination.

Iqtidar Alam Khan's biography of Humayun's brother, *Mirza Kamran* (Bombay, 1964) is also useful. One of the best treatments of the Surs is I. H. Siddiqi, *History of Sher Shah Sur* (Aligarh, 1971) and by the same author *Afghan Despotism in India* (Aligarh, 1969).

AKBAR

The official history of the reign is by Abul Fazl, *Akbar-Nama* (Delhi, 3 vols., reprint 1977) in the Beveridge translation. Frequently cited is the accompanying imperial manual, the *Ain-i Akbari* translated by H. Beveridge (Lahore, reprint 1975). Distinctly unofficial is the unsympathetic Abdul Qadir

Badauni, *Muntahkhabu-t Tawarikh* (Calcutta, 3 vols., 1864–9). A. Monserrate *Commentary ... on his journey to the Court of Akbar* translated by J. S. Hoyland (London, 1922) is an informative visitor's account. In a provocative synthesis, Douglas E. Streusand, *The Formation of the Mughal Empire* (Delhi, 1989) sets out a new interpretation of the evolution of Mughal political institutions under Akbar. K. A. Nizami, *Akbar and Religion* (Delhi, 1989) systematically analyzes. N. A. Siddiqi, *Land Revenue Administration Under the Mughals 1700–1750* (Aligarh, 1970) treats the deterioration of the revenue system in north India.

IMPERIAL ADMINISTRATION, MILITARY, AND DIPLOMACY

For administrative, political, and economic geography consult Irfan Habib, *An Atlas of the Mughal Empire* (Delhi, 1982). The atlas, the product of inspired scholarship, contains detailed political and economic maps of each province. For the revenue system and imperial institutions generally Irfan Habib's *The Agrarian System of Mughal India* (London, 1963) is indispensable. I. H. Qureshi, *The Administration of the Mughul Empire* (Karachi, 1966) is clear and concise. The most informative treatment of the Mughal nobility is M. Athar Ali, *The Mughal Nobility Under Aurangzeb* (Aligarh, 1966) and consult also Athar Ali, *The Apparatus of Empire* (Delhi, 1985) an exhaustive compendium on the nobility prior to 1658. H. Beveridge and B. Prashad have translated the large biographical dictionary of the Mughal nobility, Shah Nawaz Khan, *The Maathir-ul-Umara* (New Delhi, 2 vols., reprint edition 1979). See S. N. Sinha, *Subah of Allahabad Under the Great Mughals* (Delhi, 1974) and B. C. Ray, *Orissa Under the Mughals* (Calcutta, 1981) for provincial administration. The excellent study by S. P. Gupta, *The Agrarian System of Eastern Rajasthan (c. 1650 to c. 1750)* (Delhi, 1986) is based upon analysis of the voluminous archival sources from this region. See also S. A. A. Rizvi, *Religious and Intellectual History of the Muslims in Akbar's Reign* (New Delhi, 1975); J. F. Richards, "The Formulation of Imperial Authority Under Akbar and Jahangir" in J. F. Richards, ed., *Kingship and Authority in South Asia* (Madison, 1978) is also useful. Shireen Moosvi has intensively analyzed the statistical material found in the *Ain-i Akbari* and ancillary sources in *The Economy of the Mughal Empire c. 1595* (Delhi, 1987). The question of Akbar's illiteracy is discussed in an important article by Ellen Smart, "Akbar, Illiterate Genius," *Kaladarshana* (1981), pp. 99–107.

JAHANGIR

A new critical study of Jahangir is badly needed. The standard biography, Beni Prasad, *History of Jahangir* (London, 1922) is outdated. Jahangir's own account is to be found in the A. Rogers and H. Beveridge translation, *The Tuzuk-i Jahangiri* (Delhi, 2nd. edn., 2 vols. in one, 1968). An excellent example of the Indo-Muslim "Mirrors for Princes" literature is Sajida Alvi's *Advice on the Art of Governance* (Albany, 1989), the text and translation of a treatise written in Jahangir's reign. A fascinatingly candid Mughal nobleman's autobiography is Mirza Nathan, *Baharistan-i Ghaybi* (Gauhati, 2 vols., 1936) translated by M. I. Borah. Thomas Roe gives us an astute foreign view of Jahangir and his court in W. Foster, ed., *The Embassy of Sir Thomas Roe to India 615–1619* (London, rev. edn, 1926).

SHAH JAHAN

The standard history of the reign, long out-dated, is Banarsi Prasad Saksena, *History of Shah Jahan of Dihli* (Allahabad, reprint of 1932 edition, 1973). The massive official chronicles of Shah Jahan's reign have not been translated, but W. E. Begley and Z. A. Desai, eds., *The Shah Jahan Nama of 'Inayat Khan* (Delhi, 1990) have published a translation of an abridged version of those histories. The better traveller's accounts include Sebastian Manrique, *Travels of Fray Sebastian Manrique 1629–1643* (Cambridge, 1927) and Peter Mundy, *Travels, Vol. 2: Travels in Asia, 1630–1634*, ed. R. C. Temple (London, 1914).

AURANGZEB

The standard biography is by Jadunath Sarkar, *History of Aurangzib* (Calcutta, 5 vols., 1912–24). This is still the most reliable full political and military narrative that we possess. S. Moinul Haq, *Khafi Khan's History of Alamgir* (Karachi, 1975) translates the best narrative history of Aurangzeb's reign. Jadunath Sarkar has translated Saqi Mustaid Khan, *Maasir-i Alamgiri* (Calcutta, 1947), a history of the reign that is more terse and official. S. C. Dutta, *The Northeast and the Mughals (1661–1714)* (New Delhi, 1984) is an evenhanded treatment of the political and military history of this neglected region. See also Gautam Bhadra, "Two Frontier Uprisings in Mughal India" in Ranajit Guha, ed., *Subaltern Studies II: Writings on South Asian History and Society* (Delhi, 1983). Provincial studies include Anjali Chatterjee, *Bengal in the Reign of Aurangzib 1658–1707* (Calcutta, 1967) and J. F. Richards, *Mughal Administration in Golconda* (Oxford, 1975). Satish Chandra, *Medieval India, Society, the Jagirdari Crisis and the Village* (Delhi, 1981) brings together a set of powerful essays touching major themes and issues in later imperial history.

The half century of Aurangzeb's reign is rich in descriptive accounts by European sojourners and residents in India. A fascinating, and generally reliable, history of Aurangzeb's half century by a participant is N. Manucci, *Storia do Mogor or Mogul India* (Calcutta, 4 vols., 1907–8) translated by William Irvine. The best-known European account is that of Francois Bernier, *Travels in the Mogul Empire AD 1656–1668* (Delhi, reprint of rev. 2nd. edn., 1968) translated by A. Constable. H. H. Das, *The Norris Embassy to Aurangzib* (Calcutta, 1959) summarizes and quotes extensively from the journals of the English ambassador to the Mughal court at the turn of the century. Jagdish Sarkar's *The Life of Mir Jumla* (New Delhi, 2nd rev. edn., 1979) has a detailed description of a remarkable career.

BAHADUR SHAH TO MUHAMMAD SHAH

The best narrative is still William Irvine, *Later Mughals* (New Delhi, 2 vols. in one, reprint edition, 1971). Bengal in this period is covered in Abdul Karim, *Murshid Quli Khan and His Times* (Dacca, 1963). Satish Chandra, *Parties and Politics at the Mughal Court, 1707–1740* (New Delhi, 2nd. edn. 1972) analyzes the politics of the center. A brilliant, incisive discussion of imperial decline in this period is Muzaffar Alam, *The Crisis of Empire in Mughal North India* (Delhi, 1986). See also Muzaffar Alam, "Eastern India in the Early Eighteenth Century 'Crisis': Some Evidence from Bihar" in *The Indian Economic and Social History Review*, 28 (1991), 43–72.

One of the few works to analyze the Mughal military system is that of Dirk H. A. Kolff, *Naukar, Rajput and Sepoy: The Ethnohistory of the Military Labour Market in Hindustan, 1450–1850* (Cambridge, 1990). For an unequalled perspective on Mughal military operations see Jagdish Sarkar, *The Military Despatches of a Seventeenth Century Indian General* (Calcutta, 1969).

Mughal relations with the other two large early modern Islamic states are of great interest. Most recently we have the excellent study by N. R. Farooqi, *Mughal–Ottoman Relations* (Delhi, 1989) and Riazul Islam, *Indo–Persian Relations: A Study of the Political and Diplomatic Relations Between Mughal Empire and Iran* (Tehran, 1970).

THE ECONOMY AND INTERNATIONAL TRADE

The first volume of Tapan Raychaudhuri and Irfan Habib, eds., *The Cambridge Economic History of India* (Cambridge, 1982) is largely devoted to Mughal India. John F. Richards, ed., *The Imperial Monetary System of Mughal India* (Delhi, 1987) is a useful approach to questions of money and coinage. A seminal article on Mughal commerce is B. R. Grover, "An Integrated Pattern of Commercial Life in the Rural Society of North India During the 17th–18th Centuries" in *Proceedings, Indian Historical Records Commission*, 37 (1966), 121–53. Ashin Das Gupta, *Indian Merchants and the Decline of Surat c. 1700–1750* (Wiesbaden, 1979) is a scholarly, gracefully written analysis of the decline of the great Mughal port.

For urbanization see the relevant sections in Raychaudhuri and Habib, above. Systematic excavation of potentially rich urban, town, and village sites has only begun for medieval and Mughal India. The benefits of intense, cooperative research may be seen in the essays in Michael Brand and Glenn D. Lowry, eds., *Fatehpur Sikri* (Bombay, 1987). Stephen P. Blake, *Shahjahanabad: The Sovereign City in Mughal India, 1639–1739* (Cambridge, 1990) provides an excellent analysis of Shah Jahan's new city and its evolution over a century. Much descriptive material from the major histories and European travelers has been assembled in H. K. Naqvi, *Mughal Hindustan: Cities and Industries 1556–1803* (Karachi, 1958) and by the same author *Urbanization and Urban Centers Under the Great Mughals* (Simla, 1972). Gavin Hambly,

Cities of Mughal India: Delhi, Agra and Fatehpur Sikri (New York, 1968) is a readable, well-illustrated volume.

The India trade has been an important field within the massive academic industry devoted to the study of early modern Europe. Many able scholars have made good use of the copious sources found in the archives of Europe. For the Portuguese, the best recent synthesis is M. N. Pearson, *The Portuguese in India* (Cambridge, 1987), vol. 1.1 in *The New Cambridge History of India*. The definitive work on the English East India Company is K. N. Chaudhuri, *The European Trading World of Asia and the English East India Company 1660–1760* (Cambridge, 1978). For a broad synthesis see by the same author, *Asia Before Europe: Economy and Civilization of the Indian Ocean from the Rise of Islam to 1750* (Cambridge, 1990). For a review of the Dutch from the perspective of the metropolis, see Jonathan I. Israel, *Dutch Primacy in World Trade 1585–1740* (Oxford, 1989). An invaluable regional study is Om Prakash, *The Dutch East India Company and the Economy of Bengal, 1630–1720* (Princeton, 1985). See also Susil Chaudhuri, *Trade and Commercial Organization in Bengal, 1650–1720* (Calcutta, 1975). An excellent study of the southeastern trade under the Mughals is S. Arasaratnam, *Merchants, Companies, and Commerce on the Coromandel Coast 1650–1740* (Delhi, 1986). For an earlier period see Sanjay Subrahmanyam, *The Political Economy of Commerce: Southern India, 1500–1650* (Cambridge, 1990). Edward Alpers points out the importance of maritime trade between western India and eastern Africa in this period in "Gujarat and the Trade of East Africa, c. 1500–1800," *The International Journal of African Historical Studies* 9 (1976), 22–44.

CULTURAL, ETHNIC AND LOCAL HISTORY

S. A. A. Rizvi, *Muslim Revivalist Movements in Northern India in the Sixteenth and Seventeenth Centuries* (Agra, 1965) is a detailed study of religious change in Indian Islam. Rizvi's two-volume *A History of Sufism in India* (Delhi, 1983) is a comprehensive treatment of the Sufi orders in Mughal India. Yohanan Friedmann, *Shaykh Ahmad Sirhindi* (Montreal, 1971) adopts a revisionist approach to Sirhindi. See also Aziz Ahmad, *Studies in Islamic Culture in the Indian Environment* (Oxford, 1964). Asim Roy, *The Islamic Syncretistic Tradition in Bengal* (Princeton, 1985) highlights the distinctive character of the expansive, rice-growing, frontier-settling Bengali Islam in this period.

The literature on the Sikhs is extensive. The most recent overview can be found in J. S. Grewal, *The Sikhs in the Punjab* in *The New Cambridge History of India*. See also by the same author, *Guru Nanak in History* (Chandigarh, 1969) and W. H. McLeod, *Guru Nanak and the Sikh Religion* (Oxford, 1968). An excellent biography of the last Sikh guru is J. S. Grewal and S. S. Bal, *Guru Gobind Singh* (Chandigarh, 1967).

Newly invigorated historical studies on the Rajputs have begun to meld detailed information from archival sources with the Rajput chronicles and bardic poetry. Kunwar Refaqat Ali Khan, *The Kachhwahas Under Akbar and Jahangir* (New Delhi, 1976) has compiled useful data on the Jaipur house. Richard Fox, *Kin, Clan, Raja, and Rule* (Berkeley, 1971) has modelled the life cycle of Rajput lineages in the Gangetic plain. See Norman P. Ziegler, "Some Notes on Rajput Loyalties During the Mughal Period" in Richards, ed., *Kingship and Authority*. Satya Prakash Gupta, *The Agrarian System of Eastern Rajasthan (c. 1650–c. 1750)* (Delhi, 1986) is a convincing example of the value of the archival sources preserved in various Rajput capitals. See also R. P. Rana, "Agrarian Revolts in Northern India during the Late 17th and Early 18th Century," *The Indian Economic and Social History Review* 28 (1981) 287–326 for a valuable case study. Robert C. Hallissey, *The Rajput Rebellion Against Aurangzeb* (Columbia, 1977) reinterprets the Rajput wars.

The most entrancing history of the Marathas is that written by a British colonial officer in western India, James Grant Duff, *History of the Mahrattas* (New Delhi, 2 vols. in one, reprint edition, 1971) first published in the early nineteenth century and incorporating data from sources now lost. The best overview of the Marathas is to be found in Stewart Gordon, *The Marathas, 1600–1800* (forthcoming) in *The New Cambridge History of India*. For a full narrative see G. S. Sardesai, *New History of the Marathas* (Bombay, 3 vols., 1957). Jadunath Sarkar, *Shivaji and His Times* (Bombay, reprint edition, 1973) is still a useful narrative. A. R. Kulkarni, the distinguished Maratha historian, reviews the structures of society, state, and economy in *Mahrashtra in the Age of Shivaji* (Poona, 1974). For details on a neglected period see A. R. Kulkarni, *The Mughal–Maratha Relations: Twenty-Five Fateful Years (1682–1707)* (Pune, 1983). See also Andre Wink, *Land and Sovereignty in India: Agrarian Society and Politics Under the Eighteenth Century Maratha Svarajya* (Cambridge, 1986).

M. C. Pradhan's anthropological study, *The Political System of the Jats of Northern India* (Bombay, 1966) points to the need for systematic research among lineage, clan, and family records. Two important documentary collections reinforce this point: B. N. Goswamy and J. S. Grewal, *The Mughals and the Joghis of Jakhbar* (Simla, 1967) and J. S. Grewal, *In the By-Lanes of History: Some Persian Documents from a Punjab Town* (Simla, 1975).

GARDENS, PAINTING, ARCHITECTURE

The visual appeal of Mughal gardens, painting, and buildings has encouraged a large literature of handsomely produced volumes. Only a few can be mentioned here. For gardens see Sylvia Crowe, et al. *The Gardens of Mughul India* (New Delhi, 1972). A stimulating interpretation of the changing uses for gardens is in James L. Wescoat, Jr., "Gardens Versus Citadels: The Territorial Context of Early Mughal Gardens" in J. D. Hunt, ed., *Landscape and Garden History: Issues, Approaches, Methods* (Washington DC, 1991). For painting under Jahangir and Shah Jahan see Milo Beach, *The Grand Mogul: Imperial*

Painting in India 1600–1660 (Williamstown, 1978), also Milo C. Beach, *Mughal Painting* (forthcoming) in *The New Cambridge History of India*. Wayne Begley, "The Myth of the Taj Mahal and a New Theory of Its Symbolic Meaning," *The Art Bulletin* (March, 1979) offers a revisionist interpretation of the tomb complex. See also by Begley, "Ahmad, Ustad" in Adolf K. Placzek, *Macmillan Encyclopedia of Architects* (New York, 1982). Catherine B. Asher, *Mughal Architecture* (forthcoming) in *The New Cambridge History of India* contains a complete treatment of Mughal building. See Ebba Koch, *Shah Jahan and Orpheus* (Graz: Akademische Druck-u. Verlagsanstalr, 1988) for a stimulating analysis of European influences in Mughal architecture under Shah Jahan.

INDEX

INDEX